D1156733

Photographic Gelatin

I

Photographic Gelatin

PROCEEDINGS OF THE SECOND SYMPOSIUM ON PHOTOGRAPHIC GELATIN HELD AT TRINITY COLLEGE, CAMBRIDGE, AUGUST–SEPTEMBER, 1970

Edited by

R. J. COX

Fellow of the Royal Photographic Society, London, England

1972

Published for The Scientific and Technical Group of the Royal Photographic Society by

ACADEMIC PRESS: LONDON AND NEW YORK

ACADEMIC PRESS INC. (LONDON) LTD.
24/28 Oval Road
London, NW1

U.S. Edition published by
ACADEMIC PRESS INC.
111 Fifth Avenue,
New York, New York 10003

Library of Congress Catalog Card Number: 79–170758

ISBN: 0–12–194450–6

Set in 11/12pt. Monotype Baskerville, printed by letterpress, and bound in Great Britain at the Pitman Press, Bath

Contributors

H. Ammann-Brass, *Laboratory of Photographic Chemistry and Technology, Fribourg, Switzerland.*
D. Bermane, *CIBA Photochemical Ltd., Fribourg, Switzerland.*
H. Borginon, *Agfa-Gevaert N.V., Mortsel, Belgium.*
B. P. Brand, *Imperial Chemical Industries Ltd., Manchester, England.*
K. Bühler, *CIBA Photochemical Ltd., Fribourg, Switzerland.*
R. V. Cole, Jr., *G.A.F. Corporation, Binghampton, New York, U.S.A.*
S. Couprié, *Société Kodak-Pathé, Vincennes, France.*
H. G. Curme, *Eastman Kodak Co., Rochester, New York, U.S.A.*
A. de Cugnac-Pailliotet, *Société Kodak-Pathé, Vincennes, France.*
E. Dubiel, *Foton Photochemical, Warsaw, Poland.*
G. Ender, *Agfa-Gevaert AG, Munich, W. Germany.*
Marilyn M. A. Faust, *Eastman Kodak Co., Rochester, New York, U.S.A.*
W. D. Fellows, *Eastman Kodak Co., Rochester, New York, U.S.A.*
M. C. Gadet, *Société Kodak-Pathé, Vincennes, France.*
D. J. Genova, *Eastman Kodak Co., Rochester, New York, U.S.A.*
S. Ghosh, *Northwestern University Medical School, Chicago, U.S.A.*
A. M. Hodot, *Société Kodak-Pathé, Vincennes, France.*
K. Hori, *Fuji Photo Film Co., Ltd., Ashigara, Japan.*
H. Irie, *Chiba University, Japan.*
T. Ishida, *Chiba University, Japan.*
M. F. Johnson, *Eastman Kodak Co., Rochester, New York, U.S.A.*
P. Johnson, *Department of Biochemistry, Free School Lane, Cambridge, England.*
W. D. Kamm, *Eastman Kodak Co., Rochester, New York, U.S.A.*
A. Katsev, *Cinema and Radio Research Institute, Sofia, Bulgaria.*
E. Klein, *Agfa-Gevaert AG, Leverkusen, W. Germany.*
G. H. Klinger, *G.A.F. Corporation, Binghampton, New York, U.S.A.*
A. M. Kragh, *Ilford Ltd., Ilford, Essex, England.*
D. W. LaPalme, Jr., *G.A.F. Corporation, Binghampton, New York, U.S.A.*
J. D. Lewis, *Ilford Ltd., Ilford, Essex, England.*
A. Libický, *CIBA Photochemical Ltd., Fribourg, Switzerland.*
W. D. Marrs, *Gelatin and Glue Research Association, Birmingham, England.*
W. M. McKernan, *Croda Food Products, London, England.*

R. S. MILLER, *Eastman Kodak Co., Rochester, New York, U.S.A.*
T. MIURA, *Fuji Photo Film Co., Ltd., Ashigara, Japan.*
E. MOISAR, *Agfa-Gevaert AG, Leverkusen, W. Germany.*
F. MOLL, *Agfa-Gevaert AG, Leverkusen, W. Germany.*
K. NAGAO, *Fuji Photo Film Co., Ltd., Ashigara, Japan.*
S. NAGATOMO, *Fuji Photo Film Co., Ltd., Ashigara, Japan.*
D. R. NELLIST, *Kodak Ltd., Harrow, Middlesex, England.*
R. OHI, *Fuji Photo Film Co., Ltd., Ashigara, Japan.*
Y. OHYAMA, *Mitubishi Paper Mills Ltd., Kyoto, Japan.*
F. ORBAN, *University of Liège, Belgium.*
HATTIE O. OTTO, *Eastman Kodak Co., Rochester, New York, U.S.A.*
M. PANCHEVA, *Cinema and Radio Research Institute, Sofia, Bulgaria.*
N. PANGELOVA, *Cinema and Radio Research Institute, Sofia, Bulgaria.*
J. POURADIER, *Société Kodak-Pathé, Vincennes, France.*
E. ROCHE, *Agfa-Gevaert AG, Leverkusen, W. Germany.*
M. ROCHE, *Imperial Chemical Industries Ltd., Manchester, England.*
A. SPÜHLER, *CIBA Photochemical Ltd., Fribourg, Switzerland.*
M. D. STERMAN, *Eastman Kodak Co., Rochester, New York, U.S.A.*
B. E. TABOR, *Kodak Ltd., Harrow, Middlesex, England.*
I. TOMKA, *CIBA Photochemical Ltd., Fribourg, Switzerland.*
E. TOJO, *Fuji Film Photo Co., Ltd., Ashigara, Japan.*
Y. TSUBAI, *Chiba University, Japan.*
A. G. TULL, *Technicolour Ltd., West Drayton, Middlesex, England.*
A. VEISS, *Northwestern University Medical School, Chicago, U.S.A.*
D. WINSTANLEY, *Imperial Chemical Industries Ltd., Manchester, England.*
P. D. WOOD, *Gelatin and Glue Research Association, Birmingham, England.*
B. J. M. WOODS, *Croda Food Products, London, England.*
N. YAMAMOTO, *Fuji Photo Film Co., Ltd., Ashigara, Japan.*
H. ZORN, *Agfa-Gevaert AG, Munich, W. Germany.*

Foreword

This volume comprises most of the papers presented at a conference organized by the Scientific and Technical Group of the Royal Photographic Society which took place at Trinity College, Cambridge, during 1970. The decision to issue a volume was taken after the conference, so that prior preparations were not made and, regrettably, a very few of the papers appear in abstract form only. The conference was one of a regular annual series organized by the Group during the summer over several years, covering in turn the range of subjects of interest to the photographic scientist. It was the second to be held on photographic gelatin. The first took place at Selwyn College, Cambridge, in 1967 and another is planned on the same topic for 1974.

Gelatin has been for nearly a hundred years, and remains today, the main vehicle for the light sensitive silver halide in silver based photography. Practically all commercial materials that have ever been made have been formulated with gelatin. It is appropriate here, especially for readers who are not connected with the manufacture of this kind of light-sensitive material, to give a brief account of its introduction and some explanation of the breadth of interest to those concerned with photography. For a fuller account of the introduction of gelatin, the reader is referred to *The History of Photography*, by H. and A. Gernsheim (1969, Thames and Hudson, London), from whom the figures quoted in the table below have been taken.

Although many early attempts were made to produce plates using gelatin, widespread use did not come about until the 1880's. Up till this time, the favoured process was the wet collodion process, using cellulose nitrate as a vehicle. The early dry plates were often unreliable and although they were more convenient than wet collodion, the latter had a speed advantage which was decisive for studio work and so was preferred by the professionals. In 1877, at an Edinburgh exhibition, of 824 exhibits, 729 were produced by wet collodion—leaving less than one hundred by all other processes, including the various dry and damp collodion processes then current.

In the period 1878–9 Bennet and others discovered that the speed of gelatin-silver bromide dispersions could be increased and brought to a standard value by holding at an elevated temperature. Once these processes had been learnt and incorporated in the commercially available dry plates, progress was very rapid indeed, as can be seen from these figures for the annual exhibitions of the Photographic Society of Great Britain for the years 1880–82.

Table

Negative processes used for the prints exhibited at the annual exhibition of the Photographic Society of Great Britain (forerunner of the RPS)

RPS Exhibition	*Negative processes used on prints* Gelatin	Wet Collodion
1880	653	518
1881	1619	319
1882	1416	21

The decline in the wet collodion process occupied only a very few years, and led directly to the birth of an industry supplying sensitized goods. The speed advantage offered by these early materials is not certain; it could have been in the region of twenty to forty times that of wet collodion. Kennet, however, remarks that he had to hold back the speed of his plates in order to stay in business, as the early users consistently over-exposed or fogged them with yellow safelights.

The reasons for the increased speed obtainable by digestion of gelatin-silver bromide dispersions did not begin to become known until after the lapse of some decades, although it was rapidly appreciated that the effect depended on the gelatin used. "Good" gelatins gave controllable increase in speed, "bad" gelatins either very little increase or uncontrollable increase leading to fogging. Gelatins came to be classified according to their relative "activity" although it was also recognized that a single classification only applied to a given formula or photographic situation showing that more than a single factor was involved. Gelatins were either selected or blended to suit the product. The idea that specific photographic effects were due to microcomponents and not to the gelatin molecules themselves grew slowly, over the years, in the absence of real certainty. It was strengthened by the continuing discovery of synthetic addenda which could influence the properties of the coating when added in tiny amounts.

The most important microcomponent is thiosulphate which occurs in microgram amounts and is widely held to be responsible for the increase in sensitivity obtained by heating the silver bromide dispersion. It was these minute quantities of material rather than the bulk properties of the gelatin that gave it a decisive advantage, at the time, over the other vehicles then available. Only then was it possible to prepare materials reproducibly, which were stable on storage and sensitive enough for a wide application. All three factors were necessary for commercial production of sensitive materials

Small amounts of nucleic acid (10^{-3}—10^{-6}) also occur. These affect the growth of silver bromide crystals and can influence the properties of the product in various ways. Such substances are known as restrainers. There is continuing interest today in these micro-constituents, and their effect on crystal growth, which is reflected in the papers presented to the conference.

The macromolecular properties, including gelation, also assume a considerable importance technologically. Gelation is regularly used to immobilize the freshly coated layer and thus obtain even layers, most necessary for modern colour products which may contain more than a dozen such layers. Almost all photographic layers are treated with chemical cross-linking agents (usually referred to as hardeners) either by addition during manufacture or during processing in order to influence the physical properties of the layer. These interests are all illustrated in the papers included in this volume.

London
November, 1971

J. W. JANUS

The Science Committee of the Royal Photographic Society

Chairman	MR. J. W. JANUS
Vice-Chairman	MR. G. W. SMITH
Hon. Treasurer	MR. R. J. COX
Hon. Secretary	MR. C. J. V. ROBERTS
Representatives of Council	MR. K. R. WARR MR. J. G. C. STEELE
Committee	MR. L. BUTLER MR. R. COLMAN MR. D. DEARNLEY DR. V. G. W. HARRISON MR. P. NUTTALL-SMITH MR. J. G. C. STEELE

The Science Committee of the Royal Photographic Society consists of the Committee of the Scientific and Technical Group of the Society together with two representatives of Council. Its function is to plan, at the highest level, events concerned with scientific and technical photography.

The Scientific and Technical Group of the Royal Photographic Society seeks to encourage and stimulate interest in scientific and technical aspects of photography. An important activity of the Group is the publication of *Photographic Abstracts*, a journal which contains abstracts of papers and patents in the field of photographic science and technology.

Further details of the future programme of the Scientific and Technical Group of the Royal Photographic Society, and forms of application for membership can be obtained from:

The Hon. Secretary,
Scientific and Technical Group,
Royal Photographic Society,
14 South Audley Street,
London W1Y 5DP

Contents

The Gelatin Gel

Deuterium-Hydrogen Exchange in Gelatin Films*

S. GHOSH and A. VEIS

Northwestern University Medical School, Department of Biochemistry,
303 *East Chicago Avenue, Chicago, Illinois* 60611, *U.S.A.*

* This study has been carried out under Contract No. 12–14–100–8933(73) with the Agricultural Research Service, U.S. Department of Agriculture, Administered by the Eastern Marketing and Nutrition Research Division, 600 E. Mermaid Lane, Philadelphia, Pennsylvania 19118, U.S.A.

ABSTRACT. When a solution of gelatin is quenched to a temperature T_q below the melting temperature, T_m, of collagen, the gelatin forms segments with the collagen fold form. For $25° < T_q < 40°C$ the growth of the collagen-fold is limited and does not proceed above a certain level. Thin films of gelatin were cast on Irtran 2 windows of infra-red liquid cells by evaporating gelatin solutions at the quenching temperature. The kinetics of deuterium-hydrogen exchange of such films, as well as of similar films of native acid-soluble collagen, were studied at 1550 cm^{-1} with a view to finding the regions responsible for the initiation of the collagen fold. Studies at different pD showed the rate to be minimum around pD = 3·5 and not diffusion limited for the thin films employed. As in the case of dissolved low molecular weight gelatin, the exchange kinetics at 40°C required at least 2 and that at 25°C at least 3 first order rate constants. The ratio of the intensities of the Amide I and Amide II bands, as well as the relative sizes of each class of the exchangeable groups may be utilized to monitor the state of renaturation of gelatin in a film. The kinetically distinct groups may be assigned to the apolar amino acid rich regions, polar regions and region rendered less accessible to D_2O due to the formation of the collagen-fold interchange helix.

INTRODUCTION

It is now well established that upon cooling a solution of gelatin below some characteristic temperature close to the melting temperature. T_m, of tropocollagen molecules, each molecule forms local regions with collagen-like structure[1]. This process is called collagen-fold formation and is an expression of the equilibrium between disordered, denatured gelatin chains and the ordered, native collagen compound helix structure. The renaturation process is of basic as well as of practical importance; on one hand, it is a good model for considering the *in vivo* assembly of collagen molecules, while on the other hand, the physical properties of gelatin films are determined by the nature of the collagen-fold units and the extent of structure formation.[2]

At $T > T_m$ gelatin molecules are essentially in the random coil conformation regardless of the molecular weight. Collagen-fold formation involves the transformation of independent chain segments by interchain associations into the triple helical structure typical of collagen. Gels form when the collagen-fold units form a three dimensional network linking all molecules. Although it has received a great deal of attention, the molecular mechanism of the random → helix transition is still not clear. Current views stem primarily from the work of Harrington and von Hippel[4] and of Flory and Weaver.[5] The key element in the process is the negative temperature dependence of the renaturation process which indicates that fold-formation is similar to a nucleated crystallization phenomenon.[5]

In the Flory and Weaver scheme,[5]

$$C \overset{1}{\rightleftharpoons} I \overset{2}{\rightleftharpoons} \tfrac{1}{3}H$$

segments of random coil chains (C) assume independent transient helical conformations (I) and these immediately associate to form triple chain helices (H). In this situation, reaction step 1 is rate limiting. The collagen-like structure is then presumed to grow from either end of the helix nucleus H in a distinct propagation step.

The structure and extent of collagen-folding in both gelatin films and solutions has been examined by several workers.[6],[7],[8] In most of this work fold-formation was induced by marked undercooling, that is, at T much below T_m, even if the equilibrium temperature was subsequently closer to T_m. At such low undercooling temperatures, e.g. 0° to 4°C, fold-formation continues for a long time and obviously involves both nucleation and propagation processes. Warming to the final equilibration temperature introduces further complications.

It was our intent to separate nucleation and propagation steps and study the nucleation process alone. This required that experiments be carried out under conditions where the temperature be held constant throughout a measurement and at T sufficiently close to T_m that helix propagation was not likely.

Veis and Legowick[9] found that if the cooling or quenching temperature, T_q, is kept within $T_m - T_q < 15°$, a constant level of optical rotation regain is rapidly achieved, suggesting that helix propagation does not occur under these conditions. Schnell and Veis[10] made use of this observation to study fold-formation in low molecular weight gelatin solutions by the hydrogen-deuterium exchange technique of Linderstrom-Lang.[11] The present work was an extension of the same approach using high molecular weight fractions of gelatin in films.

EXPERIMENTAL PROCEDURES

A. Gelatin fractions

An acid-precursor pig skin gelatin (Grayslake Corp.) with an iso-electric pH of 9·0 was fractionated by a salt-ethanol procedure.[12] Three fractions were collected at varying ethanol/water ratios. The gelatin was recovered by precipitation from the coacervate phase with acetone. After removal of the acetone, the gelatins were redissolved in water, deionized by ion-exchange chromatography and then lyophilized.

B. Rat skin acid soluble collagen

Acid soluble collagen was used as a control for examination of the completely native protein. Rat skins were extracted with citrate or acetate buffers and the extracted protein then purified by reprecipitation with NaCl, according to the procedure of Piez *et al.*[13]

C. Buffers

All measurements were made using 0·01 M Na citrate buffers made up in H_2O or D_2O. The pH was varied by adjustment with citric acid. The pD of the D_2O buffers was calculated as pD = pH + 0·4.

D. Infra-red spectra

The degree of hydrogen bonding and internal fold formation in gelatin films was studied by the D—H exchange technique utilizing the amide II, N—H deformation band at 1550 cm^{-1} in the infrared region of the spectrum. Since this technique looks specifically at the N—H bond of the protein, the rate and extent of exchange at this bond can be related directly to the structure in the peptide chains. Measurements were made in a Beckman IR-12 spectrophotometer.

Gelatin films were prepared from 1% gelatin solutions prepared in citrate buffer at the proper pH in H_2O. The solutions were heated to 70°C for 10 minutes and then put in a water bath at 40°C. For experiments at lower temperature, T_q, an aliquot was transferred directly to a bath at T_q. After equilibrating at T_q for 0·5–1 hr, 25 μl of solution was spread on one side of an Irtran 2 window and allowed to dry at T_q. The temperature was monitored by a surface thermistor. The calculated film thickness was of the order of 1·0 μ. The window with dry gelatin film was then assembled into a liquid cell and put in the constant temperature cell jacket in the IR-12 spectrophotometer.

Similar films were formed from acid soluble collagen except that the collagen was not denatured before being spread as a film. That is, the 70° and 40°C heating steps were omitted.

In each case, a similar cell filled with citrate buffer in D_2O was used as a reference. D_2O buffer at T_q was injected into the sample cell. For the native acid-soluble collagen, the spectrum was taken at T_q between 1400–1700 cm^{-1} and repeated periodically. The film with D_2O covering it was then heated to 40°C and held until all structure had melted out. The complete spectrum was then taken.

The gelatin films had very little initial order so that the spectrum was not of much use. In these cases, upon injection of the D_2O over the film, the 1550 cm^{-1} band was followed as a function of time using the expanded scale. The 1650 cm^{-1} band (C = 0 stretch) was monitored from time to time to see that there was no drift of the baseline. At the end of the exchange at T_q, when the transmission at 1550 cm^{-1} became constant, the temperature of the cell holder was increased to 40°C (40°C $> T_m$) to melt out any residual collagen-fold in N—H hydrogen bonding. The cell was then cooled back to T_q after all H's had exchanged and the 1550 cm^{-1} band transmission measured. The spectrum from 1400–1700 cm^{-1} was also taken.

RESULTS AND DISCUSSION

The IR spectrum of a film of acid-soluble collagen is shown in Fig. 1. Curves 1 and 2 refer to the native form at $T_q = 25°$. There is a slight difference between transmission of the 1550 cm^{-1} band at 7 and 45 minutes after introduction of the D_2O. This is probably due to a slight amount of disordered material in the sample but after 45 minutes the transmission at 1550 cm^{-1} remained constant. Heating the film *in situ* to a temperature above 40°C melts out the structure, all amide H's rapidly exchange and, after a few minutes spectrum 3 of Fig. 1 is obtained. Comparison of spectra 1 and 3 shows the expected marked decrease in intensity of the N—H band at 1550 cm^{-1} and the concomitant appearance of the N—D deformation band at 1450 cm^{-1}. Either of these changes could be used to monitor the D—H exchange but it is easier to establish the baseline for the 1550 cm^{-1} band. There is also a slight shift of the C=0 band at 1650 cm^{-1} to lower frequency following denaturation but the absorbance is unchanged. Hence, this absorbance can be used to determine base line stability in an exchange kinetics experiment or to monitor the concentration of collagen or gelatin.

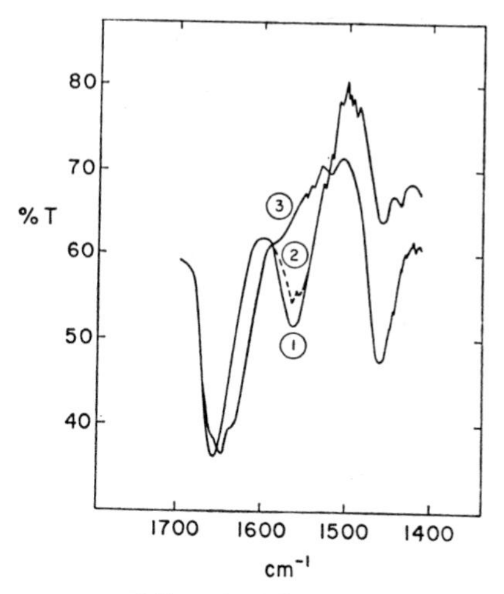

Fig. 1. Absorption spectra of film of acid-soluble collagen in D_2O at pD 3·6. Spectrum 1. Native collagen, seven min after addition of D_2O to the film. Spectrum 2. Native collagen after 45 min exposure to D_2O. This spectrum coincides with spectrum 1 in all details except in the dashed-line region near 1550 cm^{-1}. Spectrum 3. Film after exposure to elevated temperature for denaturation and complete exchange, followed by cooling to initial film temperature.

Films formed from gelatin under the conditions used, $T_m - T_q <$ 15°, contain so little structure that measurements of the spectrum at different time intervals were of little direct value. The 1550 cm^{-1} band was monitored for analysis of the exchange kinetics in this case.

A typical exchange run is shown in Fig. 2. As indicated, it required about one minute after introduction of the D_2O before all adjustments could be made to the 1550 cm^{-1} band on the expanded scale of the spectrophotometer. The transmittance at zero time could not be determined. However, the exchange could be measured quite easily to a constant value. Heating to 40°C to melt out the remaining collagen-fold units and subsequent recooling to T_q allowed the direct measurement of H-bonded fold-units. It was necessary to cool the cell back to T_q after melting out the collagen-fold to avoid dimensional changes within the cell.

The D—H exchange is an acid-base catalyzed reaction[(14)] and should show a minimum rate at a certain pD. The exchange kinetics were examined at several pD from gelatin films prepared at 40°C and which were stabilized against swelling and solution by the addition of a drop of formaldehyde. Exchange was measured at 30°C. The data are plotted in Fig. 3 in terms of time for 90% exchange *v.* pD. A

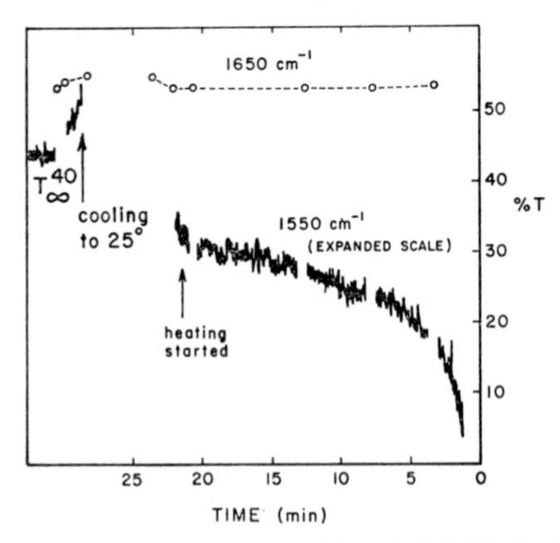

Fig. 2. Kinetic analysis of the 1550 cm^{-1} band (N–H) during an exchange run. The expanded scale trace of the percentage transmission at 1550 cm^{-1} follows the exchange out of H at 25°C. At the arrow labelled heating started the cell jacket was raised to 40°C. After exchange was complete in the re-melted film, the cell was cooled back to 25°C to provide the final transmission reading for completely exchanged gelatin, T^{40}. The dashed line with open circles represents the C═O absorbance at 1650^{∞} cm^{-1} measured at intervals throughout the run, the measurements at each point corresponding at each point to the gaps in the trace of the 1550 cm^{-1} transmission.

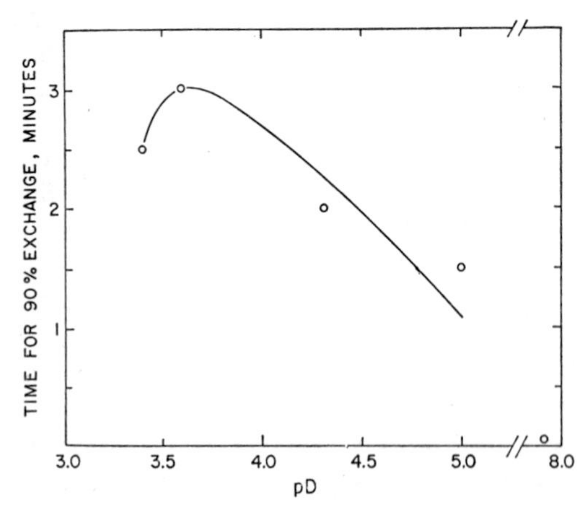

Fig. 3. The effect of pD on the time required for 90% exchange. In gelatin films at pD 7·6 exchange is complete before measurements can be made.

minimum rate was noted at pD ~3·6 and all subsequent measurements were done at this pD. Equally important was the observation that at pD 7·9 exchange was virtually complete as soon as measurements could be made, <1 minute. This shows that the lower rates of exchange seen at the other values of pD were not dependent on diffusion and film thickness.

For the analysis of exchange kinetics, the Amide II transmittance values were converted to absorbancy A_t, according to the formula

$$\Delta A_t^T = A_\infty^{40} - A_t^T = \log \frac{T_\infty^{40}}{T_t^T}$$

The term ΔA_t^T is proportional to the concentration of amide —H in the *unexchanged* state. Log ΔA_t^T plotted against time should give a straight line for a first-order exchange process. As shown in Fig. 4, the exchange

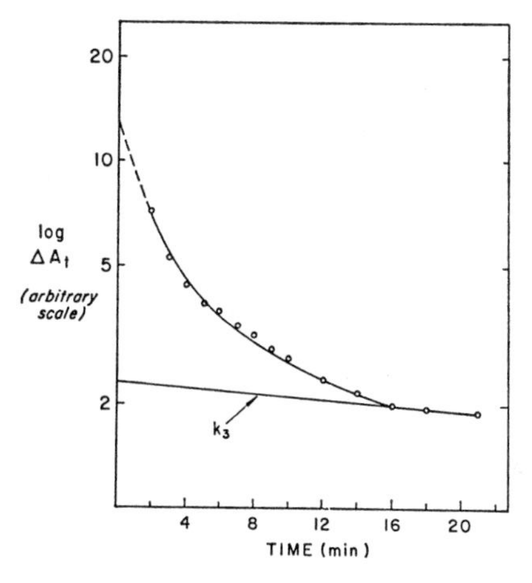

Fig. 4. Kinetic data for exchange in a gelatin film, pD 3·6, 25°C. ΔA_t^{25} is defined by log T_∞^{40}/T_t^{25}. The slope of the final linear region is k_3.

data do not follow a straight line. Much information in the literature does show that H—D exchange reactions are first order, hence, the interpretation to be placed on the raw exchange data is that these data represent the sum of a set of simultaneous first order reactions. A linear plot is attained near the end of the reaction, and the single first order reaction being followed here, represented by the line with slope k_3, can be subtracted from the initial exchange curve. Similarly, in Fig. 5, the difference curve can then be examined as the sum of two first order reactions and the separate reaction rate constants, k_2 and k_1 determined.

Exchange studies at 40°C where there was no collagen-fold yielded data which could be interpreted as the sum of two first order reactions. At $T_q < T_m$ three rate constants were required to reproduce the exchange curve. There was, moreover, at $T_q < T_m$ always a small difference between A^{40}_{∞} and $A^{T}_{\infty}q$ indicating a small extent of fold formation and the production of a group of hydrogens no longer

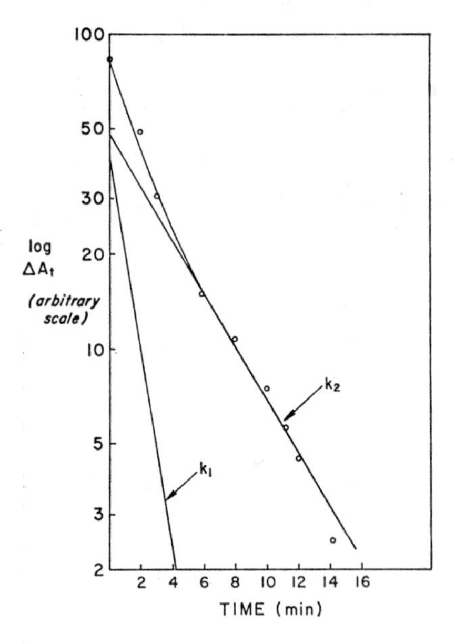

Fig. 5. Analysis of the kinetic data of Fig. 4. The points represent the curve of Fig. 4 from which the slowest reaction, represented by rate constant k_3, had been subtracted. The resulting curve is analyzed in terms of two simultaneous reactions, with constants k, and k_2.

capable of exchanging with deuterium. The total exchangeable hydrogen content was determined from the difference between A^{40}_{∞} and $A^{T}_{0}q$. The absorbance at zero time, $A^{T}_{0}q$, was calculated from the ratio of absorbances at the Amide I and Amide II bands for native collagen (Fig. 1, spectrum 1) and the absorbance at the Amide I band by the gelatin undergoing D—H exchange. From the total exchangeable hydrogens ($A^{40}_{\infty} - A^{T}_{\infty}q$) and the calculated group rate constants the fraction of hydrogens in each class were calculated. The rate constants and group fractions are presented in Table 1 for exchange at 40° and 25°C. These values are compared with the data of Veis and Schnell[10] using low molecular weight gelatin in solution and the lyophilization techniques of Linderstron–Lang. Veis and Schnell used gelatin fraction III. Fraction I, of higher molecular weight, was used in the current work.

Table 1

D-H **Exchange in gelatin**

Method employed	*First order rate constants and class sizes*				
	40°C		25°C		
	k_1	k_2	k_1	k_2	k_3
	$\times 10^2$ sec^{-1}			$\times 10^2$ sec^{-1}	
Film	2·5 55%	1·36 45%	1·26 37%	0·40 37%	0·03 26%
Lyophilization, solution technique	1·34 57%	0·6 43%	0·6 28%	0·17 28%	0·04 44%

At 40°C the data are remarkably similar with respect to the relative group contents and the relative ratios of k_1 to k_2. The film exchange rate constants are more rapid than those of the solution exchange experiments confirming the previous conclusion that diffusion in these thin films was not rate-limiting. Veis and Schnell[10] have suggested that the two classes of exchangeable hydrogens seen in gelatins at 40°C where no collagen-fold structures are present result from the differences in the basicity of the amide groups in the peptide backbones in different chain regions. Since collagen peptide chains contain alternating regions of polar and apolar character it may be that the differences in side chain polarity affect the backbone exchange rates.[14]

When collagen-fold units were present, that is, whenever some H— was in the non-exchangeable class as at 25°C, there was always the appearance of a third class of hydrogens with rate constant k_3. Table 1 shows that the fraction of group 3 hydrogens is quite large, much larger than the extent of actual fold-formation as indicated by optical rotation regain studies.[10] It is of interest also to note that, in spite of the correspondence of the exchange in films and solution at 40°C, at 25°C group 3 is smaller in the films than in solution.

It would appear that the new, slowly exchanging class of hydrogens is related to the regions of collagen-fold and represent regions contiguous to the helical folded units in which associated but non-helical chain segments are less accessible to solvent for exchange. The molecular picture is shown schematically in Fig. 6. The regions immediately adjacent to the fold units are those with restricted chain mobility and are the regions where helix propagation would take place at lower T_q. The lower value of the group 3 hydrogens in the film as compared to solution may be related to the difficulty in mobility of the chains in

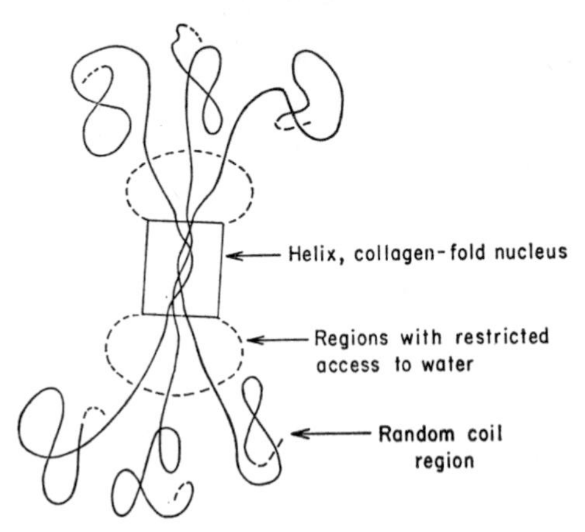

Fig. 6. Schematic diagram of the three regions of the gelatin collagen-fold system showing the different accessibility of the folded-regions to solvent from the bulk of the random chain regions.

the solid to become organized into fold units. However, this remains a point to be investigated since it is not clear that this difference may not also be due to the differences in experimental technique.

References

(1) Veis, A., "The Macromolecular Chemistry of Gelatin", pp. 267–416, Academic Press, New York (1964).
(2) Bradbury, E. and Martin, C., *Proc. Roy. Soc., London,* **A214,** 183 (1952).
(3) Veis, A. and Cohen, J., *J. Polymer Sci.,* **26,** 113 (1957).
(4) Harrington, W. F. and von Hippel, P. H., *Arch. Biochem. Biophys.,* **92,** 100 (1961).
(5) Flory, P. J. and Weaver, E. S., *J. Amer. Chem. Soc.,* **82,** 4518 (1960).
(6) Robinson, C. in "Nature and Structure of Collagen", p. 96. (Ed. J. T. Randall), Butterworths Ltd., London (1953).
(7) Ferry, J. D. and Eldridge, J. E., *J. Phys. Chem.,* **53,** 184 (1949).
(8) Bensusan, H. B. and Nielsen, S. O., *Biochemistry,* **3,** 1967 (1964).
(9) Veis, A. and Legowick, J. T., in "Structure and Function of Connective and Skeletal Tissues," p. 70. (Ed. S. Fitton-Jackson), Butterworths Ltd., London (1965).
(10) Veis, A. and Schnell, J., "Symposium on Fibrous Proteins", p. 193. (Ed. W. G. Crewether), Butterworths Ltd., London (1967).
(11) Hvidt, A. and Linderstrom-Lang, K. U., *Biochim. Biophys. Acta,* **14,** 574 (1954).
(12) Veis, A., Anesey, J. and Cohen, J., *Arch. Biochem. Biophys.,* **98,** 104 (1962).
(13) Piez, K. A., Eigner, E. A. and Lewis, M. S., *Biochemistry,* **2,** 58 (1963).
(14) Klotz, I. M. and Mueller, D. D., *Biochemistry,* **8,** 12 (1969).

Velocity and Equilibrium Aspects of the Sedimentation of Agar Gels

P. JOHNSON

Colloid Science Laboratory (Department of Biochemistry), Free School Lane, Cambridge

ABSTRACT. When a gel is subjected to a centrifugal field of sufficient magnitude, the motion of the gel surface which ensues may be followed readily and used to characterize gel behaviour. Eventually the motion slows down and ultimately ceases, the system showing no further change as long as the experimental conditions, particularly the speed, remain constant. The "equilibrium" condition can even be approached from another direction. The present paper deals with the gel concentration distribution during centrifugation, comparing it with typical solution systems. It deals also with the final "equilibrium" distribution from which, for favourable systems, swelling pressure data may be derived.

INTRODUCTION

Previous papers from this laboratory[1],[2],[3] have dealt in some detail with the sedimentation rate of gels in the ultracentrifuge. This paper is concerned generally with the processes occurring in the ultracentrifuge cell, with the concentration distribution and how it changes with time and, finally, how it leads to an equilibrium state in the cell. It will be shown also how this state can be used as a means of investigation of swelling pressure and its relation with concentration.

CONCENTRATION DISTRIBUTION IN FLOWING GEL

It is helpful to recall the main features of sedimentation for a monodisperse solute in normal solutions. Below a sedimenting boundary, the concentration (c) remains constant with increasing radial distance, (x), (in the plateau region) until close to the cell base (Fig. 1). With increasing time (t), the boundary moves and the concentration in the plateau region decreases according to

$$c = c_0 \,.\, \mathrm{e}^{-2s\omega^r t} \qquad (1)$$

where c_0 is the concentration at time $t = 0$, ω is angular velocity and s is the sedimentation coefficient. For the validity of this description, it is essential that solute is deposited continuously at the cell base or at least concentrated there where it is effectively removed from the system. Corresponding with the changing plateau concentration with increasing time, some change in sedimentation coefficient is also observed but this is usually small.

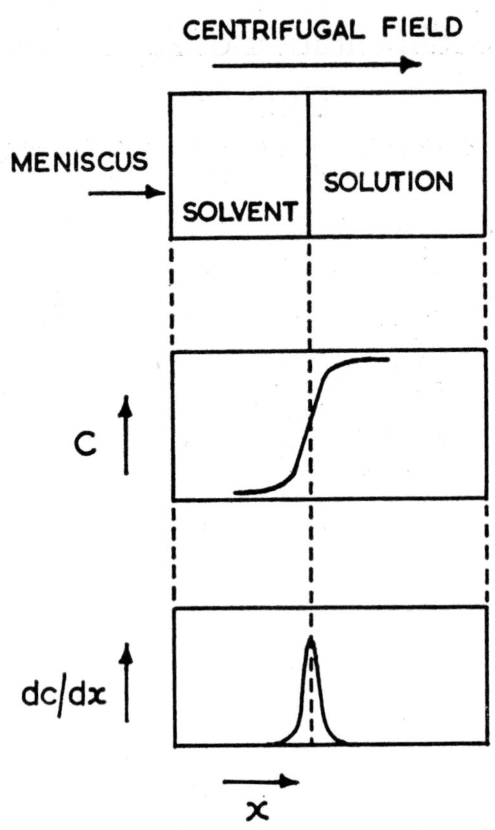

Fig. 1. The main features of sedimentation for a monodisperse solute in normal solution.

This picture applies to a simple case of sedimentation velocity in its earlier stages, but not necessarily to its later stages, nor to a region near the base of the cell. As the concentration increases near the base, the process of back diffusion becomes increasingly significant and eventually, if the field is applied for a long enough time, a state of equilibrium will be set up in which no further net sedimentation occurs, i.e. sediment-ation is balanced by diffusion. In such a balance, it is well known that the concentration varies with radial distance in a manner described by the usual equilibrium equations (Fig. 2).

Thus the plateau region of constant solute concentration gives way at long times or at the longer radial distances to the distribution of solute concentration approaching the equilibrium state, the details of the transition being determined by the nature of the solute system and the magnitude of the field.

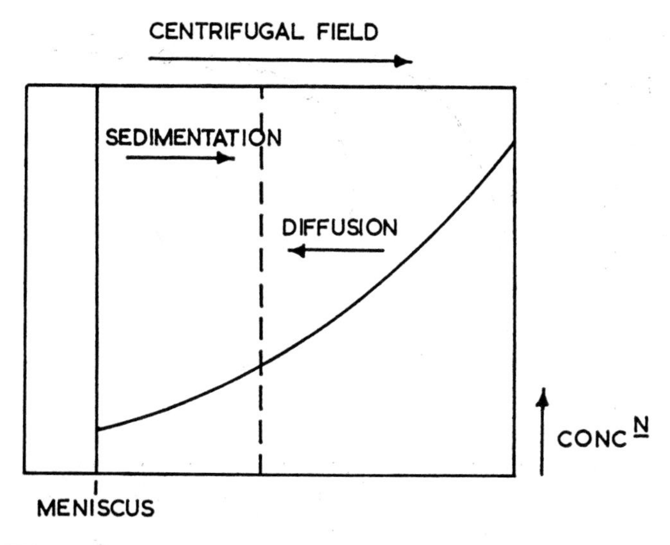

Fig. 2. Sedimentation equilibrium in normal solution.

A similar situation exists also for gel sedimentation in that both velocity and equilibrium aspects are apparent, but it is clear also that important differences occur. Thus it seems that the gelling material is not removed from the system at the cell base during sedimentation but remains effective throughout both aspects of sedimentation, though confined to a continuously decreasing volume.[1] At the end of an experiment the gelling material may be quantitatively removed as a coherent gel pad whose thickness is greater the lower the centrifugal field applied. If not removed from the cell, the pad will swell (Fig. 3) in the supernatant liquid to approach its original condition, after which it will behave in sedimentation just as in the first case. This retention of the gelling solute within the sedimenting system constitutes an important difference from "true" liquid solution systems, though any non-gelling solute which may occur (e.g. in most gelatins) within a gel may be removed at the base of the gel column as in the solution case.

Associated with this property is the considerable rise in average gelling solute concentration which must occur with the movement of the gel boundary—a further important difference from "true" solution systems where a decrease in concentration, though of much smaller magnitude, occurs. This increase in concentration with time causes the considerable decrease in sedimentation rate observed (see later) which also has no counterpart in true liquid solution.

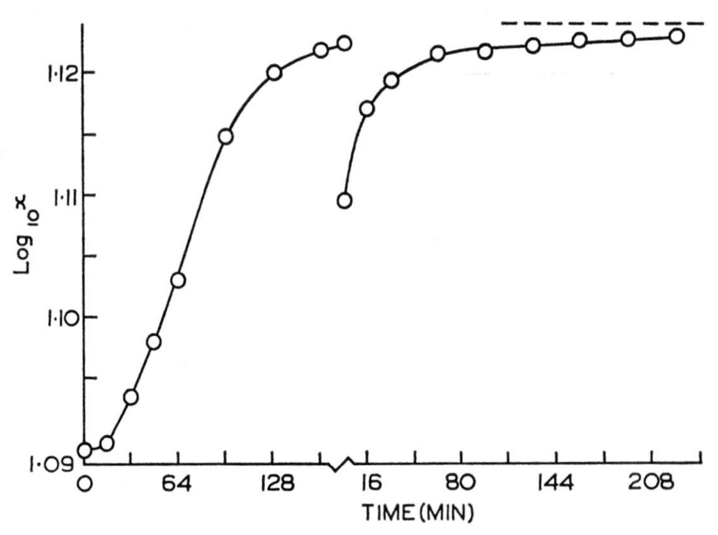

Fig. 3. Plot of $\log_{10} x$ *v.* t for the sedimentation of a ½% agar gel at 17·5°C in phosphate-NaCl buffer at pH 7·8, $I = 0{\cdot}1$ and 6803 rev/min. After 176 min, the rotor was decelerated and the cell allowed to stand for 15 h at 18°C before accelerating to the above conditions again (– – – – equilibrium level).

A similarity with the solution case is, however, the apparent constancy of concentration throughout the "plateau" region of the cell at any given time in the earlier stages of sedimentation. Svedberg and Pedersen[(4)] argued that a redistribution of solvent occurs in which solvent is squeezed out at the base of the gel column (owing to greater hydrostatic pressure) whilst swelling occurs at the top. On experimental grounds, it seems that this process is not involved significantly in the earlier stages of sedimentation, during which there are strong reasons for considering the gel concentration to be constant over a large portion of the gel column.[(3)] Thus although scattered light makes sedimenting gels rather opaque, in some very clear gels and particularly in the early stages of sedimentation, the schlieren trace (dn/dx *v.* x, where n is refractive index) remains horizontal at a very low (if not zero) level from the gel interface down almost to the cell bottom. A similar indication was also obtained by observing the sedimentation of a gel to which was covalently attached a suitable dyestuff (Procion Brilliant Red 2BS). The resulting optical density across the gel and its variation with the time (Fig. 4) clearly confirmed the constancy of the dye concentration (and therefore that of the gel) at a given time and its increase with time. A more quantitative proof was obtained by investigating the variation of s_T values (s_T being the sedimentation rate reduced to unit field at temperature T) with column length of gel.

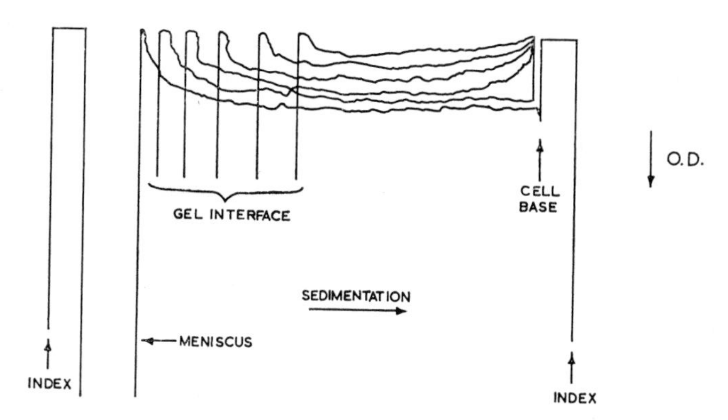

Fig. 4. Microdensitometer traces of photographic negatives taken during the sedimentation of a Procion (Brilliant Red 2BS) dyed gelatin gel at 18°C and 59 780 rev/min. Ordinate—optical density in arbitrary units. Abscissa—radial distance in cell. (From Johnson and King.[3])

If the gel concentration is to remain constant throughout its volume, it follows that during flow, small volume elements along a radius must be deformed in proportion to their length in the direction of the field. Thus the observed s_T value should be proportional to the column length, as is accurately observed (Fig. 5) for a range of temperatures and conditions. Nor is the s_T value affected by introducing a column of supernatant liquid above the gel, so that total hydrostatic pressure seems relatively unimportant. Further, observations on layers of one gel upon another of different concentration were entirely explicable in terms of the s_T values of the separate gels.

Thus in the velocity stages of gel sedimentation it seems that, apart from minor local irregularities of concentration arising from cell imperfections, density inhomogeneity, etc. (e.g. from adsorbed materials or included particles), the concentration across the cell below the boundary may be taken as approximately constant as in true solution sedimentation (though increasing markedly with time). In dealing further with the variation of sedimentation rate with concentration, this is now assumed (see below).

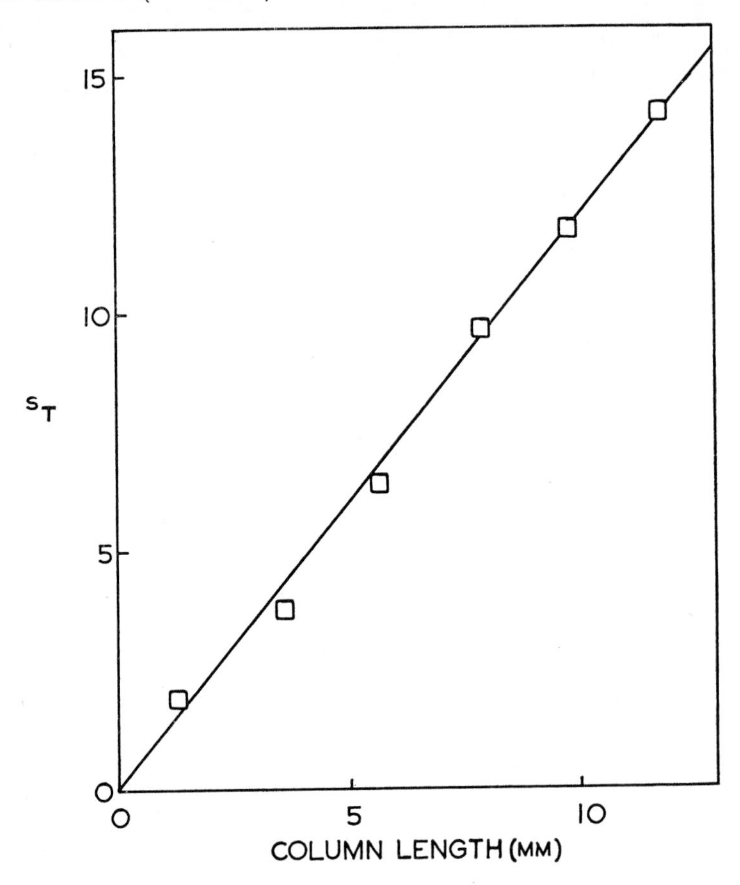

Fig. 5. The dependence of s_T upon column length for aqueous 2% gelatin gels at 10°C and 52 640 rev/min. (From Johnson and King.[3])

However, at a relatively early time, the schlieren trace may be seen to bend upwards steeply near the very base of the gel column. With increasing time, this bending upwards becomes more gradual and occurs further and further from cell base. In many cases the trace becomes very indistinct or disappears, and continuous observation of the schlieren trace becomes impossible. However, these observations are consistent with what is now known regarding the "approach to equilibrium" and equilibrium distribution of gel concentration (see later).

EQUILIBRIUM ASPECTS OF GEL SEDIMENTATION

From Fig. 3, it was clear that if the centrifugal field is applied for a long enough period, then an equilibrium level for the gel interface is reached. In this situation it seems that a balance has been achieved

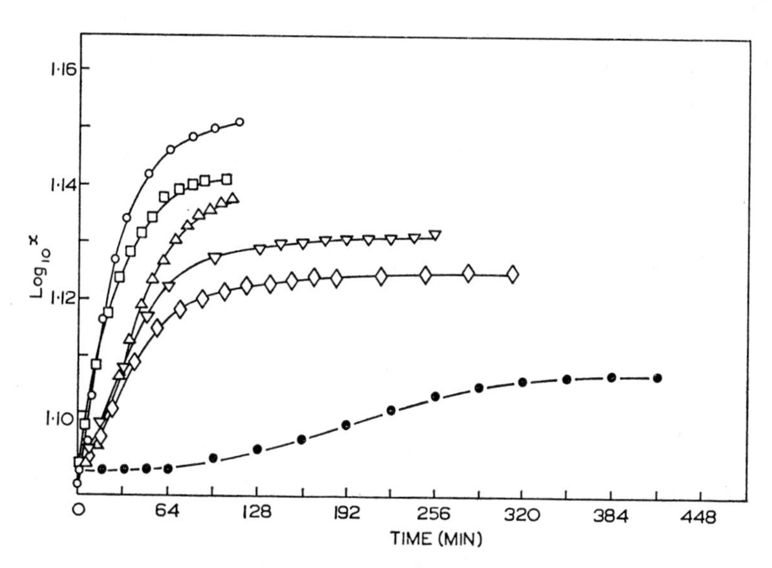

Fig. 6. The dependence of final equilibrium level on rotational speed for 1% Difco Agar gels in phosphate-NaCl buffer at pH 7·8, $I = 0·1$.

	Rotational Speed (rev/min)	*Maturing Time* (h)	*Temperature* (°C)
○	17 980	$\frac{1}{2}$	17·1 ± 0·1
□	12 590	$\frac{1}{2}$	21·7 ± 0·1
△	12 590	16	19·9 ± 0·1
△	9230	$\frac{1}{2}$	20·2 ± 0·1
◇	9230	45	18·8 ± 0·1
●	6803	$\frac{1}{2}$	18·0 ± 0·4

between sedimentation and swelling within the gel column. With increasing centrifugal field, such a balance is reached in shorter gel columns (Fig. 6) and on the other hand, at a given field, increase in concentration of the gel results in longer equilibrated gel columns (Fig. 7).

Before proceeding further, it was considered essential to demonstrate the true equilibrium nature of the levels reached after long times. Accordingly the "equilibrium" level for a 3% agar gel was approached from "opposite directions" (Fig. 8). Thus in one experiment the gel was spun for many hours at 23 150 rev/min in the usual manner but in a further comparison experiment, overspeeding was utilized. Thus the

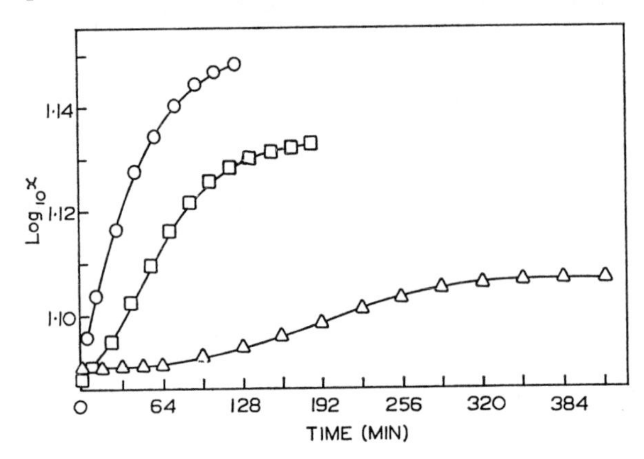

Fig. 7. The dependence of final equilibrium level on gel concentration for Difco Agar Gels in phosphate-NaCl buffer at pH 7·8, $I = 0{\cdot}1$ and at 6803 rev/min.

	Agar Concentration (%)	*Temperature* (°C)
○	$\frac{1}{4}$	18·4 ± 0·7
□	$\frac{1}{2}$	18·1 ± 0·3
△	1	18·1 ± 0·3

same type of gel was first spun at 42 040 rev/min so that the gel column was shortened below the equilibrium length appropriate to the lower field, and then at 23 150 rev/min for an extended period. It seems clear that in both processes, the same equilibrium length of column is approached at long times, and that genuine equilibrium rather than merely very slow rate of change is indicated. Thus it seemed profitable to probe further into the nature of this equilibrium state.

Concentration distribution was of obvious interest but the most obvious method of deriving this information was made impossible by the fading of the schlieren trace after the early stages of sedimentation. This occurred much too early and too abruptly to be caused by mere increase in the gel concentration and is thought to be caused by increased light scattering within the gel. This probably arises as a result of the flow occurring which must be at a coarser level than molecular. Such increased scattering must inevitably interfere with absorption optical methods as well as schlieren so that, at those stages where this complication exists, other methods of concentration determination are required. It seems conceivable that where no further net flow occurs, then optical methods might again be useful and this possibility is being investigated.

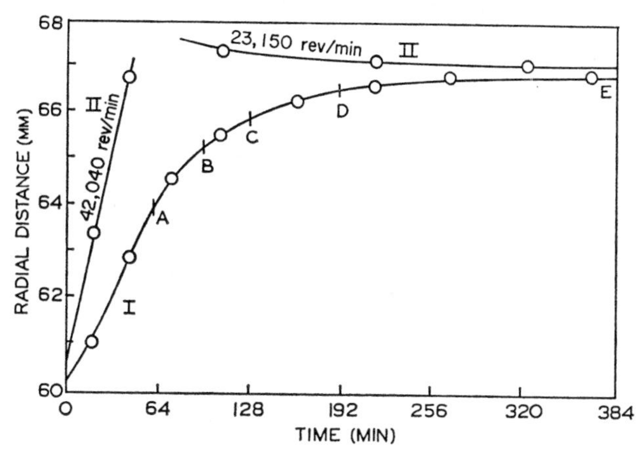

Fig. 8. Demonstration of true equilibrium nature of final level in gel sedimentation for washed Oxoid Ionagar in water, initially at concentration of 3 g/100 ml of H_2O. Curve 1. Plot of radial position of gel interface against time at 23 150 rev/min. Points A – – – – E represent stages of sedimentation which are further considered in Fig. 10. Curve 2. Speed as indicated on curve.

In earlier work (Johnson[1]), the relative unimportance of elastic processes in gel sedimentation was demonstrated, and in more recent work it has been confirmed, for the conditions used, that the equilibrium column length, as indicated during spinning at low speed (from the position of the gel-solvent interface and the known position of the base of the cell relative to the index marks), was not significantly different from the length observed directly in the cell after stopping the ultracentrifuge. Thus it was feasible to sample the gel column at different heights and to use analytical methods to measure the concentration of the gelling material. A sledge type (moving sample) microtome was used to slice the gel column after supporting in paraffin wax, slices not thinner than 100 microns being used. Instead of using total solute content to indicate concentration, which would have required gel slices of identical or accurately known dimensions, it was decided to measure gel density, a method which should be independent of slice dimensions. Fig. 9 shows clearly that the density is linearly related to the gel concentration. Accordingly, small discs were cut from the gel slices and their densities were measured by a density gradient column set up according to the method of Tung and Taylor[5],[6] and Salo and Kouns.[7] Benzene and carbon tetrachloride were the organic liquids chosen to avoid swelling effects, and a linear column was readily obtained as shown by the calibration with sucrose/water solutions of known density.

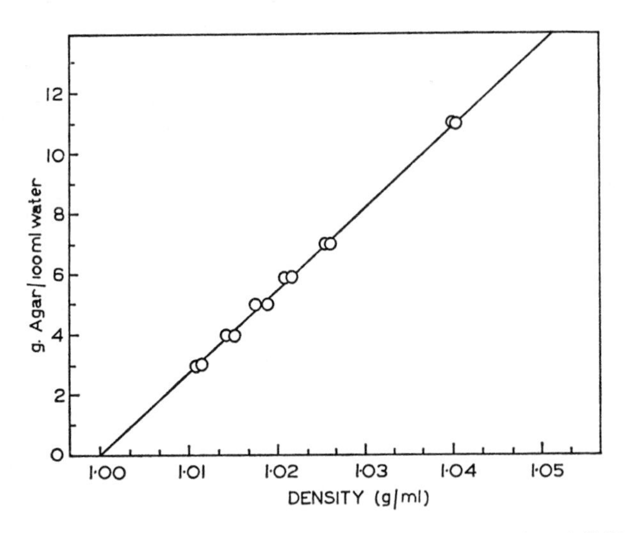

Fig. 9. The dependence of gel density (g/ml) on gel concentration (g/100 ml water) for washed Oxoid Ionagar.

Columns in which $d\rho/dx$ (x in cm) was about 0·001 were used so that the densities of unknown sucrose solutions could be determined to ±0·0001. The accuracy of determining gel densities was somewhat less (±0·0002) but this allowed gel concentration to be determined to ±0·05 g/100 ml.

Fig. 10(a) and (b) shows the changing distribution of agar concentration with the duration of spinning. At point A, we have clearly the remains of the plateau of constant concentration associated with the sedimentation velocity phase. However, this is shortly replaced by the continuously changing concentration of the later curves, and finally by curve E which is very close to equilibrium. In this case, a short region near the meniscus, where the concentration remains constant, apparently occurs but it seems possible that this may arise from artefacts in the curved meniscus region. Further work on this point is required.

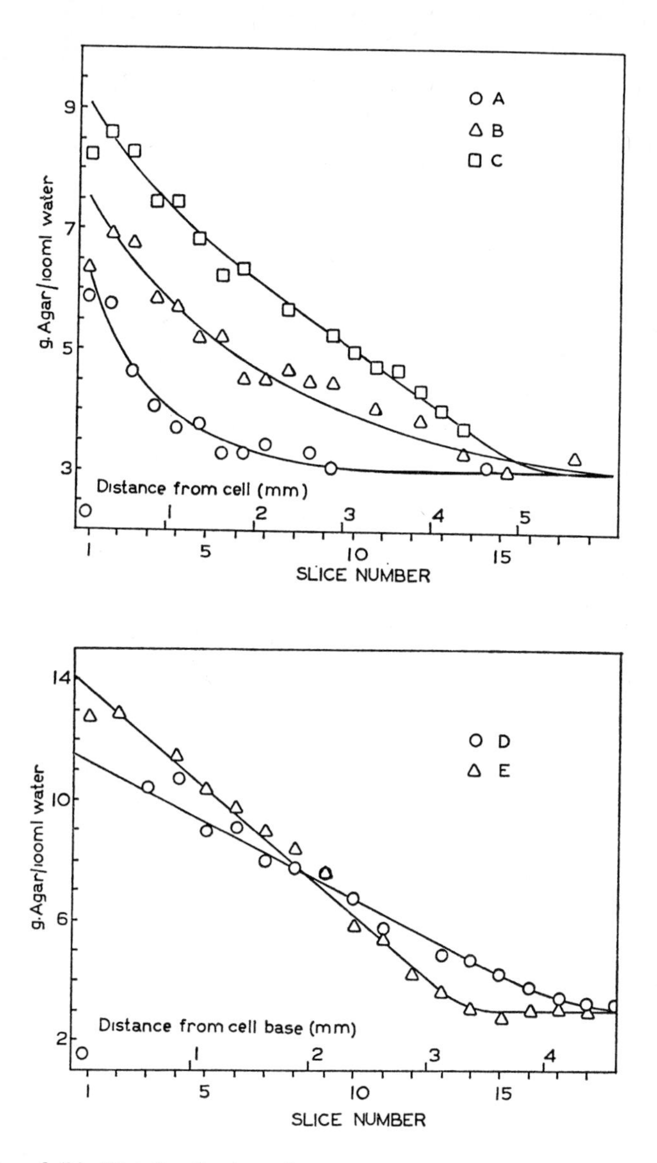

Fig. 10(a) and (b). The distribution of concentration in the cell at different times of sedimentation for washed Oxoid Ionagar in water at 23 150 rev/min. Letters A – – – – E refer to positions of the gel interface shown in Fig. 8.

Results to date have been of a preliminary nature only and their complete reliability has to be established. A step in this direction has been taken by integrating over the whole cell and comparing total agar calculated with that taken initially. Agreement within 5% has been obtained. However, much further work is yet required before the results obtained can be utilized with confidence.

UTILIZATION OF GEL CONCENTRATION DISTRIBUTION

Consider a small cylindrical element of a gel column of thickness dx in a radial direction (Fig. 11). At equilibrium for the whole system, this element is in equilibrium with it surroundings. The concentration of

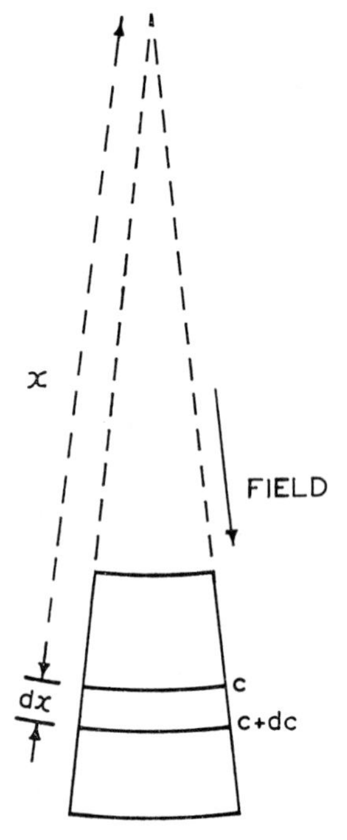

Fig. 11. Equilibrium in a sector-shaped gel column.

gelling material increases from c at radius x to $c + dc$ at $(x + dx)$ and in both positions the swelling pressure associated with these concentration levels (or, in other language, the tendency to diffuse of the solute) is balanced by the effect of the centrifugal field. As argued by Svedberg and Pedersen[4] the latter is related not to the total hydrostatic pressure but to the partial pressure, P_p, at a given distance x from the axis of rotation where

$$P_p = \omega^2 \int_{x_0}^{x} c(1 - \bar{v}\rho)x \, dx \tag{2}$$

where x_0 is the distance from the gel meniscus to the centre of rotation, c is the concentration in g/ml at distance x, $\bar{v}$ is the partial specific volume of the solute and ρ is the gel density.

On the other hand, the swelling pressure P_s of a gel is, according to Freundlich,[8] given by

$$P_s = P_0 c^k \tag{3}$$

where P_0 and k are constants for the particular gel system. Fig. 12

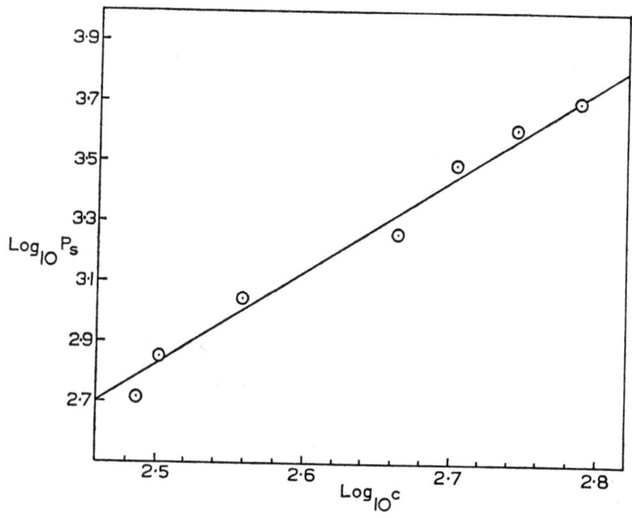

Fig. 12. Plot of $\log_{10} P_s$ v. $\log_{10} c$ for Freundlich's[8] gelatin-water data.

contains Freundlich's data for aqueous gelatin gels plotted as $\log_{10} P_s$ v. $\log_{10} c$, from which $k \approx 3$.

At equilibrium we have

$$\frac{\partial P_p}{\partial x} \, . \, dx = \frac{\partial P_s}{\partial x} \, . \, dx \tag{4}$$

i.e.

$$\omega^2 c(1 - \bar{v}\rho)x = kP_0 c^{k-1} \frac{dc}{dx}$$

or

$$\frac{\omega^2(1 - \bar{v}\rho)}{kP_0} x \, . \, dx = c^{k-2} \, dc$$

Integrating between x_0, the position of the gel-solvent interface and some position in the gel x, we obtain

$$\frac{\omega^2(1-\bar{v}\rho)}{2kP_0}[x^2 - x_0^2] = \frac{1}{(k-1)}[c^{k-1} - c_0^{k-1}] \tag{5}$$

If $k = 2$, then this equation reduces to

$$\frac{\omega^2(1-\bar{v}\rho)}{4P_0}(x^2 - x_0^2) = c - c_0 \tag{6}$$

and if $k = 3$, we obtain

$$\frac{\omega^2(1-\bar{v}\rho)}{3P_0}(x^2 - x_0^2) = c^2 - c_0^2 \tag{7}$$

In accordance with equations (6) and (7), c and c^2 are each plotted against x^2 in Fig. 13 and it seems very clear that k must be approximately 2, though it should be noted that k is not necessarily integral.

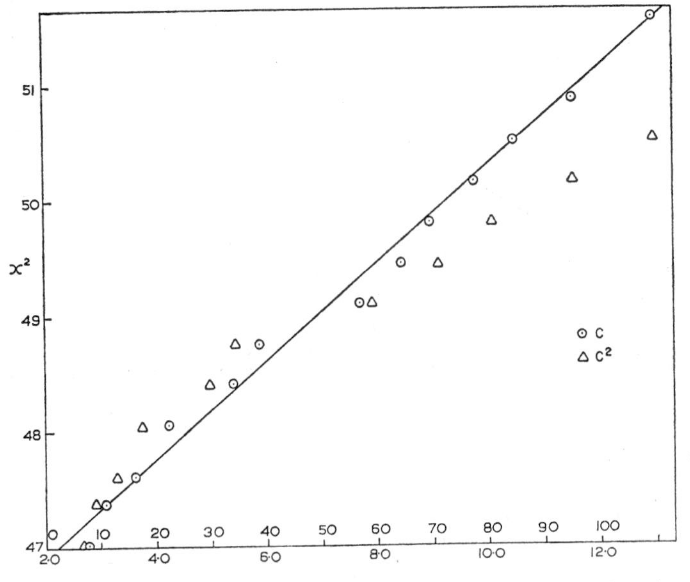

Fig. 13. Plot of c (or c^2) $v.$ x^2 for Ionagar concentration distribution given by curve E of Fig. 10.

However, using the slope of the linear plot of c $v.$ x^2, P_0 is evaluated as $2{\cdot}52 \times 10^7$ (where c is g/cm^3 solvent and P is in dynes/cm^2).

These conclusions are preliminary only and more experimental data is required to obtain reliable P_0 values. P_0 values tabulated by Freundlich for other systems are, however, of a similar magnitude, when account is taken of the concentration and pressure units employed. Thus for gelatin in water, his P_0 value becomes $2 \cdot 7 \times 10^7$.

ACKNOWLEDGEMENT

I am indebted to Mr. R. W. Turvey for the equilibrium results reported in this paper.

References

(1) Johnson, P., *Proc. Roy. Soc. London*, **A278,** 527 (1964).
(2) Johnson, P. and Metcalfe, J. C., *Eur. Polym. J.*, **3,** 423 (1967).
(3) Johnson, P. and King, R. W., *J. Photogr. Soc.*, **16,** 82 (1968).
(4) Svedberg, T. and Pedersen, K. O., "The Ultracentrifuge", p. 29, Oxford Press, (1940).
(5) Tung, L. H. and Taylor, W. C., *J. Polym. Sci.*, **17,** 441 (1955).
(6) Tung, L. H. and Taylor, W. C., *J. Polym. Sci.*, **19,** 598 (1956).
Tung, L. H. and Taylor, W. C., *J. Polym. Sci.*, **21,** 144 (1956).
(7) Salo, T. and Kouns, D. M., *Anal. Biochem.*, **13,** 74 (1965).
(8) Freundlich, H., "Colloid and Capillary Chemistry", p. 674, Methuen (1926).

Kinetics and Equilibria of Swelling of Gelatin Layers in Water

A. LIBICKÝ and D. BERMANE

Ciba-Geigy Photochemical Ltd., Fribourg, Switzerland

ABSTRACT. The kinetics of swelling in water of hardened and unhardened model gelatin layers have been investigated by means of thickness determinations with the aid of a modified Wallace Indentation tester. The swelling curves can, as a first approximation, be expressed by means of a second order rate equation, with the equilibrium swelling h_∞ and the initial velocity of swelling V_0 as parameters. The temperature dependence of V_0 and the limiting value of swell ratio S_∞ are discussed for non-crosslinked and crosslinked gelatin layers, in the temperature range 10–30°C. It is demonstrated for a non-crosslinked gelatin, that S_∞ decreases as a linear function of dry thickness (4–24 μ), whereas V_0 is practically independent of it.

INTRODUCTION

The degree of crosslinking of gelatin is one of the critical factors which influence the mechanical and physico-chemical properties of photographic layers. Information on gelatin crosslinking is generally obtained by means of relatively simple measurements, such as those of the melting point, rigidity modulus, scratch resistance and water absorption.

The point in common to all these methods of investigation is that the value of the crosslinking dependent variable is determined when the material is in the swollen state. The necessity of swelling a material in order to determine to what extent it is crosslinked leads to the obvious conclusion that swelling itself may be a factor of primary importance. It was therefore considered worthwhile to carry out a systematic study of the kinetics and equilibria of swelling of gelatin layers in water.

The swelling of gelatin layers has been investigated by several authors, using various experimental techniques, e.g. weight determination of amount of water absorbed,[1] estimation of volume change in the case of isotropic swelling[2] and estimation of change of thickness,[3] double refraction[4] or infra-red absorption in the case of uniaxial swelling.

Several empirical rate equations have been reported for describing the kinetics of swelling and are given below in forms convenient for direct comparison.

$$K_1 = \frac{1}{t} \log \frac{h_\infty}{h_\infty - h} \tag{1}$$

(1907) Sheppard and Mees.[5]

$$K_2 = \frac{1}{t^{\frac{1}{2}}} \log \frac{h_\infty}{h_\infty - h} \tag{2}$$

(1947) Bromberg and Maltseva.[6]

$$K_3 = \frac{1}{t^b} \log \frac{h_\infty}{h_\infty - h} \tag{3}$$

(1948) Dumansky *et al.*[7]

$$K_4 = \frac{1}{t} \cdot \frac{h \, . \, h_\infty}{h_\infty - h} \tag{4}$$

(1964) Robinson.[8]

Here, h indicates the vertical swelling at time t and h_∞, the equilibrium swelling attained for $t \rightarrow \infty$. Relationship (1) corresponds to a first order rate equation. Its agreement with experimental results is often very poor.[6] The equations (2) and (3) were obtained by introducing corrections to the first relationship; they become identical when the parameter $b = \frac{1}{2}$, as was actually the case for the materials investigated by Dumansky and co-workers.[7]

Relationship (4) is formally equivalent to a second order rate equation. Its application to the experimental results has the advantage with respect to the first three equations, that the value of h_∞ is not arbitrary, but may be directly evaluated from the equation, for the boundary condition that $t \rightarrow \infty$.

Preliminary investigations showed a reasonable fit of our experimental data with equation (4). A more detailed study of the validity of this relationship and its physical interpretation was therefore undertaken and its results are discussed below.

Experimental data plotted according to Robinson[8] gave straight lines as shown in Fig. 2. This can be expressed by equation (5) as:

$$t/h = a + bt \tag{5}$$

where $a = 1/K_4$, and

$$b = 1/h_\infty \tag{6}$$

Thus, the values of h_∞ and K_4 are given by the slope of the line and its intersect respectively.

The physical significance of K_4 can be shown by rearrangement and differentiation of (5). One obtains:

$$\mathrm{d}h/\mathrm{d}t = a/(a + bt)^2 \tag{7}$$

which for $t \to 0$ reduces to

$$\lim_{t \to 0}\left(\frac{\mathrm{d}h}{\mathrm{d}t}\right) = \frac{1}{a} = K_4 = V_0 \tag{8}$$

K_4 thus represents the extrapolated initial velocity of swelling, hereafter referred to as V_0.

By substituting for a and b in equation (7), from (8) and (6) respectively, one finds:

$$\mathrm{d}h/\mathrm{d}t = V_0(1 - h/h_\infty)^2 \tag{9}$$

so that a logarithmic plot of $\mathrm{d}h/\mathrm{d}t$ against $(1 - h/h_\infty)$ should have a slope equal to 2 and an intersect value of $\log V_0$.

To evaluate the swelling data of various layers, one must take into account the difference in their dry thickness d. This can be achieved by defining the respective volume concentrations of gelatin and water in the swollen layer system as:

$$C_{\mathrm{gel}} = d/(h + d) \tag{10}$$

and

$$C_{\mathrm{H_2O}} = h/(h + d) \tag{11}$$

so that whatever the degree of swelling of the system the sum of C_{gel} and $C_{\mathrm{H_2O}}$ remains equal to unity.

Inasmuch as V_0 represents the initial velocity of swelling, $-V_0/d$ expresses the initial change of volume concentration of gelatin. This can be shown by rearrangement and differentiation of equation (10) with respect to time and substitution for $\mathrm{d}h/\mathrm{d}t$ into equation (9). This results in

$$\frac{\mathrm{d}C_{\mathrm{gel}}}{\mathrm{d}t} = -\frac{V_0}{d}\left(\frac{C_{\mathrm{gel}} - C_{\infty\mathrm{gel}}}{1 - C_{\infty\mathrm{gel}}}\right)^2 \tag{12}$$

where

$$C_{\infty\mathrm{gel}} = \frac{d}{h_\infty + d}.$$

Approximation of equation (12) for $t \rightarrow 0$ then gives:

$$\lim_{t \to 0} \left(\frac{dC_{gel}}{dt} \right) = -\frac{V_0}{d} \tag{13}$$

The constants a and b in equation (5) can also be expressed by means of the time τ at which swelling reaches the value of $h_\infty/2$. By substitution for h and b in equation (5) and following rearrangement one obtains:

$$a = \tau / h_\infty \tag{14}$$

and by comparison with (8) and (6):

$$\tau = a/b = h_\infty / V_0 \tag{15}$$

Equations (9) and (13) expressed with the aid of (15) then give

$$\frac{dh}{dt} = \frac{1}{\tau \, . \, h_\infty} (h_\infty - h)^2 \tag{16}$$

and

$$\lim_{t \to 0} \left(\frac{dC_{gel}}{dt} \right) = -\frac{h_\infty}{\tau \, . \, d} \tag{17}$$

The reciprocal value of the gelatin volume concentration is called the swell ratio and it is only a matter of convenience to refer for example to the equilibrium swell ratio S_∞ or equilibrium gel concentration $C_{\infty gel}$.

Although both equations (13) and (17) give a means of comparing swelling velocities of layers of various thickness, the found values are basically extrapolated ones and direct comparison with experimental data is not possible. A correlation between calculated and experimental data can, however, be achieved by evaluating the time necessary for a layer to expand to a given swell ratio.

For such comparisons, the value of $S = 2$ ($C_{gel} = 0{\cdot}5$) has been arbitrarily chosen. In this case, $h = d$ so that substitution from (14) and (9) into (5) gives

$$t_{S=2\cdot 0} = \tau \left(\frac{h_\infty}{h_\infty - d} \right) = \tau \left(\frac{1}{S_\infty - 2} \right) \tag{18}$$

EXPERIMENTAL

Measurement of swelling

As the swelling of thin gelatin layers coated on hydrophobic substrates is practically one-dimensional, the volume changes occurring can be sufficiently well characterized by measurements of changes in thickness of the coated layers.

These measurements were carried out with a Wallace H7 identation tester, using a technique similar to that described by Taylor and Kragh.[9] The instrument was modified in view of recording the data and reducing errors due to temperature changes of the sample holder. The apparatus is shown in Fig. 1.

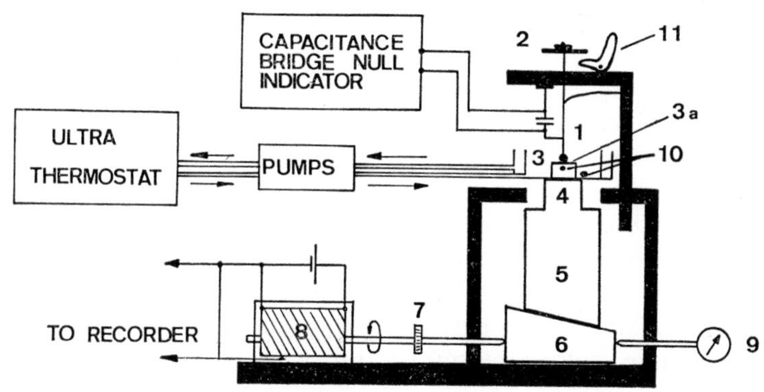

Fig. 1. Wallace H7 Indentation Tester (Modified) Apparatus. Key: 1, sensor; 2, load; 3, sample holder; 3a, sample; 4, 5 and 6, precision movement table; 7, hand screw; 8, potentiometer; 9, micrometric gauge; 10, Pt-resistance thermometers; 11, lever and time base switch.

Measurements of thickness, respectively of swelling, consist in evaluating the shift of position of table 4, necessary to maintain the spring balanced sensor 1 in a constant position and simultaneously in touch with the sample surface (3a).

The sensor is coupled to the mobile part of a balanced capacitance bridge circuit. Any change of sensor position causes the circuit to become out of balance which is indicated by an acoustic or optical signal. The disappearance of the signal thus indicates that the electronic circuit has been returned to its former equilibrium.

The difference in readings from the gauge 9 before and after the gelatin layer has either been removed from the support or left to swell, give the dry thickness or the swelling of the gelatin.

As it was found that the velocity of swelling is substantially reduced during the period of contact of the sensor with the layer, measurements were carried out in the shortest time possible (1–3 s). Between measurements, the sensor was lifted by means of the lever 11 about 3 mm above the sample surface. The individual measurement times were excluded from the time of swelling by synchronizing the time base of the recorder with the actual time of swelling of the layer. This was achieved by working a relay switching the time base, with a microswitch monitored by the lever for lowering the sensor into its measuring position.

To record the measurements of swelling, the screw 7 initiating the table shift was connected to a slide-wire potentiometer 8 fed from a constant voltage source and branched into a Y-T recorder. Its sensitivity was adapted to give a 4–5 mm/μ recording (according to the size of the chart) and a 50μ per scale chart. The instrument gauge 9 was used for calibrating the recorder.

The short time repeatability of a single measurement was usually in the range of $\pm 0{\cdot}1\mu$, if the dead path of the wedge system (components 5 and 6) was avoided. Values of equilibrium swelling from 30 to 180μ could be reproduced within $\pm 3\%$. Values of dry thickness in the range 5–25μ were normally reproducible to $\pm 0{\cdot}2\mu$.

The sample holder 3 was constructed of plexiglass as a concentric overflow reservoir with two departments. The interior one, into which the water was conducted directly, had a free volume of $\sim$15 ml. Distilled water was cycled between a thermostatically controlled bath and the sample holder by means of two peristaltic pumps. Flow velocities were variable in the range from 0 to 250 ml/min.

The temperatures of the sample holder at 2 mm under the surface of the sample and that of the water in its interior department could be continuously measured by means of two Pt-resistance thermometers 10. Either of these temperatures could be recorded with the desired precision onto the same chart as the swelling data. The sample holder used had a temperature coefficient of 1·8μ/°C. Corrections of measured dry thickness were therefore introduced for changes of temperature $\Delta T \geqslant 0{\cdot}1$°C.

Materials

The experiments were carried out on model gelatin layers of various thickness either with or without the crosslinking agent (CLA) 2·4 dichlor-6-*p*-sulphanilino-1,3,5-triazine (content 1·9 g or 7·65 g/100 g gelatin). Besides this the layers contained 0·8 g/100 g gelatin of a magenta dye for visual control of coating homogeneity. The measurements were mostly performed on samples from a limed-bone gelatin with a Bloom strength of 260 g. Comparative data were also obtained from a limed-hide gelatin with a Bloom strength of 140 g. The layers, with a total dry thickness in the range 4–25 μ were slit-coated at speeds of 3·5–4·4 m/min from solutions of pH $\sim$5·6, maintained at 40–45°C and containing 8–16 g gelatin/100 ml solution. Under these conditions, uncrosslinked single layers could be prepared with a thickness of up to ~20 μ, whereas crosslinked ones up to only ~10 μ. Thicker crosslinked coatings were thus always prepared by multiple coatings with complete drying taking place between coatings.

All layers were set at 0°C, dried in a 2-zone dryer with air conditioning at 27°C, 10% RH and 45°C, 10% RH respectively, then conditioned at 20% and 80% RH. The total drying time was of the order of 20 min. The samples were spooled, then stored before measurement in a controlled room at 20°C and 60–65% RH. Measurements were carried out in the same room after the samples had been left freely exposed to the room atmosphere for at least 24 h (but usually for a considerably longer period). The layers were coated on a 200 μ thick triacetate base.

The table in Fig. 12 shows the main data of the layers used. Although the sample marked as No. 1650 was a 4-layer system, the predecessors with 1, 2 and 3 layers were available, and the results of the measurements performed on them are also reported.

RESULTS AND DISCUSSION

Validity of Robinson's equation

In order to verify the validity of Robinson's equation (5), the swelling data obtained with both uncrosslinked and crosslinked gelatin layers were evaluated by means of several approaches.

(a) Fig. 2 shows the results obtained by plotting t/h against t for a series of uncrosslinked layers of one gelatin with a dry thickness ranging from 4–23 μ, the number n of layers increasing from 1 to 4.

(b) The calculated and experimental values of the halftime of swelling τ were also compared. The calculated ones were obtained from equation (15) and least square analysis of the whole kinetic curve, whereas the experimental values were evaluated by linear interpolation between times corresponding to the swellings closest to $h_\infty/2$.

The results relating to uncrosslinked and crosslinked materials are shown as a function of temperature of swelling in Fig. 3. For the uncrosslinked material (1649) there is an average agreement to within 4% between the calculated and experimental half times over the whole experimental range, but for the hardened material (1927) there is a systematic negative deviation of the calculated values with an average of about 12% for the range 10–30°C.

In spite of the reasonable agreement between the calculated and experimental values of τ for both types of layers, one sees that the behaviour of unhardened layers is more complicated.

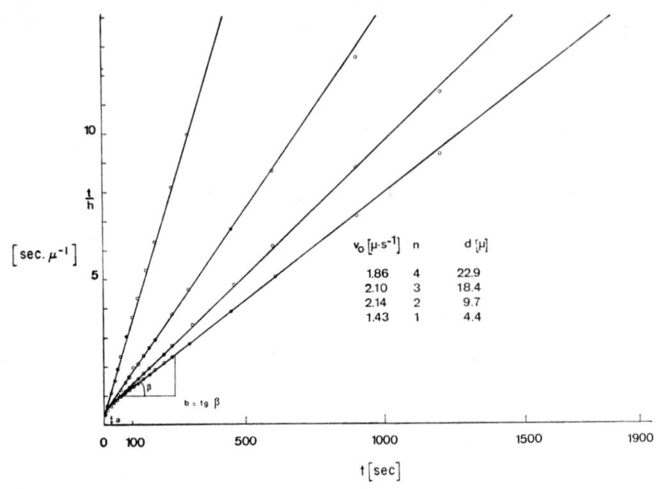

Fig. 2. Verification of Robinson's equation. Swelling of unhardened gelatin layers at 20°C; material: 1650; h: swelling; t: time.

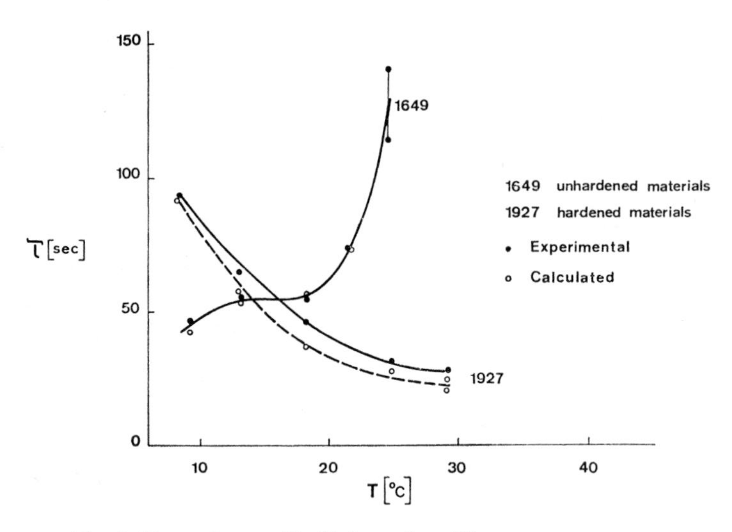

Fig. 3. Dependence of half time of swelling on temperature.

(c) A better understanding of the type of deviations obtained follows from a logarithmic plot of dh/dt against $(1 - h/h_\infty)$, according to equation (9).

Figs. 4 and 5 relate to uncrosslinked layers:

at a given temperature the fit for thick layers is better than for thin ones. The mean value of the slope ranges from 3 to 2 for thicknesses increasing from 3·5 μ to $\sim$24 μ;

at a given thickness (of $\sim$20 μ) a good fit with a mean slope practically equal to 2 is obtained at temperatures below 18°C. At higher temperatures the curve becomes deformed. Higher slope values are found for $1 - h/h_\infty$ close to 1 (corresponding to low swelling), while lower slopes are obtained for $1 - h/h_\infty < 0{\cdot}5$.

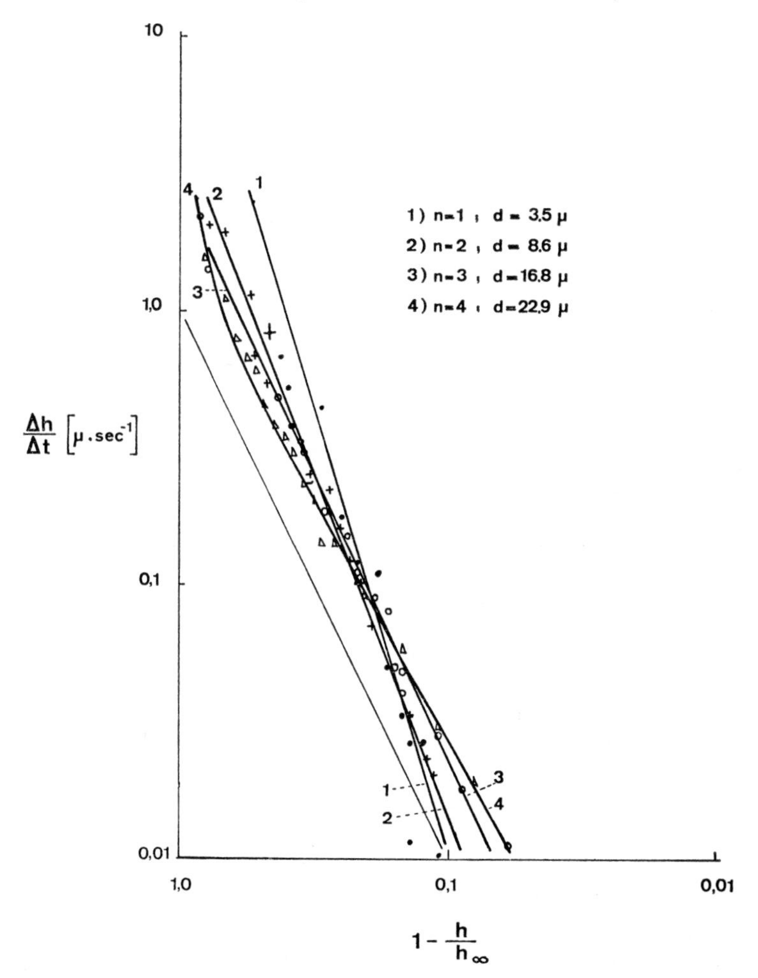

Fig. 4. Dependence of velocity of swelling on the degree of swelling—unhardened layers. Constant temperature. Material: 1650; $t = 20{\cdot}5$°C.

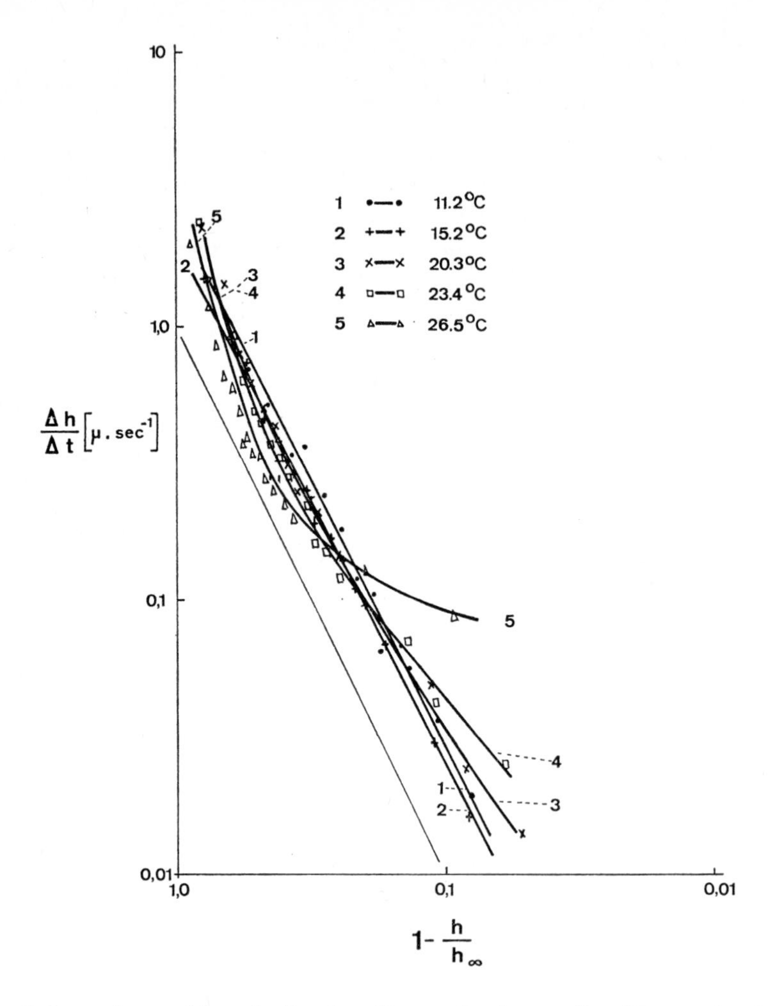

Fig. 5. Dependence of the velocity of swelling on the degree of swelling—unhardened layers. Constant layer thickness. Material: 1649; $\bar{d} = 20\mu$; $n = 1$.

Fig. 6 presents the data obtained at various temperatures for the crosslinked material: during swelling at 10°C there is a progressive change of slope from ~1 to 2. With increase of temperature, the initial slope value increases but remains smaller than 2. As the deviations of the initial slope value are systematically negative, recalculation of the data was attempted with a first order rate equation. This, however, lead to a worse overall fit than found originally.

(d) Further information on the adequacy of the fit of equation (5) is found by comparing the calculated and experimental swelling curves directly. Such comparisons are shown in Figs. 7, 8 and 9. The fit for the

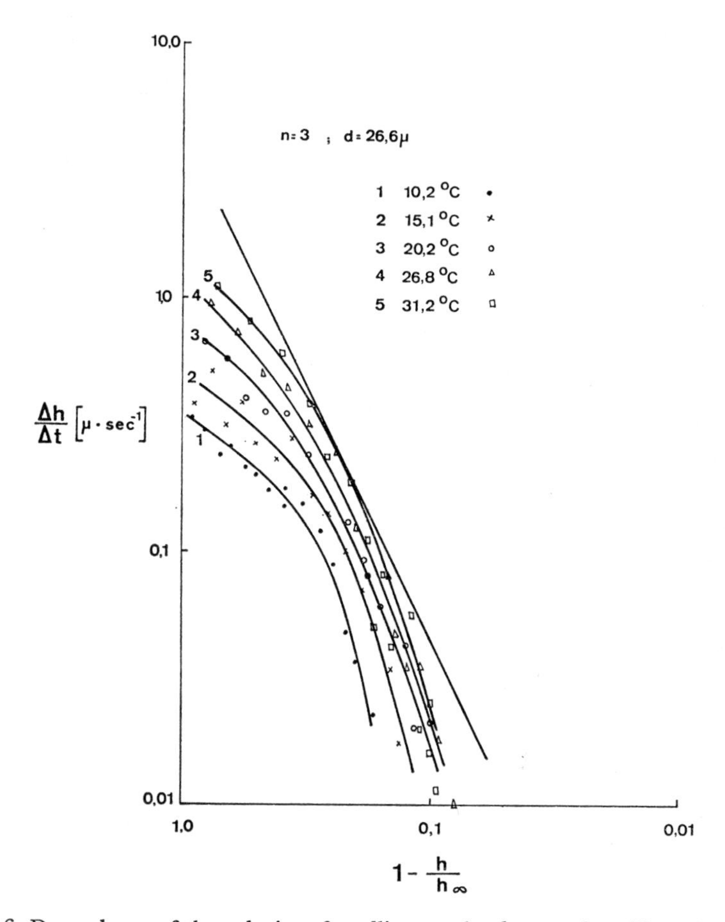

Fig. 6. Dependence of the velocity of swelling on the degree of swelling—hardened layers. Constant layer thickness. Material: 1927.

unhardened materials 1650 and 1649 at room temperature or lower is rather good, while the hardened material (1927) shows a systematic deviation.

On the basis of the experimental evidence so far obtained, it is clear that the kinetics of swelling in water is rather complex and that a second order rate equation is not a theoretically appropriate relationship.

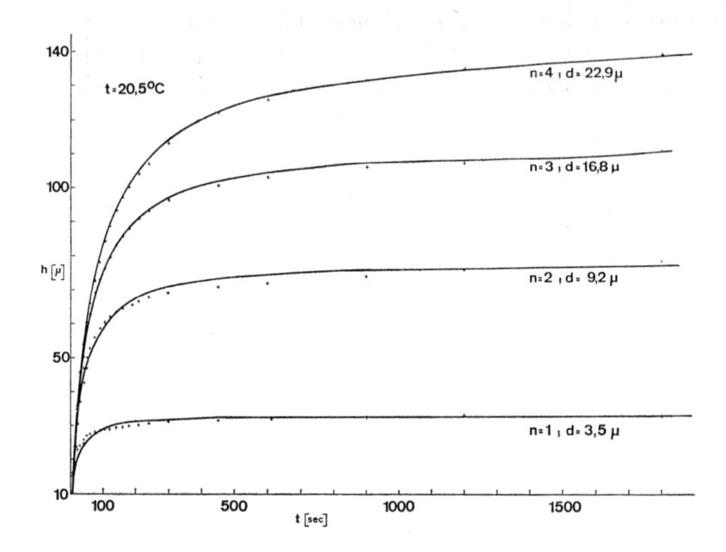

Fig. 7. Experimental values of swelling and calculated swelling curves of unhardened layers—constant temperature. Material: 1650.

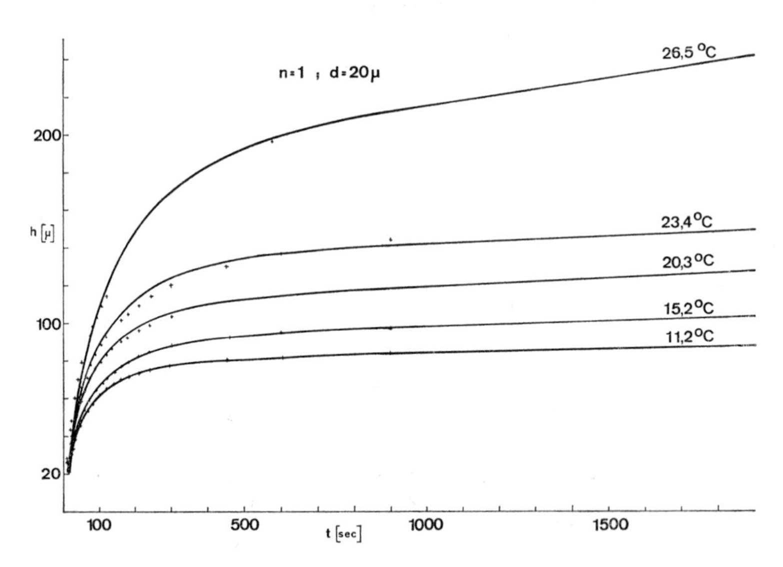

Fig. 8. Experimental values of swelling and calculated swelling curves of unhardened layers—constant layer thickness. Material: 1649.

Due to the fact that systematic but different deviations in the order of the rate equation are found for both unhardened and hardened gelatin layers, one sees that a simple equation such as

$$\frac{\mathrm{d}h}{\mathrm{d}t} = V_0 \left(1 - \frac{h}{h_\infty}\right)^p \tag{19}$$

wherein p is a constant cannot be applied. If one considers p to be a variable, then it is dependent at least on both the degree of crosslinking and temperature. Evidently, a new approach would be needed in order

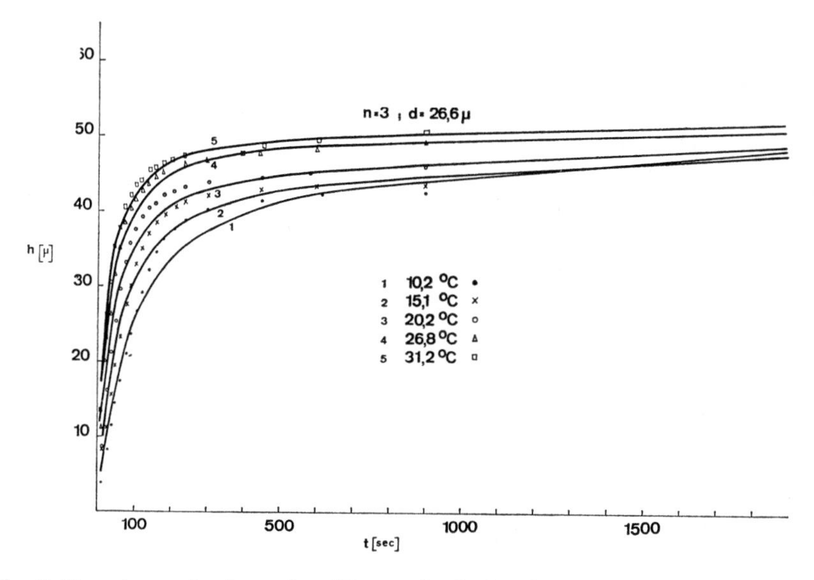

Fig. 9. Experimental values of swelling and calculated swelling curves of hardened layers—constant layer thickness. Material: 1927.

to separate these parameters. This calls for a suitable model for describing the kinetics of swelling which is, in turn, determined by unveiling the complexity of gelatin structure.

Temperature coefficient of V_0

The difference between the temperature coefficient of V_0 for the well hardened and unhardened materials is noteworthy in spite of the difficulties in interpretation of the results, due to the mentioned imperfect fitting of experimental data to the calculated curves.

Fig. 10 shows the dependence of log V_0 on reciprocal temperature for the region 10–31°C for a hardened material (curves 1A, 1B), and 11–25°C for an unhardened one (curve 2). In the case of the hardened material, the values of V_0 increases very significantly with temperature, whereas those of the unhardened ones remain practically unchanged.

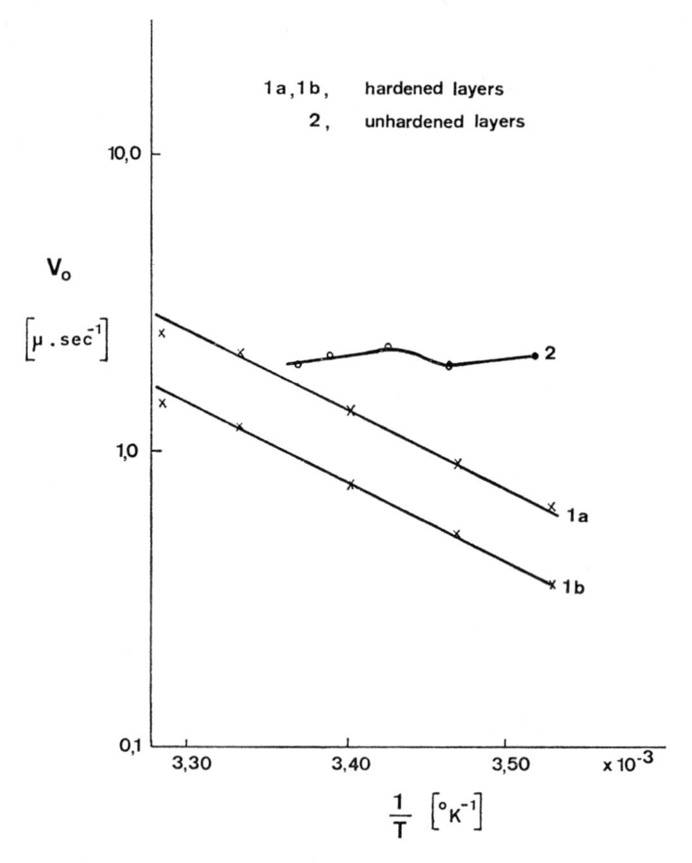

Fig. 10. Temperature dependence of V_0. Curves 1a, 1b: material 1927, $\bar{d} = 26{\cdot}6\mu$; $n = 3$. Curve 2: material 1649, $\bar{d} = 20{\cdot}0\mu$; $n = 1$.

As the slope of the curves 1A and 1B are reasonably constant for the hardened material, one may attempt to calculate the activation energy of swelling. The obtained value $E_A = 12{\cdot}1 \pm 3{\cdot}5$ kcal/mol is not substantially influenced by calculating the initial velocities V_0 from least square analysis (1A) or by extrapolating them graphically (1B) from the $\log(\Delta h/\Delta t)/\log(1 - (h/h_\infty))$ curves shown in Fig. 6.

The activation energy of swelling of the crosslinked material was also calculated from the temperature coefficient of $t_{s=2 \cdot 0}$; the individual values of $t_{s=2 \cdot 0}$ were found by linear interpolation between data corresponding to swellings nearest to $h = d$. Within the limits of error the same result as mentioned above was found, indicating that the experimental values of $t_{s=2 \cdot 0}$ reflect the calculated values of V_0 rather well.

Swelling time and layer thickness

Fig. 11 shows the relationship between the dry thickness of unhardened layers and the swelling time to expand them either:

to a preselected swelling (curves 1 to 3, corresponding respectively to swellings up to 25 μ, 15 μ, 10 μ)

or

to a preselected swell ratio of 2 (curve 4).

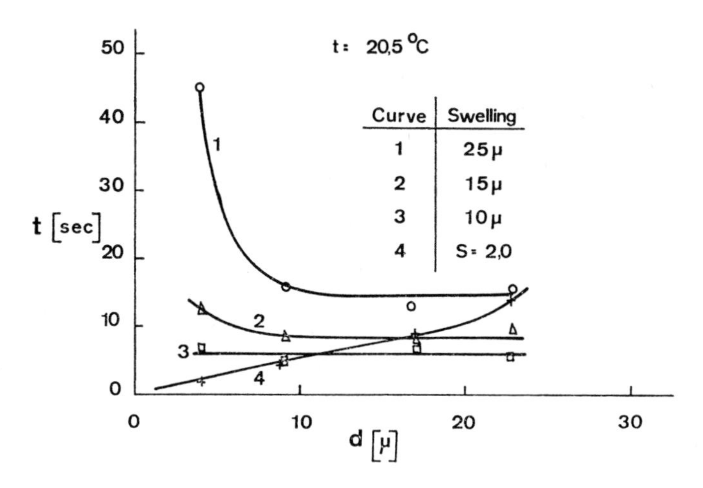

Fig. 11. Time for swelling to a defined value as a function of dry layer thickness. Material: 1650.

It is interesting to notice that, at low levels of swelling, there is no significant difference in swelling times between samples, the thickness of which ranges from 4 to ~24 μ.

The time necessary to attain a swell ratio of 2 at constant temperature (curve 4) seems to be proportional to the dry thickness d at a power between 1 and 2.

Confirmation of the results shown by curve 4 would call for a more precise evaluation at the early stages of swelling, in particular for an investigation on the role of permeation of water into the system.

Permeation coefficient of water into gelatin

As a first approximation, the values of V_0 can be used to estimate the permeation coefficient of water into gelatin layers. Assuming $V_0 = 1$ μ/s, the amount of water passing through a surface of 1 $cm^2 = 10^{-4}$ g $= 5{\cdot}56{\cdot}10^{-6}$ mol and the permeation coefficient $D' = 5{\cdot}6{\cdot}10^{-6}$ cm^2/s. The values of V_0 measured so far range from $0{\cdot}5 - 10$ μ/s, thus giving values of $D' \simeq 3{\cdot}10^{-6} - 6{\cdot}10^{-5}$ cm^2/s.

As the coefficient of self-diffusion of water for the temperature range in question (250–300°K) is about 3–$4{\cdot}10^{-4}$ cm^2/s, the largest value of permeation coefficient measured up to date is still $\sim 5 \times$ smaller than the self diffusion coefficient of water.

Although rather large changes of D' have been found, no particular dependence of the permeation coefficient on the degree of crosslinking irrespectively of temperature is evident. Both the smallest and the largest values of D' were found for layers with a high degree of crosslinking.

As significant changes of D' are due to the presence of compounds influencing Donnan equilibria of gelatin, this could be an interesting subject for further investigation.

Swelling at equilibrium

Fig. 12 shows the temperature dependence of equilibrium swelling: curves 1, 2, 2a and 3 relate to unhardened layers. The difference between curves 2 and 2a is due to ageing of the material for 1 year at 20°C and 60% RH.

Curves 4 and 5 correspond to materials containing 25% of the CLA concentration normally used for crosslinking under the given experimental conditions. Curve 6 corresponds to the concentration of CLA normally used.

It can be seen that uncrosslinked materials have larger equilibrium swell ratios and temperature coefficients of equilibrium swell ratio than partially crosslinked layers. These in turn have larger values than layers treated with a large excess of CLA. Thus both the equilibrium swell ratio and its temperature coefficient, at a given temperature, characterize the degree of crosslinking and the stability of the crosslinks.

The difference in swell ratio between curves 1, 2 and 3 of Fig. 12 is related to differences in total dry thickness, as shown by Fig. 13. The thickness range was obtained either by means of single layers ($n = 1$) or by multi-layers systems ($n = 2$, 3 or 4), according to the procedure described in section on Materials.

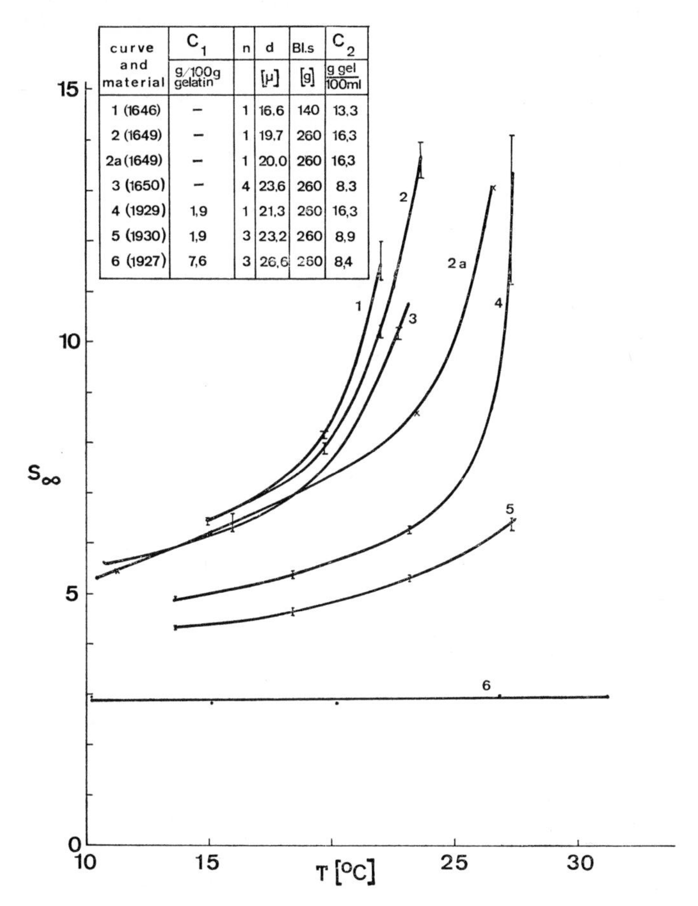

curve and material	C_1 g/100g gelatin	n	d [μ]	Bl.s [g]	C_2 g gel/100ml
1 (1646)	–	1	16,6	140	13,3
2 (1649)	–	1	19,7	260	16,3
2a (1649)	–	1	20,0	260	16,3
3 (1650)	–	4	23,6	260	8,3
4 (1929)	1,9	1	21,3	260	16,3
5 (1930)	1,9	3	23,2	260	8,9
6 (1927)	7,6	3	26,6	260	8,4

Fig. 12. Dependence of S_∞ on temperature. Key: C_1, concentration of CLA. n, number of layers. d, total dry thickness. Bl.s, Bloom strength of gelatin. C_2, concentration of gelatin solution at coating stage.

For unhardened layers, it is striking to notice that the degree of equilibrium swelling is a unique function of dry thickness. It is not significantly dependent either on the gelatin Bloom strength or the number of layers, neither does the difference in concentration of gelatin at the coating stage (as shown by the table given in Fig. 12) produce deviations in the dependency of swell ratio on dry thickness.

As the multi-layer system behaves as a single layer of the same total thickness, this leads to the conclusion that the degree of swelling is not dependent on the history of the gelatin layer. One may therefore assume that the degree of swelling is controlled by crosslinks formed in the final stages of drying, e.g. when the volume concentration of gelatin is near its maximum.

Moreover, there is no apparent interface effect hindering crosslinking between individual layers of one gelatin; otherwise swollen multilayers would have a different degree of swelling than simple layers of the same dry thickness.

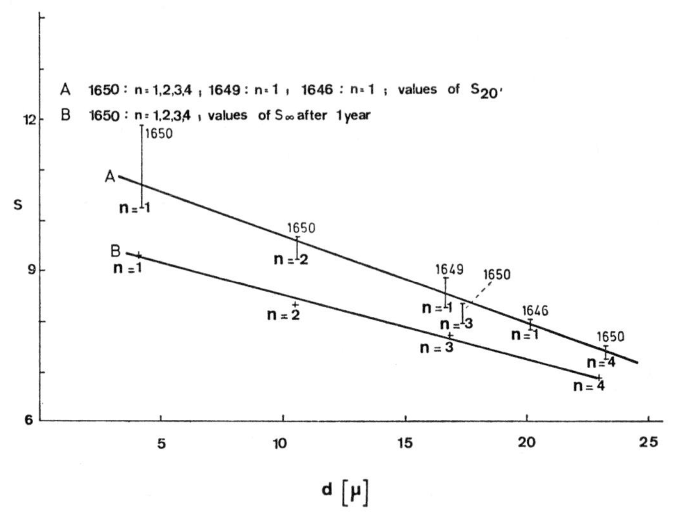

Fig. 13. Dependence of equilibrium swelling on dry thickness of unhardened layers. *n* indicates the number of layers comprising the total dry thickness.

The results plotted in Fig. 13 lead to the empirical equations:

$$S_{\infty} = 9{\cdot}75 - 0{\cdot}13d \tag{20}$$

$$h_{\infty} = 8{\cdot}75d - 0{\cdot}13d^2 \tag{21}$$

valid for d ranging from 4 to 24 μ.

The mechanism by means of which thicker layers have a smaller swelling than thinner ones is not clear. One may, however, assume that the gelatin layer near to its dry state behaves as a single macromolecular species, the properties of which are dependent on dry thicknesses. It is well known that under experimental conditions, different from our own, the equilibrium swell ratio is a function of the concentration of gelatin solution during coating.[10] It thus remains an open question to what degree the behaviour of our layers was influenced by the setting and drying conditions employed.

CONCLUSIONS

From this work the following conclusions may be drawn:

1. The kinetics of swelling of gelatin layers in water can be investigated by means of point-to-point measurements performed with a modified Wallace indentation tester.

2. The second order rate equation (9) is not a theoretically appropriate relationship. Nevertheless it is often applicable as a good approximation for characterizing the swelling of both crosslinked and uncrosslinked gelatin layers by means of the parameters h_∞ and V_0 or τ. Layers of various thickness can then be compared by means of the parameters S_∞ and V_0/d or for example, $t_{s=2\cdot0}$.

3. The values of V_0 and $t_{s=2\cdot0}$ varied in the range of 0·5–10 μ/s and 2–100 s for the temperature range 10–30°C and dry thickness from 4–26 μ. At a given temperature, no relationship between V_0/d or $t_{s=2\cdot0}$ and the degree of crosslinking was found. The sign and magnitude of the temperature coefficients for both V_0 and $t_{s=2\cdot0}$ were, however, dependent on the degree of crosslinking. An activation energy of swelling $E_A = 12\cdot1 \pm 3\cdot5$ kcal/mol was found for crosslinked layers with a value of $S_\infty \sim 2\cdot9$. Further information would be necessary in order to evaluate the complex behaviour of uncrosslinked materials.

4. The values of S_∞ and its temperature coefficient are closely related to the degree of crosslinking of gelatin layers. The degree and thermal stability of hardening can thus be evaluated by means of swelling measurements.

5. For layers containing no CLA, S_∞ decreased as a linear function of dry thickness d, independently of concentration of the gelatin solution, gelatin Bloom strength and number of coated layers; it is therefore suggested that intercrosslinking between layers is not hindered by surface effects; the relationship between S_∞ and d can be explained by assuming that the amount of crosslinks increases considerably as the material approaches the dry state, at which it behaves as a single macromolecular species.

ACKNOWLEDGEMENTS

We are indebted to Dr. F. Trautweiler for helpful criticism and permission to publish our results.

During the course of this work, we have benefited from many discussions with our colleagues. We are grateful to Mr. N. Metzger for carrying out most of the experimental determinations and to Mr. F. Lehre for preparing the materials.

References

(1) Winter, Chr., *Acta Chem. Scand.*, **8,** 1053 (1954).
(2) Moll, F., "Mitteilungen aus dem Forschungslaboratorium der Agfa-Leverkusen", p. 215, München, Springer Verlag (1961).
(3) Jopling, D. W., *Sci. Ind. Photogr.*, **23,** 253 (1952).
(4) Bromberg, A. V. and Merekalov, S. A., *J. Appl. Chem. USSR*, **23,** 1361 (1950).
(5) Sheppard, S. E. and Mees, C. E. K., "Investigations on the Theory of the Photographic Process", Longmans, London (1907).
(6) Bromberg, A. V. and Maltseva, O. S., *J. Appl. Chem.*, **20,** 422 (1947).
(7) Dumansky, A. V., Mezhenny, Ya. F. and Nekryach, E. F., *Kolloid Zh.*, **10,** 193 (1948).
(8) Robinson, J. D., *J. Phot. Sc. and Eng.*, **8,** 220 (1964).
(9) Taylor D. J. and Kragh, A. M., *J. Phys. D., Appl. Phys.*, **3,** 29 (1970).
(10) Frieser, H., Heimann, G. and Eger, H., *Photogr. Korresp.*, **100,** 143 (1964).

Reticulation in Gelatin Layers

E. TOJO, K. NAGAO, T. MIURA and S. NAGATOMO
Research Laboratories Ashigara, Fuji Photo Film Co. Ltd., Minamiashigara, Kanagawa, Japan

ABSTRACT. The course of development of reticulation was followed by using a phase contrast microscope. Cross-sections of reticulated layers were measured optically by the focusing method; the valleys on the surface were very steep. Vertical and lateral swell ratios of reticulating layers were also measured. Based upon the above observations, a mechanism of reticulation in which emphasis is laid on the role of expansive force in the hardened surface layer has been proposed.

INTRODUCTION

More than fifty years ago Sheppard[1] reported the nature and cause of reticulation in his paper published in 1918. But since that time very few scientific papers have appeared on the reticulation. This is rather surprising when we consider the significance of reticulation as a frequent trouble in the processing on the one hand, and as a basis of the well-known collotype method on the other hand.

Sheppard proposed that the reticulation is caused by an excessive swelling when the simultaneous action of swelling and hardening agents is present. Smethurst[2] emphasized the rôle of the surface hardening and showed reticulation is caused by lateral compression. His mechanism seems to be the one that is generally accepted now. But certain aspects of reticulation are not consistent with his mechanism; according to his model and analysis, the shape of incipient reticulation should be shallow sine curves, but in fact it is not.

For the purpose of elucidating the mechanism of reticulation, the most important step is to make precise observation and quantitative measurement in the water of reticulated layers. These data constitute the major part of the present paper.

EXPERIMENTAL

Method of Observation

Gelatin coatings were made on glass plates in the usual way with or without the addition of a hardener. They were swollen in water and examined under a microscope, the temperature of the water being raised gradually. The arrangement is shown schematically in Fig. 1.

The surface of gelatin layers in the swelling bath is generally hard to observe because of the small difference in the refractive indices between the swollen gelatin and the water. This difficulty is overcome by use of a phase contrast microscope. In some experiments silver bromide grains were incorporated in the coatings, or fine carbon black powder was dusted on the surface before swelling in order to aid the observation.

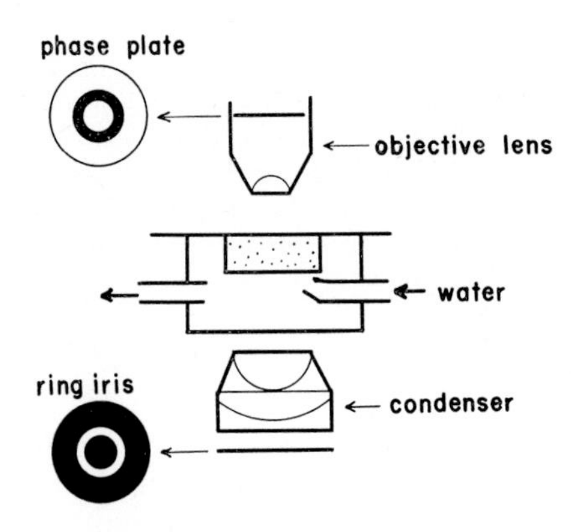

Fig. 1. Experimental method.

The depth or vertical length was measured by the fine focusing adjustment of the microscope graduated in microns.

Development of Reticulation

Fig. 2(a), (b), (c) and (d) show photographs of a reticulating surface taken successively at the same point; the temperature and elapsed time are also indicated. Reticulation started from some particles or defects on the surface as short lines of depression; see (a). The lines grew in length and perhaps in depth, and joined up with each other; see (b) and (c). At last the lines were widened and some of them vanished as if they were absorbed, leaving a larger and more uniform pattern; see (d). It may be noted that the depressions were very sharp from the beginning. Another such example is shown in Fig. 3(a), (b) and (c) but in this case, the coating contained a small amount of silver bromide particles.

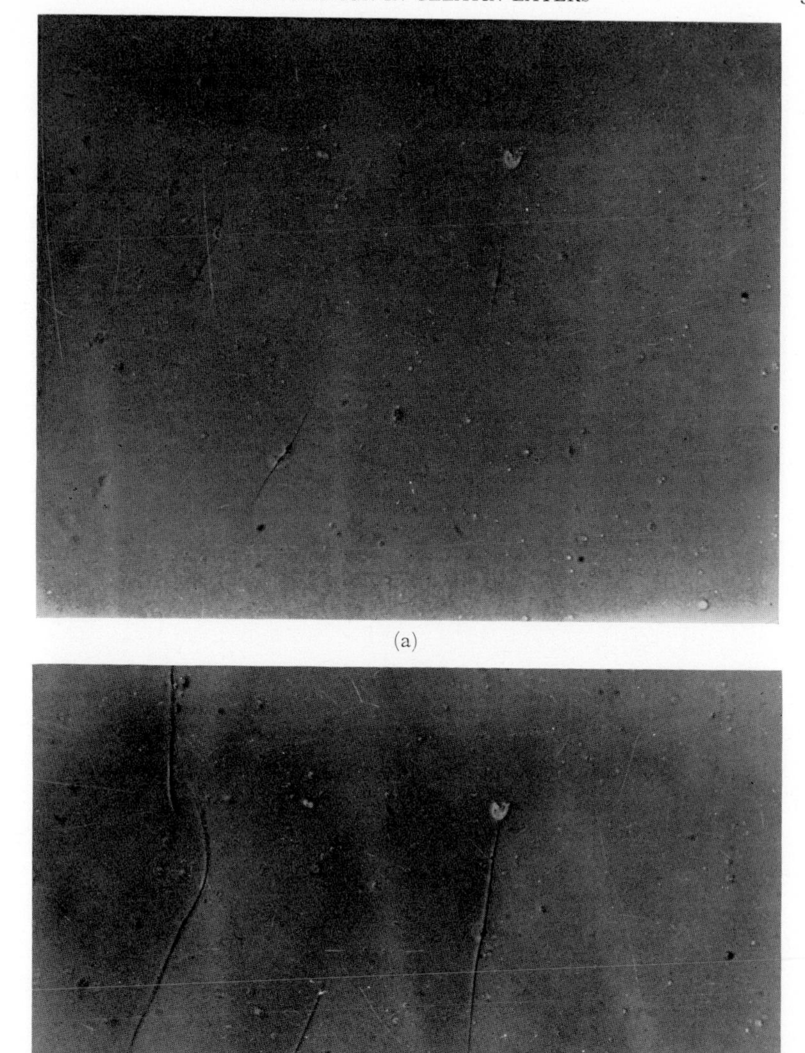

(a)

(b)

Fig. 2. Development of reticulation. (a) 29·3°C, 64 min. (b) 29·3°C, 67 min. (c) 29·4°C, 72 min. (d) 30·4°C, 90–100 min.

(c)

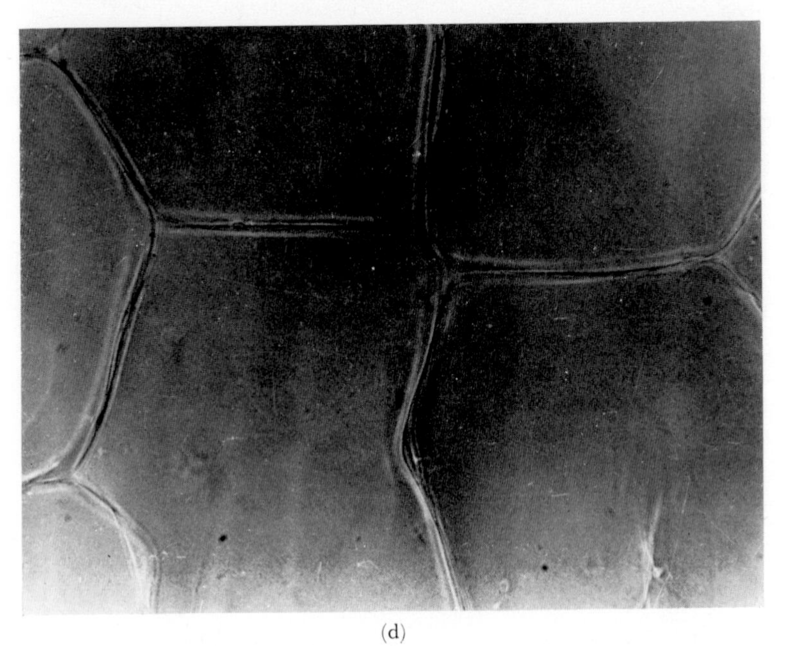

(d)

Fig. 2.

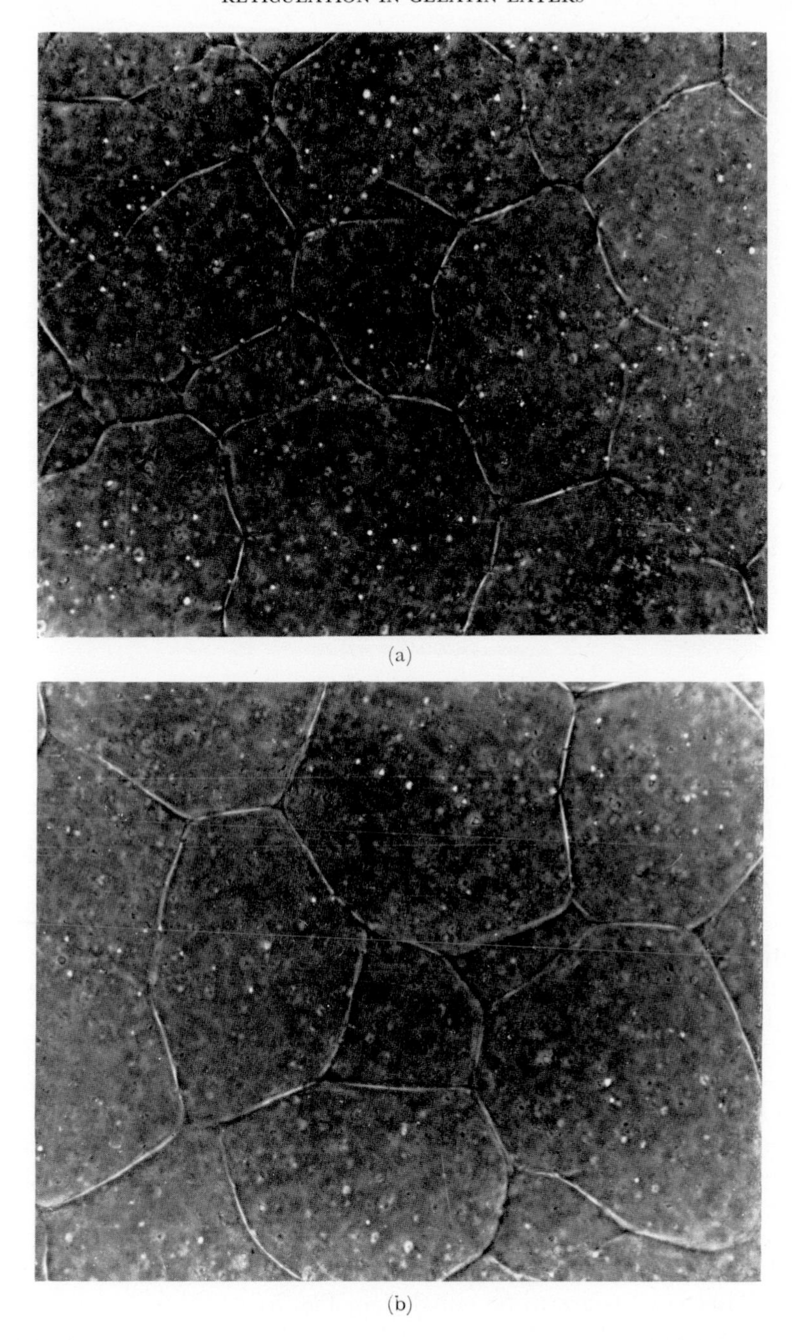

(a)

(b)

Fig. 3. Development of reticulation. (a) 30·0°C. (b) 30·2°C. (c) 30·4°C.

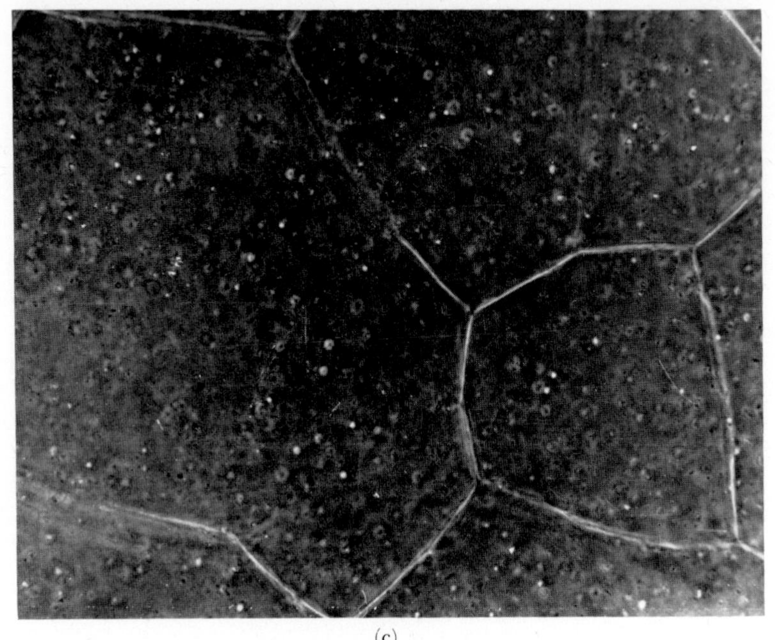

(c)
Fig. 3.

Measurement of Cross-section

The four photographs shown in Fig. 2 indicate that the valleys of reticulation are narrow and steep. This is illustrated also by the photographs shown in Fig. 4(a) and (b). In this observation the surface was dusted before swelling with fine powder of carbon black and then the coating was swollen. Photographs were taken focused at varying depths. In Fig. 4(a) the focus is on the "plateau" of reticulation, the original surface being indicated by the presence of black grains. In Fig. 4(b) the focus is halfway up the valley, of which both walls are shown standing almost vertically and as if they were touching each other.

In order to determine the exact shape of cross-sections, the positions or depths of the surface were measured point by point by the focusing method. The results are plotted in Fig. 5(a), (b) and (c) in which the positions of the surface before swelling are shown in broken lines. The change with time of the position of the surface is also shown in Fig. 5(a). Three points are to be noted from Fig. 5:

1. The valleys are very steep.

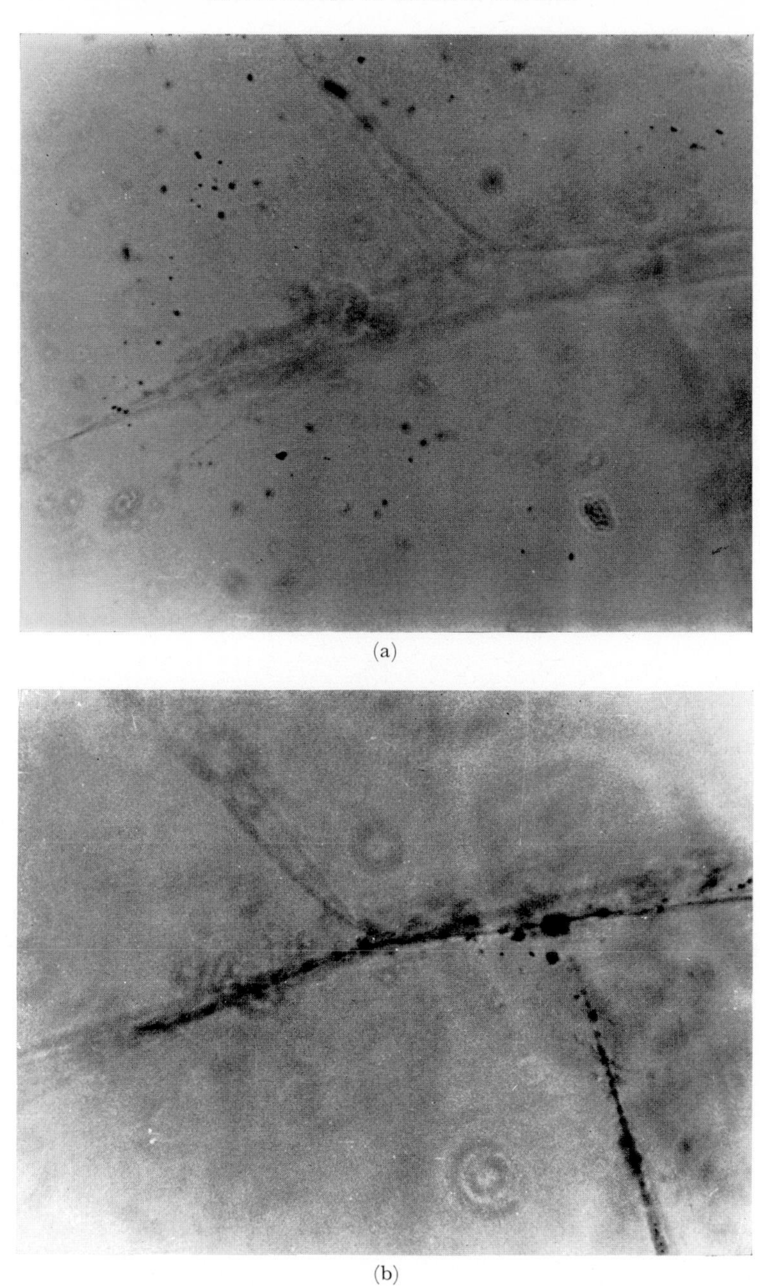

(a)

(b)

Fig. 4. Micrograph of reticulation dusted with carbon black. (a) focused on the surface. (b) focused halfway up the valley.

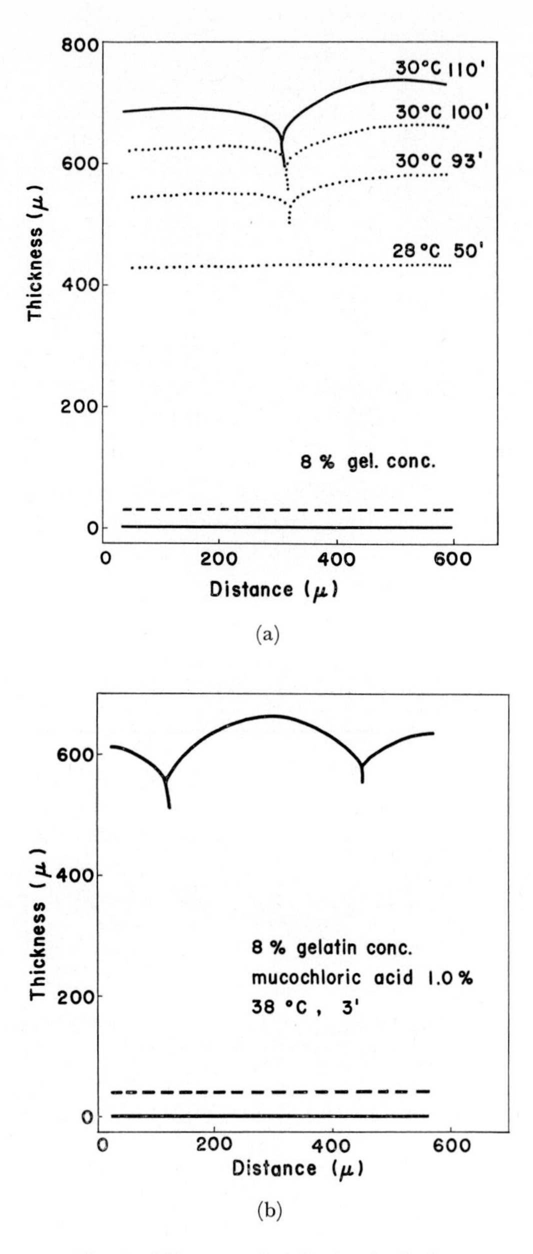

(a)

(b)

Fig. 5. "Cross-sections" of reticulation.

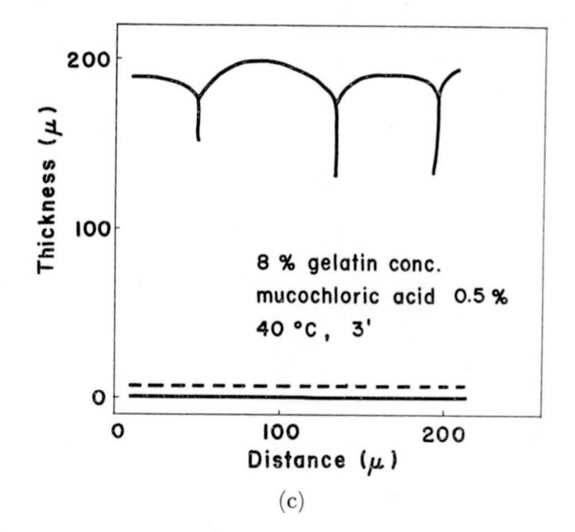

(c)

2. The valleys are sometimes very deep, reaching to about one third of the swollen thickness.

3. The grain size or distance between the neighbouring valleys of the reticulation is somewhat smaller than the swollen thickness.

Photographs of thin sections of reticulated gelatin films are shown in Fig. 6(a) and (b). In these photographs the hardened layers which were coloured with colloidal silver for the sake of distinction, are represented dark. Although the sectioning method has the disadvantage of possible deformation, it is helpful in visualizing what has happened in a reticulated layer.

Stretching Tendencies of Reticulated Layers

There are very strong indications for the presence of lateral compression in the reticulated layers. The stretching tendencies were evaluated by measuring the length along the reticulated surface and comparison with its original length. This ratio was about 1·4:1 for the early stage of reticulation and more than 2:1 for the later stage. This corresponds, by the square of these ratios in length, to 2 and 4 times respectively an expansion in area.

When the swollen layers were made free from the substratum by cutting between them, the layers did in fact expand by this ratio.

Model Experiment

A model experiment was undertaken in order to prove that the lateral compression actually produces reticulation. Gelatin solution was coated on a two-dimensionally stretched thin rubber membrane. After the coating was set, the membrane was released; it contracted with the coating on it. The surface of the gelatin coating became uneven and a pattern somewhat resembling reticulation was produced.

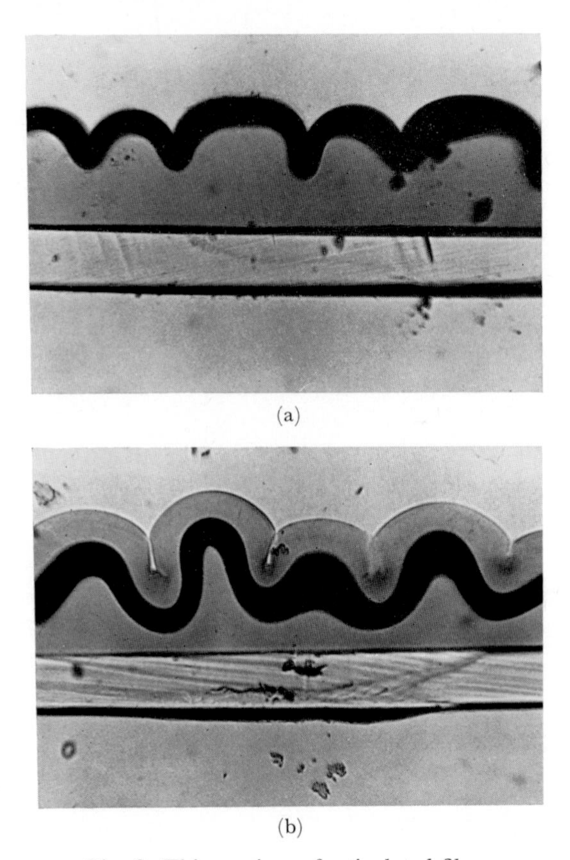

(a)

(b)

Fig. 6. Thin sections of reticulated films.

Reticulation and Vertical Swelling

Gelatin coatings were swollen in water and the temperature was raised gradually. The vertical swelling was measured by the focusing method and also at the same time the change on the surface was observed. The results are shown in Fig. 7. The vertical swelling increased slowly at first and then a sudden increase occurred at around 29°C. At this point, the first appearance of reticulation was recognized, and when the temperature of water was raised a little, the reticulation developed rapidly and covered the whole surface. The coincidence of the appearance of reticulation and the sudden increase in swelling seems to indicate that the reticulation released the internal stresses and thus made the layer swell more.

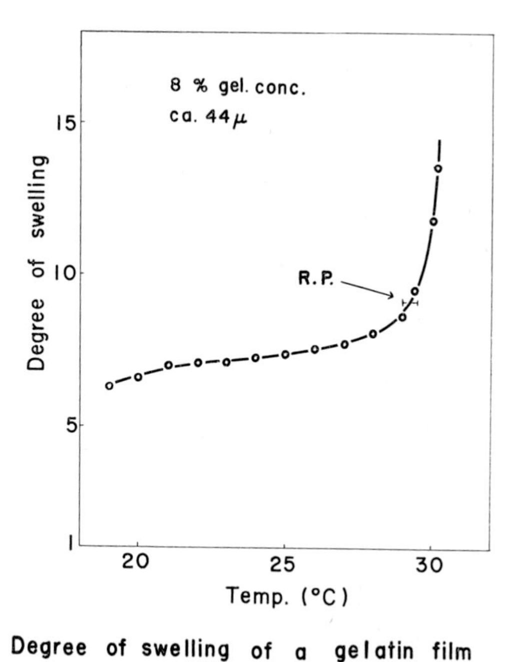

Degree of swelling of a gelatin film

Fig. 7. Relationship between vertical swelling and reticulation.

Effect of Surface Hardening

Smethurst[2] has shown surface hardening facilitates the production of reticulation by applying an alcoholic solution of formaldehyde on the coated surface. In the collotype process the hardening is also supposed to be limited only to the surface layer, owing to the large extinction coefficient of chromate for ultra-violet rays.

We tried to confirm the effect of surface hardening by use of one of the non-diffusible hardeners, which have become available in recent years. Seven three-layered coatings were prepared, each containing the same amount of the non-diffusible hardener in total but differing in the distribution among the layers. These coatings were swollen in a solution of sodium carbonate and the reticulation temperatures were measured.

The results shown in Fig. 8 clearly demonstrate the effect of surface hardening.

Distribution of hardener *							
	1/3	—	—	1	1/4	1/4	1/2
	1/3	—	1	—	1/4	1/2	1/4
	1/3	1	—	—	1/2	1/4	1/4
Base							
R.P. (°C) (in Na_2CO_3 soln.)	75	36	34	29	72	60	34

*) Non-diffusible hardener.

Fig. 8. Reticulation points of differently hardened layers.

CONCLUSIONS

Conditions for Reticulation

The conditions favouring the production of reticulation are summarized as follows:

1. Swelling in the bulk; this reduces the rigidity of the gel.
2. Strong tendency to lateral expansion.
3. Presence of hardened surface layer; this condition is not absolutely necessary but makes reticulation very easy to occur.
4. Adhesion to the substratum.

There is little need to explain the first and second conditions for reticulation. It is enough to point out that films made under such conditions that cause them to swell a lot in a lateral direction have always lower reticulation points, i.e. a high coating concentration and an elevated drying temperature.

Mechanism of Reticulation

Although it is not a necessary condition to harden the surface layer for the production of reticulation, since without the action of hardener coatings also reticulate, a coating with a hardened surface layer provides a very good model for the understanding of the mechanism of reticulation. Such a model is illustrated in Fig. 9. The important point is that there is a strong expansive force in the hardened layer. Let us consider the two factors of the stress, the strain and the modulus (rigidity). If the ratio of the lateral swelling to the vertical does not change appreciably with the degree of swelling, the compressive strain in the plane of coating will be proportional to the swelling, while the rigidity of the layer which is proportional to the square of the gelatin concentration, falls more rapidly with the increase in swelling. Thus by a simple mathematical calculation, a maximum of the expansive force is expected to exist at a not so small concentration of gelatin.

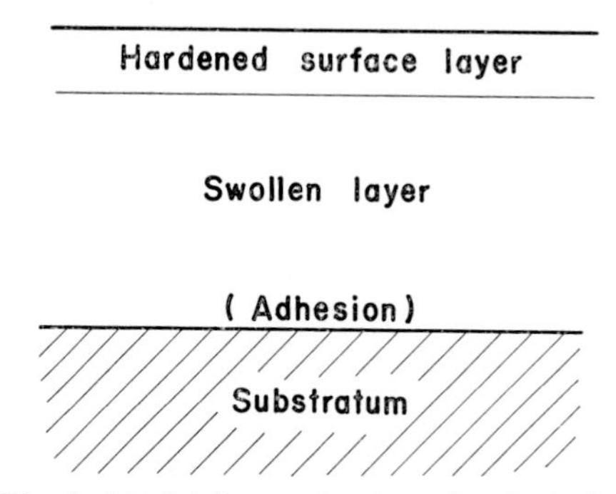

Fig. 9. Model for mechanism of reticulation.

When the degree of swelling of a gelatin coating exceeds this point of the maximal expansive force (this is the case under ordinary conditions), the hardened layer has, in spite of the less swelling, a larger expansive force than the more swollen inner parts.

The system shown in Fig. 9 becomes unstable when the strong expansive force is supported by weaker gel adhering to the substratum and may easily buckle to reticulate.

The reason why reticulations always appear as depressions and not as projections is not yet fully understood. But if the rigidity modulus of gelatin gel is larger for stretching than for compression (this is likely because the elasticity of gelatin gel is essentially rubberlike and deformation at reticulation is fairly large), that deeply depressed shape of reticulation is a very natural consequence, because if, by chance, the surface at any point is depressed slightly, this tendency (of reticulation) is greatly advanced by the balance of the forces to form deep depressions.

References

(1) Sheppard, S. E. and Elliott, F. A., *Ind. Eng. Chem.*, **10,** 727 (1918).
(2) Smethurst, P. C., *Brit. J. Photogr.*, **96,** 371 (1949).

The Gelation and Rupture Properties of Gelatin Gels

W. M. MARRS and P. D. WOOD

G.G.R.A. Laboratories, Warwick Street, Birmingham 12*

ABSTRACT. A new method for the determination of the gelation time of gelatin solutions is described. The gelation times and rupture loads of gelatins with both limed-hide and acid-pigskin precursors have been measured as functions of pH. The forms of these functions are discussed in the light of current ideas on the gelation process and the structure of gelatin gels.

INTRODUCTION

The rheological properties of gelatin gels and the kinetics of gel formation are areas of particular interest to many industries (e.g. photographic and food) using gelatin gels. The rheology of gelatin gels is moreover closely correlated to the rate of gelation of gelatin solutions since both properties are manifestations of the formation of cross-linking bonds involving secondary forces generally believed to be hydrogen bonds. It is an area of study in which not a great deal of accurate experimental information is available. Gelatin is a material whose physical and chemical properties vary considerably depending upon the nature of the collagen precursor and the method by which it is prepared. The experimental difficulties involved in the preparation of gelatin gels are considerable and reproducibility is notoriously difficult to achieve. The gelation kinetics of gelatin solutions are not well understood due largely to the absence of an adequate method for determining the gelation point of gelatin solutions.

These phenomena have been studied at the G.G.R.A. laboratories. The rupture properties of gelatin gels from various sources have been investigated. We have subsequently studied the rates of gelation of gelatin solutions. The results of these studies are presented in this paper in an attempt to describe the processes by which gelatin gels are formed, and which contribute to their solid state properties. The rheological

* Now part of B.F.M.I.R.A., Randalls Road, Leatherhead, Surrey.

work on gelatin gels was originally initiated on behalf of the food industry with a view to characterizing more accurately the rheological properties of edible gelatins. The food industry also sponsored the initial investigations into the gelation time of gelatin solutions.

GELATION

The gelation of gelatin solutions is a process that has not been widely studied. A great deal of work has been performed on both gelatin solutions and gelatin gels, but the transition region, the gelation point, is not well documented. There lie inherent difficulties in defining the gelation point since the thermodynamic nature of the transition is still in question. It is thought by some workers that the transition is a co-operative phenomenon and bears some resemblance to the glass transition. More recent evidence suggests that the gelation process is simply the outward manifestation of a crosslinking process involving the formulation of secondary bonds, probably hydrogen bonds. The reverse process, sometimes called the melting transition, seems to occur over a much narrower range of temperature and the notion of cooperative process or glass transition is generally applied to the melting rather than to the gelation process.

There exists a temperature above which a gelatin solution does not gel. This temperature is a function of ionic strength, pH and the type of gelatin used. Below this temperature, a crosslinking process takes place leading to an increase in solution viscosity and finally to gelation. The rate at which crosslinking secondary force bonds are formed is a continuously increasing function of decreasing temperature. The gelation time is that at which the viscosity of the gelatin solution tends asymptotically to infinity. This point coincides with the onset of elastic behaviour.

The methods which have been used to determine the gelation time of gelatin solutions fall into one of two categories; those based on the behaviour of the viscosity of the solution close to the gelation point and those based on the appearance of rigidity after the gelation point has been passed. Hodgetts and Norman[1] described an instrument for the determination of gelation time by viscosity measurement, and other similar gelation timers have been marketed. The method developed by Janus[2] is of the second type, depending upon the onset of solid state behaviour of drops of gelatin solution. This method is particularly suitable for measuring the relatively short gelation times of concentrated solutions of gelatin. Drops (0·03 ml) of the gelatin solution were placed at suitable intervals of time on a level hollow metal bar maintained by circulating water at 20°C. The gelation time was deduced by rotating the bar through 90° and observing how many of the drops remained on the bar.

The various gelation time methods already in use were carefully examined and it was decided that a new method, suitable for use with the relatively dilute edible gelatin solutions, was required. The method should be based on the viscosity behaviour of the solution and should be free of any complications introduced by changes in the surface of the solution such as "skinning". The method used was based on the free-falling sphere principle* which states that the terminal velocity of a sphere falling under the influence of a constant force is directly proportional to the viscosity coefficient of the liquid through which the sphere passes. The spheres in this case were drops of carbon tetrachloride, immiscible in water, and were introduced under the surface of the gelatin solution by means of a hypodermic syringe. Any complications due to surface changes were in this way avoided. The method will be described in detail later.

The detection of the gelation point using an external force presents an inherent difficulty in that this force, used to demonstrate the presence of a gel, perturbs the gelation process itself. Therefore referring again to the falling sphere method, the sphere should be as light as possible so as to minimize the perturbation of the gelation process. In this respect, the use of carbon tetrachloride is advantageous since it is much lighter than glass or other readily available materials.

GELATIN GEL RUPTURE

The stress-strain characteristics of gelatin gels have been measured extensively. Both static and dynamic experiments have been performed on bars, strips and cylinders of gelatin gels by Veis.[3]

The purpose of the present work was to investigate the rupture properties of edible gelatin gels under a constant rate of strain and to measure the effect of changes in pH and of ionic strength on these properties. The work stems in part from the investigations of Saunders[4] who fractionated gelatins and measured the rheological properties of both the high and low viscosity fractions. The high viscosity fraction was rubbery and tough in texture while that of the low viscosity material was brittle and easy to crumble. Saunders determined the rigidity modulus of both materials at high strains and discovered that it was little affected by the molecular weight of the gelatin fraction. He concluded that the differences in physical properties were due to a

* See Appendix.

variation in rupture strength of the material and that the rupture strength became an additional parameter relevant to the physical properties of gelatin gels. The rupture properties of gels have not been properly investigated before the research by Saunders. Experiments in which rupture at the interface between a gel and test piece have been recorded but those in which rupture has occurred completely within the gel have not been reported in any detail. Cobbett[7] suggested that the rupture of a gelatin gel at an interface wholly within the gel was of greater significance than that at the interface of the gel and the test piece.

The method employed by Wood[8] was based on the method of Cobbett and Ward[11] with modifications to the apparatus enabling the strain to be measured electronically and recorded continuously.

EXPERIMENTAL

Gelation time

The gelation time can be defined as the point in time at which the viscosity of a gelatin solution at constant temperature becomes infinitely large. It is not possible in practice to measure an infinitely large viscosity, but since the viscosity of a gelatin solution increases rapidly with time near the point of gelation, it is possible to determine a time very close to the gelation time by measuring a point on the steeply rising portion of the viscosity/time curve. In principle, the method is similar to those of Hodgetts and Norman[1] and of Eiloart,[6] the important difference being the magnitude of the applied force used to determine the solution viscosity. The method described here employs a relatively small external force which minimizes the perturbation of the gelation process.

Apparatus

The apparatus is shown in Fig. 1. A thick-walled pyrex test tube containing the gelatin solution under investigation is fitted with a hypodermic needle assembly. This consists of a hypodermic needle (Luer type, 26 G) connected to a nylon tube and housed in a glass tube which can be fitted into the pyrex tube. The hypodermic needle is fed through the nylon tubing from a reservoir containing carbon tetrachloride. The flow rate of carbon tetrachloride from the hypodermic syringe can be regulated by the adjustment of the height of the reservoir. The whole assembly is clamped in position in a thermostatically controlled water bath, the temperature of which is accurate to $\pm 0{\cdot}002°C$.

Two stop-watches are required; one to measure the absolute time and the other to measure the rate at which drops of carbon tetrachloride are discharged into the gelatin solution.

Procedure

The gelatin solution was prepared by soaking the gelatin pieces in water at room temperature for several hours and then raising the temperature to above 40°C when the gelatin readily dissolved. The

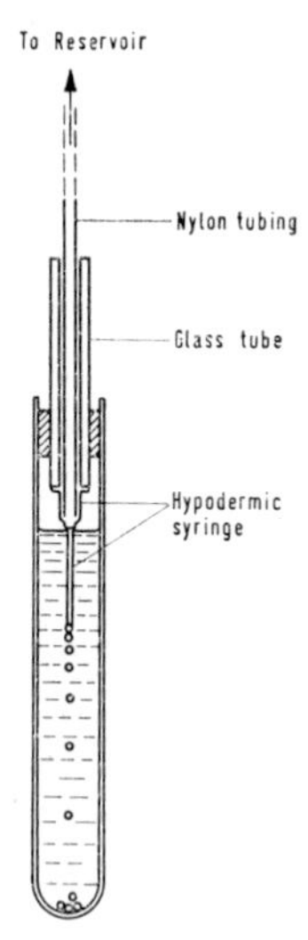

Fig. 1. The gelation-time assembly. The situation at the gelatin point is shown, the emerging drop being in contact with the preceding drop.

selection of pyrex tubes in which the gelation takes place is important since the cooling rate of the gelatin solution is an essential factor in the gelation process. A number of tubes were selected from a batch of thick-walled pyrex test tubes which had the following dimensions: length 153 mm ± 2·0 mm; external diameter 18·5 mm ± 2 mm; wall thickness 13·0 mm ± 2 mm.

The gelatin solution was prepared and the necessary adjustment made to the pH, ionic strength and concentration; the solution (20 ml) was then transferred to the pyrex tube by means of a pipette. The pyrex tube and its contents were maintained in a water bath at 40°C ±0·1°C for 6 min and then transferred to the water bath at 23°C ±0·002°C. At this moment, the absolute time stop watch was started.

The glass reservoir containing carbon tetrachloride was placed in another part of the bath. The reservoir was fitted with an outlet tube to which was attached a length of nylon tube. The nylon tube was connected to the hypodermic needle and the whole assembly carefully filled with carbon tetrachloride from the reservoir. The hypodermic needle was then inserted into the pyrex tube so that the tip was situated at a predetermined depth below the surface of the solution. This depth was simply the length of the needle itself. Drops of carbon tetrachloride were falling from the needle into the solution, and the height of the reservoir was adjusted so that the drop rate was one every 6 secs, timed by the other stop watch.

As gelation took place, the increasing viscosity of the solution caused the distance between the falling drops to diminish. A point was reached when the viscosity of the solution had increased to the point where the drops of carbon tetrachloride were almost stationary in the liquid, and a drop emerging from the needle came into physical contact with the preceding drop. The instant, recorded on the first stop watch, at which this contact was seen to take place was taken as the gelation time and was found to be a reproducible parameter of the gelation process. The validity of the method depends upon the drop size being constant since the velocity of fall is directly proportional to the solution viscosity only if the drop radius is constant. The results show the maximum error associated with this technique to be $\pm 3\%$.

The reliability of the method was estimated by making a simple statistical analysis of two sets of gelation time data. It was felt that the normal distribution function would best describe the data; values of the standard deviation were calculated and used in the evaluation of the distribution function. The reproducibility experiments were performed using an acid-treated pigskin gelatin (No. 281) in a 3·52% solution (on a dry weight basis) made up in distilled water. The pH of the solution was 5·8 and the gelation time of the solution was determined at 20°C after thermostatting at 40°C for 15 min. The determination was repeated nine times. The second set of data was obtained using an identical gelatin solution and a gelation temperature of 25°C instead of 20°C. The gelation time was determined thirteen times. Both sets of data are recorded in Table 1. The standard deviation, σ, was calculated for each set of data. A series of experiments was performed using the acid-treated pigskin gelatin (No. 281) to determine the variation of the gelation time of the gelatin solution as a function of pH. The gelatin solution (3·52% concentration on a dry weight basis) was prepared using sodium chloride solution (0·15 M) as solvent. The solution was maintained at 40°C in an open water bath. Samples (20 ml) of gelatin solution were transferred to a beaker (50 ml capacity) and the pH adjusted using sodium hydroxide solution (1 N) or hydrochloric acid (1 N). The additions of acid or alkali were made using a micropipette and the volumes employed noted. The volume of the gelatin solution was then made up to 25 ml with sodium chloride solution (0·15 M). In

Table 1

Gelation time data for an acid-treated pigskin gelatin (No. 281) in a 3·52% solution at pH 5·8

Temperature 20°C		*Temperature* 25°C	
Gelation Time x (sec)	$(x-\mu)^2$	*Gelation Time* x (sec)	$(x-\mu)^2$
192	9	565	100
195	36	584	81
188	1	590	225
190	1	555	400
183	36	584	81
189	0	575	0
187	4	558	289
192	9	575	0
187	4	567	64
Standard deviation $\sigma = 3{\cdot}3$ (sec)		571	16
		591	256
		576	1
		585	100
		Standard deviation $\sigma = 11$ (sec)	

μ is the mean value of the gelation time, x
σ is the standard deviation and is the positive square root of the variance σ^2, where

$$\sigma^2 = \frac{1}{n}\sum_{n=1}^{n}(x-\mu)^2$$

this way, a series of gelatin solutions of constant concentration, constant ionic strength and of known pH were prepared, and their gelation times determined at a temperature of 23°C. The experiment was repeated using a gelatin solution prepared with distilled water instead of sodium chloride solution. The effect of changing the ionic strength of the solution on the pH/gelation time profile can be seen in Fig. 2.

The pH/gelation time profile for a gelatin (No. 342) having a limed-hide precursor was also determined. In these experiments, a solution

(3·47% on a dry weight basis) was made up using distilled water as solvent at 40°C. The pH of the solution was adjusted in the same manner as previously described, and the gelation times were measured at 23°C. The results are shown in Fig. 2.

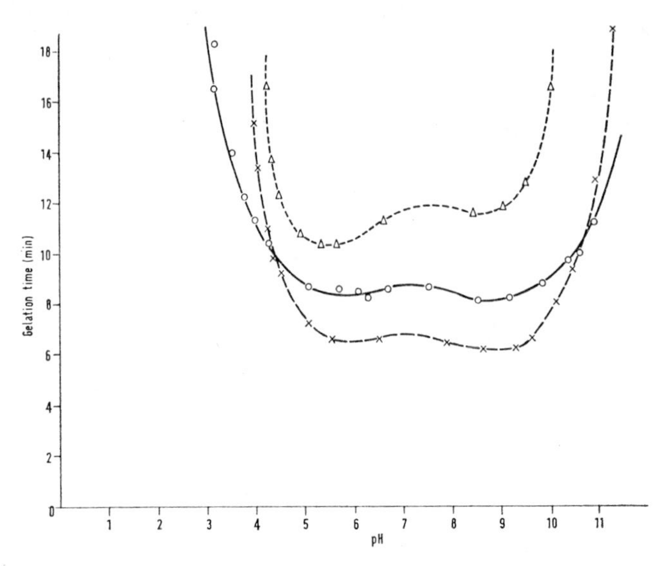

Fig. 2. The gelation time of gelatin solutions as a function of pH. Key to curves: ○——○, acid-pigskin gelatin (3·52%) in 0·5 M sodium chloride solution; X – – X, acid-pigskin gelatin (3·52%) solution in distilled water; △ – – – △, limed-hide gelatin (3·47%) solution in distilled water.

THE RUPTURE PROPERTIES OF GELATIN GELS

Apparatus

The apparatus is essentially that described by Cobbett[(11)] with a few modifications. It consisted of a horizontally positioned trough into which the test piece on a perspex platform was placed, a device for producing a constant rate extension and a system for measuring the stress within the test piece.

The trough was constructed from perspex sheet and measured 36 in long, $2\frac{1}{2}$ in wide (inner dimension) and $1\frac{1}{4}$ in high, and was fitted with a lid. The trough was held at constant temperature by the circulation of a refrigerated liquid through a coil resting on the bed. A silicone oil of sufficient quantity to submerge the perspex platform was added to the trough, the oil serving as a lubricant to provide a frictionless barrier between the gelatin and the perspex platform on which it rested.

A rack and pinion mechanism provided the constant extension rate required and a rate of 0·536 cm sec^{-1} was used throughout these experiments. A length of $\frac{1}{16}$ diameter steel rod connected the rack to one end of the gelatin test piece by means of a bridge made from perspex. The bridge was located by two pins passing through a wood-slip embedded in the end of the test piece.

The other end of the test piece was connected by means of a similar steel rod to a tensile load transducer (type UF1 by Ether Ltd.) with a total armature displacement of ±0·0015 in, for measuring the relatively small stresses in the gelatin test piece. A transducer was employed in place of Cobbett's optical system in an attempt to increase the accuracy of the instrument and record continuously the output from the transducer up to the point of rupture. A stabilized d.c. supply unit was used in conjunction with the transducer, the output of which was fed into a recording potentiometer (Linear—log type by Beckman Instruments Inc.). Three interchangeable transducers operating in the load ranges ±114 g, ±454 g and ±908 g, respectively were employed in these experiments.

Procedure

The gelatin gel test pieces were prepared by casting the gel in a dumb-bell shaped mould. At the ends of the mould, wood-slips (2 in^2) were positioned prior to the introduction of the gelatin solution. Each gelatin test piece carried a woodslip at each end which enabled the test piece to be fixed in the extension apparatus by the perspex bridges. The test pieces rupture at a plane in the gelatin gel rather than at the gelatin—wood interface.

The moulds were constructed from perspex sheet, and each machined sheet was positioned between two blank sheets to complete the mould. Six of these units were clamped together enabling six gelatin test pieces to be prepared at a single operation. The perspex sheet was machined to a tolerance of ±0·001 in and the width of the six sheets in a mould varied by ±0·002 in.

The gelatin solution was prepared after pre-soaking the gelatin at room temperature. A drop of anti-foaming agent (Siotol AF, manufactured by ICI Ltd.) was added to the gelatin solution and, after the appropriate adjustment of pH and other variables, the solution was made up to the required concentration. The solution was then degassed under reduced pressure. The wood slips were soaked in the gelatin solution prior to insertion in the mould, where they were located by means of nickel-plated steel rods. The appropriate faces of the perspex mould sheets were coated with a release-agent, and the mould assembly clamped in position. The gelatin solution (at about 50°C) was introduced into the mould assembly and the assembly allowed to stand for 5 min to allow air bubbles to escape. The mould assembly was then placed in a constant temperature bath at 10°C for 18 h.

The mould was removed from the constant temperature bath and the assembly dismantled. The perspex sheets were removed; a gelatin

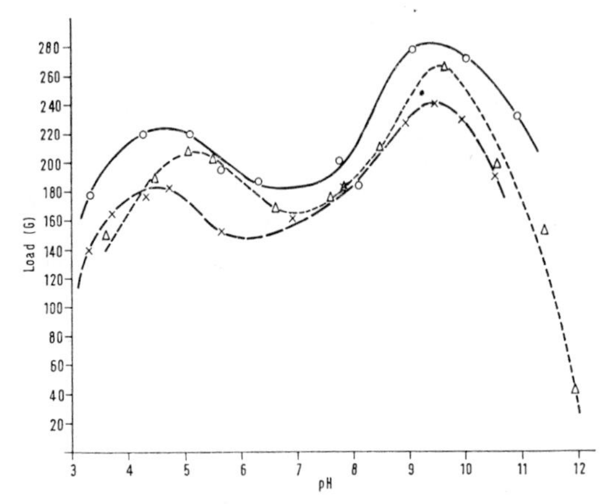

Fig. 3. The rupture load of limed-hide gelatins as a function of pH. Key to curves: ○——○, limed-hide gelatin, No. 304; X – – X, limed-hide gelatin, No. 296; △ - - - △, limed-hide gelatin, No. 213. In each case at 10% concentration and at 10°C.

test piece was lifted from the backing plate, transferred to the trough and coupled to the perspex bridges. The lid was placed on the trough. The temperature of the oil in the trough was maintained at 10°C throughout the experiment. The extension of the test piece was now effected at a rate of 0·536 cm sec^{-1}, and the stress was recorded by the potentiometer up to the point of rupture. A small proportion of the test pieces failed at the wood-gelatin interface; the results in such cases were discarded. An average rupture load value was calculated from the results of six test pieces from each gelatin system.

The rupture properties of a number of different gelatins were measured over the pH range 3 to 12. The rupture load of three limed-hide gelatin gels is shown as a function of pH in Fig. 3. The concentration of the gelatin solutions was 10% (weight of air-dried gelatin) and a maturing temperature of 10°C was used. It was not found possible to use the same conditions for two of the acid-pigskin gelatins (Nos. 280, 281) due to the limited range of the transducer; gelatin No. 280 was matured at 20°C, having a concentration of 10% whilst gelatin No. 281 was used at a concentration of 5% and matured at 10°C.

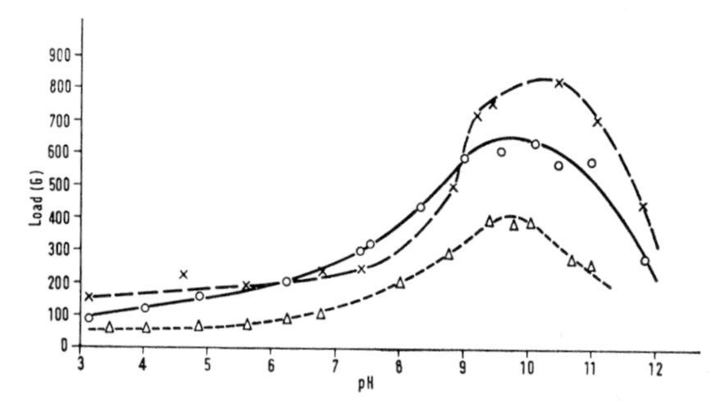

Fig. 4. The rupture load of acid-pigskin gelatins as a function of pH. Key to curves: ○——○, acid-pigskin gelatin, No. 280 (10%) at 20°C; X – – X, acid-pigskin gelatin, No. 313 (10%) at 10°C; △ – – – △, acid-pigskin gelatin, No. 281 (5%) at 10°C.

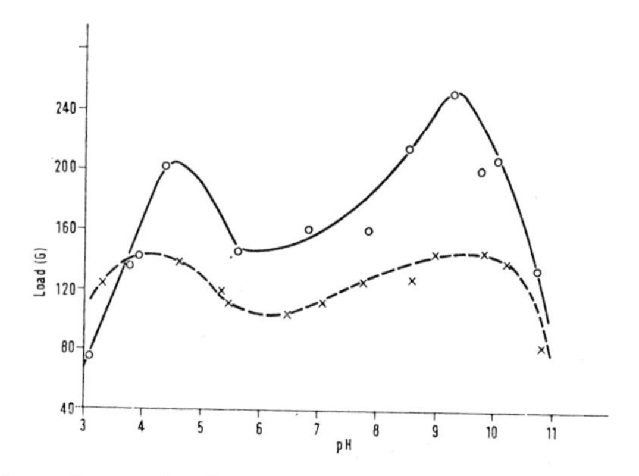

Fig. 5. The effect of neutral salt on the rupture load/pH profile of a limed-hide gelatin. Key to curves: ○——○, limed-hide gelatin, No. 304, deionized; X – – X, limed-hide gelatin, No. 304, in 0·19 M calcium chloride solution.

The results for these materials, and the acid-pigskin gelatin No. 313, are shown in Fig. 4. The effect of calcium ions on the pH/rupture load profile is depicted in Fig. 5, where the profile for a deionized limed-hide gelatin (No. 304) is compared with that of the gelatin made up with a 0·19 N solution of calcium chloride. The results obtained with the ossein gelatins have not been shown here. At a concentration of 10% and a maturing temperature of 10°C, the rupture loads were generally much lower than those of the hide-gelatins and the experimental percentage error correspondingly greater. The rupture loads were in the region 120 g to 180 g and were substantially constant over the pH range 3 to 12.

Discussion

Some general remarks can be made about the pH dependence of both the gelation time and the rupture load of the gelatins used, and on the effect of the ionic strength on these profiles. The gelation time of the gelatin solutions increased very rapidly towards the extremes of the pH range, that is, below pH 4·5 and above pH 9·5. The gelation time goes through shallow minima near these pH values, rising slightly at pH 7. The effect of pH on the rupture load for the limed-hide gelatins reflects this pattern in reverse, falling rapidly below 4·5 and above pH 9·5. The rupture load goes through a minimum near pH 7. The acid-pigskin gelatins however, display quite different behaviour. Their rupture loads are of the same order of magnitude at the lower end of the pH range, but rise steadily as the pH increases to reach a maximum at about pH 9·5. Their rupture loads at the maximum are far higher than those of the limed-hide gelatins. The actual values displayed in Fig. 4 cannot be directly compared with the corresponding values for the limed-hide gelatins, since at a comparable concentration (10%) and temperature (10°C), their rupture loads were beyond the scope of the transducers employed.

The effect of ionic strength on the form of the pH/gelation time curve can be seen in Fig. 2. The gelation time is increased in sodium chloride solution (0·15 N) in the pH range 4·5 to 10·8 but is decreased below pH 4·5 and above pH 10·8. The form of the pH/gelation time curve retains its approximate symmetry about pH 7. The two curves intersect at pH 4·5 and pH 10·8, the gelation time being unaffected by the change in ionic strength at these pH values. The positions of the minima and maxima do not appear to be affected by the change in ionic strength. The pH/rupture load curve for the limed-hide gelatin (No. 304) is displaced to lower values on the rupture load axis by the presence of calcium chloride (0·19 N), in the pH range 3·5 to 10·8. The rupture load is increased below pH 3·5 but the experimental evidence does not confirm a similar cross-over point at pH 10·8. Further measurements at the higher end of the pH range would be necessary to clarify this point. Again, the effect of ionic strength on the pH/gelation time for the acid-pigskin gelatin (No. 281) is reflected by the effect on the pH/rupture load curve for the limed-hide gelation (No. 304). It would appear that the minima of the pH/gelation time curves correspond approximately to the maxima of the pH/rupture load curves and that the forms of the two types of curve are, in general terms, complimentary. The pH/rupture load curves for the acid-pigskin gelatin, however, cannot be compared with those of the limed-hide gelatin, and they bear no resemblance to the pH/gelation time curve for the acid-pigskin gelatin.

CONCLUSIONS

Although it would be a formidable task to review the work that has been done on the mechanism of gelation, a number of facts have emerged which could serve to illuminate the results presented here. It is well established that the gelation of gelatin solutions is essentially similar to the gelation of many other polymeric materials, both natural and synthetic. Ferry[8] demonstrated the use of statistical methods for the elucidation of the kinetics of gelation of gelatin solutions. Random collisions between active groups in the polymer chain result in the formation of crosslinks which in the case of gelatin are stabilized by secondary forces. The rate at which crosslinks are formed determines the time taken for the critical number of crosslinks to be formed, i.e. the gelation time. Furthermore, statistical theory predicts that the gelation point occurs when the fraction p_c, of active groups involved in crosslinks is given by,

$$p_c = \frac{1}{\rho(\lambda\omega - 1)}$$

where ρ is the fraction of groups in the macromolecule that are active, or able to form crosslinks, and $\lambda\omega$ is the weight-average number of monomer units per macromolecule.

Bonding

Thus, the gelation point, and hence gelation time, is a function of weight-average molecular weight and the number of active groups per macromolecule. This simple treatment suggests that the gelation time is a meaningful parameter in that it is related to the rate at which crosslinks between gelatin molecules are formed.

The formation of intermolecular crosslinks is by no means the only process involved in the gelation of gelatin solutions. Boedtker and Doty[9] demonstrated the formation and growth of light scattering centres termed aggregates during the gelation process, and reasoned that such aggregates were the result of intramolecular bonding, or cyclical bonding. At high gelatin concentrations, the rate at which intermolecular crosslinks are formed exceeds that at which aggregates are formed, and gelation proceeds rapidly giving gels of low aggregate content. At low concentrations, however, a greater proportion of bonding contributes to aggregate formation and gelation proceeds more slowly giving gels of high aggregate content. Gelation at low temperatures produces more highly crosslinked gels with a low aggregate content. Boedtker and Doty suggested that electrostatic forces were not involved in the formation of aggregates and it was thought that secondary forces were involved. There has been much evidence to suggest that the aggregates were ordered structures and later work has confirmed that the crystallites present in aggregates have the collagen-fold configuration and involve multiple chain segments. The groups involved in the collagen-fold region appear to be non-polar and include both proline and hydroxyproline. Gelation then, is accompanied by at least two processes; the formation of the collagen-fold configuration involving both the segments of different macromolecules and those of a single macromolecule. The intermolecular bonding leads to crosslinks being formed which inhibits the intramolecular bonding process, and crosslinking is achieved at the expense of aggregate formation.

The rate at which crosslinking bonds are formed is related to the gelation time but no information about aggregate formation can be obtained from gelation time data. The nature of the bonding is responsible for the form of the pH/gelation time function as shown in Fig. 2. The form of the curves for both acid-pigskin and limed-hide gelations is almost symmetrical about pH 7 with minima appearing at about pH 5·5 and pH 9·0. The minimum at pH 5·5 for the limed-hide gelatin is lower than that at pH 9. The minimum gelation time for the acid-pigskin gelatin at pH 9, on the other hand, is slightly less than that at pH 5·5. The difference is not so marked in the case of the acid-pigskin gelatin. These results suggest that the electrostatic state of the gelatin molecule is not of prime importance as far as gelation is concerned, although it may have a minor effect on the pH/gelation time function.

Isoionic pH values

The isoionic pH of both limed-hide and acid-pigskin gelatins is different from pH 7·0. Janus, Kenchington and Ward[10] measured the isoionic pH values of a number of gelatins using an ion-exchange technique. Gelatin solutions containing protein molecules and both hydrogen and hydroxyl ions only were prepared and such solutions are, by definition, isoionic. Their results showed that alkali-precursor gelatins had an isoionic pH of about 5 while acid-pigskin gelatins had an isoionic pH of about 9. It is also known that the isoionic pH of deionized gelatin solutions is almost equal to the isoelectric pH of the solutions, and that the radius of gyration of the molecule is a minimum at this pH value. The net charge on the gelatin molecules is zero at the isoelectric point. On the basis of these facts, it would seem that the net charge on gelatin protein molecules cannot be closely correlated to the gelation time of gelatin solutions, since the variation in gelation time is not symmetrical about the isoelectric point but is symmetrical about the point of neutrality, pH 7·0. This is true for both acid-pigskin and limed-hide gelatins. However, it is clear from the data presented in Fig. 2 that the minimum at the isoelectric points of the two types of gelatin has a lower value than the second minimum point. This may indicate a much smaller effect of the net charge on the gelation time of gelatin solutions.

Although the isoionic pH values of limed-hide and acid-pigskin gelatins are widely different, light scattering techniques have shown that acid-pigskin gelatins display anomalous behaviour.(11) The information obtainable from light scattering measurements is used to determine molecular dimensions and net charge on molecules. Acid-pigskin gelatins are found to display zero net charge at pH values somewhat lower than the isoionic pH. It has been suggested that the strong absorption of ionic species by the gelatin molecules may account for this behaviour. Limed-hide gelatins behave normally in that the minimum reduced scattering value coincides with the isoionic pH and zero net charge. The minimum reduced scattering value for acid-pigskin gelatin occurs at about pH 6·2 instead of the isoionic pH 9·0. The isoelectric pH of acid-pigskin gelatin can be much lower than the isoionic pH.

Isoelectric pH values

Under certain conditions, then, the isoelectric pH values of both acid-pigskin and limed-hide gelatins can be within a pH unit of each other. This, however, would not account for the symmetry of the pH/gelation time curves about the point of neutrality, pH 7·0, when the isoelectric points of the two types of gelatin are in the range pH 5·0 to pH 6·0. A more likely explanation is that the rate of crosslinking is related to the concentration of ionic species in solution. Von Hippel and Wong(13) investigated the effect of neutral salt concentration on the rate of collagen-fold formation in gelatin solutions and concluded that ionic species modify the interactions between water and protein molecules which stabilize the collagen-fold configuration. This may also be true of hydrogen and hydroxyl ions. It must be remembered that Von Hippel and Wong determined the degree of collagen-fold formation from optical rotation data which did not distinguish between intra- and inter-molecular bonding. In this work, only the bonding leading to cross-linking contributes to the gelation process. However, the symmetry of the pH/gelation time curve above pH 7·0 supports the suggestion that the rate of collagen-fold formation is a function of the concentration of ionic species present in solution which are capable of interacting with the structured water associated with the collagen-fold. The presence of neutral salt has the effect of suppressing the pH variation of the gelation time. The similarity between the pH/gelation time curves for both limed-hide and acid-pigskin gelatins support this theory since the chemical constitutions of the two types of gelatin are almost identical and the same chemical groups are probably involved in the crosslinking process. The differences in secondary structure which exist between the two types of gelatin do not affect the rate of collagen-fold formation, which accompanies gelation.

Rupture properties

Although the pH/gelation time data do not suggest that there are fundamental differences between the two types of gelatin as far as the gelation process is concerned, their rupture properties are fundamentally different. There is a great deal of evidence from our results to suggest that the structures of the two types of gelatin molecules are different. Limed-hide gelatin consists of protein molecules having a random linear configuration, which behave as linear polyampholytes in solution. Acid-pigskin gelatin, however, cannot be represented as a similar single chain structure, and it has been suggested by Veis *et al.*[12] that some of the covalent crosslinks of the parent collagen are retained by the gelatin. The acid-pigskin gelatin molecules probably consist of a number of peptide chains held together by covalent crosslinks. These networks of peptide chains also display ion-binding properties differing from limed-hide gelatins in the isoelectric regions. An acid-pigskin gelatin does not undergo configurational changes as the pH is changed from the isoelectric pH in solution and this suggests the presence of a constraining action of the type that crosslinks would impose.

Veis *et al.*[12] have discussed the structure of acid-pigskin gelatins at some length and have described this type of gelatin in terms of "melted soluble collagen". The ion-binding properties displayed by the acid-pigskin gelatins may be formally explained by the Donnan equilibrium that exist between ions in solution and ions absorbed by a fixed array of charged groups. These structural differences between acid-pigskin and limed-hide gelatins are evidently playing some part in the difference in their rupture properties. In particular, the presence of covalent bonds between polypeptide molecules is of importance. The acid-pigskin gelatins appear to consist of a lateral array of polypeptide molecules held together by covalent crosslinks and structurally stabilized by electrostatic interactions between oppositely charged groups on adjacent polypeptide molecules. In general terms, this model is compatible with the results presented here. The rupture properties of gelatin gels reflects both the number of links per unit volume of gel and the bond strength of these linkages. The high rupture loads of the acid-pigskin gelatin gels in the region of pH 9·0 suggests that the types of bonds existing in this pH region are different from those found at lower pH values. The fact that the rate of crosslinking appears to be almost the same at pH 9·0 as at pH 5·0 indicates that electrostatic interactions with the collagen-fold structure of the type proposed by Veis *et al.* may be responsible for the high rupture loads of acid-pigskin gelatin gels in the region of pH 9·0.

References

(1) Hodgetts, G. B. and Norman, D. E., *J. Sci. Instrum.*, **44,** 963–965 (1967).

(2) Janus, J. W., in *Recent Advances in Gelatin and Glue Research* (Ed. G. Stainsby), pp. 214–218, Pergamon Press, Oxford (1958).

(3) Veis, A., *The Macromolecular Chemistry of Gelatin*, Academic Press, London and New York (1964).

(4) Saunders, P. R., Supplement to Research Report All, pp. 11–14, G.G.R.A. Publication (1956).

(5) Wood, P. D., Research Report A44, G.G.R.A. Publication, September (1969).

(6) Eloart, T. M. B., *Adhes. Age*, **Ma7** (1963).

(7) Cobbett, W. G., G.G.R.A. Publication A27, April (1961).

(8) Ferry, J. D., *Advan. Protein Chem.*, **4,** 1 (1948).

(9) Boedtker, H. and Doty, P., *J. Phys. Chem.*, **58,** 968 (1954).

(10) Janus, J. W., Kenchington, A. W. and Ward, A. G., *Res. Appl. Ind.*, **4,** 247 (1951).

(11) Cobbett, W. G. and Ward, A. G., *Rheol. Acta*, **7,** No. 3, 217–222 (1968).

(12) Veis, A., Anesey, J. and Cohen, J., in *Recent Advances in Gelatin and Glue Research* (Ed. G. Stainsby), pp. 155–163, Pergamon Press, Oxford (1958).

(13) Von Hippel, P. H. and Wong, K., *Biochemistry*, **1,** 664–674 (1962).

Appendix

The terminal velocity, V, of a free-falling sphere through a liquid, is a function only of the viscosity coefficient, η, of the liquid, the radius, r, of the sphere and the difference between the liquid and sphere densities, $(\rho_l - \rho_s)$. The constant of proportionality includes the acceleration due to gravity, g, since this together with the density difference determines the force on the sphere.

The exact relation between these variables is not of interest here, but the form of the relation can be deduced most conveniently and the proportionality written in the following manner

$$v \propto \eta^a[(\rho_l - \rho_s)g]^b r^c$$

where a, b and c are power indices.

The values of a, b and c can be found by equating the expressions on both sides of the proportionality symbol. This dimensional analysis leads to the equation

$$LT^{-1} = M^{(a+b)}L^{(-a-2b+c)}T^{(-a-2b)}$$

where M is mass, L is length and T is time.

The indices can be equated giving

$$\begin{aligned} 0 &= a + b \\ 1 &= -a - 2b + c \\ -1 &= -a - 2b \end{aligned}$$

from which the values of a, b and c are found to be $a = -1$, $b = 1$, $c = 2$.

The terminal velocity is therefore given by,

$$v \propto \eta^{-1}(\rho_l - \rho_s)gr^2$$

The velocity of the falling drop of carbon tetrachloride is inversely proportional to the viscosity coefficient of the gelatin solution. The absolute value of the velocity has not been measured in these experiments. Instead, a point in time has been measured when the velocity of a falling drop is less than its diameter divided by the time interval between two adjacent drops. At this point, an emerging drop comes into contact with the preceding drop. The reproducibility of the method depends upon both the drop rate and drop diameter being constant at the gel point. The reproducibility of the method is within acceptable limits and any variations which may take place in drop size or drop rate do not effect the gelation time to any great extent. This is due to the very rapid increase in the solution viscosity as the gelation point is approached.

The Gelatin Molecule

Determination of Gelatin Molecular Weights and Shape by Scattered Light Measurements

B. E. TABOR

Research Laboratories, Kodak Ltd., Wealdstone, Middlesex

ABSTRACT. Weight average molecular weights ($\bar{M}w$) and scattered light dissymmetry ratios (Z) have been determined for a large number of acid and alkali process gelatins and gelatin fractions by an enzymic digestion difference technique. The extension of this technique to obtain a Zimm plot of the angular distribution of the scattered light has also been demonstrated.

Some sources of error that can arise with the digestion technique are indicated and criteria are suggested for judging the validity of the results obtained. A comparison of $\bar{M}w$ and Z for those gelatins which satisfy these criteria supports the idea of the molecule as a random coil. The $\bar{M}w$ data has been used to establish a dilute solution viscosity/molecular weight relationship which is such as to indicate a branched molecule.

A Critique of Gel Filtration Chromatography as a Method of Characterizing the Structure of Photographic Gelatin

D. W. LaPALME, Jr., G. H. KLINGER and R. V. COLE, Jr.
G.A.F. Corporation, Binghampton, New York 13902, U.S.A.

ABSTRACT. A review of gel filtration chromatography as a method of characterizing the structure of photographic gelatin in dilute aqueous solutions will be presented. The methods described by Leiner, Hermel, and Chevé were found to give reproducible results. Based on our experimental work and the results reported by the aforementioned authors, we conclude that the gel filtration technique can at best only characterize the secondary structure of gelatin, i.e. the distribution of gelatin aggregates. The determination of aggregate size on an absolute scale is impossible because of the lack of knowledge of the molecular composition of the aggregates. The parameters influencing the shape of the elution chromatogram such as pH, temperature, gelatin concentration, thermal path and solvent composition will also be discussed.

Extended Molecular Characterization of Photographic Gelatin by Analytical and Preparative Gel Chromatography, Acrylamide Gel Electrophoresis and Light Scattering

I. TOMKA, A. SPÜHLER and K. BÜHLER

CIBA Photochemical Limited, 1701 Fribourg, Switzerland

ABSTRACT. Preliminary experiments by gel electrophoresis of gelatins have shown a discontinuous molecular size distribution of their components. On this basis we analysed the molecular mass spectrum of gelatins by gel chromatography and electrophoresis. These methods had to be adapted to the unique properties of gelatin which are: high tendency of association, adsorption on the surface of the separation media, and the sensitivity of the hydrodynamic volume of the gelatine molecules to pH and ionic strength. The numerous components of the gelatins required optimization of the separation methods.

The dispersity of the fractions won by repeated gel chromatography has been checked by gel electrophoresis. These fractions were characterized by light scattering and in some cases also by the limiting viscosity number and ultracentrifugation. Gel chromatography on the analytical scale has been calibrated by hydrodynamic volume determinations of gelatin fractions and other monodisperse protein solutions.

The resolution on the analytical scale has been completed by a mathematical analysis of the elution diagrams. Here also the skewness of the peaks has been studied.

The resolved components of many photographic gelatins (alkaline degraded) could be classified in three groups: associates of soluble collagen molecules, soluble collagen components and peptides.

The associate character of the components of the first group could be shown by denaturation with urea and following electrophoresis and limiting viscosity number determination. These associates are of the lateral type and their molecular weights are in the range of $5 \times 10^5 \rightarrow 10^7$. The components of the second group could be identified by molecular weight determination and electron-microscopic identification of the cross-striation pattern of native contrasted fibrils with those prepared from the gelatin fractions. The peptides have in general molecular weights below those of the soluble collagen components. The applications of these methods are: the qualitative molecular mass analysis of photographic gelatins, the analysis of the gel and sol fractions of gel sedimentation made by P. Johnson, and the comparison of our results with those of C. R. Maxey on isoelectric focusing electrophoresis of photographic gelatins.

Column Chromatographic Separation of Gelatin Hydrolysates and their Interactions on Silver Halide Crystals

E. DUBIEL

Foton Photochemical Establishment, Warsaw, Poland

ABSTRACT. Enzymatically hydrolysed gelatin was fractionated on columns filled with fine grade Sephadex G50 or G25 and chosen fractions tested in regard to their sensitizing properties by addition to aqueous silver halide suspensions.

Twenty per cent gelatin solutions were treated with Exocoll, a commercial enzyme obtained from animal pancreas, or with pure trypsin. After given times of enzyme action, the gelatin hydrolysates were put upon the column and fractionated according to molecular size. The presence and the approximate quantity of polypeptides in 4·5 ml fractions were indicated spectophotometrically by UV measurements at 230 and 260 nm. Comparison of the optical density curves showed that pure trypsin degrades gelatin only moderately and that these hydrolysates have reached their end-point after about 2 hours. Exocoll, in contrast, consists of an ill-defined mixture of enzymes and it degrades gelatin continuously over several days and correspondingly to a greater degree. In spite of the difference in the course of hydrolysis, the UV absorption curves of the fractions resulting from chromatographic separation were relatively similar. The qualitative resemblance appears not only to the fractions of the different gelatins but extends to the regions of fractionation according to molecular size, on Sephasex G50 from 1500 to 30 000 molecular weight and on Sephadex G25 from 1000 to 5000. It is presumed that the fractionation results not only from the size, that is, length of polypeptide chain, but is also influenced by the structural differences and chemical properties of the separated polypeptides.

A medium sensitivity, ammoniacal silver bromo-iodide suspension was precipitated without gelatin in the presence of a non-ionic surfactant, and then physically ripened and washed. Equivalent volumes of combined fractions, corresponding to the distribution curve were added to these silver halide crystals and mixed in. After sedimentation, the supernatant was poured off and the silver halide crystals re-dispersed in gelatin. Finally, the sensitometric changes were evaluated by comparison with the unsensitized sample. The sensitizing effect occurs as changes in fog and sensitivity to varying extents with all polypeptide-containing samples. The sensitization is not always proportional to the polypeptide content. Likewise, there is no clear relationship between the size of sensitizing substance and the sensitization effect. The sensitizing properties of fractions in the region of about 1000 to 15 000 molecular weight, following fractionation either on Sephasex G50 or on Sephadex G25, appear, however, to be the most interesting for future investigation.

On the Interactions Between Gelatin and Glycerol

J. POURADIER and A. M. HODOT

Centre de Recherches de la Société Kodak-Pathé, Vincennes (94), *France*

ABSTRACT. Glycerol, introduced as a plasticizer in gelatin, reduces its hygroscopicity. This action is due to the blocking of the reactive sites of gelatin, each molecule of glycerol solvating, probably caused by one of its own OH functions, one hydrophilic group of gelatin.

INTRODUCTION

Glycerol can be either a plasticizer or a solvent for gelatin, depending on its relative concentration. These two effects denote the existence of strong molecular interactions between glycerol and gelatin, interactions which have repercussions on the other properties of gelatin, particularly on its affinity for moisture. This affinity is lowered by the presence of glycerol (see Fig. 1 where the results obtained with a limed calf skin

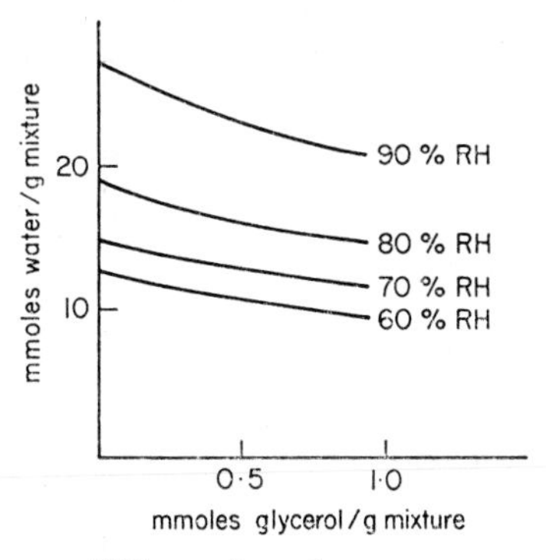

Fig. 1. Influence of Glycerol on the water vapour sorption by a limed calf skin gelatin

gelatin are plotted), and a simple calculation shows that the amount of water fixed by a mixture of gelatin and glycerol is always inferior to the quantity retained at the same humidity by the two materials taken separately.

The influence of glycerol on the affinity of gelatin for water can be ascribed to a partial, or to a total, blocking of some hydrophilic groups of the protein. In order to define the blockage mechanism, we have studied the sorption of water by samples of gelatin containing various amounts of glycerol.

EXPLANATION

The amount of water fixed by gelatin in equilibrium with the ambient humidity increases with the vapour pressure and the graphic representation of this variation gives a sigmoid. This shape of curve, which has been observed with several macromolecular and colloidal substances, does not correspond to a single mechanism and, to explain it, it is necessary to consider, at least, two interaction processes, one or the other prevailing according to the surrounding vapour pressure[1-5]. The interpretation of the lower part is rather easy and this has been shown in a previous paper[6]. Authors Brunauer, Emmett and Teller[7] agree that it is possible to admit a mechanism as is explained below in B.E.T. equation (1).

$$\frac{p}{p_0 - p}\frac{1}{a} = \frac{1}{a_m C} + \frac{C-1}{a_m C}\frac{p}{p_0} \tag{1}$$

where a is the amount of water fixed (expressed in this paper in mmole/g of absorbant) for the vapour pressure p

p_0 is the vapour pressure at saturation

a_m is the amount of water bound when a monomolecular layer covers all the surface

C is a parameter depending on the binding energy between the absorbant and the absorbed molecules in the first layer

Harkins and Jura equation

When the vapour pressure increases, the B.E.T. equation is no longer applicable and it becomes necessary to use a new equation. In the case of gelatins, the water sorption can satisfactorily be represented by the Harkins and Jura equation[6].

$$\log \frac{p}{p_0} = K - \frac{A}{a^2} \tag{2}$$

in which a, p and p_0 have the same meanings as above.

A and K are parameters depending on the compounds present.

Influence of B.E.T. relation

By the association of this equation with the B.E.T. relation, Liang[8] has shown that A is equal to the square of a_m

$$A = a_m^2 \tag{3}$$

This identification is very promising, because it gives a means of calculating a_m from the part of the isotherm corresponding to the high pressures. The calculation has been carried out for several proteins[9], and for gelatins the results obtained by considering the high R.H. (relative humidity) part of the isotherm are in a very good agreement with those obtained from the B.E.T. analysis of the lower part (Tables 1 and 2).

Table 1

Agreement between "a_m" values calculated from the lower and the upper parts of the isotherm (different gelatins)

	Temp. 0°C	a_m mmole H_2O/g *gelatin*	
		Low R.H.	*High R.H.*
Hide gelatin acid treatment	25°	4·99	4·90
Hide gelatin acid treatment	40°	4·96	4·87
Lime ossein	27°	5·35	5·43
Calf skin gelatin	27°	5·58	5·63

Table 2

Agreement between "a_m" values calculated from the lower and the upper parts of the isotherm (calf skin gelatin at 25°C and at different pH)

pH	a_m mmole H_2O/g *gelatin*	
	Low R.H.	*High R.H.*
2·0	4·22	4·11
2·9	4·54	4·44
4·79	5·05	4·95
6·10	5·39	5·29
7·89	5·58	5·38
10·02	5·66	5·51

Sorption of water

Strictly speaking, the B.E.T. and the Harkins and Jura equations are only applicable to systems showing *adsorption*, but the agreement between the figures corresponding to low and high R.H. shows that, from a purely mathematical point of view, these two equations give an accurate account of the sorption of water vapour by gelatins. In these conditions, the analysis of the isotherms enables us to calculate the parameter "a_m" which represents the state of hydration when each free hydrophilic site of gelatin is occupied by a molecule of water.

This mathematical analysis of the isotherms has been applied to gelatin samples containing known amounts of glycerol and the results are given in Table 3.

Table 3

Influence of glycerol on the amount of water retained by gelatin

% *glycerol in the mixture*	mmole *glycerol per* g *of mixture*	a_m mmole *water per* g *mixture*	mmole *water per* g (*separated constituents*)	*Difference between 3rd and 4th columns*
0·00	0·000	5·80	5·80	0·00
1·15	0·125	5·65	5·75	−0·10
2·27	0·247	5·41	5·71	−0·30
4·44	0·483	5·09	5·62	−0·53
8·51	0·925	4·63	5·46	−0·83

Considering the sorption isotherms, it is easy for each sample to determine the R.H. corresponding to "a_m" and, referring to the gelatin and glycerol isotherms, to calculate the quantity of water retained under the same moisture environment by the two substances in a separate condition (4th column of Table 3). In the range of glycerol concentrations, "a_m" is always smaller than the values corresponding to the separated substances. The difference (5th column) represents the mutual blocking by gelatin and glycerol, of a part of their hydrophilic groups.

The plot of this difference as a function of the glycerol content in the mixture gives values which, within experimental errors, yield a straight line passing through the origin and having a slope about unity (Fig. 2). This relationship shows that each molecule of glycerol introduced into the mixture prevents the binding of a water molecule.

CONCLUSIONS

As, at humidities corresponding to "a_m" ($p/p_0 \simeq 0{\cdot}2$), the retention of water by pure glycerol is small, and in every case less than 2×10^{-1} mole/mole glycerol, it appears that the main effect is due to a blocking of the hydrophilic groups of the gelatin. The solvation of these groups by glycerol produces a lowering of their affinity for water and the one water mole for one glycerol mole relationship mentioned above

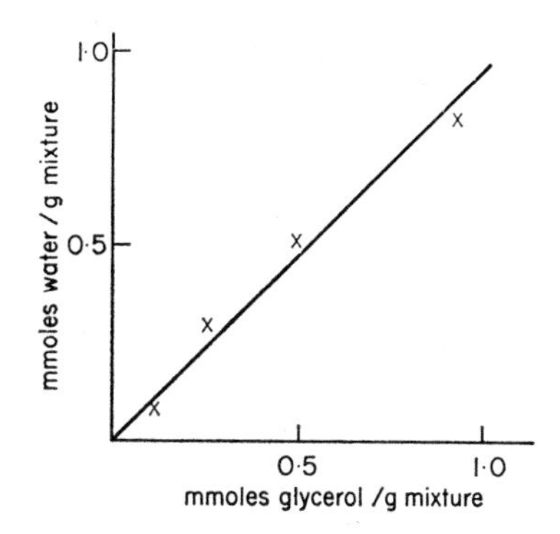

Fig. 2. Blocking of the reactive sites of gelatin by glycerol

shows that, in spite of its three alcohol functions, each glycerol molecule solvates only one group of the gelatin. This limitation is probably due to the spacings separating the hydrophilic groups of gelatin, these groups being *too* distant to allow the association of two of them with the same glycerol molecule.

References

(1) Bull, H. B., *J. Amer. Chem. Soc.*, **66,** 1499–1507 (1944).
(2) Jura, G. and Harkins, W. D., *J. Amer. Chem. Soc.*, **68,** 1941–1952 (1946).
(3) Simha, R. and Rowen, J. W., *J. Amer. Chem. Soc.*, **70,** 1663–1665 (1948).
(4) Rowen, J. W. and Simha, R., *J. Phys. Chem.*, **53,** 921–930 (1949).
(5) Cutler, J. A. and McLaren, A. D., *J. Polym. Sci.*, **3,** 792–794 (1948).
(6) Pouradier, J., *J. Chim. Phys.*, **67,** 229–234 (1970).
(7) Brunauer, S., Emmett, P. H. and Teller, E., *J. Amer. Chem. Soc.*, **60,** 309–319 (1938).
(8) Liang, S. C., *J. Phys. Chem.*, **55,** 1410–1412 (1951).
(9) Dunford, H. B. and Morrison, J. L., *Can. J. Chem.*, **32,** 558–560 (1954).

The Crosslinking of Gelatin

Contributions of Chemical Crosslinks and Ordered Structure to the Physical Properties of Swollen Gelatin Films

M. F. JOHNSON, W. D. FELLOWS, W. D. KAMM,
R. S. MILLER, HATTIE O. OTTO and H. G. CURME

Research Laboratories, Eastman Kodak Co., Rochester, New York 14650, U.S.A.

ABSTRACT. Chemical crosslinks in gelatin films formed by reaction with bisacryloylurea have been quantitated using amino acid analysis and radiochemical techniques. Swollen hot-dried, crosslinked films were found to show the same specific optical rotation as gelatin solutions at 40°C and are felt to be without ordered structure. The number of crosslinks in hot-dried films was calculated from tensile measurements on the swollen films using rubber elasticity theory. These figures agreed well with the chemical analysis. Hot-dried and cold-dried films at the same level of bisacryloylurea showed roughly the same amount of reaction with the bisacryloylurea. However, the moduli of elasticity of the swollen cold-dried films were three to ten times greater than those of hot-dried films containing the same number of chemical crosslinks. The crosslinks in the cold-dried films maintain levorotation indicative of ordered structure at temperatures and volume fractions at which similar structure in uncrosslinked gels and in hot-dried films has melted.

Similar work has been carried out using ^{14}C-tagged formaldehyde as the crosslinking reagent. Levels of both free and bound formaldehyde were found to be much higher than the actual number of physical crosslinks.

INTRODUCTION

It is generally agreed that there are two structural features which contribute to the physical properties of crosslinked gelatin films. These are the ordered structure (collagen helix,[1] oriented to some degree in the plane of the sheet[2]), which may be induced by chilling the melt and drying it cool, and the chemical crosslinks introduced by crosslinking agents, or "hardeners". It is the purpose of the present work to devise methods of measuring the relative or absolute amounts of these structural features in the films, and assess their contribution to the physical properties of the films in the swollen state.

EXPERIMENTAL

The gelatins used were commercial lime-processed ossein gelatins. Number-average molecular weights of the two gelatins used, determined with a Melabs osmometer,[3] were 101 200 and 89 200.

The crosslinking agents were added to the gelatin solutions at 40°C and pH 6·0. The coating concentrations were 12–13% gelatin. The solutions were immediately coated onto cellulose acetate film. "Hot-dried" films were held on a coating block at a temperature of 49°C under a nylon cover during drying; "cold-dried" films were chilled to 5°C for 3 min after coating, then dried at ambient temperature. Exceptions to these procedures were those films referred to in Fig. 1. These were dried, at the temperature indicated, on a coating block without a cover.

Optical rotation of the gelatin films was used as a measure of their content of ordered structure. The increase of levorotation of cool gelatin solutions over a base level ($[\alpha]_D^{40°} \approx -140°$) characteristic of the disordered (random coil) form has been established as being due to formation in the gelatin of helical collagenlike elements.[1],[4] Cold-dried gelatin films show ORD curves qualitatively similar to those of cold solutions of gelatin or soluble collagen[5],[6] and show X-ray scattering patterns with many of the features of collagen patterns.[2] The collagenlike volume elements in these films show orientation in the plane of the sheet.[2] It has not been clearly established, however, why the rotation of these films[6],[7] is substantially higher than that of solutions of soluble collagen.[8] The optical rotation of the dry films was measured under ambient conditions. The optical rotation of the swollen films was measured in a thermostatted cell. Both an Adam-Hilger polarimeter and a Perkin-Elmer Model 141 polarimeter were used for these measurements.

Tensile properties of the swollen films were measured with an Instron Tensile Tester, model TTB, equipped with an immersion unit and auxiliary thermostatting, using "A" or "B" load cells. Lateral swelling of the films was measured optically and vertical swelling by a thickness gauge. Values of rotation, modulus and tensile properties at 40°C were measured after approximately 30 min of swelling, but were nearly constant over a period of 1 h, except for the initial 10–15 min swelling. Degradation of the films at 50°C in some cases was somewhat faster.[9]

Counts of crosslinks obtained by tensile testing of swollen hot-dried films crosslinked with bisacryloylurea (BAU) were compared with those of chemical crosslinks found by amino acid chromatography. For the latter analyses, crosslinked gelatin films were hydrolysed in 6 N

HCl for 22 h at 110°C. Hydrolysates were analysed by a variation of the method of Moore, Spackman and Stein,[10] using a Beckman Spinco Model 120B amino acid analyser. The resulting chromatograms were quantitated using standardized procedures for integrating the areas under the elution peaks and relating these to concentration for the individual amino acids via an extinction factor previously determined for each amino acid.

Chemical crosslinks could be calculated by dividing by two the number of residues reacting with the acryloyl groups, were it not for the fact that some of the molecules of the crosslinking agent will have reacted at only one end, leaving an unreacted double bond at the other. To correct for this effect, mercaptoacetic acid (MAA) labelled with ^{35}S was made to react with the swollen crosslinked films. The films were then washed with water, hydrolysed with an enzyme (Takamine HT, Miles Laboratories), and the reacted mercaptoacetic acid was determined by liquid scintillation counting.

Analyses for formaldehyde could not be carried out by amino acid analysis since the crosslinks are hydrolysed along with the gelatin and amino acids are recovered unaltered. As a result, radioactive tagging methods similar to those used by Bowes, Cater and Ellis[11] in their studies of collagen were employed. The films crosslinked with ^{14}C-tagged formaldehyde were hydrolysed with Takamine and counted by scintillation counting. The formaldehyde content was determined in the films as coated, after washing to constant levels with water, and after washing to constant levels with 1 M hydroxylamine at pH 5.

RESULTS

Fig. 1 shows the specific rotation of the dry films which had been dried at the temperatures indicated on the horizontal axis. Films dried at 45°C or higher showed values of $[\alpha]_D$ of about $-90°$ when dry or $-140°$ when swollen (if hardened) at 40°C. Since the latter value is that characteristic of gelatin solutions at 40°C, and since the swelling of these films was nearly isotropic, it is presumed that they contained no ordered structure.

Swollen hot-dried films with values of $[\alpha]_D$ of $-140°$ at 40°C showed rubberlike stress-strain behaviour at this temperature; the density of physical crosslinks was calculated for these samples from the stress-strain data using the theory of rubberlike elasticity,[12] modified for systems that are in equilibrium with excess solvent during deformation.[13] The stress on cold-dried films measured at 40° or 50°C increased much more rapidly with extension than predicted by rubber-like elasticity theory and no calculations of crosslink density were made from physical data on these samples.

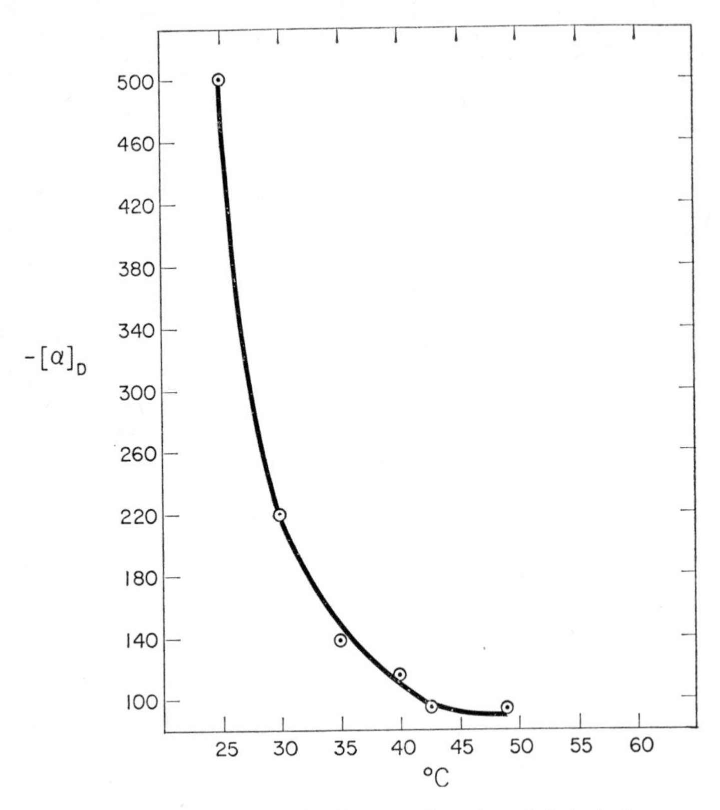

Fig. 1. Specific rotation of dry gelatin films as a function of their drying temperature.

Reduction in the areas of the lysine (LYS), hydroxylysine (HYL), and histidine (HIS) peaks were observed after reaction between gelatin and bisacryloylurea in the films. At the same time new peaks were found corresponding to monocarboxyethyllysine (MCELYS), dicarboxyethyllysine (DCELYS) and corresponding reaction products of HYL and HIS with BAU. The LYS derivatives were positively identified by isolation, esterification and analysis by mass spectrometry.(14) It was also demonstrated that MCELYS and DCELYS eluted without diminution in peak height after subjection to the 22 h hydrolysis in 6 N HCl at 110°C. It is thus demonstrated that the mode of crosslinking, at least in the case of LYS, is addition of the ε-amino group across the double bond of BAU; the urea moiety of the hardener is cleaved from the acryloyl group during the HCl hydrolysis.

In the case of films crosslinked with BAU, chemicla crosslinks were calculated as:

$$\text{Chemical crosslinks} = \frac{\text{reacted residues} + \text{DCELYS-MAA}}{2} \quad (1)$$

In this formula, "reacted residues" are the total moles of LYS, HYL and HIS in the gelatin found to have reacted with the BAU. This calculation ignores the doubly substituted HYL and HIS; in view of the low levels of these amino acids compared with LYS, this correction is probably small. Table 1 shows results of a typical analysis; the loss in LYS is seen to be in fair agreement with the amount of MCELYS and DCELYS found. The valves are in millimoles per gram of gelatin (mmoles/g).

Table 1

Results of a typical analysis. The values are in mmoles/g of gelatin

BAU added	*LYS*	*HYL*	*HIS*	*MCELYS*	*DCELYS*	*MCELYS + DCELYS*	*MAA*
			Found				
None	0·296	0·066	0·043				
0·148 (not incubated)	0·228	0·033	0·015	0·048	0·012	0·060	0·038
			Reacted residues				
0·148 (not incubated)	0·068	0·033	0·028				

Chemical crosslinks (calculated by equation (1)) = 0·048

Physical crosslinks = 0·027

Residual formaldehyde levels after water and hydroxylamine washing were almost identical, indicating that hydroxylamine, an aldehyde scavenger, does not reverse the reaction with gelatin. A typical analysis of formaldehyde-crosslinked films after keeping 1 day at 25°C, ambient RH ("fresh") or sealed in a bag at 25°C, 50% RH, and incubated at 49°C for 3 days, is shown in Table 2. A fraction of the formaldehyde volatilizes off during drying. Over half of that left is seen to readily wash out of the fresh coat, but less from the incubated coat. The "crosslinks" were calculated by rubberlike elasticity theory and represent a small fraction of the tightly bound formaldehyde.

Table 2

Bone gelatin crosslinked with formaldehyde (FA)
The values are in mmoles/g of gelatin

	Fresh	*Incubated*
FA added	0·667	0·667
Total FA found	0·418	0·379
FA after water wash	0·182	0·276
Crosslinks	0·033	0·057

Fig. 2 shows reacted residues for sets of cold- and hot-dried films crosslinked with BAU, as well as chemical crosslinks calculated by equation (1) for the hot-dried films and physical crosslinks calculated from elasticity theory. The hot- and cold-dried films show very nearly

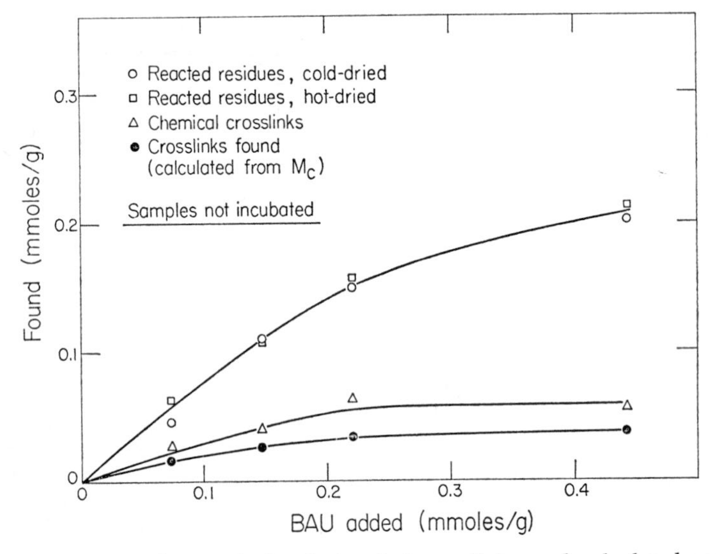

Fig. 2. Reacted residues, calculated chemical crosslinks, and calculated crosslinks from 40°C tensile data (from M_c, molecular weight between crosslinks) as a function of amount of BAU added to unincubated gelatin films.

the same amount of reaction. More chemical crosslinks are found than are calculated from elasticity theory; the ratio (physical crosslinks)/(chemical crosslinks) ranges from 0·45 to 0·57 in this series. Fig. 3 shows similar data for the same films after incubation. Increased degree of reaction is noted as well as physical crosslinking; however, a decrease in the ratio (physical crosslinks)/(chemical crosslinks) is found: the ratio for the incubated samples ranges from 0·36 to 0·40. This and other observations point to some hydrolysis of the bisacryloylurea crosslinks during moist incubation or holding in warm water.

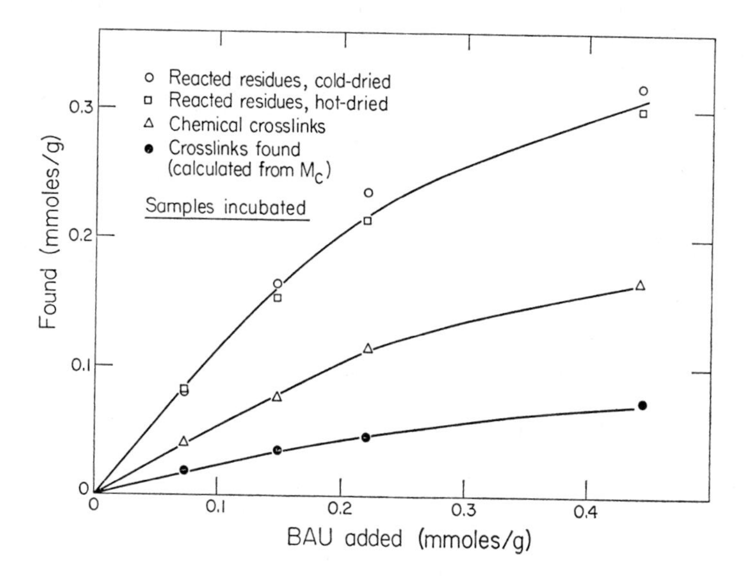

Fig. 3. Reacted residues, calculated chemical crosslinks, and calculated crosslinks from 40°C tensile data (from M_c, molecular weight between crosslinks) as a function of amount of BAU added to incubated gelatin films.

Fig. 4 shows similar data for the films crosslinked with formaldehyde. The ratios (physical crosslinks)/(bound formaldehyde) range from 0·18 to 0·38 in these coatings. By comparison with the BAU-crosslinked coatings, it would appear that not all the bound formaldehyde participates in crosslinking, or that more than one formaldehyde residue may participate in a crosslink.

The contribution of the ordered structure produced by cold drying to the tensile properties of a set of films is shown in Fig. 5. These films were all cold-dried in the same manner, but differed in the amount of BAU added to them. The cold-dried films showed values of $[\alpha]_D$ ranging from $-560°$ to $-620°$ when dry.* These values of levorotation dropped when the coatings were swollen at 40° or 50°C, the amount of levorotation retained increasing with increased level of crosslinking.

* Very little change in specific rotation of any of the dry films was noted on incubation.

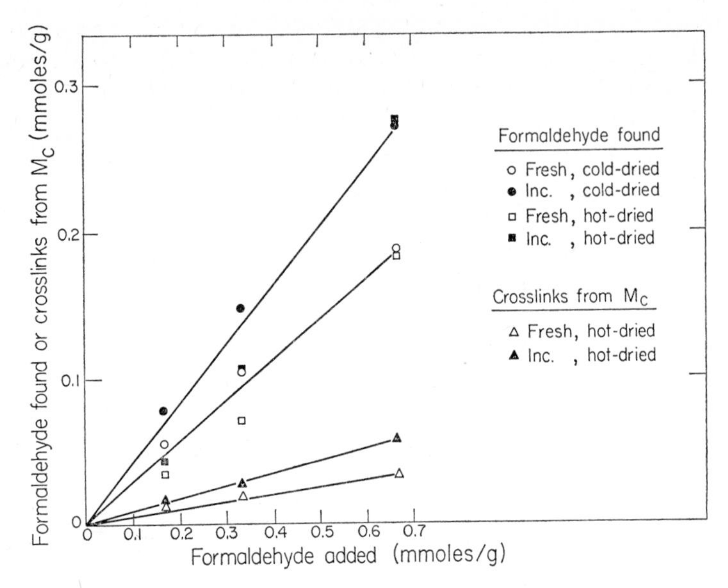

Fig. 4. Formaldehyde found after water washing, and crosslinks calculated from 40°C tensile data (from M_c, molecular weight between crosslinks) as a function of amount of formaldehyde added.

The main curve in Fig. 5 shows the in-plane tensile modulus of these swollen films as a function of their rotation; clearly, the modulus of the films is strongly dependent on the amount of ordered structure (as indicated by $[\alpha]_D$) remaining after swelling. The two points to the left of the main curve represent a plot of the in-plane moduli of hot-dried films crosslinked with the same range of BAU concentrations as the cold-dried films; the level of crosslinking agent in the most highly crosslinked hot-dried film is the same as in the most highly crosslinked cold-dried film. Fig. 6 compares the in-plane tensile moduli of swollen hot-dried and cold-dried films as a function of the number of chemical crosslinks found in them. It is seen that the cold-dried films have moduli three to ten times higher than hot-dried films containing the same number of chemical crosslinks.

Fig. 7 is a plot of the rotation of crosslinked cold-dried and hot-dried films and of uncrosslinked gelatin gels as a function of their volume fraction. (The films were allowed to swell in an excess of water, but the gelatin solutions were at constant volume except for the temperature coefficient of expansion.) Whereas the hot-dried films and the gels clearly show rotations characteristic of solutions at 40°C over the volume fraction range studied, the crosslinks in the cold-dried films maintain

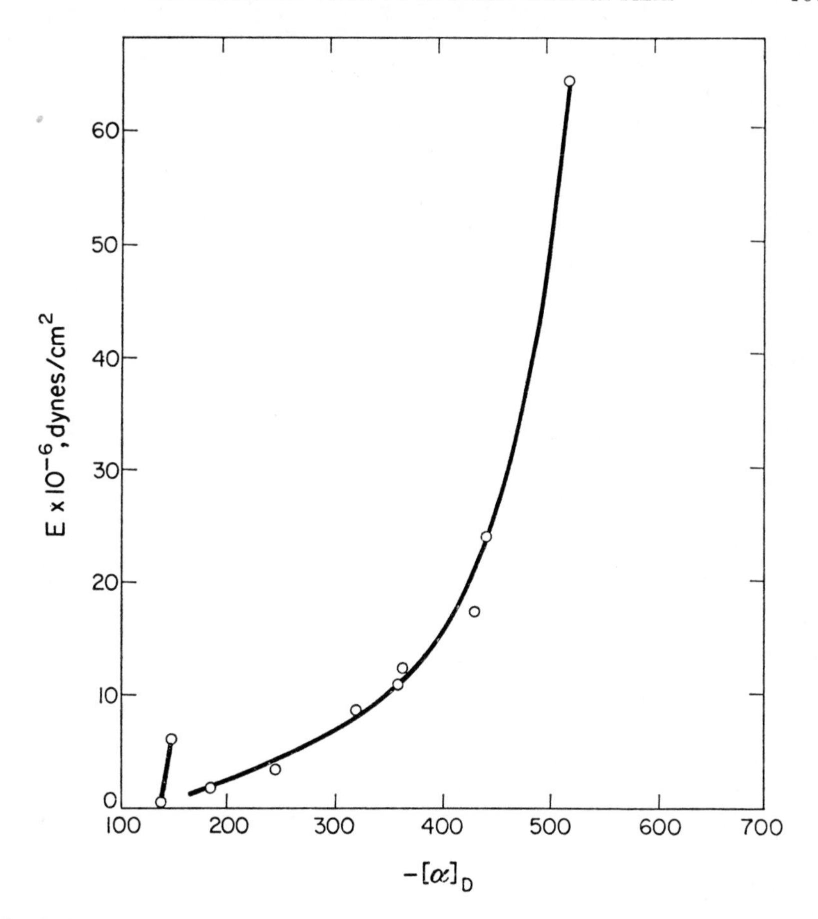

Fig. 5. In-plane tensile modulus of swollen gelatin films at 40°C as a function of their specific rotation. Main curve: all films cold-dried in same manner and differing in level of BAU added. Two points to the left: films hot-dried covering same concentration range of BAU as films shown on main curve.

higher rotations indicative of ordered structure over the same range of volume fractions, the degree of rotation increasing as the number of crosslinks increases. This is clear indication that volume fraction is not the sole factor determining the temperature of melting of ordered structure in swollen films, and that a simple application of Flory's equation(15) relating melting point to volume fraction in swollen crystalline polymers is not appropriate in these crosslinked systems. Rather, the observations probably represent an illustration of Flory's principle(12) that crosslinks introduced into an ordered structure can

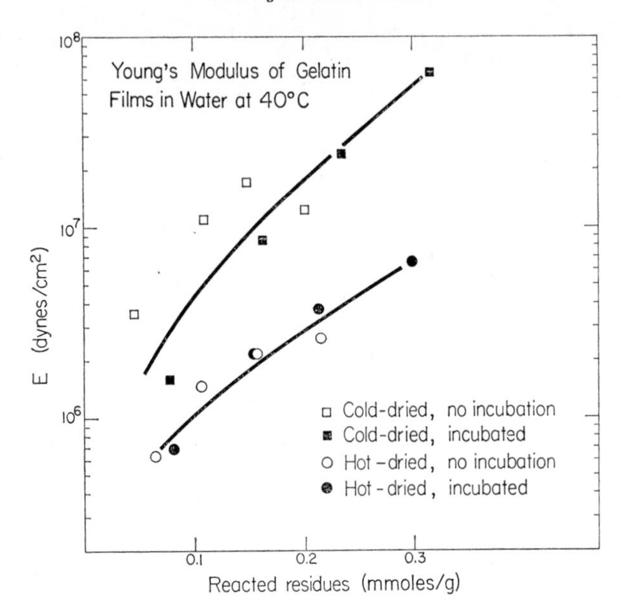

Fig. 6. Tensile moduli of swollen cold-dried and hot-dried gelatin films as a function of residues reacted with BAU.

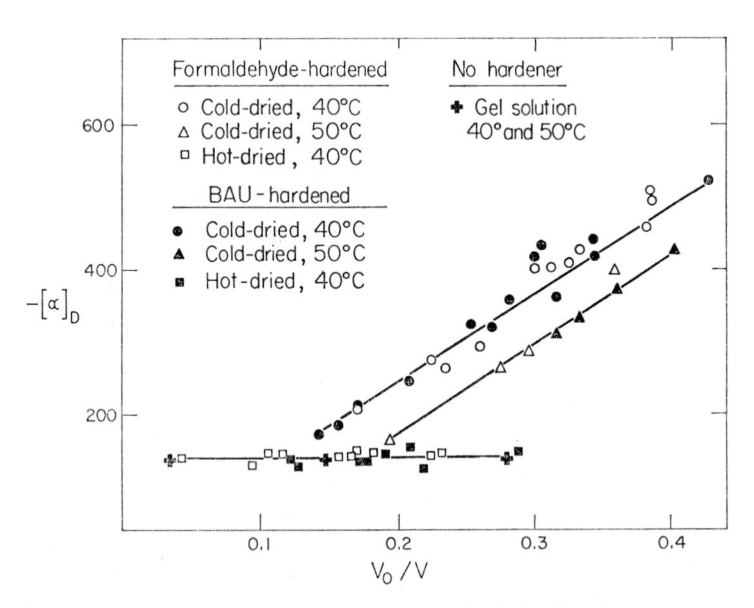

Fig. 7. Specific rotation of hot-dried and cold-dried gelatin films in excess water, and of gelatin solutions as a function of their volume fraction.

increase the melting temperatures of the structure by decreasing the entropy of fusion. It is apparent that the contribution of the crosslinks to the mechanical properties of these systems is neither the simple provision of further junction points in the network nor the mere repression of the swelling. Rather, their function is the stabilization of the ordered structure (including collagen helix, and perhaps some orientation of the chains in the plane of the sheet) at temperatures at which these features would melt out in the absence of the crosslinks.

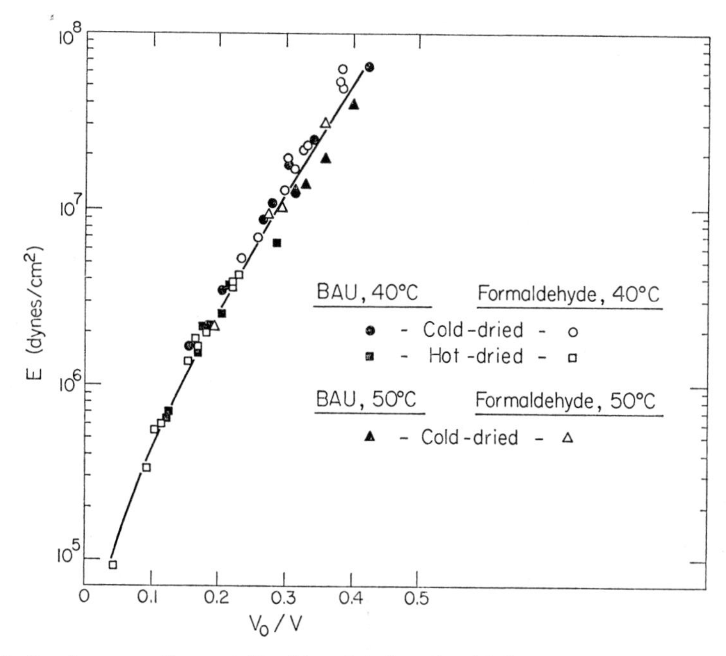

Fig. 8. In-plane tensile moduli of hot-dried and cold-dried gelatin films in excess water as a function of their volume fraction.

An in-plane modulus of intermediate value can be achieved either by using a high level of crosslinking agent with hot-drying, or much less of the crosslinking agent coupled with cold-drying. Fig. 8 shows a plot of the in-plane moduli of all films studied against their volume fraction. Very interestingly, data for both the hot-dried and the cold-dried films fall on the same plot. Apparently, regardless of the presence or absence of ordered structure and despite differences in anisotropy, the total volume swell and the modulus in the plane of the sheet are measures of the same characteristic of the films, that is, the tendency of the chains in the films to resist deformation. A similar plot for in-plane tensile strength of the films is shown in Fig. 9. The data suggest that the hot-dried films may have a lower tensile strength than the cold-dried films at the same volume fraction.

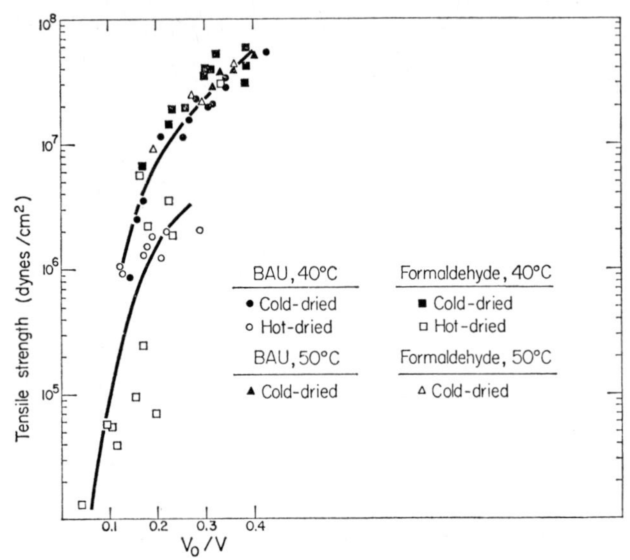

Fig. 9. In-plane tensile strength values of hot-dried and cold-dried gelatin films in excess water as a function of their volume fraction.

ACKNOWLEDGEMENT

The authors are grateful to Miss Prudence Costich for her aid in the design of the tensile testing experiments.

References

(1) Veis, A., "The Macromolecular Chemistry of Gelatin", Academic Press, New York (1964).
(2) Bradbury, E. and Martin, C., *Proc. Roy. Soc. London*, **A214,** 183 (1952).
(3) Genova, D., private communication.
(4) Cohen, C., *J. Biophys. Biochem. Cytol.*, **1,** 203 (1955).
(5) Sterman, M. D., private communication.
(6) Coopes, I. H., *J. Polym. Sci.*, in press.
(7) Robinson, C. and Bott, M. J., *Nature* (*London*), **168,** 325 (1951).
(8) Doty, P. and Nishihara, T., in "Recent Advances in Gelatin and Glue Research", p. 92. (Ed. G. Stainsby), Pergamon Press, New York (1958).
(9) Sterman, M. D., Faust, M. A., Genova, D. J., Curme, H. G. and Johnson, M. F., see this book.

(10) Moore, S., Spackman, D. H. and Stein, W. H., *Anal. Chem.*, **30,** 1185 (1958).
(11) Bowes, J. H., Cater, C. W. and Ellis, M. J., *J. Amer. Leather Chem. Ass.*, **60,** 275 (1965).
(12) Flory, P. J., *J. Amer. Chem. Soc.*, **78,** 5222 (1956).
(13) Puett, D., Ciferri, A. and Rajagh, L. V., *Biopolymers*, **3,** 439 (1965).
(14) Biemann, K., Seibl, J. and Gapp, F., *J. Amer. Chem. Soc.*, **83,** 3795 (1961).
(15) Flory, P. J., "Principles of Polymer Chemistry", p. 569. Cornell University Press, Ithaca, New York (1953).

Effect of Chemical Crosslinks on the Thermal Stability of Conformation in Swollen Gelatin Films

M. D. STERMAN, MARILYN A. FAUST, D. J. GENOVA, H. G. CURME and M. F. JOHNSON

Research Laboratories, Eastman Kodak Co., Rochester, New York 14650, U.S.A.

ABSTRACT. The temperature dependence of tensile modulus, swelling, and specific optical rotation of cold-dried gelatin films hardened with formaldehyde and swollen in water has been determined over the temperature range 10–60°C. Results indicate the following: (1) The films undergo structural transitions over the temperature range studied, with the transitions broadening and shifting to higher temperatures as the hardener level is increased. (2) Chemical crosslinks stabilize ordered structure in the films in a manner more specific than merely reducing swell. This is indicated by the fact that crosslinked, cold-dried films maintain high levorotation not found in hot-dried films or in uncrosslinked gelatin at the same temperatures and *volume fraction.* (3) The combination of chemical crosslinks and ordered structure contribute far more to the modulus of elasticity and to the suppression of swell than chemical crosslinks alone.

INTRODUCTION

Several factors have been recognized as affecting the melting points of crystalline regions in polymers swollen with diluent. Flory[1] showed that the melting temperature, T_m, of the crystalline regions in a swollen polymer is related to T_m^0, that of the unswollen polymer, through the relationship

$$\frac{1}{T_m} - \frac{1}{T_m^0} = \frac{R}{\Delta H_0}\frac{V_0}{V_1}(v_1 - \chi_1 v_1^2) \quad (1)$$

where ΔH_0 is the heat of fusion per mole of crystalline polymer repeat unit, V_0 the molar volume of the repeat unit, V_1 the molar volume of the solvent, v_1 the volume fraction of solvent and χ_1 the solvent-polymer interaction parameter. In deriving equation (1), the polymer was assumed to be uncrosslinked. Flory[2] also demonstrated theoretically that crosslinking an ordered system decreases the entropy of fusion and thus tends to raise the melting point, provided crosslink formation does not alter the heat of crystallization. Flory and Garrett[3] showed the melting point of swollen crosslinked collagen to be only 2° or 3°C higher than that of uncrosslinked material at the same volume fraction, and Witnauer and Fee[4] showed a slightly larger increase in shrinkage temperature comparing crosslinked and uncrosslinked collagen at the same volume fraction. It has long been known[5],[6] that crosslinked gelatin layers swollen in excess water "melt" (or, more properly, disintegrate) at higher temperatures than do uncrosslinked layers. However, in very few cases[7] have any attempts been made to ascertain whether crosslinks play any role outside of their control of volume fraction and hence melting point through equation (1). Neither has any effort been made to separate changes in conformation from irreversible crosslink hydrolysis or main-chain degradation in the "melting" process. In the present work, films were cold-dried, crosslinked, subsequently swollen in excess water, and their swell, optical rotation and tensile properties measured as a function of temperature. As in the previous work,[8] the optical rotation of the films has been taken to be a measure of the ordered structure, including the collagen-like helix. Decreases in levorotation and tensile moduli are interpreted as being caused by the transition from ordered to disordered forms. The properties of the cold-dried films are compared with those of films crosslinked in their hot-dried (random) conformation, and those of gelatin solutions which had not been chemically crosslinked and were maintained at constant volume fraction. The thermal instability of formaldehyde crosslinks[9] above 60°C prevented an unambiguous determination of the temperatures at which the cold-dried films lost all ordered structure, but these temperatures are nevertheless clearly demonstrated to be as much as tens of degrees higher than corresponding temperatures for the uncrosslinked gelatin solutions at the same volume fractions.

EXPERIMENTAL

The cold-dried films were prepared by swelling and melting the lime-processed commercial gelatin previously described,[8] adjusting the pH to 6, adding formaldehyde as the crosslinker, coating onto film support, and drying with flowing air at a wet bulb temperature of about 20°C for 6 min. Dry films were about 0·0015 in. thick. Films were held at 25°C, 100% RH for 24 h before testing.

Measurements of optical rotation, swell and tensile modulus were made in a manner similar to measurements previously described.[8] Different samples of the same films were used at each temperature. The temperatures of testing ranged from 10° to 80°C. In most of the work reported below, each film sample was immersed in excess water at a given temperature for 15 min before measurements were begun. This period of time permitted near-equilibrium swell, yet it held to a minimum the crosslink hydrolysis which is observed with formaldehyde-crosslinked films, at temperatures above 60°C.[9] A number of experiments were performed after longer times of swelling in order to explore the time dependence of the measured properties. In these experiments samples were held at a given temperature for intervals of time from 15 min to 7 h before measurement of rotation, modulus and swell.

Gelatin solutions at volume fraction gelatin of 0·035 and 0·280 (at 40°C) were prepared, cooled at 2°C for 20 h and their rotation observed. The temperature was increased stepwise, with holding periods before measurement of 60 min at each temperature below 40°C, and 30 min at each temperature above 40°C. Birefringence in the 2 mm cell prevented making meaningful readings of rotation of the 0·280 volume fraction solution at temperatures below 30–33°C.

RESULTS

The experiments on time dependence showed that values of rotation, swell and modulus changed slowly with time at temperatures up to 40°C. However, the value of the tensile modulus of the film crosslinked with 0·05 mmole formaldehyde per gram of gelatin decreased to half its back-extrapolated zero-time value in 100 min at 50°C, and in less than 30 min at 60°C. The more highly crosslinked films showed substantially slower degradation. Several experiments with films crosslinked with glutaraldehyde showed that their modulus values decreased in hot water much more slowly than those of formaldehyde-crosslinked films, indicating that crosslink rather than main-chain degradation was responsible for the deterioration of the formaldehyde-crosslinked films. Due to uncertainties introduced by this crosslink degradation, values of rotation and modulus observed above 60°C are not reported.

Fig. 1 shows the specific rotation of the films after they had been swollen at the temperature indicated for 15 min. The amount of formaldehyde added to each melt before coating is indicated. Broadening of the order-disorder transitions with shifting to higher temperatures is evident as the amount of crosslinker is increased. Upon thermal cycling between 40° and 60°C, films regained a large fraction, but not all, of the levorotation at 40°C which had been lost at 60°C.

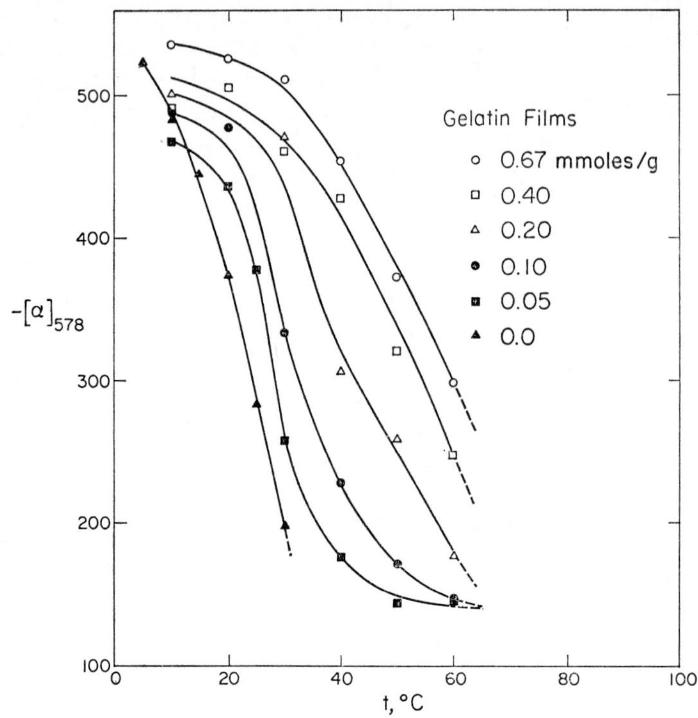

Fig. 1. Specific rotation of cold-dried gelatin films crosslinked with levels of formaldehyde indicated, determined after swelling in water 15 min at the temperature of measurement.

Fig. 2 shows the volume fractions of these films as a function of temperature. Fig. 3 shows the specific rotation of the uncrosslinked gelatin gels and solutions. In both cases, as the temperature is increased, the order-disorder transition is essentially complete at temperatures of 40–45°C, at which temperatures $[\alpha]_{578}$ is approximately $-140°$. Decrease in levorotation as the temperature is further increased is simply the temperature dependence of rotation of the random coil form. (The latter has been postulated[(10),(11)] to retain some elements of structure above the melting temperature.) Reference to Fig. 1 shows that the only cold-dried crosslinked film which has achieved the rotation characteristic of the random coil form at 50°C is that crosslinked with 0·05 mmole formaldehyde per gram of gelatin. Even at 60°C, the three most highly crosslinked films show values of levorotation substantially in excess of that of the random coil. The volume fractions of these three films at 60°C range from 0·26 to 0·33, thus overlapping the volume fractions of the uncrosslinked gelatin solutions.

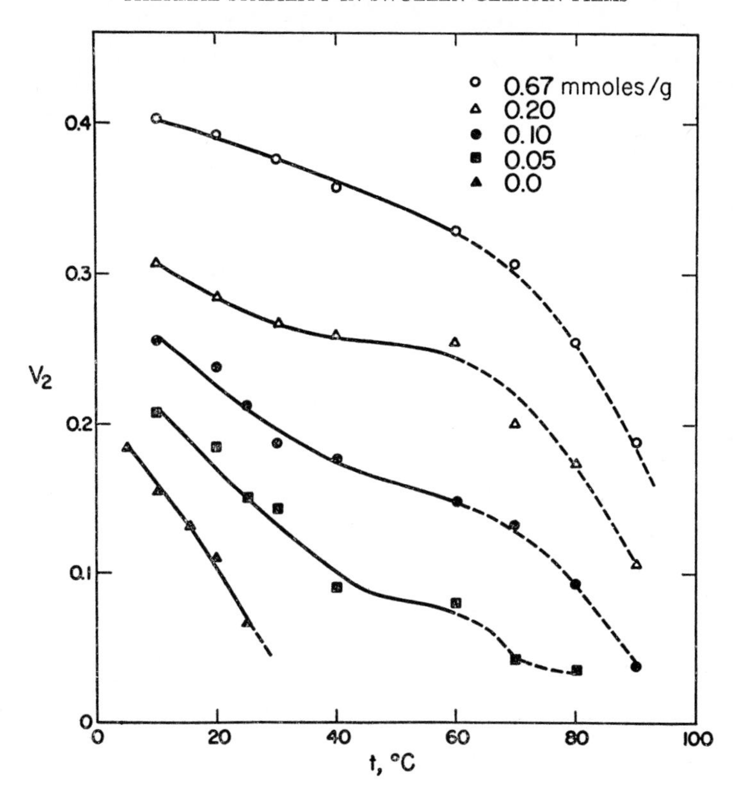

Fig. 2. Volume fraction of cold-dried gelatin films crosslinked with levels of formaldehyde as indicated, determined after swelling in water 15 min at the temperature of measurement.

Fig. 4 shows the modulus of elasticity (based on swollen cross section) of the same set of swollen films measured under the same conditions. The near-horizontal lines drawn from 40°C are estimated values of the moduli of hot-dried films containing the same amounts of bound formaldehyde[8] as contained by the cold-dried films. The modulus values of the cold-dried films appear to be approaching those of the structureless hot-dried films at 60°C, but in no case have they reached these low limiting values. This is further evidence that the temperature at which the order-disorder transition is complete is increased by the presence of crosslinks in cold-dried systems.

The complications of thermal degradation have prevented determination of the temperatures at which the last of the ordered structure has melted in the cold-dried films. However, other means of defining melting points permit further comparisons between the crosslinked and

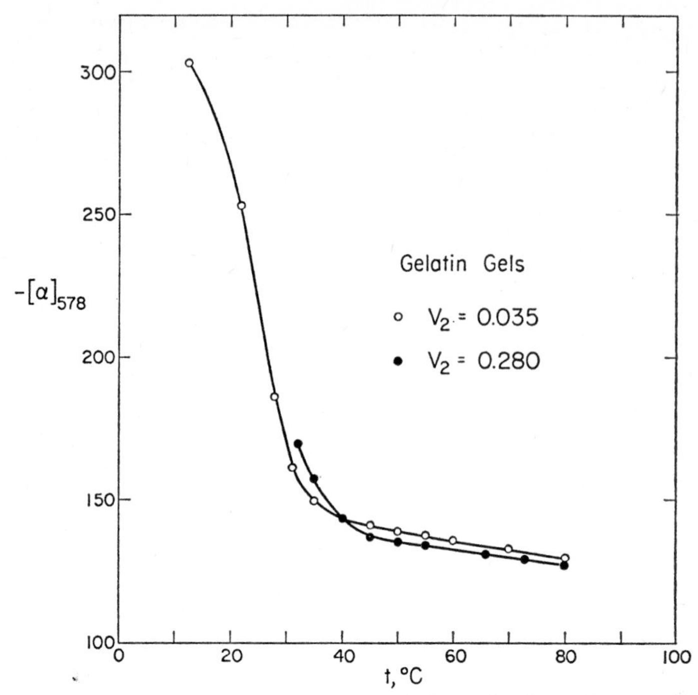

Fig. 3. Specific rotation of gelatin solutions at indicated volume fractions, held 20 h at 2°C, then warmed stepwise, as indicated in the text.

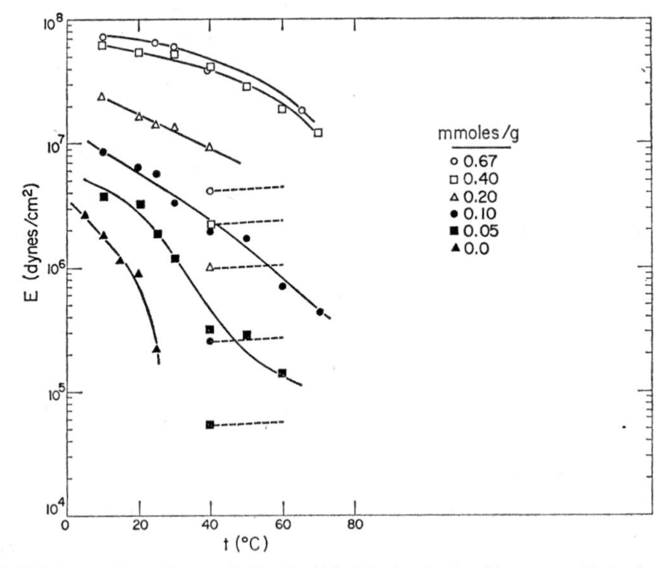

Fig. 4. Solid lines: Tensile moduli of cold-dried gelatin films crosslinked with levels of formaldehyde indicated, determined after swelling in water 15 min at the temperature of measurement. Dotted lines: Tensile moduli of swollen hot-dried films containing the same levels of bound formaldehyde.

uncrosslinked systems. For this purpose, the melting temperature may be defined as the temperature at the midpoint of the curves of log modulus or specific rotation versus temperature. Thus, in Fig. 5 the melting temperatures (defined in this manner) of crosslinked films and uncrosslinked gels, are plotted against the volume fractions at these temperatures. Because of difficulties with birefringence at the lower

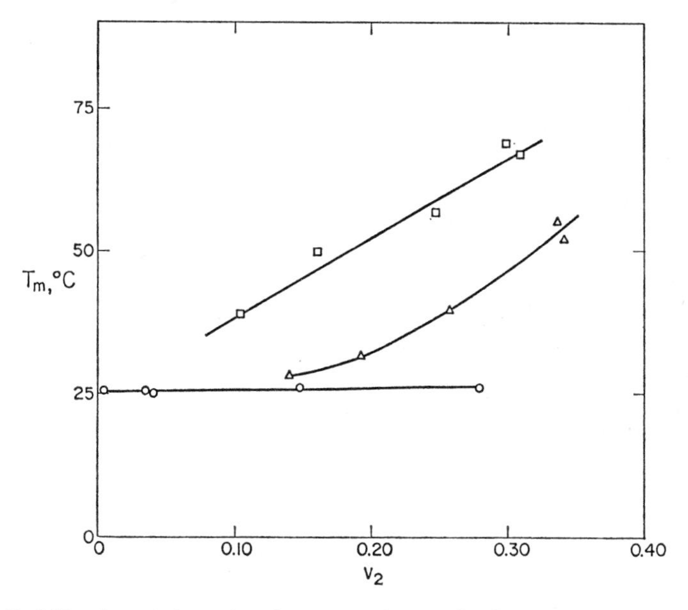

Fig. 5. Stabilization of the ordered structure in gelatin films by chemical crosslinks, as shown by the melting temperatures and corresponding volume fractions of crosslinked films and uncrosslinked gels. The melting temperature is the temperature at which:

(1) □, $\log E = (\log E^{10}_{\text{cold-dried}} + \log E^{40}_{\text{hot-dried}})/2$ for films;
(2) △, $[\alpha]_{578} = ([\alpha]^{10}_{578} + 140)/2$ for films; or
(3) ○, $[\alpha]_{578} = ([\alpha]^{10}_{578} + 140)/2$ for gels.

temperatures with the gels of higher volume fraction, the midpoints for these systems are estimated from extrapolation of the specific rotation curves to low temperatures. While the melting points of the uncrosslinked gels, as defined in this manner, show virtually no concentration dependence, those of the crosslinked films show considerable concentration dependence and lie well above those of the uncrosslinked gels. The results clearly indicate that chemical crosslinks stabilize ordered structure in the films in a manner more specific than merely reducing swell. This stabilization, as seen in Fig. 5, amounts to at least a 15°C increase in melting temperature in the case of well-crosslinked films and may actually be much more than this. It is reasonable to postulate that the reduction of the entropy of melting which results from crosslinking the ordered structure[2] is an important factor in this stabilization.

References

(1) Flory, P. J., "Principles of Polymer Chemistry", p. 569. Cornell University Press, Ithaca, New York (1953).
(2) Flory, P. J., *J. Amer. Chem. Soc.*, **78,** 5222 (1956).
(3) Flory, P. J. and Garrett, R. R., *J. Amer. Chem. Soc.*, **80,** 4836 (1958).
(4) Witnauer, L. P. and Fee, J. G., *J. Amer. Leather Chem. Ass.*, **54,** 374 (1959).
(5) Pouradier, J. and Burness, D. M., in "Theory of the Photographic Process", 3rd ed. (Ed. T. H. James), Macmillan, New York (1966).
(6) Tamura, M., Kurata, M. and Fujita, K., *Photogr. Sci. Eng.*, **3,** 277 (1959).
(7) Pchelin, V. A., Grivor'eva, N. V. and Izmailova, V. N., *Dokl. Akad. Nauk SSSR,* **151,** 134 (1963).
(8) Johnson, M. F., Fellows, W. D., Miller, R. S., Kamm, W. O. and Curme, H. G., see this book.
(9) Jopling, D. W., *Rheol. Acta,* **1,** 133 (1958).
(10) Sterman, M. D., unpublished work.
(11) Coopes, I. H., *J. Polym. Sci.,* in press.

Cross-linking of Gelatin by 2,4-dichloro-6-hydroxy-*s*-triazine

R. OHI, N. YAMAMOTO and K. HORI

Research Laboratories Ashigara, Fuji Photo Film Co. Ltd., Minamiashigara, Kanagawa, Japan

ABSTRACT. The cross-linking of gelatin by 2,4-dichloro-6-hydroxy-*s*-triazine (DCT-Na) was studied.

Among the amino acids which constitute gelatin, lysine was highly reactive against DCT-Na while the others were not.

The gelatin cross-linked with DCT-Na was acid-hydrolyzed and analysed by means of two-dimensional paper chromatography and an automatic amino acid analysing apparatus.

The amounts of 1-1 and 1-2 reaction products of DCT-Na with lysine in the hydrolysate were determined against the authentic samples which had been prepared by reaction of lysine with DCT-Na.

These data suggest a mechanism of the cross-linking reaction of gelatin by DCT-Na.

INTRODUCTION

It is generally accepted that the hardening of gelatin by an organic hardener is due to cross-linking between gelatin molecules(1). Thus the reaction of gelatin with, for instance, a bifunctional hardening agent should lead to the formation of gelatin-hardener linkage of type I and II.

Gelatin-hardener-gelatin (cross-link) (I)
Gelatin-hardener (pendant type) (II)

If hydrolysis of the peptide linkage of the hardened gelatin could be successfully carried out without affecting the gelatin-hardener linkage, the analyses of the hydrolysate should tell us the site where the cross-linking reaction had occurred. In this study, the reaction of gelatin with the sodium salt of 2,4-dichloro-6-hydroxy-*s*-triazine was investigated. From the hydrolysate, two species containing the triazine nucleus were isolated. Determination of their chemical structures followed by the quantitative analysis allowed an estimate of I/II ratio.

EXPERIMENTAL

Materials

The sodium salt of 2,4-dichloro-6-hydroxy-*s*-triazine (DCT-Na) was prepared by partial alkaline hydrolysis of trichloro-*s*-triazine[2].

Gelatin: Commercial lime-processed inert type gelatin was used.

Amino acids: Commercial analytical grade reagents were used without further purification.

Authentic samples of 5-lysine derivatives of hardener were used.

2,4-Bis(5-amino-5-carboxypentylamino)-6-hydroxy-*s*-triazine (III) was prepared by the following procedure. Lysine was converted to its cupric complex, which was then treated with the sodium salt of 2,4-dichloro-6-hydroxy-*s*-triazine. The product was freed from cupric ion by H_2S.

2(5-amino-5-carboxypentylamino)-4,6-dihydroxy-*s*-triazine (IV) was prepared by a similar procedure, except that the sodium salt of 2-chloro-4,6-dihydroxy-*s*-triazine was used instead of the sodium salt of 2,4-dichloro-6-hydroxy-*s*-triazine.

Hardening of gelatin in aqueous solutions

	No. 1	*No.* 2
Gelatin	10 g	10 g
Water	75 ml	150 ml
DCT-Na	0·33 g	2 g
pH	8–9	8–9
Temperature	70–80°C	40–50°C
Time	1 h	3 h
Mole ratio of DCT-Na/lysine of gelatin	1/2	3/1

Acid hydrolysis of gelatin

6N-HCl at a temperature of 110°C for 12 h

Analyses

QUALITATIVE ANALYSIS

Two-dimensional chromatograms were obtained by the combination of paper-electrophoresis and paper-chromatography.

Paper-electrophoresis: 2500 V, 80 min

Solvent pyridine: acetic acid: water 1:10:99

Paper-chromatography:

Solvent butanol: acetic acid: water 4:2:1

QUANTITATIVE ANALYSIS

Elution chromatograms were obtained using the Hitachi-Perkin-Elmer Model KLA-3B automatic amino acid analyser.

Results and discussion

Two-dimensional chromatograms of the hydrolysate of the hardened and unhardened gelatin are illustrated in Figs. 1–3. Comparison with

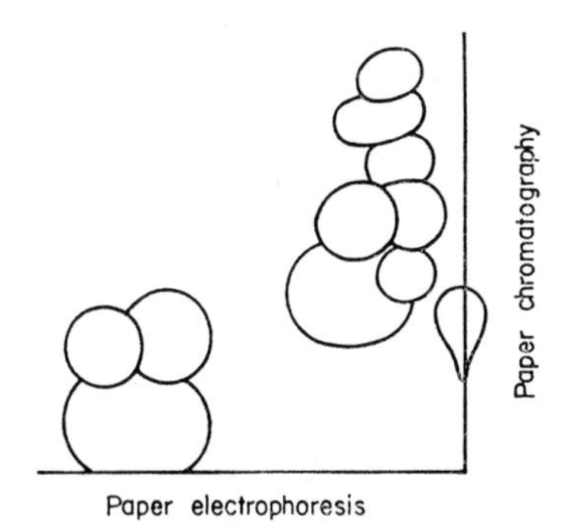

Fig. 1. Two-dimensional chromatogram of the hydrolysate of unhardened gelatin.

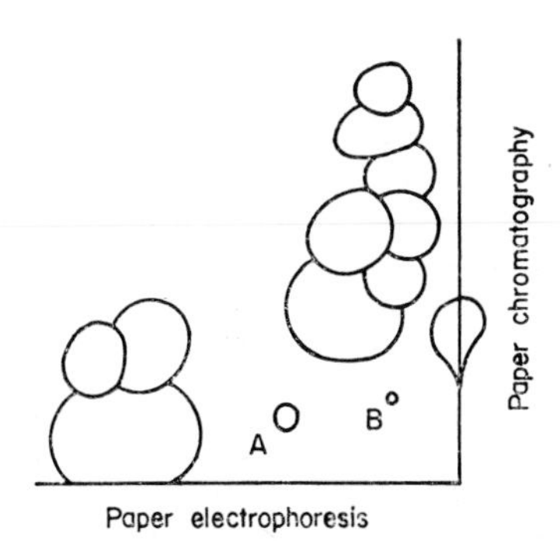

Fig. 2. Two-dimensional chromatogram of the hydrolysate of hardened gelatin (No. 1).

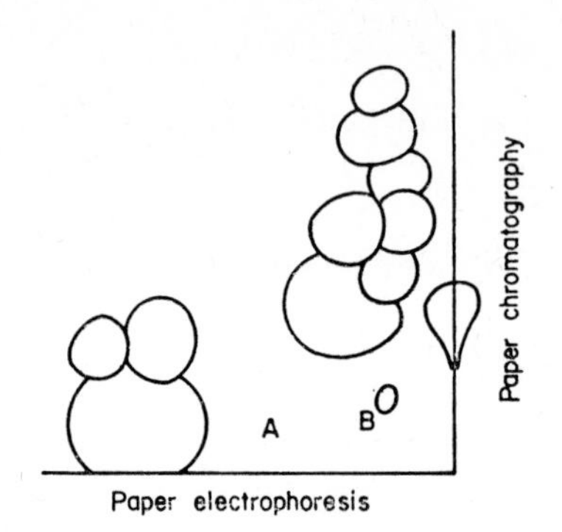

Fig. 3. Two-dimensional chromatogram of the hydrolysate of hardened gelatin (No. 2).

the authentic samples demonstrated that spot A originated from (III) and spot B from (IV).

Elution chromatograms of the hydrolysate of the hardened and unhardened gelatin are illustrated in Figs. 4–6. Comparison of the

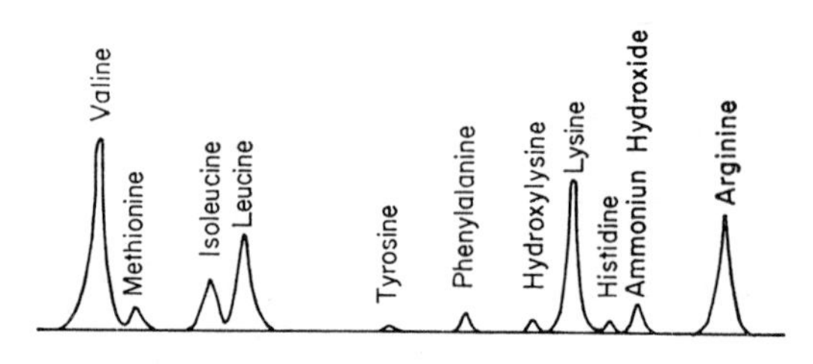

Fig. 4. Elution chromatogram of the hydrolysate of unhardened gelatin.

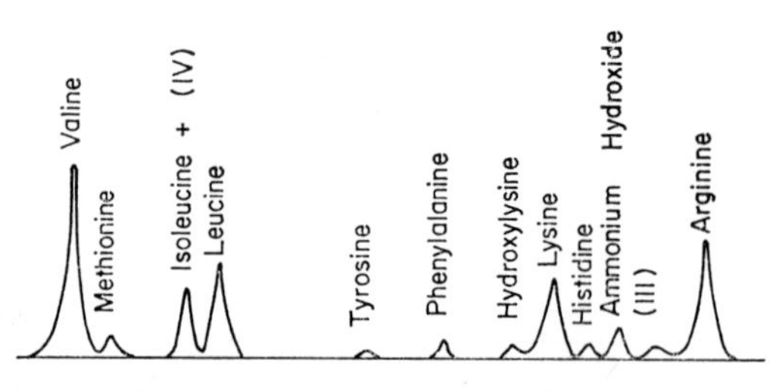

Fig. 5. Elution chromatogram of the hydrolysate of hardened gelatin (No. 1).

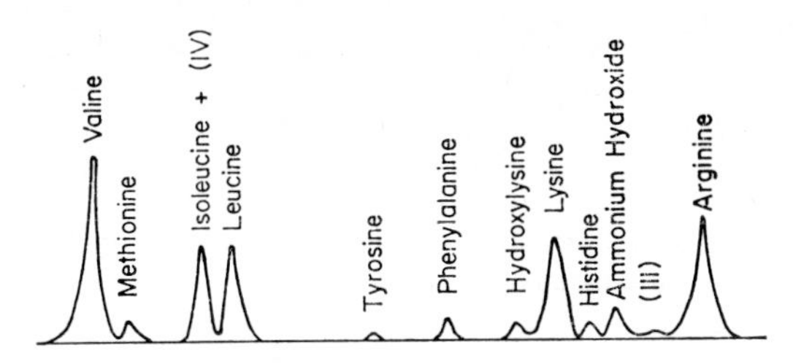

Fig. 6. Elution chromatogram of the hydrolysate of hardened gelatin (No. 2).

three chromatograms indicated the decrease of lysine and the apparent increase of isoleucine in the hydrolysate of the hardened gelatin. In addition, a new peak was observed in the chromatograms of the hydrolysate of the hardened gelatin.

As the added authentic sample of III gave the identical peak in the chromatogram of the unhardened gelatin, the conclusion that III is responsible for the new peak is justified.

The peak of isoleucine proved to fall on the identical place of the chromatogram as does the peak of IV, which turned out to be responsible for the apparent increase of isoleucine in the hydrolysate.

The amounts of III, IV and lysine in the hydrolysates of the hardened and unhardened gelatin are shown in Table 1.

Table 1

Amounts of III, IV lysine in the hydrolysates of hardened, and unhardened gelatin (m mol/g gelatin)

	Hardened gelatin		*Unhardened gelatin*
	No. 1	*No. 2*	
III	0·039	0·009	—
IV	0·029	0·070	—
Lysine	0·193	0·213	0·300
2 × III* + IV + lysine	0·300	0·301	0·300

* III contains two lysine residues.

It is necessary to compensate for the survival of the lysine-hardener linkage during hydrolysis of the gelatin. This was simulated by the survival of added III and IV under similar circumstances. Compound III partly decomposes into IV and into lysine with the conversion ratio of 11·3% and 14·3% respectively. Similarly IV decomposes into lysine with 40% survival. Using these factors the extent of cross-linking in the hardened gelatin were calculated (Table 2).

Table 2
Number of cross-links in hardened gelatin (assumed molecular weight 100 000)

Hardened gelatin	
No. 1	*No.* 2
5·2	1·2

CONCLUSION

It is concluded that the hardening of gelatin by the sodium salt of 2,4-dichloro-6-hydroxy-*s*-triazine is due to the cross-linking of gelatin which occurs exclusively at the ε-amino-group of lysine moiety. The method used in this study offers a novel tool for estimating the number of cross-links in hardened gelatin.

References

(1) Pouradier, J. and Burness, D. M. in "The Theory of the Photographic Process" 3rd Ed., C. E. K. Mees and T. H. James, Eds, p. 56. Macmillan, New York (1966).
(2) British Patent 1 022 656.

Hardening Gelatin by Direct Oxidation

A. G. TULL

Technicolor Ltd., West Drayton, Middlesex

ABSTRACT. Gelatin layers may be hardened by the controlled application under alkaline conditions of certain oxidizing agents, including the normally destructive sodium hypochlorite. Permanganate and ferricyanide solutions may also be used and the latter provides a good practical method. It is believed the mechanism is a condensation between neighbouring gelatin molecules at certain reactive points.

INTRODUCTION

The procedures to be described are of so simple a character, and the reagents so commonplace that a phenomenon observed in this laboratory some 18 years ago has not been published hitherto. Confirmatory tests in the intervening period again established the validity of the mechanism and a recent review of these records prompted a brief resumption of investigations on a more formal basis. It is still believed that the information presented will be new, at least in the field of photographic science.

As the title suggests, gelatin may be hardened by the application of certain oxidizing agents, but this must be carried out under alkaline conditions. If the suggestion were made to harden a gelatin layer sufficiently to withstand boiling water by a brief treatment with sodium hypochlorite solution, the idea would probably be dismissed as inconceivable, yet this remarkable effect can be obtained provided certain conditions are observed.

TEST PROCEDURE

The materials consisted of subbed triacetate film base coated either with normal, alkali process, gelatin (pI approx. 5·0) or with acid process gelatin (pI approx. 9·0), both dissolving in water in the range 30–35°C, and both tested at the time of coating and 4 weeks subsequently to ensure that no hardener had been picked up inadvertently.* Coating weight was 13 g/m^2 approximately.

Treatment was effected by bathing film strips both in the dry condition and following a pre-soak in cold water for 30 s, thereafter washing in running cold water for 3–5 min.

For present purposes actual hardness values, even on a conventional standard, were not determined, but merely the resistance of the layers to water at 60°C and at 100°C. For most of the tests described the samples were exposed to the hot water immediately after washing without intermediate drying. In a few cases the effect of drying the treated samples before testing was also explored. The strips were subjected to water at each temperature for 30 s.

Successful results have been obtained with three different oxidizing agents, though others may be useful also, and the experiences with each are separately described. Some general principles were observed throughout the series, the most important being the concept that for cross-linking to occur, intermolecular spacing of the gelatin molecules must be favourable. In other words, undue swell of the layer must be prevented and so sufficient electrolyte must be included in the solution to control swell. Sodium sulphate is suitable or even sodium carbonate in a high concentration since the reaction only proceeds under alkaline conditions.

Concentration of the oxidizer may be very significant also, as well as the actual pH and time of treatment. Each reagent needs special study in each of these respects.

Ferricyanide

This reagent is the most versatile of the three mentioned here and gives very acceptable results with great ease. Analytical grade potassium ferricyanide was employed for the present work but is unnecessary for general use. The dependence on conditions is illustrated in the tabular summaries.

Hypochlorite

The treatment solutions made use of commercial sodium hypochlorite solution of 10–14% content of available chlorine and the dilutions indicated are in respect of this solution regarded as 100% reagent. Wash time after hypochlorite treatment was 3 min in cold water. Since the reagent is normally very destructive of gelatin, the application temperature must not be allowed to rise and is preferably kept at 16°C.

* I am indebted to Mr. J. W. Janus, of Kodak Ltd., for putting this tested material at my disposal.

Permanganate

This reagent when used in alkali as an oxidizing agent is stated to require strong alkali and there are two reactions, the first rapid:

$$MnO_4^- + e = MnO_4^{--}$$

and the second slower:

$$MnO_4^{--} + 2H_2O + 2e = MnO_2 + 4OH^-$$

Conditions can be arranged so that the first reaction predominates and there is then no precipitation of manganese dioxide.

When this concept was applied to a gelatin layer with a view to hardening it, there seemed to be no action until the pH was reduced and a brown stain of the dioxide produced. Wherever this occurred, hardening was recorded. The brown stain is quickly removed in a bisulphite solution but it was found that the degree of hardening was then also reduced. However, conditions may be found where resistance to boiling water can still be secured (without intermediate drying), but the layers are nevertheless not so tough on inspection.

Table 1—Ferricyanide

Strips treated in dry condition but tested without drying*

Gel	*Ferri Conc.* %	*Alkali*	*pH*	*Other Content*	*Time* (*min*)	*Resistance* °C 60 *deg.*	100 *deg.*
alk.	25	1% NaOH	13·35	—	1	R	R
ac.	25	1% NaOH	13·35	—	1	R	R
alk.	20	1% NaOH	13·35	—	1	R	R
ac.	20	1% NaOH	13·35	—	1	R	R
alk.	15	1% NaOH	13·35	—	1	R	R
ac.	15	1% NaOH	13·35	—	1	R	R
alk.	15	1% NaOH	13·35	—	10	S	S
ac.	15	1% NaOH	13·35	—	10	R	R
alk.	10	1% NaOH	13·35	—	1	S*	S*
ac.	10	1% NaOH	13·35	—	1	R	R
alk.	7·5	1% NaOH	13·35	—	1	S*	S*
ac.	7·5	1% NaOH	13·35	—	1	R*	R*
alk.	7·5	1% NaOH	13·35	—	10	S	S
alk.	7·5	1% NaOH	13·35	—	½	R	S
alk.	5	1% NaOH	13·35	—	1	S*	S
ac.	5	1% NaOH	13·35	—	1	S*	S
alk.	5	1% NaOH	13·35	5% Na_2SO_4	1	R	R
ac.	5	1% NaOH	13·35	5% Na_2SO_4	1	R	R

Notes: Items shown S* resisted water treatment if dried first.
If 15% solution used at 30 deg. C, alkali gel. dissolved at 100 deg. C, otherwise resists obtained.

* In Tables 1 to 4 the following abbreviations are used. *R* = resists water; *S* = soluble; alk. = alkali gelatin; ac. = acid gelatin.

Table 2—Ferricyanide

Strips pre-soaked ½ min in cold water before treatment and tested without drying

Gel	*Ferri Conc.* %	*Alkali*	*pH*	*Other Content*	*Time (min)*	*Resistance* °C 60 *deg.*	100 *deg.*
alk.	15	1% NaOH	13·35	—	1	R	S
ac.	15	1% NaOH	13·35	—	1	R	R
alk.	5	1% NaOH	13·35	5% Na_2SO_4	1	R	R
ac.	5	1% NaOH	13·35	5% Na_2SO_4	1	R	R
alk.	5	1% NaOH	13·35	5% Na_2SO_4	10	R	R
ac.	5	1% NaOH	13·35	5% Na_2SO_4	10	R	R
alk.	2·5	1% NaOH	13·35	5% Na_2SO_4	1	R	S
ac.	2·5	1% NaOH	13·35	5% Na_2SO_4	1	R	R
alk.	2·5	1% NaOH	13·1	10% Na_2SO_4	1	R	S
alk.	2·5	1% NaOH	13·1	10% Na_2SO_4	10	R	R
alk.	1	1% NaOH	13·1	5% Na_2SO_4	1	S	S
ac.	1	1% NaOH	13·1	5% Na_2SO_4	1	R	S
alk.	1	1% NaOH	13·1	5% Na_2SO_4	10	R	R
ac.	1	1% NaOH	13·1	5% Na_2SO_4	10	R	R
alk.	1	1% NaOH	13·1	10% Na_2SO_4	1	S	S
ac.	1	1% NaOH	13·1	10% Na_2SO_4	1	R	R
alk.	2·5	5% Na_2CO_3	11·1	—	1	R	R
ac.	2·5	5% Na_2CO_3	11·1	—	1	R	R
alk.	2·5	(5% Na_2CO_3	10·2	—	1	R	S
ac.	2·5	+ HCl)	10·2	—	1	R	R
alk.	2·5	(5% Na_2CO_3	9·0	—	1	S	S
ac.	2·5	+ HCl)	9·0	—	1	S	S
alk.	2·5	(5% Na_2CO_3	9·0	—	10	S	S
ac.	2·5	+ HCl)	9·0	—	10	R	R
alk.	2·5	1% NaOH	11·1	5% ferrocy.	1	S	S
ac.	2·5	1% NaOH	11·1	5% ferrocy.	1	S	S
alk.	2·5	1% NaOH	11·1	5% ferrocy.	10	S	S
ac.	2·5	1% NaOH	11·1	5% ferrocy.	10	R	S

Notes: The above ferricyanide solutions will bleach a silver image.
The hardened layers appear to resist an acid treatment.
Acid type gelatin is hardened more readily than the normal type.
Longer treatment times than 1 min can be used to offset a slow reaction.
The importance of swell control is clearly seen, but ferrocyanide is inadvisable for this purpose, presumably because it cancels the oxidation potential of the ferricyanide.
Hardened blanks when tested for residual ferricyanide, ferrocyanide, ferric or ferrous ions show a negative reaction. More exhaustive tests might be desirable to confirm this conclusion.

Table 3—Hypochlorite

Samples pre-soaked in water before treatment and tested without drying

Gel	*Soln. Conc.* %	*Alkali*	*pH*	*Other Content*	*Time* (*sec*)	*Resistance* °C 60 *deg.*	100 *deg.*
alk.	5	2·5% NaOH	13·4	10% Na_2SO_4	30	R	R
ac.	5	2·5% NaOH	13·4	10% Na_2SO_4	30	R	R
alk.	5	2·5% NaOH	13.4	10% Na_2SO_4	20	R	R
ac.	5	2·5% NaOH	13·4	10% Na_2SO_4	20	S*	S
alk.	5	2·5% NaOH	13·4	10% Na_2SO_4	10	S	S
ac.	5	2·5% NaOH	13·4	10% Na_2SO_4	10	S	S
alk.	5	2·5% NaOH	13·4	15% Na_2CO_3	30	R	R
ac.	5	2·5% NaOH	13·4	15% Na_2CO_3	30	R	R
alk.	2	2·5% NaOH	13·4	15% Na_2CO_3	30	R	R
ac.	2	2·5% NaOH	13·4	15% Na_2CO_3	30	S	S
alk.	10	2·5% NaOH	13·4	15% Na_2CO_3	30	R	R
ac.	10	2·5% NaOH	13·4	15% Na_2CO_3	30	R	R
alk.	5	1·0% Na_2CO_3	10·2	15% Na_2SO_4	30	S	S
ac.	5	1·0% Na_2CO_3	10·2 (by HCl)	15% Na_2SO_4	30	S	S

Notes: S*, this item resists water if dried first.

In this series the alkali-process gelatin hardens better and high pH is important. Swell control is essential. Longer treatment times than ½ min may be permissible, but gelatin is removed by too long an exposure to hypochlorite. On the other hand, too low a concentration of hypochlorite is ineffective.

Table 4—Permanganate

Samples used dry (D) and also pre-soaked in water (W) before treatment, then given bisulphite post-treatment and the usual wash, finally tested for hardness without drying

	Gel	*$KMnO_4$ Conc. %*	*Alkali*	*pH*	*Other Content*	*Time (min)*	*Resistance °C 60 deg.*	*100 deg.*
D	alk.	1·5	15% Na_2CO_3	11·0	—	1	S	—
	ac.	1·5	15% Na_2CO_3	11·0	—	1	S	—
D	alk.	0·75	15% Na_2CO_3	11·0	—	1	R	S
	ac.	0·75	15% Na_2CO_3	11·0	—	1	R	R
D	alk.	0·3	15% Na_2CO_3	11·0	—	1	R	S
	ac.	0·3	15% Na_2CO_3	11·0	—	1	R	R
D	alk.	0·2	15% Na_2CO_3	11·0	—	1	R	R
	ac.	0·2	15% Na_2CO_3	11·0	—	1	R	R
D	alk.	0·1	15% Na_2CO_3	11·0	—	1	S	—
	ac.	0·1	15% Na_2CO_3	11·0	—	1	S	—
W	alk.	0·2	15% Na_2CO_3	11·0	—	1	R	S
	ac.	0·2	15% Na_2CO_3	11·0	—	1	R	R
D	alk.	0·2	15% Na_2CO_3	11·0	—	3	R	R
	ac.	0·2	15% Na_2CO_3	11·0	—	3	R	R
W	alk.	0·2	15% Na_2CO_3	11·0	—	3	R	S
	ac.	0·2	15% Na_2CO_3	11·0	—	3	R	R
W	alk.	0·2	15% Na_2CO_3	11·0	10% Na_2SO_4	3	R	R
	ac.	0·2	15% Na_2CO_3	11·0	10% Na_2SO_4	3	R	R
D	alk.	0·2	(1% Na_2CO_3	10·0	10% Na_2SO_4	3	S	—
	ac.	0·2	+ HCl)	10·0	10% Na_2SO_4	3	R	S
W	alk.	0·2	(1% Na_2CO_3	10·0	10% Na_2SO_4	3	S	—
	ac.	0·2	+ HCl)	10·0	10% Na_2SO_4	3	R	S

Notes: The oxidizer concentration seems critical in this series and the acid-process gelatin responds better to the hardening action.

SUMMARY

Three practical working solutions emerge from the study, of which the ferricyanide composition is the most attractive. For a quick test of efficacy, the unhardened film should be pre-soaked in cold water, treated for the specified time and temperature in the reagents, then washed for 3–5 min and submitted at once to hot water for ascertaining the hardness obtained. Suitable solutions are the following:

Solution 1

Potassium ferricyanide	2·5 g
Sodium carbonate anhyd.	5·0 g
Water to	100 ml

Time: 1 min. Temperature probably not critical.

Solution 2

Sodium hypochlorite soln. (10–14% available chlorine)	5·0 ml
Sodium hydroxide	2·5 g
Sodium carbonate anhyd.	15·0 g
Water to	100 ml

Time: 30 s at about 16°C.

Solution 3

Potassium permanganate	0·2 g
Sodium carbonate anhyd.	15·0 g
Sodium sulphate anhyd.	10·0 g
Water to	100 ml

Time: about 3 min at about 16°C.

After treatment in the last solution, the film should be briefly washed, bathed in dilute sodium bisulphite solution, then washed finally.

SUPPLEMENTARY NOTES

The chemistry of the hardening mechanisms described is not easy to elucidate, but as a similar effect is obtained by reagents which only have an oxidizing capacity in common it is believed that reactive groups on juxtaposed gelatin molecules are reacted with each other to form a cross-link. The effect is that of polymerization of the gelatin molecules without the intervention of bridging material. This view is supported by the suppressing effect of added ferrocyanide to Solution 1 which, presumably, only affects the Redox situation and would not interfere if the ferricyanide was participating as an ion in providing cross links. So far no evidence has been found for the presence of iron in the hardened layer.

On the practical side it may prove of interest to consider the ferricyanide solution both as a silver bleach solution and overall hardening medium at one and the same time. This could be of value in certain colour film processing sequences and avoid alternations from the alkaline conditions of development to acid conditions of bleach.

ACKNOWLEDGEMENT

This paper is presented by kind permission of Technicolor Limited.

Viscometric Study of Interaction of Substantive Colour Couplers with Gelatin

B. P. BRAND, M. ROCHE and D. WINSTANLEY

Research Department, Hexagon House, Imperial Chemical Industries Limited, Dyestuffs Division, Blackley, Manchester 9

ABSTRACT. The structure of some water soluble substantive couplers has been systematically varied and their interaction with gelatin studied viscometrically. The formation of the coupler-gelatin complexes could not be ascribed to any single factor, but several factors in the coupler structure have been isolated. These factors play their part through ion-ion, ion-dipole, hydrophobic bond and hydrogen bond forces. A micellar theory is adopted to explain viscosity increases. The influence of environmental factors such as concentration of coupler and gelatin, pH, ionic strength and solvent on the micellar type structure have been investigated in order to control viscosity.

INTRODUCTION

When substantive colour couplers are added to photographic emulsions the viscosity usually increases and coating can sometimes be difficult. In some cases simple formulation adjustment such as that of pH will allow a difficult coupler to be coated in emulsion. When the formulation is too viscous the colour coupler cannot be used. A study of the causes of this interaction was undertaken in order to gain a greater control of the system. Since viscosity increases were obtained with gelatin and colour coupler alone the effect of the silver halide phase has been ignored in this work.

MATERIALS

Compounds C1–C15 were prepared by standard methods. The structures are given in Table 1. With the exception of C3 all are colour couplers. The gelatin batches B1 and B2 were blends of commercially available alkaline processed gelatins having iso-electric points around 5. Gelatins B1 and B2 contained 12·5 and 12·0% respectively of water.

Analar reagents, deionized water and freshly distilled organic solvents were used throughout.

EXPERIMENTAL

For making viscosity measurements stock solutions of 0·1 M colour coupler in deionized water were made up each day. 0·1 N NaOH was added where necessary to dissolve the colour coupler. Stock solutions of gelatin of double the final desired concentration were prepared by first allowing the gelatin to swell in deionized water for 30 min before warming the mixture to about 40°C with gentle stirring. The volume was finally adjusted to 250 ml with water. Gelatin stock solutions were freshly prepared each day. The concentrations of these solutions quoted in this paper are based on gelatin as supplied.

4 ml of 0·1 M colour coupler stock solution was pipetted with stirring into a 100 ml beaker containing 20 ml of the stock gelatin solution. The volume was adjusted to 40 ml by the addition of water and if necessary 0·1 N NaOH to give a $1{\cdot}0 \times 10^{-2}$ M solution of colour coupler in gelatin at a given pH. Solutions were stored in stoppered flasks at 35°C for 30 min before taking measurements. Viscosity measurements quoted on a particular solution were constant over a period of 4 h at $35{\cdot}0 \pm 0{\cdot}2$°C using Ostwald Nos. 1 and 2 viscometers calibrated by the standard method with water.

The apparent relative viscosity was taken as the ratio flow time of the solution to flow time of water. To determine the actual relative viscosity the densities of water and solution also need to be known. The error introduced by the neglect of the density factor can be shown to be negligible for in this study we are mainly interested in the position of the peak in the apparent relative viscosity versus coupler concentration curves. The symbol ηr will be used throughout for apparent relative viscosity.

Colour coupler C1

The ηr of 3·0% B2 gelatin solutions containing increasing concentrations of C1 were determined at pH 6·0.

A plot of ηr against increasing colour coupler concentration (C) gave a curve rising to a maximum viscosity max. ηr (see Fig. 1). Higher concentrations of C1 reduced the viscosity to values approaching that of gelatin alone. Similar curves were obtained at gelatin concentrations of 3·3, 2·5, 2·0 and 1·5% at pH 6·0. For a given stock solution of gelatin the curve up to max. ηr was reproducible, but was irreproducible after max. ηr. The value of C at max. ηr expressed as a ratio of

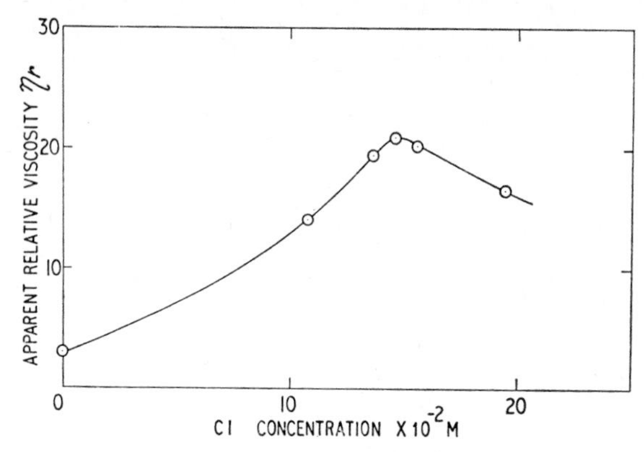

Fig. 1. Plot of apparent relative viscosity versus C1 concentration at 3·0% gelatin concentration.

colour coupler concentration to gelatin concentration was constant for a given gelatin concentration, and did not vary with different stock solutions of gelatin or different gelatin batches. However, some slight variation in absolute values or viscosity was obtained using different

Table 1

Structures of compounds

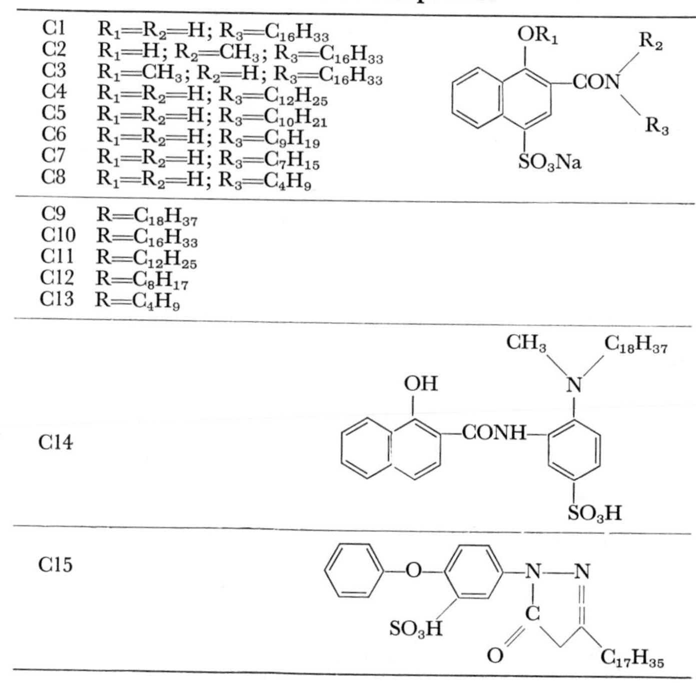

Compound	Substituents
C1	$R_1 = R_2 = H$; $R_3 = C_{16}H_{33}$
C2	$R_1 = H$; $R_2 = CH_3$; $R_3 = C_{16}H_{33}$
C3	$R_1 = CH_3$; $R_2 = H$; $R_3 = C_{16}H_{33}$
C4	$R_1 = R_2 = H$; $R_3 = C_{12}H_{25}$
C5	$R_1 = R_2 = H$; $R_3 = C_{10}H_{21}$
C6	$R_1 = R_2 = H$; $R_3 = C_9H_{19}$
C7	$R_1 = R_2 = H$; $R_3 = C_7H_{15}$
C8	$R_1 = R_2 = H$; $R_3 = C_4H_9$
C9	$R = C_{18}H_{37}$
C10	$R = C_{16}H_{33}$
C11	$R = C_{12}H_{25}$
C12	$R = C_8H_{17}$
C13	$R = C_4H_9$
C14	
C15	

stock gelatin solutions, and this was attributed to some denaturization occurring during the preparation of the solutions. Plotting C at max. ηr against gelatin concentration gave a straight line plot of slope 0·54 mmoles of colour coupler per gramme of gelatin (see Fig. 2). These results indicate that a complex between gelatin and C1 was being formed which had a constant composition at the maximum viscosity. Precipitation experiments with ammonium nitrate showed that this

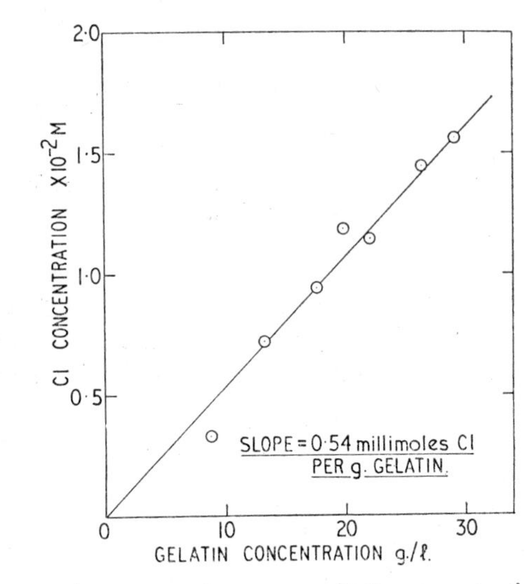

Fig. 2. Plot of C1 concentration versus gelatin concentration at max. ηr.

complex was more hydrophobic than gelatin. Thus the addition of 4 moles of ammonium nitrate to a 3·0% B2 gelatin solution containing $1{\cdot}5 \times 10^{-2}$ M C1 at 25°C precipitated at the complex whilst addition of 14 moles of ammonium nitrate to 3·0% B2 gelatin solution alone did not result in precipitation. Fig. 3 shows the sharp increase in viscosity at max. ηr obtained with increasing gelatin concentration as compared with the viscosity of gelatin alone.

Effect of structural changes of C1

(a) *Alkyl chain length*

The viscosities of 3·0% B2 gelatin solutions containing varying concentrations of the alkyl chain analogues of C1 (C4, C5, C6, C7, C8) were measured at pH 6·0 and from these plots of ηr against colour coupler concentration were drawn. The values of max. ηr determined from these curves were plotted against alkyl chain length (see Fig. 4).

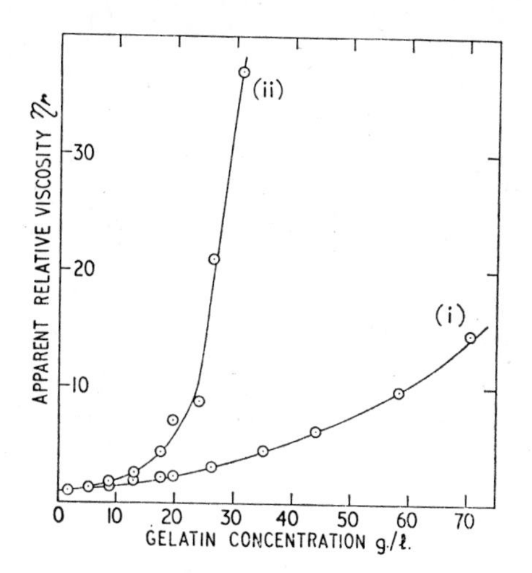

Fig. 3. Plot of (i) apparent relative viscosity (ηr) of gelatin solutions alone versus gelatin concentration. (ii) Maximum apparent relative viscosity (max. ηr) of gelatin solutions of C1 versus gelatin concentration.

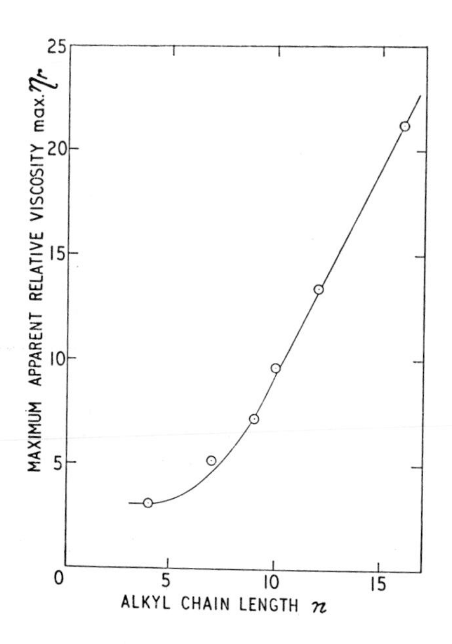

Fig. 4. Plot of maximum apparent relative viscosity (max. ηr) versus alkyl chain length (C_nH_{2n+1}) for C1.

This graph shows that for an alkyl chain length of C_7 and above, max. ηr varies linearly with increasing chain length. For the C_{12} analogue (C4) viscosities of mixtures with 2·0% and 4·0% in addition to 3·0% gelatin were determined. When the concentration of colour coupler at max. ηr was plotted against the gelatin concentrations a straight line graph of slope 0·54 mmoles of colour coupler per gramme of gelatin was obtained, thus confirming the previous result (see Fig. 2).

(b) *Naphthol and amide group*

The contributions of the C1 naphthol and amide group to the observed viscosity increase were determined by examining the derivatives of C1 which were methylated at each position separately.

(i) *N-methylation*

Viscosities of 2·5% and 3·0% B2 gelatin solutions containing varying concentrations of C2 were measured and plotted in Fig. 5 which shows

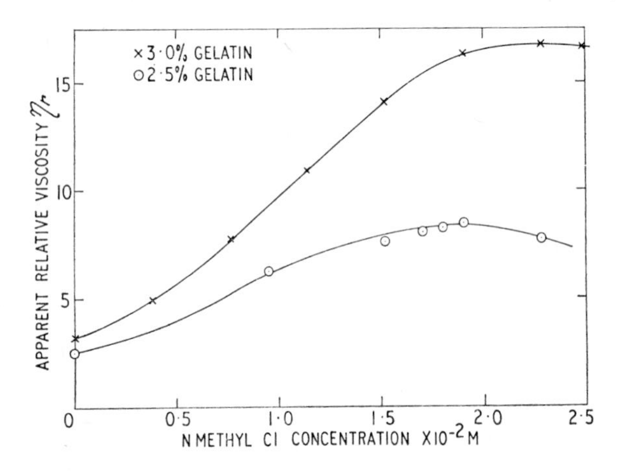

Fig. 5. Plot of apparent relative viscosity versus N-methyl C1 concentration at 2·5% and 3·0% gelatin concentrations.

that the value of max. ηr obtained from the plot of ηr against colour coupler concentration was 20% lower than the value obtained using C1 (Fig. 1). The colour coupler to gelatin ratio at max. ηr had also increased from 0·54–0·865 mmoles colour coupler per gramme of gelatin at both gelatin strengths studied.

(ii) *O-methylation*

Viscosities of 3% B2 gelatin solutions containing various concentrations of compound C3 were measured at pH 6·0 (see later for determination at other pH values), and the results plotted in Fig. 6 which shows that the value of max. ηr obtained from the plot of ηr against increased compound concentration was 30% lower than that obtained using C1 (Fig. 1). The compound C3 to gelatin ratio at max. ηr was 0·74 mmoles C3 per gramme of gelatin.

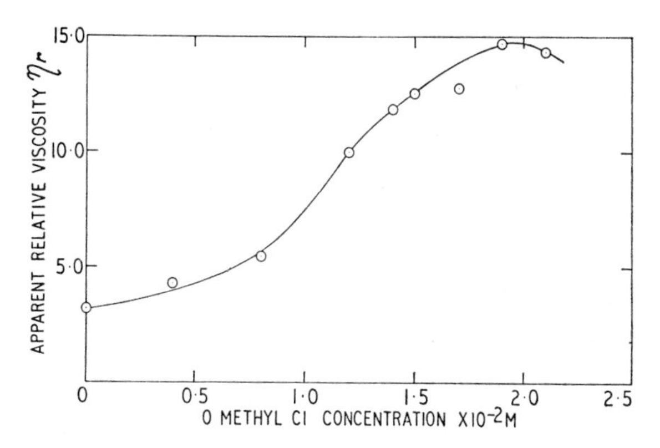

Fig. 6. Plot of apparent relative viscosity versus O-methyl C1 concentration using 3·0% gelatin.

Modification of gelatin

To increase the number of guanidino groups the gelatin was reacted with o-methylisourea according to the equation:

$$\text{Prot—NH}_2 + \text{CH}_3\text{—O—C}\begin{smallmatrix}\nearrow\text{NH}\\ \searrow\text{NH}_2\end{smallmatrix} \rightarrow \text{Prot—NH—C}\begin{smallmatrix}\nearrow\text{NH}\\ \searrow\text{NH}_2\end{smallmatrix} + \text{CH}_3\text{OH}$$

after Janus.[1]

To B2 gelatin (50 g) dispersed in water (545 ml) at 40°C was added o-methylisoureamethasulphate (12·12 g) prepared by the method described below. This quantity of reagent was double the theoretical quantity required to react with all the ε-amino groups of the gelatin. The pH which immediately fell to 5·5 was adjusted to 10·0 by the addition of 2·5 N sodium hydroxide solution (15 ml). The suspension was stirred at 40°C for 25 min at this pH before adding 10% acetic acid (25 ml) to bring the pH to 6·0.

A blank experiment in which o-methylisoureamethasulphate was omitted was carried out.

The gelatin solutions were passed down a mixed bed ion exchange column prepared as described below. The solutions were dried overnight on Melinex trays in a stream of hot air and finally at 40–50°C for 3 h to give sheets of gelatin which were ground in a C & N mill with Drikold. The preparation in which the gelatin was treated with o-methylisoureamethasulphate gave a yield of 42 g whilst that in which o-methylsoureamethasulphate was omitted gave a yield of 40 g.

Preparation of o-methylisoureamethasulphate

Dry urea (30 g) was added to freshly distilled dimethyl sulphate (63 g) and the mixture heated to 70°C over $\frac{1}{2}$ h with rapid agitation. Stirring was continued at 70°C for a further $\frac{1}{2}$ h when a clear solution had been formed. This viscous solution was stored in a desiccator over P_2O_5 before use.

The yield of product was estimated by treating a known weight of the oil with saturated aqueous sodium picrate at 90–95°C until a clear solution was obtained. The picrate which crystallized out on cooling for 2 h in an ice bath was filtered off through a pre-weighed sintered glass crucible, washed with ethanol and finally dried at 80°C for 1 h. Yield = 64·7% Theory.

Preparation of a mixed bed ion exchange column[2]

Anion exchange resin Amberlite I.R.A.400 (Cl form) (180 g) was eluted with 2 N sodium hydroxide (5 l) until free from chloride ion (silver nitrate test) then with deionized water (3 l) until alkali free to Brilliant Yellow paper before mixing with Cation exchange resin Amberlite I.R. 120 (H form) (70 g). The column consisted of two Liebig condensers connected together, with water at 40°C passing through the jacket. Gelatin solutions of concentrations $\not>$10% were passed through at a rate of not more than 120 g of dry gelatin per hour per litre of bed.

Viscosity of guanidated gelatin solutions containing C1

The viscosities of 3% guanidated gelatin solutions containing varying concentrations of C1 measured at pH 6·0 and those obtained using a 3% solution of the blank gelatin are plotted in Fig. 7. Fig. 7 shows that the ratio of colour coupler to gelatin concentration at max. ηr had increased by 0·12 mmoles of colour coupler per gramme of gelatin using guanidated gelatin. Comparison of Figs. 1 and 7 show that the viscosities of the solutions were much higher than normal. This point is considered later in this paper (see Effect of Ionic Strength).

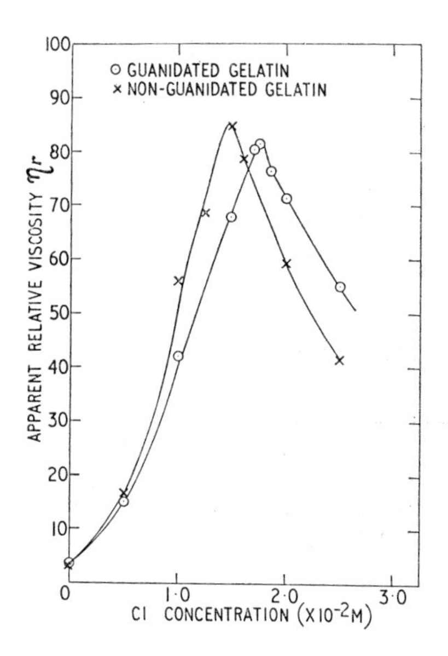

Fig. 7. Plot of apparent relative viscosity versus C1 concentration using 3·0% guanidated gelatin and 3·0% non-guanidated gelatin.

Effect of additives as viscosity reducers

Methylation of the phenolic group of the amide group of C1 gave a reduction in viscosity. This implies that hydrogen bonding is partially responsible for the viscosity increase where a colour coupler like C1 is mixed with gelatin. The effect of hydrogen bonding solvents such as dimethyl formamide and ethylene carbonate on C1 gelatin solutions was therefore studied.

The viscosities of 3% B2 gelatin solutions containing $1{\cdot}49 \times 10^{-2}$ M C1 was determined for various volume concentrations of dimethyl formamide and ethylene carbonate. Plots of viscosity against per centage dimethyl formamide and percentage ethylene carbonate showed that in both cases a sharp linear drop in viscosity occurred up to a point corresponding to a concentration of 9% (v/v) of additive thereafter falling more gradually with increasing additive concentration (see Fig. 8). Further experiments showed that the ratio of C1 to gelatin at max. ηr was not affected by dimethyl formamide.

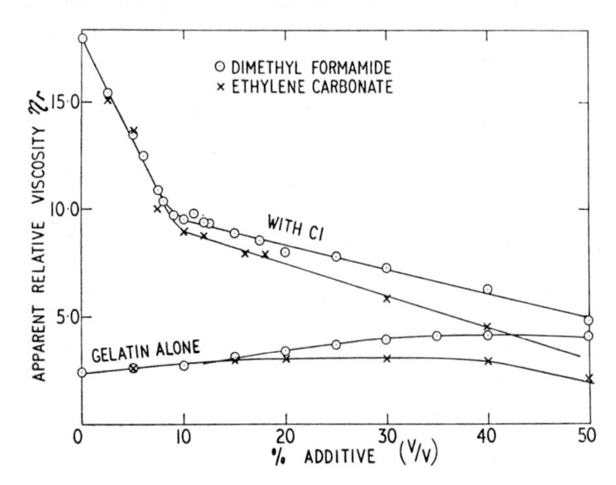

Fig. 8. Plot of apparent relative viscosity versus additive concentration for (i) a $1{\cdot}49 \times 10^{-2}$ M C1 solution in 3·0% gelatin solution, (ii) a 3·0% gelatin solution.

The effect of pH

The viscosities of 3% B1 gelatin solutions containing varying concentrations of C1 was measured at pH 6, 7, 8, 9, 10 and 11. Plots of ηr against colour coupler concentration gave curves from which the ratio of colour coupler to gelatin concentrations at max. ηr could be determined. These ratios when plotted against pH (see Fig. 9) gave a curve

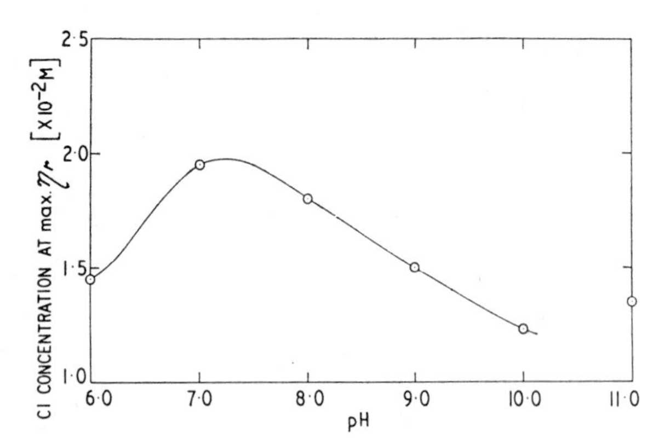

Fig. 9. Plot of C1 concentration at max. ηr versus pH using 3·0% gelatin.

rising to maximum ratio at pH 7·5 subsequently falling with further increase in pH.

The effect of pH on the interaction between the o-methyl derivative of C1 and gelatin was studied in the same way. The ratio of compound to gelatin concentration at max. ηr was obtained at each pH and is summarized in Table 2.

Table 2

Effect of pH on composition of complex of o-methyl derivative of C1 with gelatin

pH	*Concentration of compound at max. $\eta r \times 10^{-2}$* M	*Composition of complex at max. ηr mM compound/g gelatin*
6·0	1·82	0·695
7·0	2·25	0·858
8·0	2·55	0·979
9·0	2·75	1·05
10·0	2·75	1·05

Thus the substitution of the phenolic group of C1 with methyl stabilize the composition of the "complex" at max. ηr to pH changes at pH > 8.

The effect of ionic strength

It was noted that solutions of guanidated gelatin containing C1 had high viscosities. To check whether these high viscosities were due to low ionic strength an aqueous solution of B2 gelatin was passed down an ion exchange column. Viscosity measurements on a 3% solution of deionized gelatin containing various concentrations of C1 confirmed that the viscosities were high. The amount of colour coupler bound per gramme gelatin at max. ηr was slightly less than that found with standard gelatin. Addition of NaCl caused the viscosity of the solution to fall to values approaching those found with standard gelatin solutions of C1. These results show that the high viscosities could be due to low ionic strength.

Viscosities of 3·0% B1 gelatin solutions containing various concentrations of C1 were then measured at pH 6·0, 7·0 and 9·0 in the presence of 0·1 M NaCl. Results which are plotted in Fig. 10 show that at pH 6·0 and 7·0 the viscosity rose exponentially to high values with increasing colour coupler concentration. On the other hand at pH 9·0 the value of max. ηr was 45% lower than that obtained in the absence of added salt whilst the amount of colour coupler bound was increased from 0·54–0·665 mmoles C1 per gramme of gelatin.

Viscosity measurements were also carried out on 3% B1 gelatin solutions containing various concentrations of C1 at pH 6·0 in the presence of 0·05 and 0·025 M NaCl. These results which are plotted in Fig. 11 together with the results for deionized and standard B2 gelatin show the effect of ionic strength on viscosity. The addition of NaCl to a deionized gelatin solution containing C1 caused a small increase in the

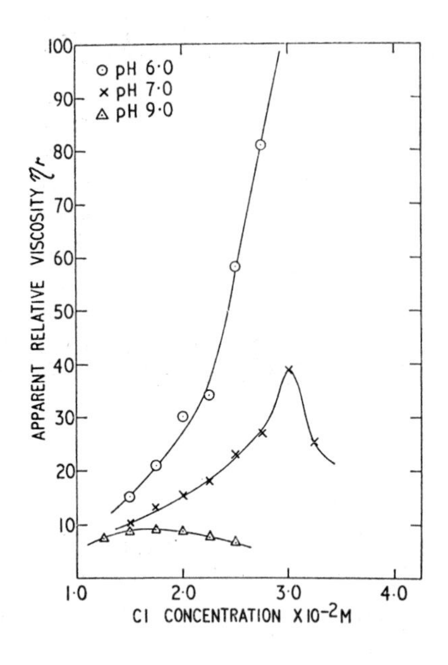

Fig. 10. Plots of apparent relative viscosity versus C1 concentration using 3·0% gelatin at various pHs in the presence of 0·1 M NaCl.

amount of C1 bound per gramme of gelatin and a decrease in viscosity to a minimum value in the presence of 0·025 M NaCl. Further increases in NaCl content caused increased binding of colour coupler and increased viscosity. It is of interest that the viscosity plot for 0·05 M NaCl shows a constant value of ηr over the C1 concentration range 1·9–2·4 × 10^{-2} M.

The addition of colour coupler to gelatin solution will cause an increase in the ionic strength. However, since it forms a gelatin coated micelle (see Discussion), it is possible that the effective increase in ionic strength is small.

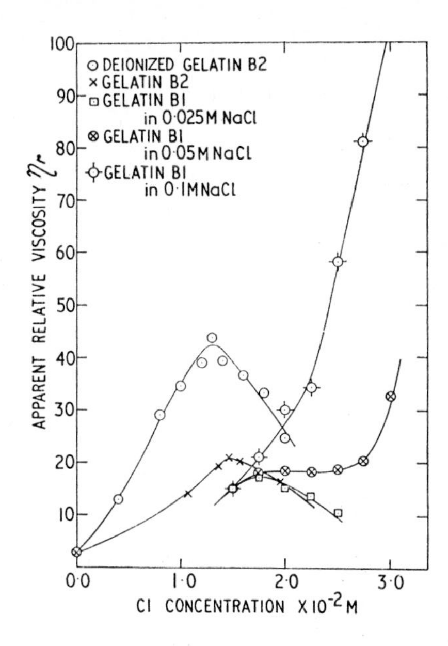

Fig. 11. The effect of ionic strength on the plots of apparent relative viscosity versus C1 concentration in 3·0% gelatin solution at pH 6·0.

Colour coupler C9

The interaction of a carboxyl group containing colour coupler with gelatin was also studied. For these experiments the colour coupler C9 was used.

The viscosities of 3·75%, 3·00% and 1·14% B1 gelatin solutions containing varying concentrations of C9 were measured at pH 9·0 (Table 3). Plots of ηr against colour coupler concentration gave curves which had poorly defined maxima. For this reason the ratio of colour coupler to gelatin concentration could not be determined accurately, but was about 0·95 mmoles colour coupler per gramme gelatin for each gelatin concentration.

Structural changes of C9

Viscosities of 3·75% B1 gelatin solutions containing varying concentrations of C10, C11, C12 and C13 were measured at pH 9·0. The colour couplers C10, C11, C12 and C13 are the alkyl chain C_{16}, C_{12},

Table 3

Viscosities of 3·75, 3·00 and 1·14% B1 gelatin solutions containing varying concentrations of C9 at pH 9·0, 35°C

Concentration of C9 × 10^{-2} M	3·75% *gelatin solution* ηr	3·00% *gelatin solution* ηr	1·14% *gelatin solution* ηr
0·00			1·719
0·20			2·020
0·40			2·361
0·60			2·569
0·80			2·655
0·90			2·689
1·00	6·28	5·96	2·666
1·20			2·689
1·40			2·689
1·50		8·35	
2·00	12·22	10·00	
2·25		10·65	
2·50	14·55	11·25	
2·75	15·20	11·35	
3·00	15·39	11·06	
3·25	14·90		
3·50		10·00	

C_8 and C_4 analogues of coupler C9. Coupler C13 (C_4 analogue) gave no appreciable viscosity increase with gelatin. In the other cases a plot of max. ηr against alkyl chain length was obtained (see Fig. 12).

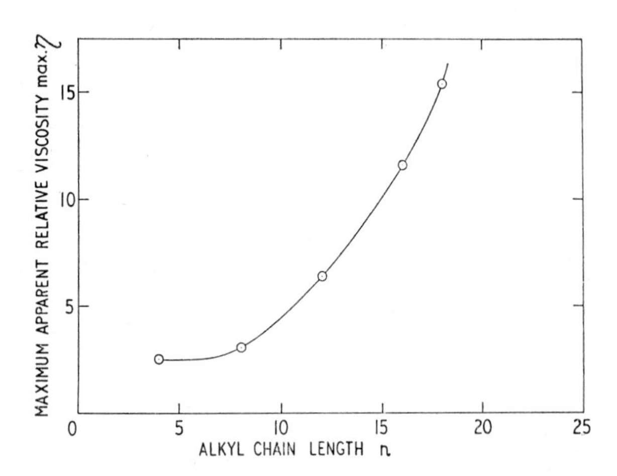

Fig. 12. Plot of maximum apparent relative viscosity (max. ηr) versus alkyl chain length (C_nH_{2n+1}) for C9.

Effect of pH

The viscosities of 3% B1 gelatin solutions containing varying concentrations of C9 were measured at pH 9·0, 10·0 and 11·0. Table 4 shows the effect of pH on the complex composition of C9 with gelatin.

Table 4

pH	*Ratio of colour coupler to gelatin concentration at max. ηr mM/g*
9·0	1·03
10·0	1·03
11·0	0·99

Effect of ionic strength

The viscosities of 3% B1 gelatin in 0·05 M and 1·00 M NaCl containing varying concentrations of C9 up to $4 \cdot 0 \times 10^{-2}$ M were measured at pH 9·0. All the viscosities were lower than those obtained in the absence of added salt. There was a gradual increase in ηr as the colour coupler concentration increased with no maximum. At colour coupler concentrations higher than $4 \cdot 0 \times 10^{-2}$ M phase separation occurred. These results showed that at high ionic strength (1·0) more C9 is bound at max. ηr as found for C1.

Colour coupler C14

Viscosities of 3% B1 gelatin solutions containing varying concentrations of C14 were measured at pH 6·0, 7·0, 8·0, 9·0 and 10·0. These results which are summarized in Table 5 below show that at pH $\geqslant$ 7·0 the amount of colour coupler bound in the complex at max. ηr is constant.

Table 5

Effect of pH on composition of complex of C14 with gelatin

pH	*Ratio of colour coupler to gelatin concentration at max. ηr mM/g*
6·0	0·665
7·0	0·855
8·0	0·855
9·0	0·855
10·0	0·855

Colour coupler C15

The previous measurements were repeated using C15. Table 6 gives the ratio of colour coupler to gelatin concentration at max. ηr for different pH values, and shows that for pH $\geqslant$ 7 the composition of the complex at max. ηr is constant.

Table 6

Effect of pH on composition of complex of C15 with gelatin

pH	*Ratio of colour coupler to gelatin concentration at max. ηr mM/g*
6·0	0·655
7·0	0·950
8·0	0·950
9·0	0·950
10·0	0·950

DISCUSSION

Viscosity measurements of gelatin solutions containing C1 gave curves similar to those obtained by Deryagin and Levi.[3] The amount of C1 bound to gelatin at pH 6·0 and at the maximum viscosity was 0·54 mmoles C1 per gramme gelatin over the gelatin concentration range 0·9–2·9%. This indicates formation of a complex of this composition. The amino and guanidino group content of gelatin is 0·94 mmoles per gramme of which 0·52 mmoles per gramme is the guanidino group.[4] Thus the guanidino groups may well be involved in linkage with C1. Guanidation of gelatin produced a product which bound 20% more C1, confirming that guanidino groups take part. As all known methods of deguanidation are considered to lead to degradation of gelatin these methods were not tried.[5] Since the amount of bound coupler in the complex decreases with increase of pH from 7–11 the simplest explanation is that C1 is mainly attached to gelatin by ion–ion attractive forces between the sulphonic acid groups and the amino and guanidino groups. The increase in the amount of C1 bound to gelatin from pH 6–7 may be attributed to gelatin chain extension facilitating binding, or alternatively to increased ion-dipole contribution. These results agree with the findings of Uhrich and Nawn, reported by Gutoff *et al.*,[6] which showed that the viscosity increase obtained on adding sodium alkyl sulphates to gelatin above its isoelectric point and in the absence of dissolved salts[15d] was due to ionic bonding between the anion and the positive protonated amino and guanidino groups of the gelatin.

That ion–ion interaction is not the only type involved was shown with experiments with the o-methyl derivative of C1. The amount bound increased from 0·69 at pH 6·0 to ca. 1·0 mmoles per gramme gelatin at pH 8·0 and thereafter remained constant with increasing pH. The attractive forces for this compound must therefore include some ion-dipole as well as the ion–ion type. For the sulphonic acid colour couplers C14 and C15 the amount of colour coupler bound increased from 0·665 at pH 6·0–0·855 and 0·950 mmoles per gramme gelatin respectively at pH 7·0. Over the pH range 7·0–10·0 the amount of coupler bound to gelatin was constant for both these colour couplers, and therefore ion-dipole interaction is the major contributive force. Similar conclusions were reached with the carboxyl colour coupler C9 where the amount of colour coupler bound was constant at ca. 1·02 mmoles per gramme gelatin over pH 9·0–11·0. Colour couplers are therefore attached to the gelatin molecule by ion–ion and ion-dipole forces. The proportions of coupler so bound depend on its structure.

The magnitude of the viscosity increase is affected by the chain length of the colour coupler. With homologues of C1 and C9, wherein the size of the ballasting group was varied, the maximum viscosity increased with increasing chain length above a certain minimum value. For C1 homologues this value was 7C atoms and for C9 homologues it was 4C atoms. The amount of colour coupler bound was not affected by chain length. Interactions between the hydrocarbon side chains are therefore also involved in the viscosity increase. Since non-polar groups can only interact with one another and with the solvent by means of van der Waals attractive forces previous discussions on the interactions between hydrocarbon side chains have only considered them in terms of these forces. On the other hand recent theories put forward by Nemethy and Sheraga claim that the interaction which occurs between two hydrocarbon chains is due to changes in the structure of associated water.[7],[8],[9] These result in the formation of a hydrophobic bond. The hydrophobic bond depends mainly on the entropy change due to changes in hydrogen bonding of the associated water. According to Nemethy and Sheraga when a hydrocarbon chain is in an aqueous environment van der Waals interaction occurs between the water and solute molecules. This promotes increased ordering of water molecules around the non-polar hydrocarbon chain ("ice-berg formation"[10]) accompanied by an increase in the degree of hydrogen bonding of the water. When a hydrocarbon chain is brought into water with an ionic group such as in a colour coupler the hydrocarbon chains associate and the colour coupler forms a micelle.[11] This is because the hydrocarbon chains which were previously surrounded by associated water come together until they touch (within their van der Waals radii) and thereby decrease the total number of water molecules in contact with them. Association of the hydrocarbon side chains occurs because of the increase in entropy due to the reduction in structure of the associated water. This theory which is attractive has been used to give a quantitative treatment of the thermodynamic behaviour of hydrophobic bonds and their role in protein structure.[9] For the purpose of this discussion the interaction which occurs between two hydrocarbon side chains will be called hereafter the hydrophobic bond. Hydrophobic bonds are therefore also involved in the viscosity increase.

The addition of 9% by volume of a strong hydrogen bonding solvent such as dimethyl formamide sharply reduced the viscosity of a gelatin solution of C1 by about 47%. This indicated the presence of hydrogen bonding in the interaction of C1 with gelatin. This view is strongly supported by the fact that the compounds N-methyl and O-methyl C1 gave solutions in 3% gelatin which were 20 and 30% lower in viscosity respectively than that obtained with C1. Methylation of the naphthol group was more effective than that of the amide group. Both compounds showed increased amounts of compound bound with gelatin. These results imply that hydrogen bonding is also involved in the interaction of C1 with gelatin.

Further increases of dimethyl formamide (9–40% v/v) gave a gradual decrease in the viscosity down to near normal values (see Fig. 8). This gradual decrease in viscosity is believed to be due to further dissociation of the complex. This may be due to displacement of the colour coupler from the gelatin by preferential adsorption of hydrogen bonding solvent or more likely to solubilization of the complex by increasing concentration of dimethyl formamide. Dimethyl formamide is a good solvent for colour couplers like C1 and in high concentrations of dimethyl formamide the micellar form of C1 would be suppressed. Similar conclusions can be reached by applying the theories of Nemethy and Sheraga. According to Nemethy a solvent additive like urea weakens hydrophobic bonds.[12] He quotes as an example of this that several workers have shown that the addition of urea increases the critical micellar concentration of micelles.[13],[14] The dissociation of the micellar type complex on addition of dimethyl formamide may similarly be due to the weakening of the hydrophobic bonds. Since it is not clear from the literature[12],[13],[14] exactly how urea acts or that hydrogen bonding solvents weaken hydrophobic bonds we prefer to consider this further dissociation of the complex, which involves hydrophobic bond breakage, to be due to solubilization. The addition of dimethyl formamide to gelatin solutions of C9 also caused substantial reduction of viscosity at pH 9·0.

Ion-dipole interaction was put forward by Pankhurst and Smith in their study of the interaction of sodium alkyl sulphates and gelatin to account for the large amount of detergent bound to gelatin.[15] Simple ion–ion interaction alone could not account for this amount. It was concluded that two types of mechanism are responsible for primary adsorption of amphipathic anions and cations to gelatin. Firstly, a purely coulombic ion–ion attraction, the extent of which depends on the net charge on the protein and the number of charged groups on the amphipathic ion, and is independent of the size of the ion. Secondly, an ion-dipole association between the amphipathic ions and the amide groups in the backbone of the protein. This mechanism is inhibited by hydrogen ions, encouraged by inorganic electrolyte and is susceptible to the size and shape of the amphipathic ion.

To account for the phenomenon of coacervation in soap solutions in gelatin, Booij put forward the concept of soap micelles coated with gelatin.[16] Dilute soap solutions contain small spherical micelles of soap molecules which change into large sandwich type micelles at increasing salt concentrations. At salt concentrations lower than that needed for coacervation there are already sandwich micelles of small extension which Booij calls precursors. At pH values above the isoelectric point coacervation occurs in a soap/gelatin system at a salt concentration smaller than that needed for soap itself. Booij therefore considers that if gelatin is added to a soap solution at a salt concentration which is high enough for some precursors to be present the gelatin will force the transformation to the large sandwich micelles. The gelatin molecules collect the precursors and induce coalescence into large sandwich micelles.

Pankhurst and Smith and Booij's theories on gelatin soap interactions were put forward to account for coacervation of the complex. The results presented in this paper show that the viscosity effects obtained between gelatin and colour couplers in solution can be equally explained on the basis of a micellar type structure. Thus the marked effect of alkyl chain and hydrogen bonding on the viscosity may be explained by linking of the adsorbed colour coupler to another gelatin molecule by the alkyl chain and hydrogen bonds, or what is more likely to another adsorbed colour coupler molecule through the interaction of the alkyl chains. Schematically we may represent the complex as:

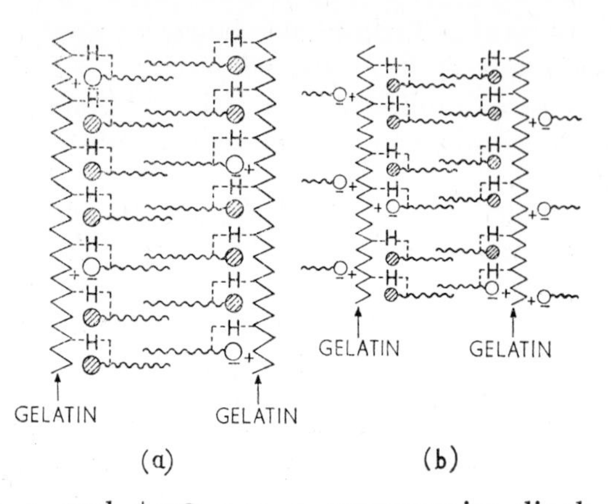

where ●∿∿∿∿ and $^{+-}$○∿∿∿∿ represent ion-dipole and ion–ion type interaction for adsorbed colour couplers and ————*H*———— represent *H* bonds. Although a sandwich type micellar complex has been drawn, the shape of the complex is not important for the purposes of the discussion. To explain why the complex is more hydrophobic than gelatin as shown by precipitation experiments with ammonium nitrate, the hydrophilic groups of gelatin could be turned into the centre of the complex as shown in complex (a). Alternatively the complex may become hydrophobic by adsorption of colour coupler to the outward facing hydrophilic groups of gelatin by ion–ion attractive forces as shown in complex (b), and as suggested by Bungenberg de Jong.(17) The addition of a colour coupler to gelatin by ion–ion interaction will also cause an uncoiling or extension of the gelatin chain due to an increase in the net negative charge on the chain. This and the formation of the micellar type structure will give the viscosity increase in gelatin colour coupler interactions. Where no viscosity increases occur the binding between gelatin molecules by the colour coupler and the extension of the gelatin chain is not sufficiently large to cause any effect. The viscosity decrease observed with increasing colour coupler concentration after the maximum viscosity has been reached is attributed to dispersion of the complexes by adsorption of the colour coupler by its alkyl chain on to the hydrophobic exterior of the complex.

The formation of the micellar type complex and its effect on viscosity is thus due to the interplay of ion–ion, ion-dipole, hydrophobic bond and hydrogen bond forces. The balance of these forces is affected by structural factors as shown strikingly by the o-methylation of C1, which increases the ion-dipole type of interaction and reduces hydrogen bonding. The viscosity is reduced because the gelatin molecules are not so tightly bound by the colour coupler in the complex.

Mazzucato *et al.* have shown[18] that fluorination of the side chain of a yellow colour coupler gave a more viscous solution with gelatin, and they have attributed this to increased van der Waal's attractive forces. In the view of the authors of this paper this increased viscosity may be due to other influences such as steric factors.

The high viscosities of gelatin solutions of C1 of lower ionic strength, made from gelatin treated with ion exchange resin, are considered to be mainly due to high extension of the gelatin chains. Addition of NaCl caused a reduction in viscosity until it reached a minimum value in the presence of 0·025 M NaCl. Further increases in NaCl content gave an increase in viscosity. The decrease in viscosity is associated with an ionic shielding of the charges on the gelatin molecule and partial coiling up or constriction of the gelatin molecule, whilst the increase in the viscosity is believed to be due to increasing insolubilization of the micellar type complex. At high viscosities visco elastic effects are noticed. Raising the pH can decrease the interaction by increasing the solubility (see Fig. 10).

No account has been taken of the silver halide phase.

The authors acknowledge helpful discussion with Mr. A. C. Farthing and thank the Directors of Imperial Chemical Industries Limited and of Ilford Limited for permission to publish this work.

References

(1) Janus, J. W., *Recent Advances in Gelatin and Glue Research*, p. 214, Pergamon Press (1958).
(2) Janus, J. W., Kenchington, A. W. and Ward, A. G., *Research*, **4,** 247 (1951).
(3) Deryagin, B. V. and Levi, S. M., *Proc. Acad. Sci. U.S.S.R.*, **79,** 283 (1951).
(4) Ward, A. G., *J. Photogr. Sci.*, **3,** 60 (1955).
(5) Bello, J., *Trans. Farad. Soc.*, **55,** 2130 (1959); *Biochem. Biophys. Acta*, **57,** 214 (1962).
(6) Guttoff, E. B., Kelly Jr., W. D., Nawn, G. H., Roth, P. H. and Steigmann, A. E., *J. Photogr. Sci.*, **16,** 124 (1968).
(7) Nemethy, G. and Sheraga, H. A., *J. Chem. Phys.*, **36,** 3382 (1962).
(8) Nemethy, G. and Sheraga, H. A., *J. Chem. Phys.*, **36,** 3401 (1962).
(9) Nemethy, G. and Sheraga, H. A., *J. Phys. Chem.*, **66,** 1773 (1962).
(10) Frank, H. S. and Evans, M. W., *J. Chem. Phys.*, **13,** 507 (1945).
(11) Brand, B. P., *J. Photogr. Sci.*, **16,** 1 (1968).
(12) Nemethy, G., *Angewandt Chemie.*, **6,** 195 (1967).
(13) Bruning, W. and Holtzer, A., *J. Amer. Chem. Soc.*, **83,** 4865 (1961).
(14) Mukerjee, P. and Ray, A., *J. Phys. Chem.*, **67,** 190 (1963).
(15) (a) Pankhurst, K. G. A. and Smith, R. C. M., *Trans. Farad. Soc.*, **40,** 565 (1944).
(b) Pankhurst, K. G. A. and Smith, R. C. M., *Trans. Farad. Soc.*, **41,** 630 (1944).
(c) Pankhurst, K. G. A., *Discussion Farad. Soc.*, **6,** 52 (1949).
(d) Pankhurst, K. G. A., *Research* (London) Supplement Surface Chemistry, 109 (1949).

(16) Booij, H. L. in Kruyt, H. R., *Colloid Sci.*, Vol. II, Chap. XIV, Elsevier Pub. Co. (1949); and Booij, H. L., *Kolloid Z.*, **136,** 16 (1953).
(17) Bungenberg de Jong, H. G., *Proc. Koninkl. Med. Akad. Wetenschap.*, **45,** 601 (1946); *ibid* **55B,** 317, 347, 360 (1952); *ibid* **56B,** 203 (1953); *ibid* **57B,** 1, 192.
(18) Mazzucato, V., Pasini, G., Talamini, G. and Bellone, D., *J. Photogr. Sci.*, **16,** 63 (1968).

The Chemical Properties of Gelatin

Colorimetric Method for Quantitative Determination of Thiosulphate Sulphur in Gelatin

G. ENDER and H. ZORN

Analytic Laboratory, Perutz Photowerke, Branch of Agfa-Gevaert AG, Munich, Germany

ABSTRACT. A survey is given of the published work of the most important methods for quantitative determination of thiosulphate sulphur in gelatin. According to the present method, gelatin is digested at a pH of 4·0–4·2 and 70°C in presence of AgBr. The quantity of silver sulphide, formed at the reaction with thiosulphate sulphur, is measured colorimetrically, while other compounds like tetrathionate, thiourea, thiosinamine etc. do not react practically under the conditions mentioned above.

INTRODUCTION

In the preparation of photographic emulsions, thiosulphate is one of the most important natural ripening substances in gelatin. A quick and reliable method for quantitative determination of thiosulphate sulphur is therefore of special interest. From the known analytical methods the following should be mentioned:

Titrimetric methods

These deal mainly with the potentiometric titration of the consumption of silver nitrate by gelatin solutions, partially in dependence on the time of reaction. Papers on these methods have been published by Abribat(1), Beersmanns and Borginon(2), Narath and Möller(3), Narath and Tiilika(4), and Titov and Rattner(5).

Colorimetric methods

These have been dealt with by Sheppard and Hudson(6), and Sutherns and Loening(7), who propose the complicated colorimetric determination of methylene-blue, formed by several steps from thiosulphate via silver sulphide and hydrogen sulphide.

The method of Requardt[8], using the oxydation of paraphenylene diamine and its N-alkyl homologues, in presence of thiosulphuric acid or hydrogen sulphide and leading to thiazine dyestuffs appears to be rather less complicated. Warburton and Przybylowicz[9] describe the formation of methylene-blue by reduction of thiosulphate in presence of *p*-dimethylaniline.

Polarographic methods

The method used by Russell[10] deals with the determination of thiosulphate in an aqueous extract of gelatin. Stefan[11] proposes the direct determination of thiosulphate in gelatin solution. The method of Timson, Kliem, Steigmann and Kelly[12] deals with the determination of thiosulphate after enzymatic decomposition of gelatin. According to Janus and Nellist[13] the determination of thiosulphate is performed after separation by an ion-exchanger.

Information from literature as well as our own experience shows that the polarographic measurements seem to be the most specific among the cited methods, but they require rather expensive equipment.

The present report deals with a simple, fast and highly specific method for the quantitative determination of thiosulphate sulphur in gelatin. This method works under reaction conditions similar to those used in the preparation of emulsions and leads to results showing a reasonable relationship to sensitometric data of the emulsions prepared with the same gelatins.

PRINCIPLES

As can be seen from Fig. 1, thiosulphate, thiourea and thiosinamine react at a pH of 4·0–4·2 and at 70°C quantitatively with silver nitrate to form silver sulphide within 2 hours, while the reaction of tetrathionate is not finished even after 6 hours. Thiourea shows a marked induction period which indicates an autocatalytical formation of silver sulphide.

On digestion with silver bromide under otherwise identical conditions (see Fig. 2) thiosulphate reacts quantitatively and very quickly to form silver sulphide, while the reaction of thiourea and thiosinamine produces practically no silver sulphide within an hour, tetrathionate only showing a weak reaction. The quantity of silver sulphide is determined colorimetrically after addition of potassium cyanide to dissolve silver bromide as well as possibly present traces of metallic silver.

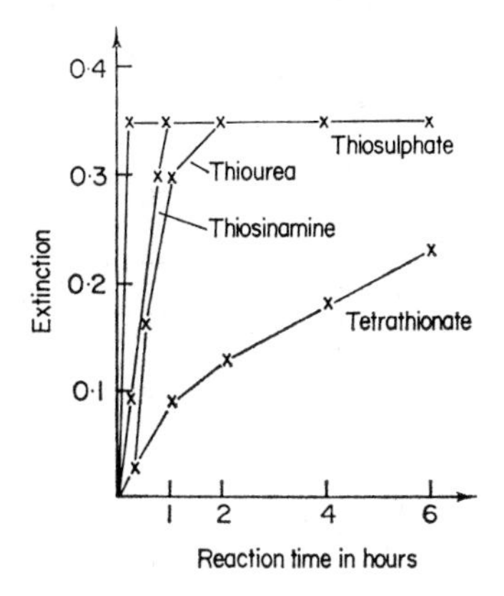

Fig. 1. Reaction of $AgNO_3$ at pH of 4·0–4·2, 70°C under formation of Ag_2S

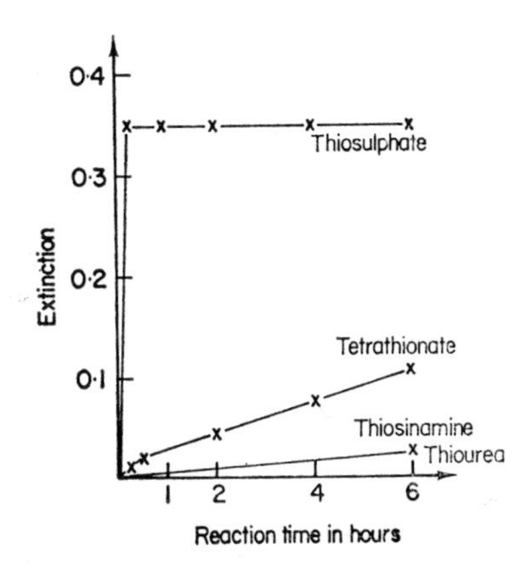

Fig. 2. Reaction of AgBr at pH of 4·0–4·2, 70°C under formation of Ag_2S

This difference in the reaction behaviour is the basis of the present method for quantitative determination of thiosulphate sulphur in gelatin.

The slow reaction of thiourea and thiosinamine with silver bromide is abruptly accelerated above a pH of 5 and, as illustrated by Fig. 3, these compounds will react like thiosulphate at a pH of 7·0.

When silver bromide is replaced by silver iodide, we find at pH 10 a behaviour (see Fig. 4) which is practically an inversion of the reaction with silver bromide at pH 4·0–4·2. This might possibly lead to a method for the quantitative determination, not only of thiosulphate, but also of

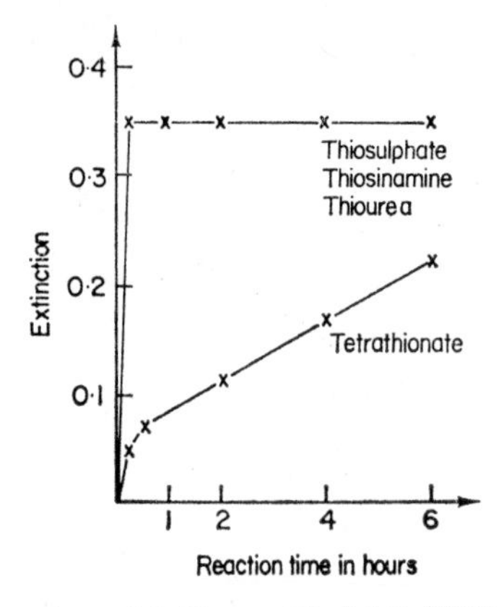

Fig. 3. Reaction of AgBr at pH of 7·0, 70°C under formation of Ag_2S

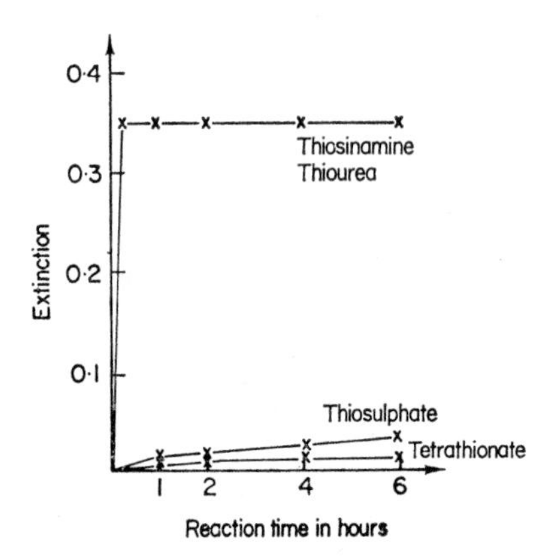

Fig. 4. Reaction of AgI at pH of 10·0, 70°C under formation of Ag_2S

other components like thiourea, polythionate and so on at different pH and pAg values. This will be subject of a future report.

On the reaction of thiosulphate with silver nitrate, silver chloride and silver bromide, only one of the two sulphur atoms of thiosulphate is involved in the silver sulphide formation. The following reactions are supposed:

$$2\ AgBr + Na_2S_2O_3 \rightarrow Ag_2S_2O_3 + 2\ NaBr$$
$$Ag_2S_2O_3 + HOH \rightarrow Ag_2S + H_2SO_4$$

EXPERIMENTAL

Reagents

1·1 N H_2SO_4 (53·944 g H_2SO_4 per litre)

1·1 N H_2SO_4/0·01 N $AgNO_3$ solution (53·944 g H_2SO_4 and 1·699 g $AgNO_3$ per litre)

0·012 N KBr solution (1·43 g KBr per litre)

3 N NaOH/0·2 N KCN solution (120 g NaOH and 13 g KCN per litre)

AEDTE* solution 20% (as solubility at room temperature is below 20%, the solution must be kept warm for use by the thermostat)

Instruments

Thermostat
Magnetic stirrer
Photometer (f.i. Zeiss Elko II)

Procedure

From the gelatin to be examined, 20 g each (±0·1 g) are weighed and put into 3 brown 250 ml bottles (with screw cap) for 1 blank and 2 measuring samples and are mixed with 70 ml of distilled water and 10 ml of 0·012 N KBr solution.

In order to avoid sticking together of the gelatin, it is recommended to stir shortly after the addition of KBr solution and water, especially when fine powdered samples are concerned. After 1 hour swelling, the gelatin is melted in a thermostat at 70°C (±1°C) for 30 min. Then to the blank sample add 10 ml of 1·1 N H_2SO_4 and to each of the 2 measuring samples add 10 ml of 1·1 N H_2SO_4/0·01 N $AgNO_3$ solution, with stirring. Then the blank and measuring samples are stoppered (with the screw cap) and kept in the thermostat for 1 hour at 70°C.

* AEDTE is the abbreviation of ethylenediaminetetraacetic acid (complex forming agent). It is added to avoid a turbidity by insoluble carbonates or hydroxides in the gelatin solution.

Once this reaction time has passed, to each of the blank and measuring samples 10 ml of AEDTE solution and 10 ml of 3 N NaOH/0·2 N KCN solution are added while stirring. Within 3 min the optical density of the samples are measured against the blank sample in 20 mm cells by a photometer with a blue filter (Zeiss S 42 E 62). Evaluation is performed by means of a calibration curve.

When adding the NaOH/KCN solution, special attention must be payed to intensive stirring, as a locally to high KCN concentration in the gelatin solution will lead to a reduction of the silver sulphide colour density.

In order to guarantee a constant final volume of blank and measuring samples, the added quantities of water and reagents must be pipetted and the bottles which carry blank and measuring samples should be kept closed between the single steps. Further attention must be payed not to prolong the reaction time of 1 hour and to perform the extinction measurements of the samples within 3 min after addition of the NaOH/KCN solution. Test series require that the single gelatin samples are melted, brought to reaction, and measured in a periodical sequence. If a gelatin contains more than 40 ppm of thiosulphate sulphur, only 10 g of such a gelatin are used and the sample is completed by another 10 g of absolutely inert gelatin. The quantity of sulphur calculated from the calibration curve has to be multiplied by the factor 2 in this case.

CALIBRATION CURVE

For the construction of the calibration curve, increasing quantities of thiosulphate are added to an inert gelatin with further addition of 60 ml of distilled water (instead of 70 ml as above), 10 ml of 0·012 N

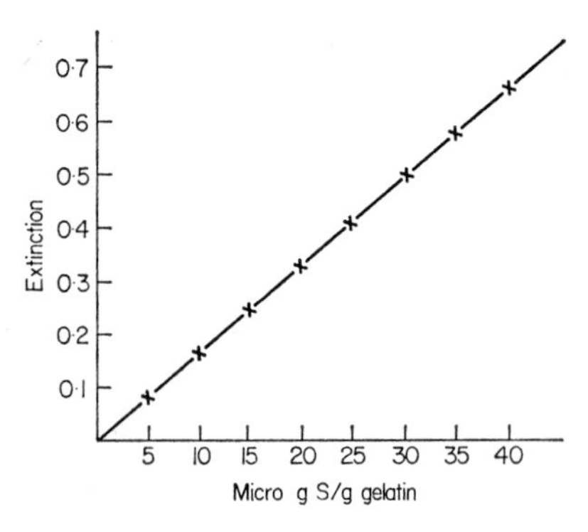

Fig. 5. Calibration curve, 0–40 ppm of thiosulphate in gelatin.

KBr solution and 10 ml of a thiosulphate solution which contains, with regard to 20 g of gelatin, 5, 10, 15 and so on up to 40 ppm sulphur, considering the fact that only one sulphur atom of the S_2O_3 ion will react with AgBr. To the blank samples of course no thiosulphate is added.

After melting, however—differing from the method given above—10 ml of 1·1 N H_2SO_4/0·01 N $AgNO_3$ solution are added to the blank samples instead of pure 1·1 N H_2SO_4. The further procedure is performed as described above.

A calibration curve for the range from 0–40 ppm of thiosulphate sulphur in gelatin is shown in Fig. 5 and the linearity of this curve proves the validity of the Lambert–Beer law.

RESULTS

In order to test the present method, gelatins of the First International Working Group (IAG) were examined. The results of these examinations are compared in Table 1 with the values which were determined polarographically by the members of the IAG.

Table 1

Comparison of IAG gelatin values determined polarographically with those obtained by Perutz

Sample	*Kodak (Harrow)* *Polarogr.*	*Agfa-Gevaert (Lev.)* *Polarogr.*	*Janus/Nellist (l.c.)* *Polarogr.*	*Perutz* *AgBr-Digest.*
		micro g S/g *gelatin*		
D.G.F. I	2·0	1·4	2·5	1·5
D.G.F. II	8·3	5·7	7	7
Hodgson A	0	0	0	$<0·5$
Leiner A	14·7	18·5	15	18
Leiner B	0	0	0	$<0·5$
Pont-Brulé I	0	0	0	$<0·5$
Pont-Brulé II	4·2	5·7	6	6
Rousselot I	0·3	0	0	$<0·5$
Rousselot II	5·8	7·1	7	10
Simeons 7572	4·9	—	3	2·5
Simeons 7573	10·5	—	11	11·5
Winterthur 6249	3·8	4·6	6	6
Winterthur 6275	0·4	traces	1	1

As can be seen from the table a very good correlation is evident between the values we obtained and the values which have been polarographically determined by other laboratories.

Certain difficulties with the present method only arise if the gelatin solution shows a rather strong turbidity created by organic substances which cannot be eliminated by the addition of AEDTE.

CONCLUSION

In conclusion it can be said that the present method offers good results according to our experiences during 3 years of application in our laboratories. The results are in a reasonable relation to the sensitometric data of each of the gelatins.

References

(1) Abribat, M., *Sci. Ind. Photogr.*, 2, **12,** 1 (1941).
(2) Beersmanns, J. and Borginon, H., *Sci. Photogr. Proc. Int. Colloq. 7th,* Liège (1959).
(3) Narath, A. and Möller, G., *Z. Wiss. Photogr.*, **61,** 17 (1967).
(4) Narath, A. and Tiilika, A., *Z. Wiss. Photogr.*, **56,** 161 (1962).
(5) Titov, A. A. and Rattner, J. M., *Tr. Vses. Nauch. Issled. Kinophotoinst.*, **8,** 20 (1948).
(6) Sheppard, S. E. and Hudson, J. H., *Photogr. J.*, **65,** 380 (1925).
(7) Sutherns, E. A. and Loening, E. E., *Wiss. Photogr. Ergeb. Int. Konf. Wiss. Photogr.*, 274 (1958).
(8) Requardt, K., *Sci. Photogr. Proc. Int. Colloq. 7th,* Liège (1959).
(9) Warburton, C. D. and Przybylowicz, E. P., *J. Photogr. Sci.*, **15,** 201 (1967).
(10) Russell, G. J., *J. Photogr. Sci.*, **4,** 94 (1956).
(11) Stefan, V., *Chem. Prum.*, **10,** 126 (1960).
(12) Timson, W. J., Kliem, P. O., Steigmann, A. E. and Kelly, W. O., *J. Photogr. Sci.*, **10,** 270 (1966).
(13) Janus, J. W. and Nellist, D. R., *J. Photogr. Sci.*, **15,** 270 (1967).

Tetrathionate in Gelatin?

D. R. NELLIST

Research Laboratories, Kodak Limited, Wealdstone, Harrow, Middlesex

ABSTRACT. Unsuccessful attempts have been made to detect tetrathionate added to enzymic hydrolysates of gelatin at pH 7. In the presence of sulphite an equivalent amount of thiosulphate is detected following the equation

$$SO_3'' + S_4O_6'' \rightarrow S_2O_3'' + S_3O_6''.$$

In the absence of sulphite or at low pH values, tetrathionate decomposes in some other way. Tetrathionate cannot therefore exist in commercial gelatin. Under the normal conditions of emulsion preparation tetrathionate will be converted into thiosulphate and cannot therefore be regarded as a sulphur sensitizer in its own right.

INTRODUCTION

The presence of thiosulphate in photographic gelatin, as a natural sulphur sensitizer, was proposed by Steigmann in 1928.[1] He later claimed to have developed tests which, when applied to extracts of alkali processed gelatins, detected thiosulphate and, in addition, trithionate.[2] The frequent presence of thiosulphate in gelatins has since been adequately confirmed and methods developed for its quantitative determination,[3]-[8] but the presence of trithionate remains to be convincingly demonstrated. That gelatin extracts contain other polythionates was shown by Wood,[9] using electrophoretic methods. He detected tetrathionate in an extract from a bone gelatin and also probably in an extract from a hide gelatin, while Russell,[3] using a polarographic method, determined tetrathionate in aqueous extracts of a large number of gelatins of various types and recorded these as evidence for the existence of the compound in gelatin.

The possible existence of tetrathionate in gelatin has implications for the polarographic method of determining thiosulphate.[6] In a base electrolyte of 0·2 M potassium nitrate for example, the half-wave potentials of thiosulphate and tetrathionate are so close that in the presence of both of these ions a single composite wave is obtained, showing anodic and cathodic branches due respectively to thiosulphate and tetrathionate.[10] These two branches can only be separated by reference to the residual current, that is the current flowing in the absence of the substances being analyzed. At the high sensitivity required for gelatin analysis, the residual current varies from gelatin to gelatin and differs significantly from the instrument zero, so that the two parts of a composite wave would be inseparable and tetrathionate could be recorded, in error, as thiosulphate.

With more concentrated solutions, such as the aqueous extracts prepared by Russell, composite waves would still be obtained but, at the lower instrumental sensitivity needed, the residual current line would be more nearly coincident with the "zero" current line, and the anodic and cathodic branches could possibly be separated without too much error.

In his paper Russell[3] does not show composite waves, the anodic and cathodic branches being shown separately (Fig. 2, Ref. 3). Indeed these were determined in different base electrolytes, the thiosulphate (anodic branch) in 0·2 M potassium nitrate and the tetrathionate (cathodic branch) in 1·0 M ammonium dihydrogen phosphate. Nevertheless Furness and Davies[10] have shown that composite waves are obtained in both these base electrolytes and in fact recommend the use of 0·2 M potassium nitrate for the determination of these compounds when they are present together in solution.

In order to assess the consequences of the presence of tetrathionate on our own polarographic determination, the effect of adding tetrathionate to gelatin has been examined.

EXPERIMENTAL

Sodium tetrathionate was supplied by K and K Laboratories, Inc. (Plainview, N.J., U.S.A.) and was 95–99% pure. All other reagents used were of Analar quality supplied by British Drug Houses Ltd.

Two gelatins were used. One was an inert bone gelatin previously deionized to remove salts, surface active material, etc. The other was a bone gelatin thought to be virtually free of sulphite. Neither thiosulphate nor tetrathionate could be detected in enzymic digests of these gelatins when they were examined polarographically.

Preparation of the enzymic hydrolysates

5 g of gelatin were swollen for 20 min in 30 ml of distilled water containing sufficient alkali or acid to bring the final pH to between 7 and 7·1 using Bromothymol Blue as an external indicator. The gelatin

was then dispersed at 45°C for 30 min. 5 ml of a solution of crystalline trypsin (Armour Pharmaceutical Co. Ltd., Eastbourne, Sussex) were then added and the solution was left at 45°C for a further 5 min. The trypsin solution was freshly prepared, as it autolyses on standing, and contained 6000 units (approximately 2 mg)/ml. In order to obtain a solution 0·2 M with respect to potassium nitrate, the sample was then made up to 50 ml in a standard flask containing 1·01 g of potassium nitrate.

Additions of tetrathionate and sulphite were made, when necessary, after the gelatin had been dispersed, and then left to stand for 20 min before the trypsin was added. Tetrathionate was added to the gelatin at various pH values, in the presence of excess of sulphite or following the complete destruction of sulphite by the addition of formaldehyde. In separate experiments, formaldehyde itself in 0·2 M potassium nitrate was shown to have no effect on the tetrathionate wave.

Digests were examined at pH 7·0 and pH 4·0. A value of 7·0 was chosen by Janus and Nellist(6) as a convenient value for determining thiosulphate directly in enzymic hydrolysates. The value of 4·0 was chosen because of the detection by Wood(9) of tetrathionate in aqueous extracts of gelatin at this pH.

In each experiment a sample of the digest was first examined without addition of tetrathionate in order to establish the position of the residual current line. A second sample was prepared with the addition of tetrathionate. Tetrathionate or thiosulphate could then be subsequently detected by the appearance of cathodic or anodic waves or both. The dropping-mercury electrode was calibrated so that the amount of thiosulphate present could be deduced from its wave-height. It should be emphasized that because of the difficulties of detecting and measuring the wave-heights at the low concentrations employed, no great accuracy or precision could be expected from the results.

RESULTS

pH 7·0

(i) *Excess sulphite*

An addition of sodium sulphite, equivalent to about 700 μg SO_2/g, was made to the digest. This is an exceptionally high value and unlikely to be exceeded very often by commercial gelatins.

Added tetrathionate could not be detected under these conditions. The cathodic wave of tetrathionate was replaced by an anodic wave due to thiosulphate, the amount of thiosulphate produced being related to the quantity of tetrathionate added (Fig. 1).

It is well known that tetrathionate and sulphite react in neutral or alkaline solutions to give thiosulphate and trithionate following the reaction:

$$SO_3'' + S_4O_6'' \rightarrow S_2O_3'' + S_3O_6'' \quad (1)$$

The yield of thiosulphate predicted by this reaction is also shown in Fig. 1 as a solid line. The agreement between the experimental points and the theoretical line is extremely good and is strong evidence that under these conditions tetrathionate does not exist.

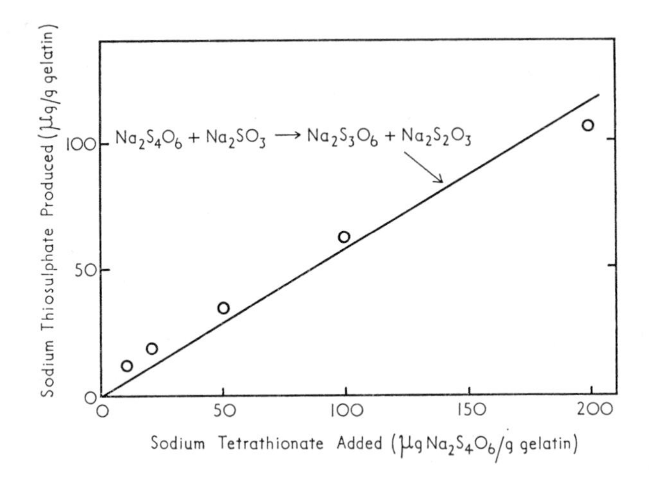

Fig. 1. Conversion of added tetrathionate to thiosulphate. Gelatin digest at pH 7·0; 700 μg added SO_2/g gelatin. The solid line indicates the result predicted by the equation shown. Experimental results are indicated by . . . ○.

(ii) *Sulphite absent*

Under these conditions a thiosulphate wave could not be detected, indicating that the conversion of tetrathionate to thiosulphate does not occur. Nevertheless the remaining tetrathionate waves are small when compared, at equal concentrations, with those obtained in 0·2 M potassium nitrate (Fig. 2). It is unlikely that this depression of the wave-height is due solely to the effect of the viscosity of the digest, which is itself low. For example, the height of a thiosulphate wave is only depressed by some 30% in a tryptic digest when compared with its height in 0·2 M potassium nitrate and one would expect any depression of a tetrathionate wave to be by about the same amount. One must therefore conclude that tetrathionate is being destroyed, thiosulphate not being among the reaction products.

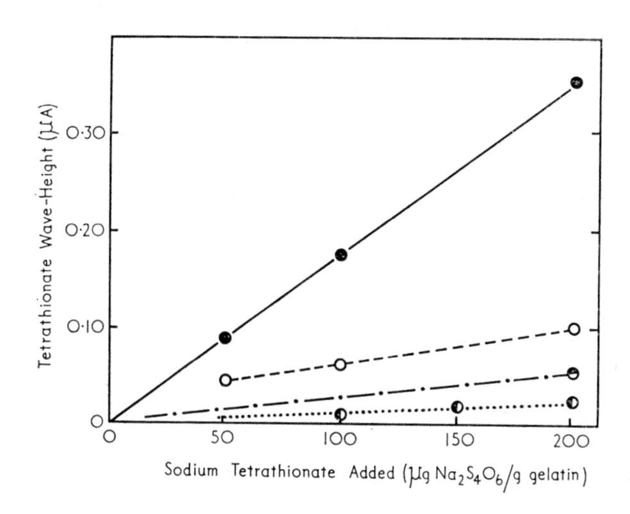

Fig. 2. Wave height of Tetrathionate in Gelatin Digests under various conditions, and also in 0·2 M KNO_3 without gelatin.

● . . . 2 M KNO_3.
○ . . . Digest at pH 4·0; no sulphite.
◓ . . . Digest at pH 4·0; 700 μg SO_2/g gelatin.
◐ . . . Digest at pH 7·0; no sulphite.

(iii) *Variation of sulphite concentration*

The amount of thiosulphate produced from an addition of 200 μg $Na_2S_4O_6$/g gelatin at various levels of sulphite addition is shown in Fig. 3. The presence in gelatin of tetrathionate in quantities as high as 200 μg/g gelatin is extremely unlikely and the experiments were therefore repeated with an addition of 50 μg $Na_2S_4O_6$/g gelatin. These results are shown inserted on Fig. 3.

The sulphite levels quoted should be regarded with caution since it is now believed that during drying of the gelatin used for these experiments, following its deionization, a quantity of sulphur dioxide was reabsorbed. Nevertheless the necessary presence of sulphite for the conversion of tetrathionate to thiosulphate at pH 7·0 is convincingly demonstrated.

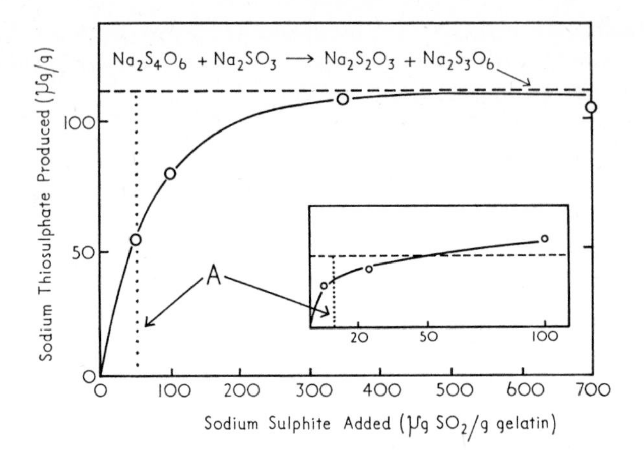

Fig. 3. Conversion of tetrathionate to thiosulphate for various sulphite additions. Gelatin digest at pH 7·0; 200 μg added tetrathionate/g gelatin. The insert shows results for 50 μg added tetrathionate/g gelatin. The dotted lines indicated by A show the quantity of SO_2 required in each case to convert the added tetrathionate, calculated from the above equation.

pH 4·0

At this level of the pH, formation of thiosulphate from added tetrathionate could not be detected either in the presence or absence of sulphite. However the sulphite level certainly affected the height of the tetrathionate wave produced (Fig. 2) and this is further evidence that these small tetrathionate waves are the result of the small equilibrium concentration of tetrathionate rather than a viscosity effect.

Effect of pH

The relation between the pH of the digest and the quantity of thiosulphate produced from an addition of 200 μg $Na_2S_4O_6$/g gelatin in the presence of excess sulphite is shown in Fig. 4. It is clear that above pH 6 the conversion is quantitative but falls away rapidly as the pH is reduced. At pH 4 no thiosulphate can be detected.

DISCUSSION

There is no doubt that, in a gelatin solution, equilibria are established between polythionates, thiosulphate and sulphite, the equilibrium position depending also on pH. The evidence presented here shows that at pH values above 6, and in the presence of sufficient sulphite, tetrathionate does not exist in gelatin solutions and is quantitatively converted into thiosulphate. Equation (1) predicts that a sulphite content equivalent to only 10 μg SO_2/g is necessary to fully convert 50 μg $Na_2S_4O_6$/g gelatin while a value of about 50 μg/g may be deduced from the rather uncertain experimental data shown in Fig. 3. No doubt the temperature and time of dispersion of the gelatin will also have a considerable effect on the conversion.

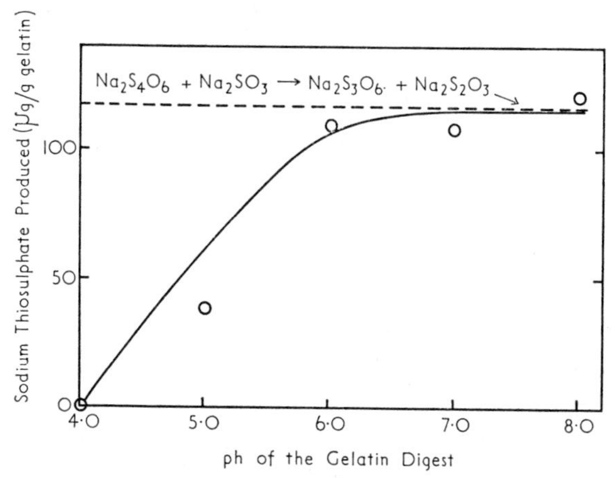

Fig. 4. Effect of pH on the conversion of tetrathionate to thiosulphate. Gelatin digest with 200 μg added tetrathionate/g gelatin; 700 μg added SO_2/g gelatin.

Because the amount of sulphite required for the conversion is small, and likely to be exceeded in normal commercial gelatins, and also because the second ripening of photographic emulsions, is carried out at pH values greater than 6, it is, perhaps, unrealistic to consider tetrathionate as a natural sulphur sensitizer. Indeed its presence in gelatin has hitherto been based only on the evidence obtained from the examination of concentrated aqueous extracts of large quantities of gelatin. These generally have a low pH, as reported by Wood,[9] and will certainly lose sulphite during the vacuum concentration procedure. Under these conditions the equilibria may well move to favour the formation of some tetrathionate and its detection in the extracts will be simply an artifact of their preparation. This view is supported by the work of Grainger and Mathewson.[11] Using an extraction procedure very similar to that published by Russell,[3] but taking certain precautions to minimize oxidation during the vacuum evaporation stage, they detected the formation of tetrathionate from thiosulphate added to a deionized gelatin.

The suggestion by Steigmann[2] that trithionate is present in some gelatins may gain credence from this work, since it is a product of the reaction shown in equation (1). Indeed, this hypothesis could be checked since trithionate is reducible at the dropping mercury electrode and its half-wave potential is considerably more negative than that of tetrathionate or thiosulphate. With a suitable choice of base electrolyte it may well be possible to determine thiosulphate and trithionate together in a single gelatin digest.

The results presented here establish that tetrathionate does not interfere with the polarographic method for the determination of thiosulphate. In the unlikely absence of sulphite the contribution of the extremely small tetrathionate wave may be neglected and in the presence of sulphite tetrathionate is quantitatively converted to thiosulphate.

References

(1) Steigmann, A., *Koll. Z.*, **46,** 57 (1928).
(2) Steigmann, A., *Sci. Industr. Photogr.*, **22,** 441 (1951).
(3) Russell, G., *J. Photogr. Sci.*, **4,** 94 (1956).
(4) Bassignana, P., Tagliafico, G. B. and Valbusa, L., *J. Photogr. Sci.*, **9,** 372 (1961).
(5) Timson, W. J., Kleim, P. O., Steigmann, A. E. and Kelly, W. O. Jr., *Photogr. Sci. Eng.*, **10,** 270 (1966).
(6) Janus, J. W. and Nellist, D. R., *J. Photogr. Sci.*, **15,** 270 (1967).
(7) Warburton, C. D. and Przybylowicz, E. P., *J. Photogr. Sci.*, **15,** 201 (1967).
(8) Stefan, V., *Chemicky Prum.*, **10,** 126 (1960).
(9) Wood, H. W., *J. Photogr. Sci.*, **2,** 154 (1954).
(10) Furness, W. and Davies, W. C., *Analyst*, **77,** 697 (1952).
(11) Grainger, F. and Mathewson, H. D., *J. Photogr. Sci.*, **13,** 269 (1965).

Reactions of Gold(I) with Gelatins

J. POURADIER, A. DE CUGNAC-PAILLIOTET
and M. C. GADET

Centre de Recherches de la Société Kodak-Pathé, Vincennes 94 (*France*)

ABSTRACT. The complexes of gold with photographic gelatin are divided into two classes according to their ease of dissociation with thiocyanate. The stable ones are attributed to reaction of the gold with impurities. The easily dissociable ones with groups on the gelatin molecule, possibly including histidine.

INTRODUCTION

Recent communications[1-3] on sensitization by noble metals have shown that the restraining action of gelatin is due to reactions occurring between this substance and the metal ions. Several constituents are liable to interfere and in order to determine the mechanism involved, we have studied the reactions of gold(I) with photographic gelatins and with their most active components.

EXPERIMENTAL

Reactions were followed potentiometrically with a gold electrode and a saturated calomel reference electrode dipping in the solution of the complex

GOLD ELECTRODE / SOLUTION { GOLD COMPLEX / EXCESS OF LIGAND } / REFERENCE ELECTRODE

Measurements were made at 63° $\pm$ 1°C.

To get significant results, it is necessary to measure potentials depending on the aurous ions concentration only. In fact, the potential of a gold electrode dipping in a solution of gelatin containing a gold(I) salt is neither stable, nor reproducible, but preliminary experiments have shown that, in agreement with the observation by Ammann–Brass[4], it is possible to obtain stable and significant values by adding a sufficient amount of alkaline thiocyanate ($(SCN^-) > 2 \times 10^{-3}$ M). The influence of thiocyanate on the response of the electrode is probably due to the mobility it gives to part of the gold. This displacement by thiocyanate of a part of the gold bound to gelatin is well shown by Fig. 1 where the potential E_{Au} is plotted against the thiocyanate concentration (logarithmic scale). After a zone of instability (hatched area), E_{Au} decreases when (SCN^-) increases and for the largest concentrations the curve is asymptotic to a straight line, the slope of which is -133 mV, i.e. the

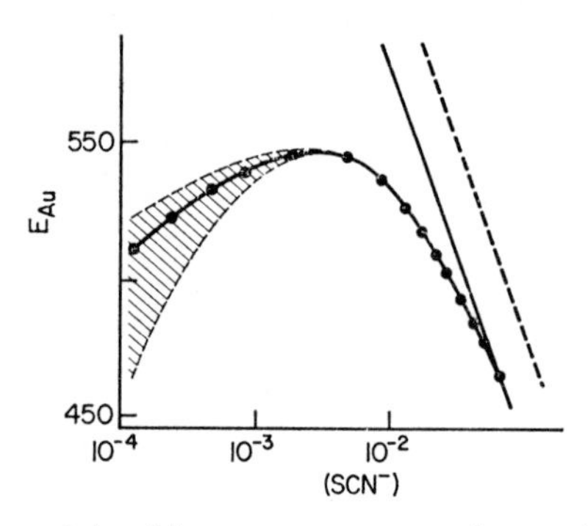

Fig. 1. Influence of the thiocyanate concentration on the response of a gold electrode dipping in a gelatin solution.

slope expected at this temperature for the aurodithiocyanate complex. This displacement is far from complete, as can be seen by comparing the results obtained with gelatin to those corresponding to aqueous solutions (dotted line) for the same amount of gold in solution. Therefore, according to their stability, the reaction products can be divided into two classes:

the weak dissociable compounds which are not modified by thiocyanate, at least up to a concentration of 5×10^{-1} M.

the more dissociable compounds able to yield aurous ions to thiocyanate when the concentration of this salt exceeds $1\text{–}2 \times 10^{-2}$ M.

The two ways of reaction can also be seen on the titration curves of gelatins by aurous salts and Fig. 2 shows the results obtained with an inert and unrestrained gelatin:

the labile sulphur content due to the thiosulphate is less than 1 ppm, and the sulphur dioxide content about 10 ppm.

The mathematical analysis of the potentiometric curve shows that the lowest part corresponds to microcomponents reacting energetically, while the highest part is associated to less reactive substances, but in larger quantity.

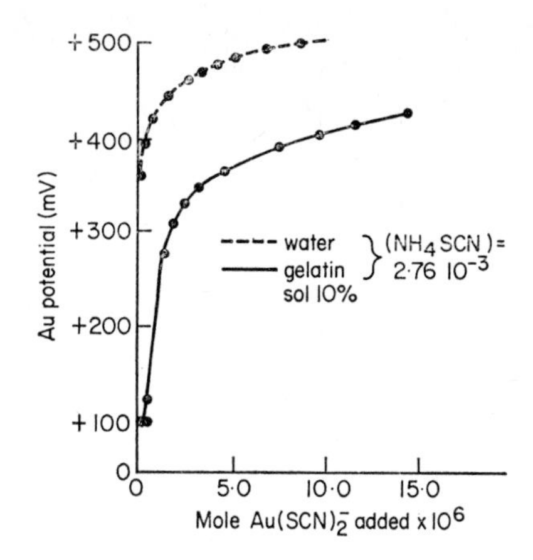

Fig. 2. Titration of an inert, unrestrained gelatin by a gold(I) salt.

Stable potential

As mentioned by Narath and Tiilikka[5], the gold electrode does not take a stable potential immediately after the addition of the gold salt to the gelatin solution, but a rather long time is needed to reach equilibrium. The time necessary to get stable values depends considerably on the amount of gold added and is longer when the additions of gold are smaller. For this gelatin, stable potentials are obtained in one hour or less when the amount of gold exceeds 5×10^{-7} mole/g of gelatin, with less than this concentration it is necessary to wait a longer time. In these conditions, titrations had to be made very slowly, chiefly at the beginning and, in our experiment, we took care to obtain potential equilibrium after each gold addition.

As explained above, the first part of the titration curve corresponds to microcomponents reacting energetically. Their content is higher in active gelatins than in inert ones, but they have been found in all gelatins even after an inertization treatment with active carbon.

Many components of photographic gelatins react with aurous salts but only a few, like thiosulphate, thiourea and sulphite[6–8] give low dissociation compounds similar to those obtained with gelatins. The co-ordination number of gold(I) being generally two, the gold ions are linked to two ligands in their stable complexes and with these chemicals they form the complexes $Au(S_2O_3)_2^{\equiv}$, $Au[SC(NH_2)_2]^+$ and probably $Au(SO_3)_2^{\equiv}$.

In the presence of gelatin, owing to the low concentration of the most reactive substances, the situation is complicated by the formation of mixed complexes. These mixed complexes can include simultaneously a very reactive ligand, for instance a thiosulphate ion, and one group of the gelatin molecule. In these conditions, the ligand and the gold ion are strongly bound to the gelatin and their mobilities are decreased.[8] They can be released by increasing the ligand concentration, since an excess of ligand displaces the gelatin from the mixed complex and gives rise to the formation of an homogeneous complex. This explains the observation by P. Faelens that gold can be washed out of a gelatin gel by a dilute thiosulphate solution.

Before leaving this type of compound, it should be noted that restrainers, like nucleic acid and their derivatives, are not reactive enough to form low dissociation compounds with gold(I) ions.

Gold complexes

Let us now consider the gold complexes having a stability near that of the aurodithiocyanate complex $Au(SCN)_2^-$. When the most reactive substances are saturated, new additions of gold give complexes which are decomposed by an excess of alkaline thiocyanate. Equilibrium between these complexes and $Au(SCN)_2^-$ allows determination of the amount of gold reversibly bound to gelatin for each value of E_{Au}. Introduction of these figures into the basis equation:

$$E_{Au} = E^{\circ}_{0-1} + \frac{RT}{F} \log \frac{(\text{conc. of gold reversibly associated with gelatin})}{(\text{concentration of ligand})^n} \quad (1)$$

(n is the number of ligands involved in the complex)

shows that the concentration of the ligand is not appreciably altered by the gold additions (up to 3 μ mole gold/g gelatin in our experiments). This means that the ligand content in gelatin considerably exceeds 3 μmole g^{-1}.

Influence of pH

In this range of gold concentrations, the potentials E_{Au} vary with the pH, but at constant pH, are little affected by the nature of the gelatin, except for low grade or very active gelatins. This observation seems to show that the second part of the titration curve is connected to the gelatin itself, rather than to its microcomponents.

The influence of the pH on the affinity of gelatin is probably due to the competition between hydrogen and aurous ions and we have to consider the ionization of the ligand

$$L + H^+ \rightleftharpoons LH^+$$

which is characterized by its pK

$$pH = pK + \log \frac{(L)}{(LH^+)} \quad (2)$$

If one or several molecules of the same ligand are bound by the metal ion, the concentration of the complex at equilibrium is related to the concentration of the active form of the ligand by equation (1): Introduction of the ionization constant in this equation leads to:

$$E_{Au} - 2{\cdot}3 \frac{RT}{F} \log (\text{gold complex})$$

$$= E^{\circ}_{0-1} - 2{\cdot}3 \frac{nRT}{F} [pH - pK + \log (LH^+)] \quad (3)$$

To determine n, we can observe that at low pH, far beneath the pK, the ligand is almost wholly associated with hydrogen ions and at constant concentration of gelatin, the complete equation can be simplified:

$$E_{Au} - 2{\cdot}3 \frac{RT}{F} \log (\text{gold complex}) = Cste - 2{\cdot}3 \frac{nRT}{F} pH \quad (4)$$

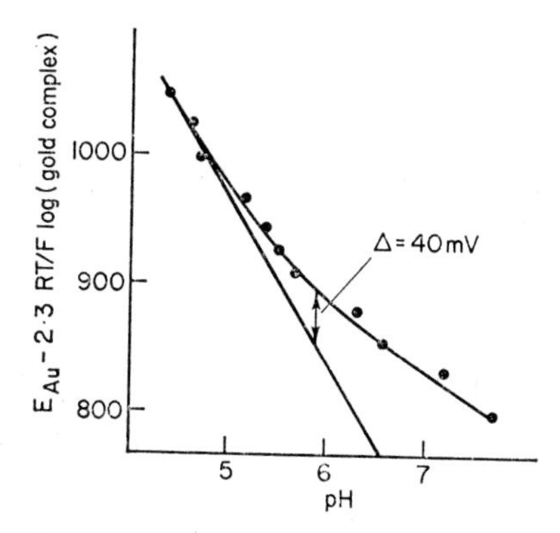

Fig. 3. Influence of the pH on the dissociation of the gelatin-gold(I) complex.

Actually, the plot of the experimental values in this system of coordinates gives at low pH (<5·0) straight lines (Fig. 3), the slopes -130 ± 5 mV of which correspond to $n = 2$.

The two ligands belong probably to the same gelatin molecule and the structure is stabilized by the formation of a chelate.

When pH = pK, half the ligand is ionized and the difference between the curve and its asymptote is $\frac{nRT}{F}$ Log 2 or 40 mV. Referring to this curve and similar ones obtained with other gelatins, this difference corresponds to pH = 5·9 ± 0·1. The only constituent of gelatin having a comparable pK is histidine (at 63°C the pK of the imidazole group of histidine is 5·55 ± 0·05).

The complete equation (3) fits experimental results up to pH ⩽6·3, but above, the agreement is not so good. The discrepancy, which increases with pH, results probably from the simplification made when it has been assumed that the two ligands are the same. In fact, due to the low concentration of histidine in gelatin (~4 10^{-5} mole g^{-1} or 3 residues for a molecular weight of 75 000), it is possible that another constituent of gelatin interferes and it is necessary to take into account this interference. This leads to a more complicated system of equations and for two ligands L_1 and L_2, we have to solve the three equations:

$$\begin{cases} E_{Au} = E^{\circ}_{0-1} + \dfrac{RT}{F} \log \dfrac{[\text{gold complex}]}{[\text{Ligand 1}][\text{Ligand 2}]} \\ \text{pH} = \text{pK}_1 + \log \dfrac{[L_1]}{[L_1H^+]} \\ \text{pH} = \text{pK}_2 + \log \dfrac{[L_2]}{[L_2H^+]} \end{cases}$$

The figures which fit best the curve of Fig. 3 and similar ones obtained with other gelatins are:

$$\text{pK}_1 = 5{\cdot}6 \pm 0{\cdot}3$$
$$\text{pK}_2 > 7{\cdot}5$$

For L_2 it would be desirable to make experiments at high pH to distinguish between lysine, hydroxylysine, arginine . . . but measurements in these conditions are disturbed by reduction and disproportionation reactions. Concerning the reduction, we must notice that, even at low pH, a platinum and a gold electrode dipping in a solution of gelatin containing aurous ions have not the same potential. The difference, which can reach 200 mV, is due to the presence in gelatin of reducers reacting very slowly with the aurous complexes.

Besides histidine, other amino-acids like methionine combine strongly with metal ions and in order to compare their behaviours, we have measured their affinity for aurous ions. The results will be published fully later and we shall only consider here the standard potentials E°_{0-1} which characterize the stability of the complexes formed.

At 63°C,

$Au(SCN)_2^-$	+640		
Au(SCN)(Meth)	+705	Au(SCN)(Hist)	+650
$Au(Meth)_2^+$	+845	$Au(Hist)_2^+$	+690
	for pH between 3·5–6·5		

(Cysteine is not considered, being not a gelatin component).

The comparison of these standard potentials shows the higher stability of histidine complexes, and explains the role of this amino-acid in the complexing of gold(I) by gelatin at pH >4.

CONCLUSION

It appears that according to the amount of gold added to gelatin, we have to consider two mechanisms of reaction of gold(I) with gelatin.

When the gold content is low, the gold ions are bound by one coordinate to a very reactive microcomponent of the gelatin and by the other to a group of the gelatin molecule. In these conditions, the microcomponent, the thiosulphate for instance, is bound to the gelatin and its reactivity is modified.

When the gold content is sufficient to saturate the most reactive substances, the excess of gold is bound to two groups of the gelatin molecule and probably forms a chelate.

Whatever the gold concentration, the same groups of the gelatin interfere. At low pH, when all the histidine is ionized, methionine is probably the principal complexing residue of gelatin. This observation is confirmed by Tavernier and De Meyer[(9)] in their study on gold(I) thioether complexes.

But at higher pH, when histidine is partly or totally undissociated, this amino-acid is more reactive than methionine and in the pH range of the chemical sensitization of photographic emulsion, gold is chiefly bound to the histidine groups of gelatin.

References

(1) Krummenerl, Th., *Z. Wiss. Photogr. Photophys. Photochem.*, **51,** 137–156 (1956).
(2) Steigmann, A., *Sci. Ind. Photogr.*, (2), **29,** 262–265 (1958).
(3) Tavernier, B. and Faelens, P., *Sci. Ind. Photogr.*, (2), **33,** 125–128 (1962).

(4) Ammann-Brass, H., Private communication.
(5) Narath, A. and Tiilikka, A., *J. Photogr. Sci.*, **9**, 303–311 (1961).
(6) Makarov, N. V. and Shchekochikhina, V. O., *Zh. Nauch. Prikl. Fotogr. Kinematogr.*, **9**, 126–127 (1964); *Sci. Ind. Photogr.*, (2), **35**, 311 (1964).
(7) Borginon, H., see this book.
(8) Pouradier, J. and Gadet, M. C., *Photogr. Korresp.*, in press.
(9) Tavernier, B. and de Meyer, A., C. R. 36*ème Congrès Intern. Chim. Indle.*, Brussels, Sept. 1966, III, 287–288.

The Gold(I)-Ion Binding of Photographic Gelatin*

H. BORGINON

Chemical Research Laboratories, Agfa-Gevaert N. V. Mortsel, (Belgium)

ABSTRACT. A potentiometric method is described for the measurement of the gold(I)-ion binding of photographic gelatin. At high pH the gold(I)-ion binding of the gelatin macromolecule can be explained on the basis of the amino acid composition. Histidine, lysine, arginine, tyrosine and methionine contribute to the binding of gold(I)-ions. At low pH however these amino acids alone do not explain the binding of gold(I)-ions. Probably a chelate is formed. Among the impurities present in geltin, which are capable of increasing the pAu, sulphite must be mentioned in the first place. Attention is also drawn to the presence of bactericides, such as phenol.

INTRODUCTION

In the literature concerning the interaction of gelatin and gold-ions it has been stated that the gold(III)-ions are reduced to gold(I)-ions by the gelatin macromolecule,[1],[2],[3] the methionine groups being mainly responsible for this reaction,[4] and that the gold(I)-ions in a subsequent reaction are complexed by gelatin.[2],[3],[5],[6]

Completely different is the viewpoint expressed by Walther[7] who concluded from polarographic measurements that gold(III)-ions are bound to gelatin, thereby supporting the earlier conception of Steigmann.[8] Gold(I)-ions however are not complexed by gelatin but react with some of the micro-components present in gelatin to form colloidal gold or gold-sulphide.

It is the purpose of this paper to give more evidence based on pAu measurements for the first hypothesis that gold(I)-ions are really bound by the gelatin macromolecule and by its impurities.

* Research sponsored by the Belgian Institute of Scientific Research in Industry and Agronomy.

EXPERIMENTAL

The pAu-measurement and its significance

pAu measurements were performed at 40°C with the aid of a gold electrode in the form of a 1 mm rod immersed in the solution to a depth of 50 mm. A saturated calomel electrode served as a reference. A bridge of saturated potassium nitrate was used to avoid contamination of the calomel electrode.

pAu-measurements are more difficult than pAg determinations for several reasons. A first difficulty is the fact that gold ions can occur as gold(III)- or as gold(I)-ions. In the practice of the chemical sensitization of a photographic emulsion the free gold(I)-ion concentration is the most important since the oxidation reduction equilibrium is practically completely shifted towards the gold(I)ions, due to the presence of large quantitities of thiocyanate ions and gelatin.

A second difficulty is that solutions of known concentration of the free gold(I)-ions are needed for the calibration of the pAu(I)-measurements which from now on will simply be called pAu-measurements. Gold(I)-ions, however never exist under the form of a completely dissociated salt but always occur as complexes.

For this investigation the calibration of the potentiometric measurements was done with a solution containing $2{\cdot}9 \times 10^{-5}$ moles of gold ions and 10^{-3} moles of thiocyanate ions per litre, together with 10^{-1} moles of potassium nitrate in order to increase the conductivity of the solution and consequently the sensitivty of the measurements.

It is possible to calculate the pAu-value of this solution both from potentiometric measurements and from the value of the complex constant of $[Au(SCN)_2]^-$.

(a) *pAu-value determined by potentiometric measurements*

For the solution used for the calibration, a potential E_x (expressed against a saturated calomelelectrode) was measured equal to 533 $\pm$ 3 mV.

Charlot[9] mentions a standard redox potential of the system Au/Au^+ equal to +1680 mV at room temperature. The exact temperature dependence is not known. Even the value of +1680 mV itself is not certain and values of +1500 or 1700 are also found in the literature. As a first approximation however, this value can be used.

The saturated calomel electrode has a standard potential at 40°C of $E_{0\,Cal} = +230$ mV.[10]

In this way the pAu may be calculated:

$$E_x = E_{0\ Au/Au^+} - E_{0\ Cal} - 2{\cdot}3\,\frac{RT}{F}\,pAu \tag{1}$$

or

$$533\ mV = (1680 - 230 - 62\ pAu)\ mV \tag{2}$$

or

$$pAu = 14{\cdot}8 \tag{3}$$

(b) *pAu-value calculated from the complex constant*

Kiehl[11] determined the complex constant of $Au(SCN)_2^-$ and found a value equal to $10^{-16\cdot9}$.

$$\frac{[Au^+][SCN^-]^2}{[Au(SCN)_2^-]} = 10^{-16\cdot9} \tag{4}$$

The added quantity of gold(I)-ions, $2{\cdot}9 \times 10^{-5}$ mole/l, is large compared with the free gold(I)-ion concentration measured: $10^{-14\cdot8}$. As a first approximation the concentration of the complex may be substituted by the total quantity of gold salt added. In the same way the concentration of free thiocyanate ions may be substituted by the total concentration of added thiocyanate since the latter (10^{-3} mole/l) is relatively large compared with the amount of thiocyanate present in the complex ($2 \times 2{\cdot}9 \times 10^{-5}$). Approximately equation (4) becomes:

$$\frac{[Au^+][1{\cdot}10^{-3}]^2}{2{\cdot}9 \times 10^{-5}} = 10^{-16\cdot9} \tag{5}$$

or

$$[Au^+] = 10^{-15\cdot4} \tag{6}$$

or

$$pAu = 15{\cdot}4 \tag{7}$$

This calculated value 15·4 differs slightly from the experimental value 14·8. A better correlation was hardly to be expected since all the values found in the literature and used in the calculations, namely the standard potentials and the complex constants, are to be taken with a certain reserve. Furthermore their temperature coefficients are not exactly known.

Last but not least, experimental errors may be due to the electrodes as well as to the solution which is not as well defined as for example a silver nitrate solution.

It is not the purpose of this paper to give exact pAu-values but merely to describe semi-quantitatively the binding of gold(I)-ions to some interesting ingredients of a photographic emulsion such as gelatin and its impurities. The calibration mentioned only serves to situate the significance of the measurements.

It is for this reason that, in the following pages, only the measured potentials will be mentioned and not the corresponding pAu.

The procedure adopted for pAu-measurements

230 ml of the calibration solution is put in a vessel, thermostated at 40°C, and the potential is measured as outlined above. This should be 533 $\pm$ 3 mV. 20 ml of the solution of the compounds under investigation are then added, the pH is adjusted to the desired value and as soon as possible the potential is measured again, always under mechanical stirring.

The amount of gold salt used, $2{\cdot}9 \times 10^{-5}$ mole/l, which is still very small, should not be smaller than used here: the adsorption of the gold-ions to the gold electrode becomes too large with respect to the amount of gold-ions present in the solution so that the concentration in the solution changes too much. This is exactly the same for the pAg-measurements of very dilute silver nitrate solutions. When the dilution becomes too high it is impossible to measure a significant pAg-value.

Even at this concentration of gold-ions, which largely exceeds the one used in a photographic emulsion, difficulties are not out of the way. Reproducible values can however be obtained when after each measurement of a sample, the gold electrode is regenerated by measuring the calibration solution again. For this solution the same potential can always be measured.

Gelatin solutions to be measured

In the case of gelatin 10% aqueous solutions were always used. 20 ml of these solutions were added to 230 ml of the calibration solution, and the pH was adjusted.

Under the term "inert gelatin" is understood gelatin which contains no or only traces of thiosulphate, nucleic acid or sulphite.

Expression of the results

The measurements of the potential are expressed as a decrease of potential ($-\Delta$ mV) compared with the one measured for the calibration solution.

RESULTS

The binding of gold(I)-ions to different gelatins at pH 5

For several inert gelatins, the pAu was measured at pH 5 as described above.

In Fig. 1 the potential decrease ($-\Delta$ mV) is given for a series of different gelatins. In general the potential decrease is larger for hide gelatins than for bone gelatins.

The differences between the gelatins are not due to some ionic impurity since they remain even after demineralization (gelatins 11 and 21).

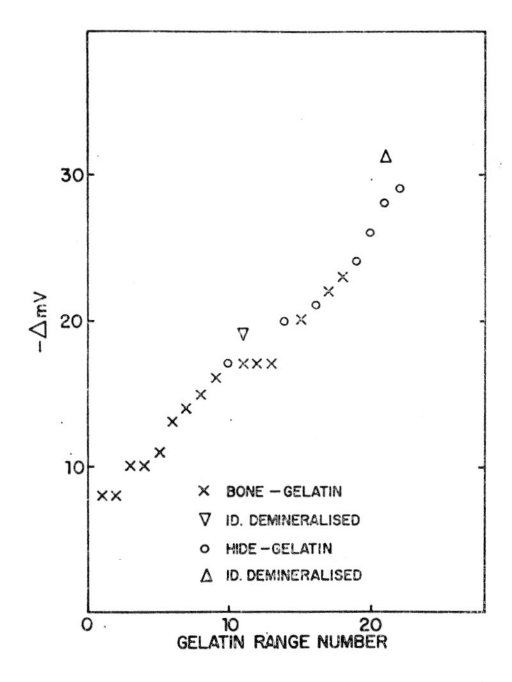

Fig. 1. Potential decrease at pH 5 for several inert gelatins.

The results of Fig. 1 could suggest the existence of two extreme types of gelatin, caused by the choice, or by the treatment of the raw material, the other gelatins being mixtures of the two extreme types. Mixtures were made of two gelatins with extreme pAu values. It was found (Fig. 2) that the gelatin that most strongly binds the gold(I)-ions, has relatively the largest effect on the measured potential decrease.

It was further observed that the difference in potential decrease almost completely disappeared when the gelatins were previously digested at pH 10 at 50°C during about 200 min. A potential decrease (at pH 5) of 15–17 mV was obtained after this treatment for all inert gelatins.

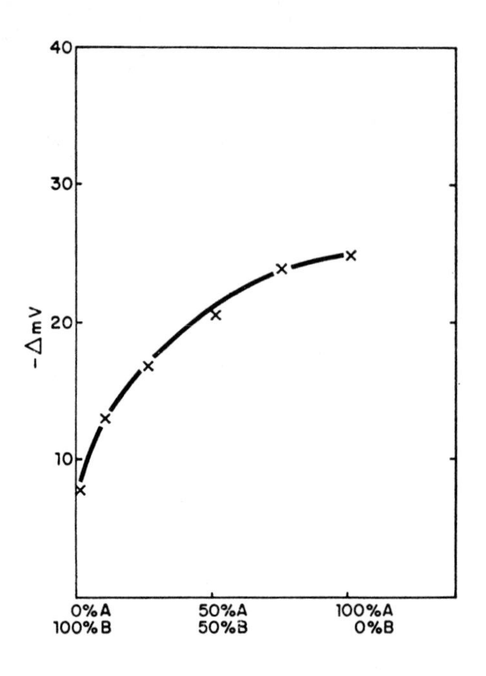

Fig. 2. Potential decrease for mixtures of gelatins.

The binding of gold(I)-ions to different gelatins at pH 9·3

For a number of the gelatins mentioned in Fig. 1, the measurements were repeated at pH 9·3. The potential decrease obtained was much larger (200–220 mV) and was reversible when the pH was lowered. This indicates a stronger binding of gold(I)-ions to the gelatin at high pH. The differences from one inert gelatin to the other were larger than at pH 5. Remarkable was that the gelatins from one manufacturer had an abnormal behaviour. The potential decrease was about 400 mV compared to 200 mV for the other gelatins. This could be attributed to the presence of phenol-like preservatives present in these gelatins.

Functional groups of the gelatin molecule involved in the binding of gold(I)-ions

In order to investigate to what kind of functional groups the gold(I)-ions are bound in the gelatin macromolecule, the most representative amino acids were studied with respect to their capacity for binding gold(I)-ions. The concentrations of these amino acids were chosen so that they correspond broadly to those wherein they occur in gelatin. The results are tabulated in Table 1.

Table 1

The binding of gold(I)-ions to different amino acids in function of the pH

Substance	*Concentration of the added solution (in %)*	*Potential decrease* ($-\Delta mV$)		
		pH 5	*pH* 7	*pH* 9
alanine	1	1	3	18
alanine	10	−3	8	171
histidine	0·1	0	17	87
arginine	1	0	4	62
lysine	0·5	−1	1	61
glutamic acid	1·5	−4	0	17
hydroxypyroline	1	−1	0	10
tyrosine	0·1	0	4	56
methionine	0·1	3	3	18
cystine	0·01	0	0	26
bone gelatin 1	10	8	90	178
hide gelatin 21	10	19	88	191
mixture containing: tyrosine 0·1%, histidine 0·07%, lysine 0·45%, arginine 0·85%		0	19	173

From the results reported on Table 1, it appears that the potential decrease, measured for gelatin at pH 9, can be explained by some of its constituent amino acids, such as the basic amino acids histidine arginine and lysine as well as tyrosine.

The other amino acids can also bind gold(I)-ions to a lesser degree, mainly by their amino groups, which are however not free in a plypeptide chain.

At pH 5 and pH 7, the binding of the gold(I)-ions by gelatin cannot be explained any more by its amino acid composition.

4. Influence of gelatin impurities on the potential measured against the gold electrode

In order to measure the influence of gelatin impurities on the binding of gold(I)-ions, the gelatins were previously digested at pH 10 at 50°C during 200 min so that the intrinsic differences in gold(I)-ion binding of these gelatins disappeared, as was shown under Result I. The potential decrease was measured at pH 5.

At pH 5 the most important gelatin impurity which influences the potential is sulphite. To a gelatin which by itself contains 10 ppm sulphur dioxide, determined according to the distillation method,[12] increased quantities of sulphite were added and the potential decrease measured. The results are mentioned in Table 2.

Table 2

ppm SO_2 *added*	$-\Delta$ *mV*
0	15
75	26
200	48
400	84

At this pH the influence of nucleic acid is negligible. The influence of the small amounts of thiosulphate present in gelatin is in most cases also very small. An addition of 150 ppm thiosulphate, or about 30 ppm labile sulphur, which is an extreme high dosis for gelatin, gives only a potential decrease of 25 mV. For normal gelatins the decrease in potential caused by thiosulphate can only be of the order of a few millivolts.

In this way the pAu-measurement can be employed for the estimation of the sulphur dioxide content of a gelatin. In Fig. 3 the sulphur dioxide determinations are shown. The correlation is not perfect, but is good enough for a rough estimation.

CONCLUSIONS

1. A method is described by which it is possible to obtain reproducible and significant values for the potential of the gold electrode in equilibrium with gold solutions containing gelatin, and the saturated calomel electrode.
2. At pH 5 small differences between several inert gelatins are detected with pAu(I)-measurements. These differences disappear after

digestion at high pH and are not due to ionic impurities since they persist after demineralization.

3. Among the gelatin impurities, sulphite interferes mostly in the pAu(I)-measurements at pH 5, in such a way that pAu(I)-determinations can be employed for a rough estimation of the sulphite content of gelatin.

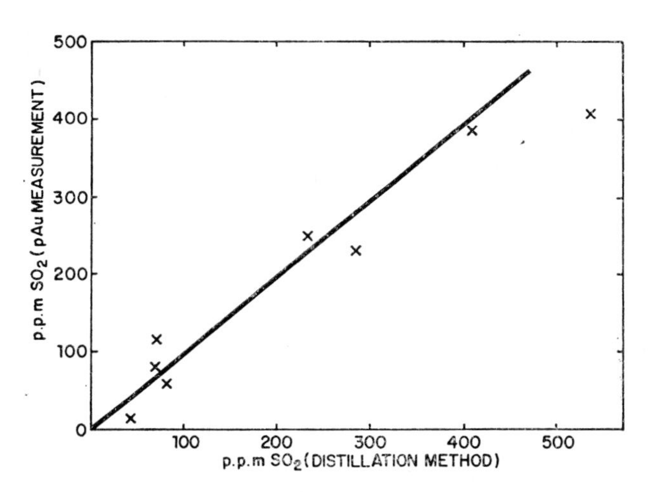

Fig. 3. Correlation between the SO^2 determination according to the distillation method and according to pAu measurements.

4. The potential measured at pH 5 or 7 for inert gelatins cannot be explained by the amino acid composition of the gelatin macromolecule.

5. At pH 9 the gold(I)-ion binding by gelatin increases considerably. This can be quantitatively explained by the presence of the imidazole groups of histidine the guanidyl groups of arginine, the ε-amino groups of lysine and the phenolic groups of tyrosine.

6. Several gelatins containing phenol-like preservatives, show a very low potential at pH 9.

References

(1) Faelens, P., *Wissenschaftliche Internationale Konferenz Köln 1956*, Verlag Dr. O. Helwich (Darmstadt, 1958), p. 258.
(2) Bontoux, J., *Annales Pharma. Françaises*, **22**, 443 (1964).
(3) Tavernier, B. and Faelens, P., *Sci. Ind. Photogr.*, **33**, 125 (1962).
(4) Pouradier, J., Maillet, A. M. and Cerisy, B., *J. Chim. Phys.*, **63**, 469 (1966).
(5) Krummenerl, Th., *Z. wiss. Photogr., Photophysik Photochem.*, **51**, 137 (1956).
(6) Narath, A. and Tiilikka, A., *J. Photogr. Sci.*, **9**, 303 (1961).

(7) Walther, D., *Veröffentlichungen der wissenschaftlichen Photo-Laboratorien Wolfen*, Band X, Verlag S. Hirzel (Leipzig, 1965), p. 37.
(8) Steigmann, A., *Brit. J. Photogr.*, 144 (1958).
(9) Charlot, G., *L'analyse qualitative et les réactions en solutions*, 4e edition, Masson et Cie (Paris, 1957), p. 267.
(10) Gladstone, S., *Textbook of Physical Chemistry*, 2nd edition, MacMillan and Co. Ltd. (London, 1953), p. 941.
(11) Kiehl, C., *Z. Phys. Chem.*, **232,** 384 (1966).
(12) Francis, A. C. and Pilgrim, A. I., *Analyst*, **69,** 90 (1944).

The Production and Photographic Properties of Gelatin Derived from Soluble Collagen

W. M. McKERNAN and B. J. M. WOODS
Croda Food Products, Bermondsey, London

ABSTRACT. A process has been developed whereby, by alkaline treatment, collagen is converted to a single uniform molecular weight fraction. The physical and photographic properties of this type of gelatin have been studied and contrasted with conventional photographic gelatins prepared from the same raw materials by the liming process.

It has been found that gelatin derived from soluble collagen by alkaline treatment contains lower quantities of photographically impurities, in particular, very low levels of restraining compounds.

Gelatin and Crystal Growth

The Influence of Gelatin on the Growth of Silver Halide Macrocrystals*

* Work undertaken under the auspices of IRSIA and the Company Agfa-Gevaert.

F. ORBAN

University of Liège, Belgium

ABSTRACT. The morphological influence of gelatin on the growth, from ammoniacal solutions, of macrocrystals of silver bromide and silver chloride has been studied.

When silver bromide grows in gelatin, tabular crystals are formed. Laue's patterns of these crystals present a well marked asterism, resulting from an intense adsorption of gelatin.

AgCl crystals are limited by (100) faces in the presence of gelatin and by (111) faces when there is no gelatin; the experimental conditions being of course identical in both cases.

Some ideas are presented concerning mechanisms that are likely to lead to the observed phenomenons.

INTRODUCTION

The influence of gelatin on the growth of the emulsion grains has frequently been studied. The morphological effects resulting from the variation of various parameters typical of the binding material (purity, concentration, nature of gelatin are known). However, the mechanisms which provoke the action of gelatin are practically unknown.

This paper presents some experimental results concerning the influence of gelatin on the growth of macrocrystals of silver bromide and silver chloride.

On the basis of these results some assumptions concerning action mechanisms of gelatin can be drawn.

EXPERIMENTAL

A powder of AgBr crystals is obtained by mixing molar solutions of KBr and $AgNO_3$ as follows:

$$KBr + AgNO_3 \rightarrow KNO_3 + AgBr$$

The precipitate is then washed carefully in order to eliminate soluble salts which are formed, and the possible small excess of one of the saline components. After drying, the powder of silver bromide is dissolved until saturation is gelatinized ammoniacal solutions at 40°C. The table summarizes the concentrations in ammonia and in gelatin.

Table 1

Sample	*Concentration in* NH_3	*Concentration in gelatin*
A	15%	0·2 mg/cm^3
B	5%	2·8 mg/cm^3
C	1%	6·6 mg/cm^3

Test solutions A′, B′, C′ without gelatin and with concentrations in NH_3 respectively equal to those of A, B, C are saturated in AgBr. After that, all the solutions are evaporated slowly at 45°C.

RESULTS

The crystals of the preparation A (0·2 g gelatin/l) and of the preparation A′ (without gelatin) are similar in shape and dimension; in this stage of concentration gelatin has apparently no influence on the crystallization process.

Fig. 1 shows the crystals of the class B. Rectangular tablets appear at the apex of the crystals. The face of great extension of these tablets is perpendicular to the fourfold axis passing by the apex of the octahedron, and is probably a (100) face. Unfortunately, the irregularity and the small dimension of these surfaces did not enable a check to be made at this point with a Wollaston's goniometer.

The dimension of these crystals varies between 0·5 and 1 mm. The crystals of the preparation B′ without gelatin are octahedrons or tetrahedrons with one apex missing. The dimension varies between 0·5 and 1 mm. The crystals are similar to those obtained from an ammoniacal solution containing 15% NH_3 and they never exhibit dendritic growth as is the case for the crystals of the class B which have the same concentration in NH_3, but which contain gelatin.

Fig. 2 shows the crystals of the class C which are much wider (2–3 mm) and more flattened (0·3 m) than those of the class B. The protuberant edges are the prolongation of the lateral faces with small surface. The tablets at the apexes have an hexagonal form, more or less regular. They are wider and thinner than those of the crystals belonging to the class B. The preparation C′ resulted in irregular crystals and they

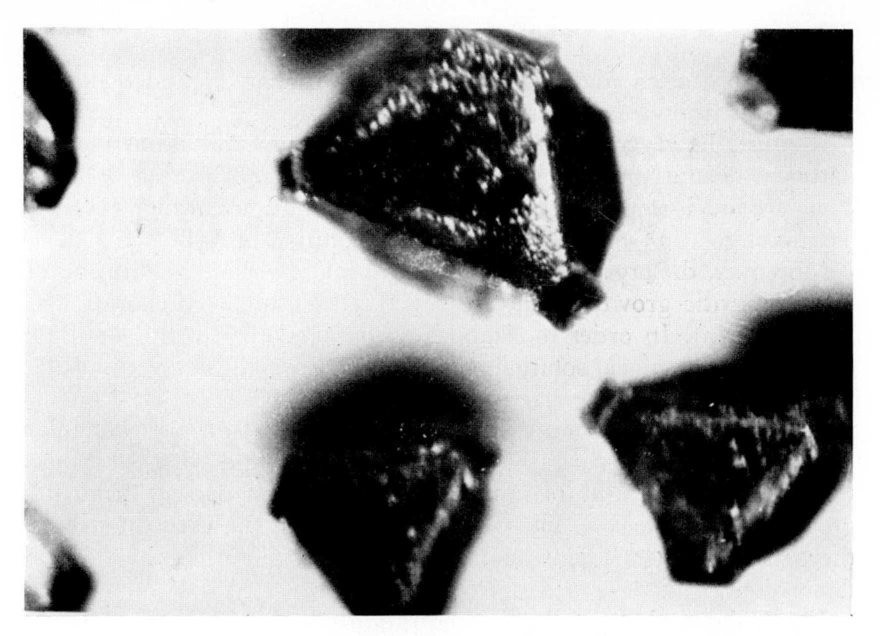

Fig. 1. AgBr crystals growing in a gelatinized (2·8 mg/cm^3) ammoniacal solution (5% NH_3).

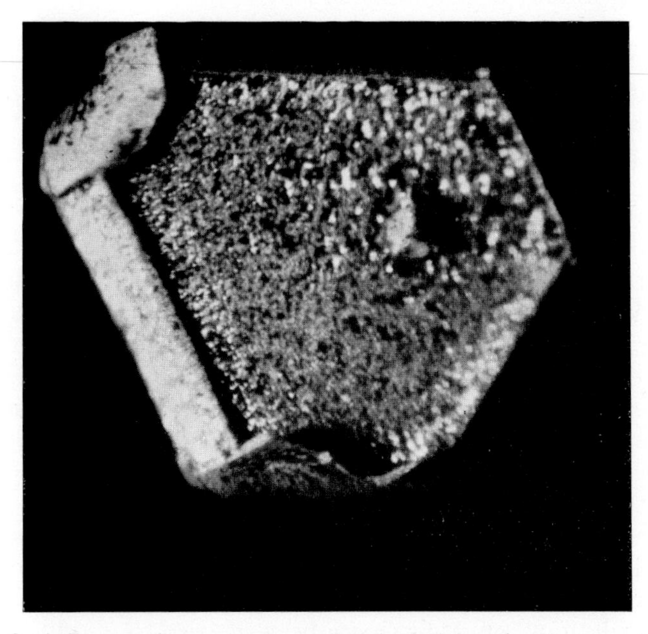

Fig. 2. AgBr crystals growing in a gelatinized (6·6 mg/cm^3) ammoniacal solution (1% NH_3).

appear more often under the form of tablets (Fig. 3) and dendrites whose dimension sometimes reaches 11 mm (Fig. 4).

It must, however, be pointed out that the greatest dimension of flattened crystals belonging to the class C′ does not exceed 0·7 mm. They are much smaller than those of the preparation C which contains 6·6 mg of gelatin per cm^3 of ammoniacal solution of AgBr.

Moreover, the crystals of the preparation C′ (without gelatin) never have dendritic growth at the apexes like those of the preparation C (with gelatin). In order to establish a comparison with the emulsion grains an ammoniacal solution of AgBr with a weight of gelatin of 3% was prepared.

At this concentration, the crystals are hexagonal or triangular tablets whose width varies between 1 and 4 mm and whose thickness varies between 0·1 and 0·2 mm; but they no longer present dendritics growth at their apexes (Fig. 5); in opposition to the preceding cases, there is no general depression of the faces, but they have local depressions.

Fig. 6 shows that, at this concentration of gelatin, the crystals are composed of superposed layers of AgBr with an incrustation of gelatin; these incrustations have appeared in the presence of pepsin mixed with some milligrammes of thiosulphate.

In Fig. 6, three perfectly linear furrows make an angle of 120°. This figure is similar to those observed by Evans and Mitchell. It is probably a dendritic growth with dislocations. This defect can also be found though not so accentuated, in hexagonal crystals (Fig. 7). Laue's patterns present a sixfold or a threefold symmetry but they never have two centres of symmetry as is the case for certain crystals which are prepared by evaporation without gelatin.

Many diagrams present an important asterism (Fig. 8). This phenomenon has never been seen in the other crystals prepared without gelatin. We suppose, like Herz, that gelatin produces internal stresses which are responsible for a distortion of the crystal lattice.

On the other hand, if the gelatin is added during the growth, tabular growth is favoured. The height of the crystals remains practically unchanged compared to what it was before addition of the binding material. In short, the crystals formed without gelatin are rather globular, but their height is smaller than their width.

In the experimental conditions described, the gelatin modifies the growth of the crystals by stopping the growth of two opposite faces.

Crystallizations of AgCl using the same techniques as those used in the crystallization of AgBr have been carried out and the most important results are summarized. When the crystallization rate is low

Fig. 3. AgBr crystals growing in ammoniacal solution (1% NH_3) without gelatin.

Fig. 4. Dendrites growing under the same conditions as in Fig. 3.

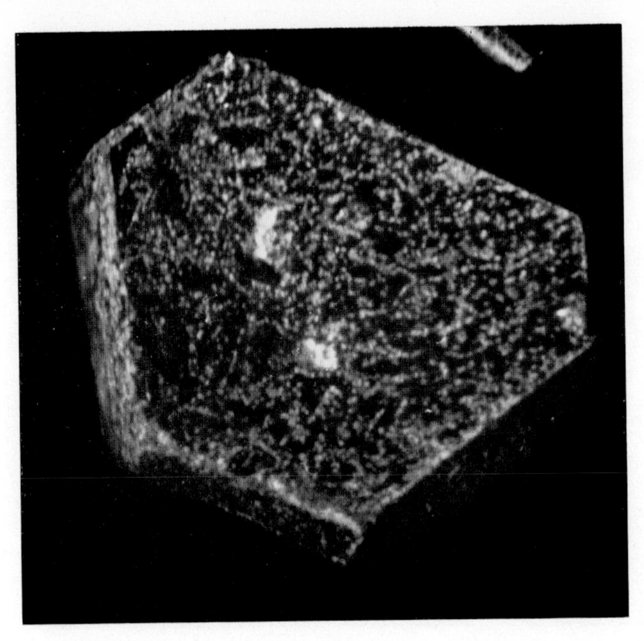

Fig. 5. Flattened AgBr crystal growing in an ammoniacal solution with 3% gelatin.

Fig. 6. This figure shows that the crystals prepared in a 3% gelatinized ammoniacal solution are composed of superposed layers. The crystal exhibit three linear furrows.

Fig. 7. Hexagonal crystal prepared in the same conditions as in Fig. 6.

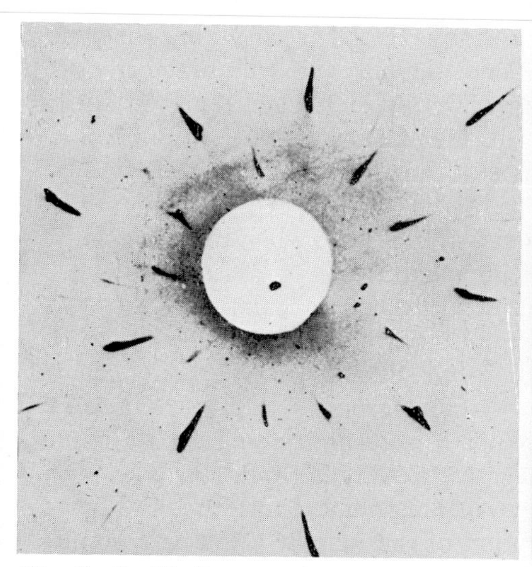

Fig. 8. R. X diagram of one Ag-Br crystal prepared in a 3% gelatinized solution. The diagram presents an important asterism.

Fig. 9. AgCl cubical crystals growing in a gelatinized (5%) ammoniacal solution.

and when there is no gelatin, the crystals of AgCl usually take an hexagonal or triangular form; a quick crystallization (by cooling) gives cubical crystals with (100) faces.

The slow crystallization with a small quantity of gelatin ($=1$ mg/cm^3) gives a certain proportion of cubical crystals.

This proportion increases when the concentration of gelatin increases. For a 5% concentration, all the crystals have a cubical form (Fig. 9). The edges of these crystals are not always equal and the angle between the faces is sometimes 10° or 15° superior or inferior to the expected 90°. There is thus a formation of vicinal faces.

DISCUSSION ON THE RESULTS

The shape of the macrocrystals of emulsion grains is frequently interpreted by the value of the pAg of the solution of precipitation.

When the pAg is large ($=8$ or 9), the Br^- ions are preferentially absorbed by the (111) faces.

The adsorption film formed inhibits the growth of these faces; the (100) faces which are growing, would finally disappear.

The (111) faces of macrocrystals prepared in ammoniacal medium could be explained by the Br^- excess.

In this case, the pAg was comprised between 7·5 and 9·9.

In fact, the questions are not as simple as they seem to be; the facts lead us to suppose that the pAg is not the only important factor.

1. AgCl crystals with (100) faces are obtained when the crystallization is rapid and AgCl crystals with (111) faces when the crystallization is slow. This shows the importance of the growth rate on the crystals' shape.

2. The AgCl crystals are limited by (100) faces when there is gelatin and by (111) faces when there is no gelatin.

3. Laue's patterns of AgBr crystals formed in gelatinous medium present a well-marked asterism, resulting from the great adsorption of the gelatin. In ammoniacal medium, i.e. alkaline, the carboxyl group of the gelatin—COOH ionizes to COO^- groups—so that the gelatin acquires a negative charge. It is not easy to understand such a great adsorption on faces which are negatively charged by Br^- ions.

When the crystallizations occur in ammoniacal medium, the complex ions can modify the adsorption of the ions Br^- and as a result, modify the intervention of the latter in the growth of the crystals; in other words, the preponderance of one type of ions would be determined by experimental conditions.

To get a precise idea of the processes which determine the formation of the faces, it seems necessary to undertake new experiments which will enable us to answer several important questions such as:

what is the nature of the ions of the crystal lattice which form the boundary (111) faces of the crystals of AgBr or AgCl?

in the case of a precipitation or a crystallization in ammoniacal medium and with a high pAg,

(a) which ion $[Ag(NH_3)_2]^+$ or Br^- is first adsorbed?
(b) do the complex ions $[Ag(NH_3)_2]^+$ accelerate or inhibit the growth of the faces on which they are fixed?

With the increasing concentration of gelatin, the crystals of AgBr are more and more flattened.

Concentrations below 0·7% provoke a dendritics growth of the edges and of the apexes. Above 1%, this dendritic growth disappears and the tabular form appears more clearly. The gelatin then creates important strains (see Laue's patterns).

These facts suggest that as gelatin is adsorbed on two opposite faces, it prevents Br^- and Ag^+ ions from depositing on these faces and so inhibits their growth.

To explain the fact that the gelatin is adsorbed more intensely on two opposite (111) faces, than on the other ones having the same indices, it must be supposed that the strength with which the gelatin adheres to the face is proportional to the surface of this face. It has been previously pointed out that the crystals prepared without gelatin were always more wide than high. This dimensional inequality must exist as soon as the germ is formed. As a result, at the beginning of the crystallization, the necessary conditions are brought together in order to allow a preferential adsorption to take place on two opposite (111) faces.

The inclusions of gelatin were produced during the ionic growth of the crystals. It suggests that the coalescence growth of macrocrystals of emulsions is not the only mechanism of imprisonment of the gelatin inside the crystalline structure.

ACKNOWLEDGEMENTS

I thank Prof. A. Hautot warmly for his judicious advice and for the encouragements I have constantly received from him.

The Influence of Different Gelatins on Crystal Habit and Grain Size of Silver Halide

F. MOLL

Agfa-Gevaert AG, Leverkusen, Germany

ABSTRACT. Electron microscopic investigations using simple chloro-bromide emulsions (7% bromide) revealed that crystal habit and grain size are decisively influenced by the amount of nucleic acids present in the gelatin. The restraining action can be strongly reduced by a treatment of the gelatin solution with active carbon. The molecular weight of the gelatin seems to influence the formation of the grains. Differences in the grain habit are observed, when gelatins degraded by various enzymes are employed.

INTRODUCTION

Photographic silver halide emulsions are usually prepared by mixing soluble silver salts and alkali halides in the presence of gelatin as protective colloid. Immediately after the mixing silver halide crystal nuclei are formed which undergo a subsequent growth process. The dispersity and shape of the crystals obtained during this growth process are governed by the properties of the liquid phase, e.g. pAg, pH and temperature, but also by the nature of the gelatin employed. Particularly the nucleic acids or their disintegration products,[(1)] present in various gelatins, exert a considerable influence as growth restrainers of silver halide grains.

The restraining properties of gelatins are usually determined by nephelometric methods as proposed by Ammann-Brass.[(2)] Tabor and Nellist,[(3)] however, emphasized that in certain cases the application of nephelometric methods could lead to erroneous results, furthermore, such nephelometric data yield only information on the mean value of the grain size distribution. It is therefore suggested that expensive electron microscopic examinations of silver halide crystals are the most reliable method of investigation the properties of gelatins.

EXPERIMENTAL METHODS

A silver chlorobromide emulsion with 7 mole per cent silver bromide was used for the experiments, since preliminary tests had revealed a greater sensitivity of silver chloride than silver bromide towards the differences between particular gelatins. The emulsions were prepared by running the silver nitrate solution into the halide-gelatin solution during five seconds. Without washing, the emulsion was physically ripened during a period of 150 min at 62°C at a pAg of 7·7 and a pH of 6·5. The emulsion contained 8% gelatin. The ratio silver/gelatin amounted to 1:6. The electron micrographs were obtained by carbon replica technique as described by Klein.[4]

RESULTS AND DISCUSSION

1. Influence of restrainers on crystal growth and grain size

Native hide gelatins usually contain more or less large amounts of nucleic acids as compared to bone gelatins. This is due to the different pretreatment of the respective raw materials during which the nucleic acids are largely removed in the acid demineralization step.[5] The restrainers present in gelatins (or, to be more exact, the nucleic acids) decrease the rate of ripening.

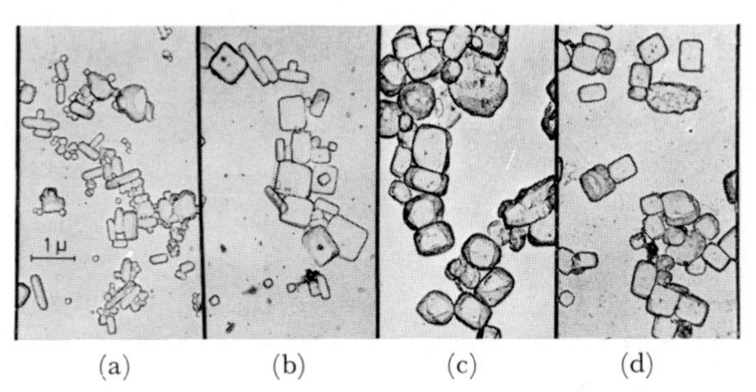

(a) (b) (c) (d)

Fig. 1. Silver halide grains obtained with a strongly restrained alkali-processed hide gelatin. (a) Untreated; (b) treated with a mixed ion exchanger; (c) treated with activated charcoal; (d) for comparison a bone gelatin.

Fig. 1 (*a*) shows the grain size distribution obtained with a commercial hide gelatin containing large amounts of restrainers. As a characteristic feature a broad size distribution appears which is typical for the action of restrained gelatins. According to their concentration the nucleic acids present are adsorbed at the grains and thus prevent their further growth. It should be noted that essentially three grain size classes exist:

(*a*) Grains with an edge length of approximately 0·5–0·7 microns. At these grains there is probably none, or only a small amount of nucleic acid adsorbed at a later stage of crystal growth.

(*b*) Cubes with an edge length of approximately 0·1 micron. The growth of these grains is restrained by adsorbed nucleic acid.

(*c*) Rod like crystals with a length of about 1 micron and a thickness of 0·2 microns. At the present time no explanation has been offered for the formation of these rodlike grains.

By treating the gelatin solution with a mixed-bed ion exchanger (3·7 parts per volume of Lewatit M 500, 1·5 parts of Lewatit S 100), obviously a part of the restraining compounds has been removed. As can be seen from (*b*) of Fig. 1, the fraction of the small crystals of the size of 0·1 micron is greatly reduced while the amount of the crystals with an edge length of 0·5–0·7 microns is increased. These crystals may be cubes or plates. An essential change of grain formation is however observed when the gelatin has been purified by activated charcoal,[6] see (*c*) in Fig. 1. (Care has to be taken that the activated charcoal is free from sulphur compounds.) The grain size distribution observed in the presence of such a gelatin is very narrow and nearly uniform crystals are obtained. This result leads to the conclusion that most of the restraining compounds have been removed. Comparison with the crystals obtained in the presence of a bone gelatin seems to confirm this assumption, (*d*) in Fig. 1.

The results of the electron micrographs agree with analytical data:

Table 1

Treatment	*Adenine* mg/kg	*Thiosulphate* mg/kg
None	40	2
Deionized	25	0
Activated charcoal	<5	0
Bone gelatin	<5	0

The grain size distribution obtained with an acid-processed pigskin is shown in (*a*) of Fig. 2. There, too, a broad size distribution can be observed with again three predominant size classes. Deionizing reduces the number of the smallest grains and increases the number of the large cubes. Treatment with activated charcoal on the other hand leads to a more or less uniform size distribution and to large crystals of cubic shape.

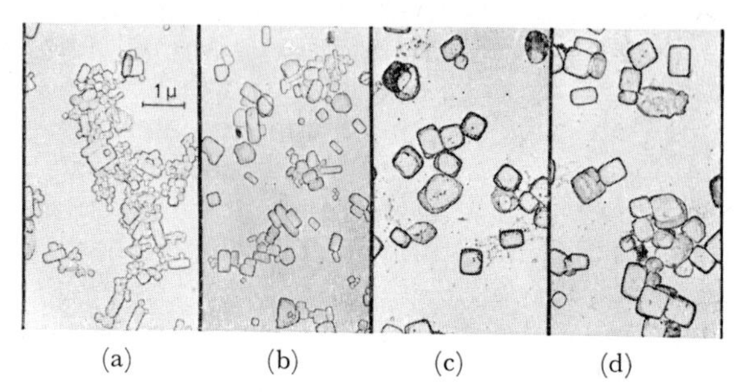

Fig. 2. Silver halide grains obtained with an acid processed pigskin gelatin. (a) Untreated; (b) treated with a mixed-bed ion exchanger; (c) treated with activated charcoal; (d) for comparison a bone gelatin.

Here again the grain shapes obtained agree with analytical data:

Table 2

Treatment	*Adenine* mg/kg	*Thiosulphate* mg/kg
None	30	5
De-ionized	18	0
Activated charcoal	<5	0
Bone gelatin	<5	0

The micrographs as well as analytical results clearly indicate that by treating the gelatins with activated charcoal a removal of nucleic acids can be achieved.

If, on the other hand, nucleic acids are deliberately added to a bone gelatin one should expect a restraining effect such as with hide gelatin.* The change of the grain shapes due to increasing additions of nucleic acids can be seen from Fig. 3.

With increasing amount of nucleic acids added to the gelatin the number of the smallest grains becomes larger. At nucleic acid concentrations of 0·1–0·5 g/kg gelatin, a tendency to develop rodlike crystals becomes apparent. At additions of 0·1 g/kg finally a nearly complete blocking of any crystal growth can be observed. If the amount of nucleic acids is further increased a change from cubic to more spherical grain shapes is observed.

* For these experiments "Natrium nucleinicum Ia" from Waldhof has been used. According to the analysis one g contained 80 mg adenine and 120 mg guanine.

The grain shapes obtained with a restrained hide gelatin containing 40 mg adenine compared with these micrographs show nearly identical results with these bone gelatins to which 0·2–0·5 g nucleic acids/kg have been added. This amount corresponds to an adenine concentration of 16–40 mg/kg gelatin according to analytical data.

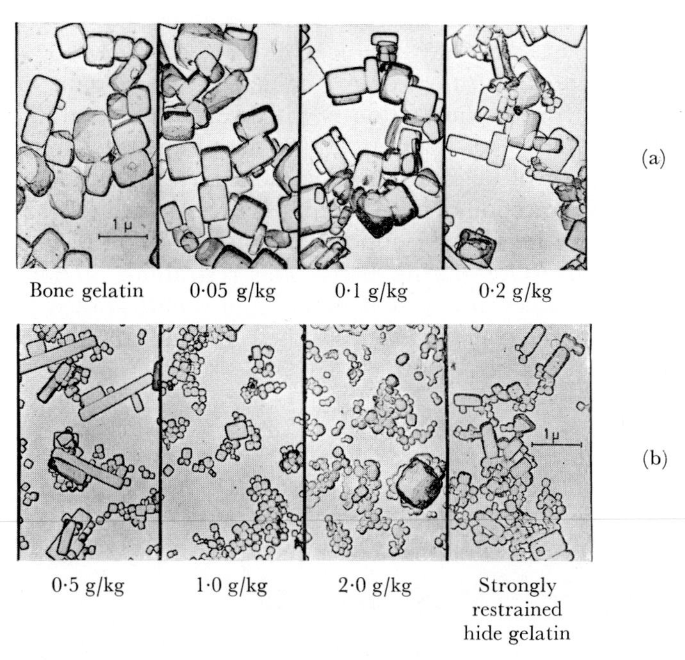

Fig. 3. Addition of nucleic acid to a bone gelatin.

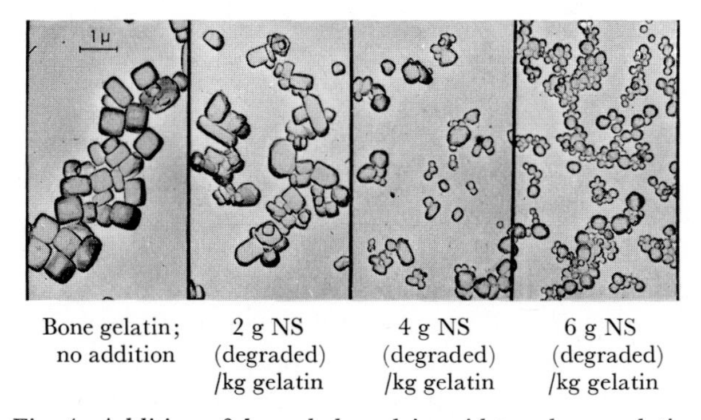

Fig. 4. Addition of degraded nucleic acid to a bone gelatin.

Generally, the action of native nucleic acids contained in gelatin differs from that of other sources which have been used as gelatin additives. Wood(7) suggests chemical differences of the various nucleic acids while Steigmann(8) as well as Russell and Oliff(9) found a dependence of the restraining action and the molecular weight of the nucleic acids.

In order to examine the effects of the molecular weight, a nucleic acid which has been hydrolytically degraded (pH 2·5, at 50°C for one h) was added to the same bone gelatin. The results are shown in Fig. 4. The restraining action is up to an addition of 2 g degraded nucleic acid/kg gelatin comparatively small and becomes pronounced only when 4 g of degraded nucleic acid have been added. If on the other hand the action of pure adenine is investigated (Fig. 5) a restraining effect can be already noticed after an addition of not more than 50 mg of the pure purine base. The restraining action of 100 mg adenine resembles nearly that of 1–2 g of non-degraded nucleic acid. According to the chemical analysis these 100 mg adenine correspond to 1·2 g nucleic acid.

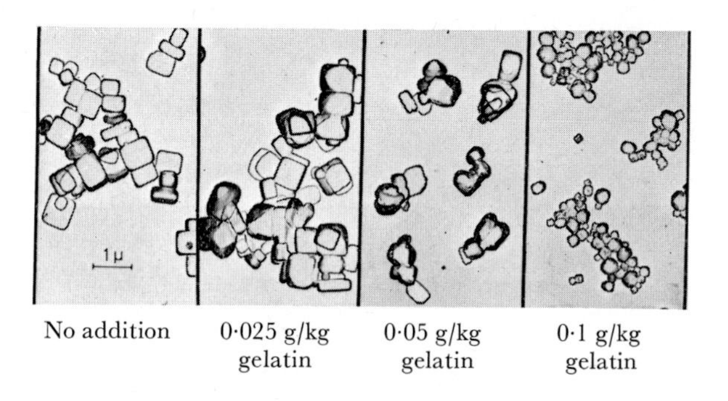

No addition | 0·025 g/kg gelatin | 0·05 g/kg gelatin | 0·1 g/kg gelatin

Fig. 5. Addition of adenine to a bone gelatin.

It seems, therefore, evident that the restraining effects of nucleic acids are mainly due to the purine base adenine contained therein, as has been already suggested.

The question why there exists a difference in the action of intact and degraded nucleic acid remains still unsolved. Perhaps the degraded products possess different adsorption properties due to steric effects or the degradation yields partly to adenylic acids which are not restrainers.(10)

2. The influence of the molecular weight of the gelatin on grain formation

No investigations of the influence of the molecular weight of the gelatin on the grain formation of silver halides have so far been published. Of course, it is possible to produce gelatins of different molecular weight; but due to the respective conditions during manufacture the nature of these gelatins may differ too. A controlled degradation of gelatins of high molecular weight can be easily done but it has to be expected that the way of degradation will have some influence on the resulting products. Finally an increase of the molecular weight can be achieved by cross-linking the gelatin. Here, too, effects due to the nature of the cross-linking agent must be expected.[14]

For these present experiments a commercial bone gelatin has been used. The degradation was performed by heating a 10% gelatin solution in a steam bath at a temperature of 90°C (pH 6·5) with constant stirring. A condenser prevented loss of water. The course of degradation was controlled by viscosity measurements of samples taken at certain intervals. Degradation was carried on until the viscosity reached at least 50% of the initial value.

In order to increase the molecular weight samples of gelatins were heated in dry state. When dry gelatin is heated, cross-linking starts and this can lead to complete insolubilization of the gelatin.[11],[12],[13] By choosing suitable temperatures and heating times (approximately 120°C and 4 h for the bone gelatin used in this case) gelatin with increased viscosity can be obtained which still is completely soluble. The molecular weight was then determined by means of an ultra centrifuge.*

Table 3

Gelatin treatment	*No.*	*Viscosity* 10% (40°C)	$\overline{M}_W$
Hydrolysis	1	9·8	54 000
Hydrolysis	2	14·2	61 000
Hydrolysis	3	16·1	72 500
Hydrolysis	4	18·4	79 500
No treatment	5	20·3	94 000
Dry heating	6	31·4	97 000
Dry heating	7	43·6	112 000

* I wish to thank Dr. Scholtan of Farbenfabriken Bayer for this experimental data.

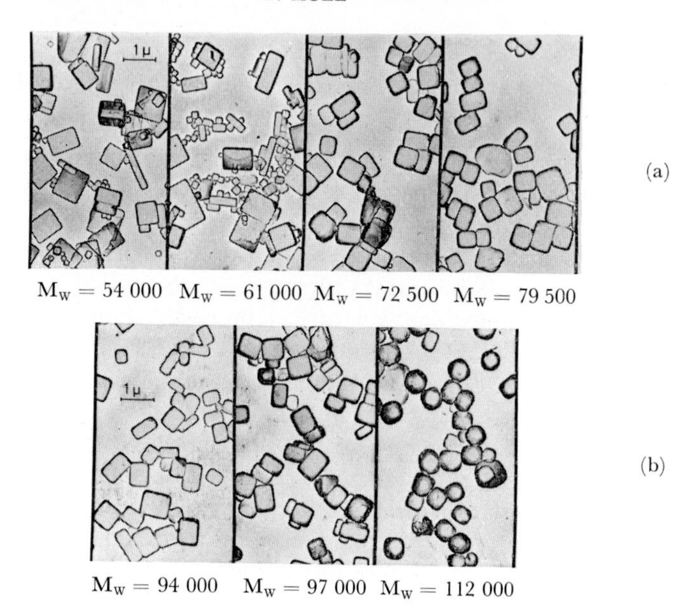

Fig. 6. Influence of the molecular weight of the gelatin on silver halide grains.

The grain shapes obtained with these gelatins are shown in Fig. 6. No apparent changes can be noticed in the molecular weight range of 72 500–97 000. At lower molecular weights the shapes typical for restrained growth (rods) as well as a broad grain size distribution can be observed. It may be assumed that certain groups which restrain crystal growth are set free by hydrolysis. A gelatin with the highest molecular weight leads to entirely different grain shapes, namely, with (111)-planes instead of cubic faces. Unfortunately a further increase of the molecular weight could not be achieved.

The changes in the molecular weight of the gelatins necessarily cause a change of the viscosity of the emulsion. This viscosity change, however, cannot be made responsible for the observed differences in grain shape, as could be shown by appropriate experiments.

It has been mentioned that both the method of gelatin degradation as well as the nature of the hydrolyzing agent (e.g. enzymes) strongly influence the shape of the silver halide crystals. Therefore the gelatin was degraded with various enzymes.

The enzymatic degradation has been performed at 35°C and at optimum pH value. The course of degradation was controlled by viscosity measurements. When the desired degree of hydrolysis had been approached the action of the enzyme was stopped by suitable means.

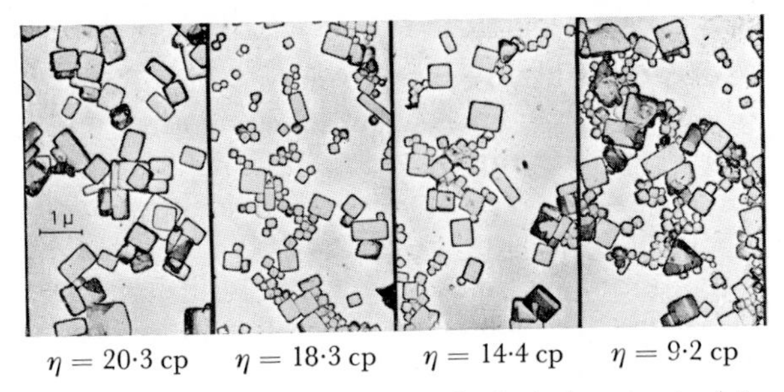

Fig. 7. The enzymatic degradation of gelatin by trypsin (viscosity of the undegraded gelatin: $=20{\cdot}3$ cp).

The grain shapes obtained with a trypsin degraded gelatin are seen in Fig. 7. Even a small degree of degradation causes a strong restraining of crystal growth. Further degradation does not markedly change the crystal shapes.

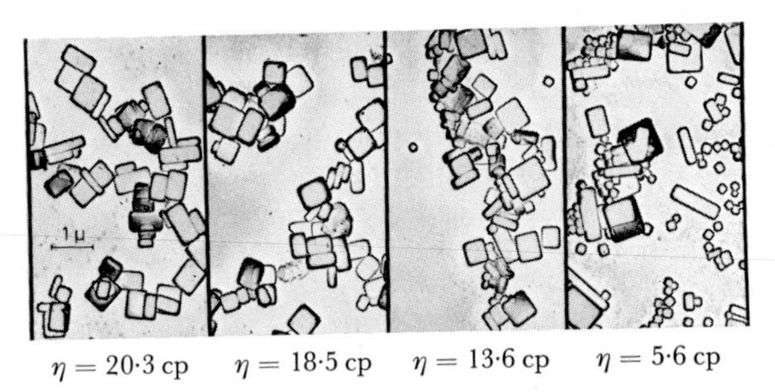

Fig. 8. Enzymatic degradation of gelatin by pepsin (viscosity of the undegraded gelatin $\eta = 20{\cdot}3$ cp).

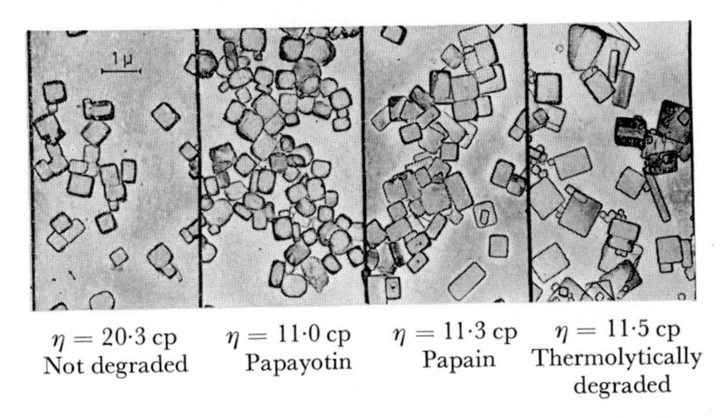

Fig. 9. Enzymatic degradation of gelatin by papayotin and papain, and for comparison thermolytically degraded gelatin.

Gelatins degraded by pepsin (Fig. 8) show similar restraining at a much higher degree of hydrolysis. No noticeable effects on the crystal shapes are observed when the enzymes papayotin* and papain have been used (Fig. 9). For comparison, the grain shapes obtained with a thermolytically degraded gelatin are once again shown in the right hand part of Fig. 9. From these results the conclusion may be drawn that according to the method of hydrolysis different groups of the gelatin chain are set free which more or less influences the course of grain growth.

CONCLUSIONS

A silver chlorobromide emulsion with 7 mole per cent bromide forms, in the presence of a pure bone gelatin, rather uniform cubes while the use of restrained hide gelatin yields different grain shapes with a broad size distribution. The restraining impurities can be removed from the gelatin by treatment with activated charcoal. A strong restraining of crystal growth is achieved by adding nucleic acids or adenine to the bone gelatin which can lead to the formation of spherical silver halide grains when the amount of restrainers is high. When the mean molecular weight of a bone gelatin is decreased by degradation processes restraining properties may appear while an increase of the mean molecular weight causes a change from cubic to octahedral growth forms of the silver halide grains.

ACKNOWLEDGEMENTS

I wish to thank Prof. Klein for the electron micrographs, Dr. Moisar for discussions and Dr. Seiz for supplying the gelatins.

References

(1) Steigmann, A., *Sci. Ind. Photogr.* (2) **27,** 422 (1956).
(2) Ammann-Brass, H., *Kolloid-Z.Z. Polym.*, **110,** 105, 161 (1948); *Photogr. Korresp.*, **106,** 21 (1970).
(3) Tabor, E. and Nellist, D. R., *Kolloid-Z.Z. Polym.*, **224,** 134 (1967).
(4) Klein, E., *Photogr. Korresp.*, **91,** 179 (1955).
(5) Russell, G., *J. Photogr. Sci.*, **15,** 236 (1967).

---

* See reference book No. M 7145 published by E. Merck AG, Darmstadt, Germany. Note in book states: Ei albumin Verdauungsvermögen 1:100; this translated means: Egg albumine has a digestive capacity 1:100.

(6) Kelly, W. D., *J. Photogr. Sci.*, **6,** 16 (1958).
(7) Wood, H. W., *J. Photogr. Sci.*, **8,** 113 (1960).
(8) Steigmann, A., *Sci. Ind. Photogr.*, **35,** 145 (1964).
(9) Russell, G. and Oliff, D. L., *J. Photogr. Sci.*, **14,** 9 (1966).
(10) Bassignana, P., Tagliafico, G. B. and Valbusa, L., *J. Photogr. Sci.*, **10,** 50 (1962).
(11) Sheppard, S. E. and Houck, R. C., *J. Phys. Chem.*, **36,** 2885 (1932).
(12) Yannas, J. V. and Tobolsky, A. V., *Nature* (*London*), **215,** 509 (1967).
(13) Polish Patent, 54549 (1965).
(14) Katsev, A., Pancheva, M. and Pangelova, N., *J. Photogr. Sci.*, (1970).

An Investigation of the Role of the Functional Groups of Gelatin on Silver Halide Crystal Growth

E. KLEIN, E. MOISAR and E. ROCHE

Agfa-Gevaert AG, Leverkusen, West Germany

ABSTRACT. The increase in the mean particle size of a dispersion of silver halide microcrystals can be governed either by recrystallization processes or by coagulation. The properties of the crystal surfaces due to adsorption phenomena as well as the electrochemical properties of the protective colloid molecules determine which particular mechanism of crystal growth predominates, as has been found by turbidimetric investigations.

INTRODUCTION

The use of gelatin in the manufacture of photographic silver halide emulsions is due to some unique properties of this binding agent. Despite its wide use in photographic practice, however, several problems concerning the action of gelatin in silver halide emulsions are still unsolved. Among these problems are the questions:

(a) In which way does pure gelatin influence the mechanism of crystal growth?

(b) What kind of groups within the gelatin chain are responsible for the interaction with silver halides?

In the present paper these problems have been investigated by nephelometric measurements of the rate of AgBr crystal growth under different conditions.(1) A bone gelatin with no detectable traces of either active sulphur compounds or nucleic acid restrainers has been used. The AgBr dispersions were prepared by rapid mixing of $AgNO_3$ and KBr solutions in the presence of gelatin or other supporting agents. The desired pAg value was established by adding a certain excess of one of the reactants. Immediately after mixing the participants a great number of crystal nuclei is formed. Secondary reactions cause a subsequent increase of the mean particle size. This change in particle distribution which is known as "physical ripening" may be either by coagulation or by recrystallization.

At first approach coagulation can be considered as a bimolecular reaction. The rate of reaction depends on the number of collisions between two particles and it therefore depends strongly on the particle concentration. Furthermore the rate depends on the mobilities of the particles and thus on the viscosity of the solution. Finally the rate of collision depends on the surface charge due to repulsion between particles of same sign of charge. These effects are summarized in an equation proposed by v. Smoluchowski:[2]

$$N_t = \frac{N_0}{1 + 2RT/3\eta N_L \,.\, N_0 \,.\, t \,.\, \exp.\,[\zeta|F/kT] \,.\, A/r}$$

where N_0 and N_t mean the numbers of initial particles and after the time t respectively, $|\zeta|$ the absolute value of the electrokinetic potential, η the viscosity, r the particle size and A the distance of attraction.

Recrystallization depends on solubility differences between particles of different size. The smaller particles have a tendency to dissolve and to deposit their matter upon the surface of the larger particles. The rate of growth is governed by the slowest step in the sequence of process:

$$\text{dissolution} \rightarrow \text{diffusion} \rightarrow \text{deposition}$$

Taking either diffusion or deposition as rate determining steps the rate of particle growth has been calculated by *C.* Wagner[3] as

$$\bar{r}_{t,D} = K[D \,.\, C_\infty \,.\, t]^{\frac{1}{3}}$$

for diffusion controlled processes and

$$\bar{r}_{t,k} = K'[k \,.\, C_\infty \,.\, t]^{\frac{1}{2}}$$

for rate determined processes with r_t = mean particle size at time t, D = diffusion coefficient, C_∞ = solubility at infinite particle size, k = rate constant of incorporation.

From these equations it follows that the rate of recrystallization is either proportional to the square root or to the cubic root of the solubility.

EXPERIMENTAL RESULTS

Influence of solubility and concentration of the solid phase

The solubility of AgBr depends on the pAg value of the solution: the solubility approaches a maximum value at the equivalence point and decreases both at smaller and at larger pAg values corresponding to the law of mass action. At extreme pAg values the solubility raises again due to complex formation.[1] The relation of pAg and solubility is shown in the solid curve of Fig. 1.

When the experimental values of the rate of crystal growth are plotted *v*. pAg, the dotted curve of Fig. 1 is obtained. At first sight there seems to be a close relation between the experimental growth rates and the solubility.

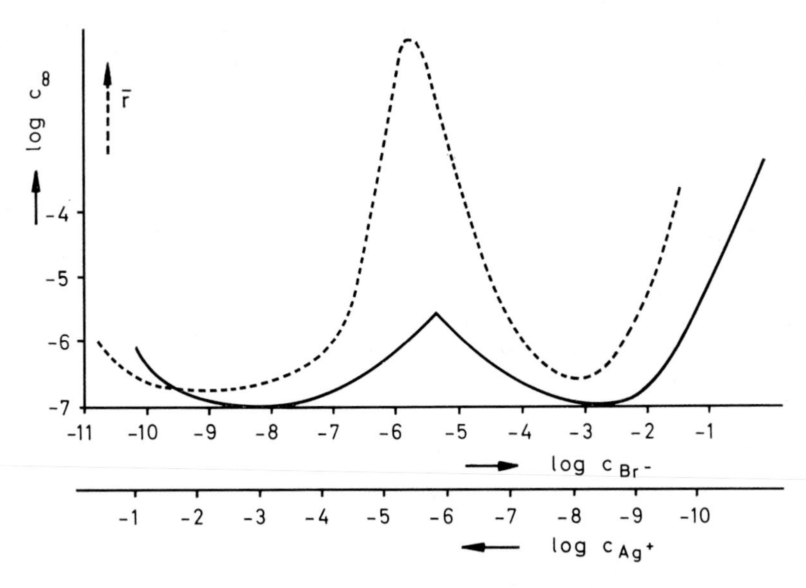

Fig. 1. Solubility (C_∞ : solid curve) and mean particle size ($\bar{r}_t$) upon 64 min recrystallization (dotted curve) *v*. bromide or silver ion concentration in solution.

Maximum growth rate coincides with the maximum of the solubility, and the minima of the speed of crystal growth are located at the very same pAg values where also the solubility attains minimum values. This apparently good agreement may be taken as evidence, that the growth of silver halide crystals occurs via diffusion or via rate controlled recrystallization processes, since the rate of these processes contrary to coagulation does depend on the solubility.

A closer examination of the two equations shown before reveals some discrepancies between theory and experiment. The ratio of maximum and minimum solubility is approximately 20:1. Therefore the ratio of the rates of crystal growth at the solubility maximum and minimum respectively should amount to $\sqrt[3]{(20)} = 2{\cdot}7$ for diffusion controlled growth or to $\sqrt[2]{(20)} = 4{\cdot}5$ in case of rate controlled growth. Actually much higher ratios are observed, a fact which can be explained by assuming an accelerated growth in the vicinity of the equivalence point. This acceleration is attributed to coagulation. Particularly in the vicinity of the equivalence point coagulation processes are possible, since here the particles carry no charge due to adsorption of excess ions, while in the regions of minimum solubility the surface charge due to adsorption of excess silver or halide ions respectively should prevent any coagulation.

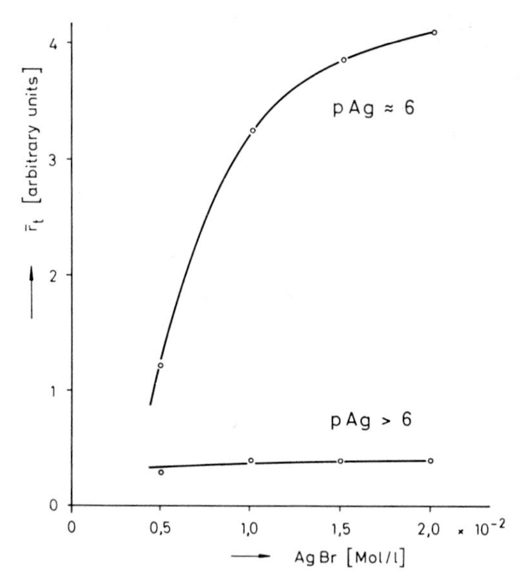

Fig. 2. Mean particle size $\bar{r}_t$ in arbitrary units *v.* concentration of the solid phase AgBr.

Further evidence of the existence of two different growth mechanisms according to the pAg value can be derived from an investigation of the dependence of the crystal growth rate on the concentration of the solid phase. The growth rate (or, more precisely, the mean particle size $\bar{r}_t$ observed after a given time t of growth) found in the region of equivalence of Ag^+ and Br^- ions (pAg ≈ 6) increases strongly with increasing AgBr particle concentration. This result is in agreement with the concept of coagulation, the rate of which strongly depends on the number of particles. On the other hand $\bar{r}_t$ remains practically independent on the particle concentration, e.g. in the presence of excess Br^- ions in solution (pAg > 6; cf., Fig. 2).

This corresponds with the concept of recrystallization, the speed of which is independent of the particle concentration and which depends merely on the cubic root of the diffusion coefficient.

Influence of surface charges

The further investigations have been restricted to pAg regions, where growth occurs via recrystallization. More insight in the role of the gelatin can be obtained, when the growth rates in the two solubility minima are measured in a wide pH region. If the growth rates τ_{min} measured at the minima at pAg < 6 and pAg > 6 respectively are plotted *v.* pH the curves in Fig. 3 are obtained. The change of the rate of crystal growth

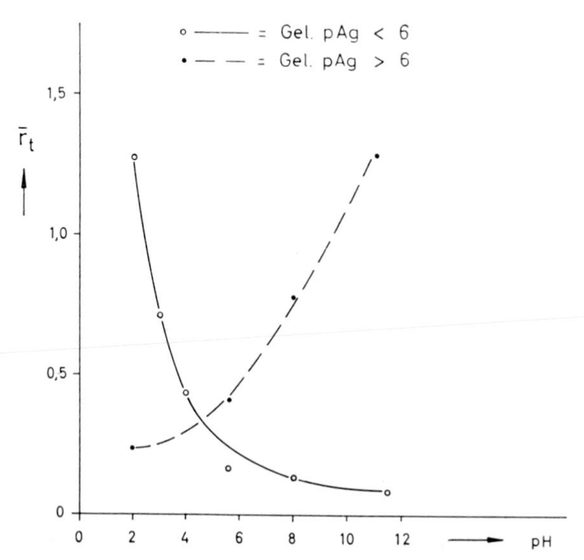

Fig. 3. Mean particle size $\bar{r}_t$ *v.* pH of the solution obtained at the pAg values for minimum solubility at pAg ≈ 3 and pAg ≈ 9 (cf. Fig. 1) in the presence of native bone gelatin as protective colloid.

with increasing pH obviously depends on the pAg of the system: the rate decreases when the pAg is low (solid curve) and it increases when the pAg is high (dotted curve).

These results can be explained when the situation at the silver halide crystal surface is considered; at low pAg values the crystals have adsorbed excess silver ions, they therefore carry a positive charge regardless of the pH value of the surrounding solution. At high pAg values their surface charge is negative due to adsorption of excess halide ions (Fig. 4(a)).

The electrochemical properties of the gelatin are not much affected by the pAg, they strongly depend, however, on the pH value.

At low pH values a protonization of free amino groups leads to an over-all positive charge of the gelatin chains, while at high pH values the gelatin molecules become anionic due to dissociation of the free carboxylic groups (Fig. 4(b)).

a

$$(AgBr)\,Ag^+_{ads.} \xleftarrow{Ag^+} (AgBr) \xrightarrow{Br^-} (AgBr)\,Br^-_{ads.}$$

pAg < 6	pAg ≈ 6	pAg > 6
positive charge		negative charge

b

$$NH_3^{\oplus}\text{-}\underset{R}{CH}\text{-}COOH \underset{H^{\oplus}}{\overset{OH^{\ominus}}{\rightleftharpoons}} NH_3^{\oplus}\text{-}\underset{R}{CH}\text{-}COO^{\ominus} \underset{H^{\oplus}}{\overset{OH^{\ominus}}{\rightleftharpoons}} NH_2\text{-}\underset{R}{CH}\text{-}COO^{\ominus}$$

Protonization	pH = IEP	Deprotonization
positive charge		negative charge
pH < IEP		pH > IEP

Fig. 4(a). Adsorption of silver and halide ions at the AgBr surface. (b) Protonization and deprotonization of gelatin.

If the properties of the gelatin and the crystal are combined it must be assumed, that irrespective of charge phenomena gelatin in any case is adsorbed by a multitude of weak non-polar bonds to the silver halide surface, probably by delivering electron pairs of the nitrogen atoms of the numerous carbon amide groups and thus filling up the octet gaps of silver ions. This more or less weak interaction is superimposed by electrostatic phenomena or, in other words, by attraction or repulsion according to the charge of the crystal and the gelatin.

When the crystal is charged positively (at low pAg) cationic gelatin (at low pH) is repulsed. This causes a decrease of the overall binding forces. The surface is less covered and hence a diffusion of silver and halide ions to the surface and consequently the incorporation into the surface are facilitated, which results in an increase of the growth rate (Fig. 5(a)).

At high pH values, gelatin is in an anionic state and is attracted by the positively charged crystal. The surface is thus blocked and a diffusion of silver and halide ions to the surface becomes difficult. Hence the growth rate decreases (Fig. 5(b)).

The same considerations for high pAg regions, when the crystal bears a negative charge due to halide ion adsorptions, lead to an inverse relation between pH and growth rate (Fig. 5(c) and 5(d)), which also has been found experimentally, as has been shown in Fig. 3.

In order to add some more evidence to prove the validity of the proposed mechanism the behaviour of modified gelatins has been investigated. If, for example, the free amino groups of the gelatin are removed, protonization can no longer occur, and the gelatin molecule remains uncharged at low pH values. Hence it can be neither attracted

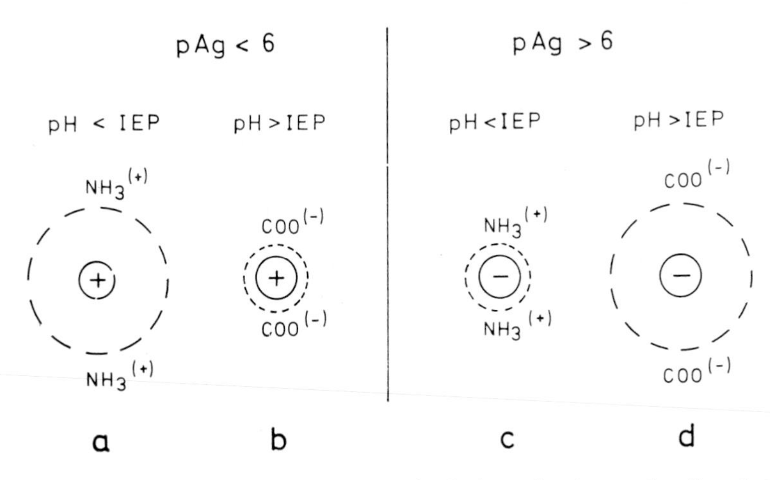

Fig. 5. Scheme of repulsion or attraction of gelatin molecules on the silver halide surface.

nor repulsed by additional electrostatic effects from a charged silver halide surface, and the rate of crystal growth ought to be here nearly equal at low or at high pH values. Ionization of the carboxylic groups, however, is still possible at high pH values, and the rates of growth should therefore diverge at high pH values depending on the charge of the crystal surface as in the case of untreated gelatin. Exactly these results are obtained when, for example, the amino groups have been blocked by reaction with maleic anhydride(4) (Fig. 6) or when they have been removed by desamination.(5)

If, on the other hand, the carboxylic groups are blocked by esterification,(6) the gelatin remains uncharged at high pH values and crystal growth becomes here independent of the crystal charge, while at low pH values a protonization of the intact amino groups leads to cation formation. Hence in this case crystal growth rate is independent of surface charges at high pH values, but becomes dependent of pAg, when gelatin cations are formed at lower pH values (Fig. 7).

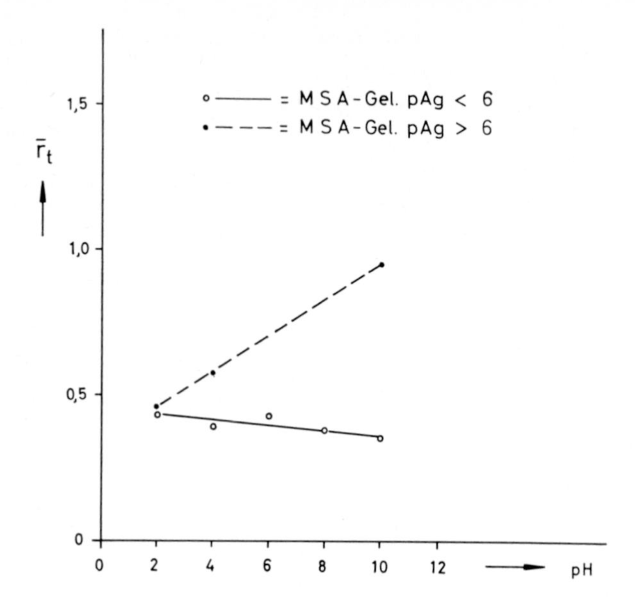

Fig. 6. Same as Fig. 3, but with gelatin treated with maleic acid anhydride.

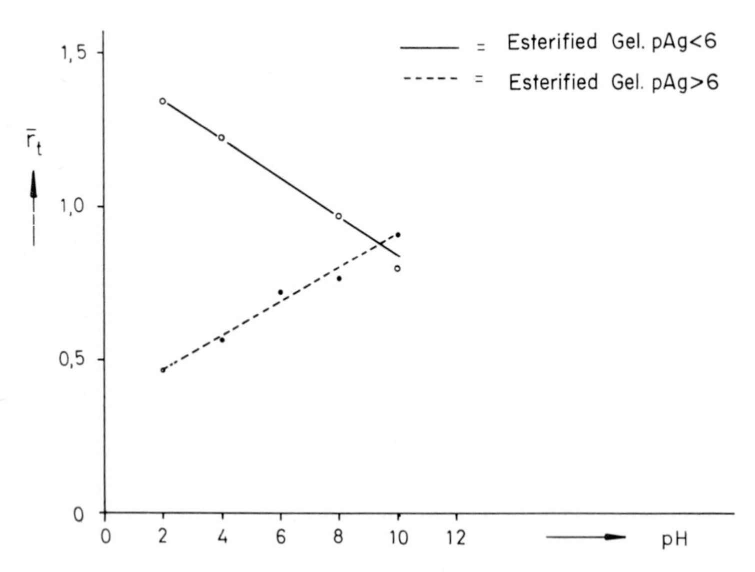

Fig. 7. Same as Fig. 3, but with esterified gelatin.

So far the explanation given for the interaction between gelatin and silver halide crystals seems to agree well with the experimental results.

The investigations have been extended to various synthetic protective colloids, some with an amphoteric character like gelatin, some being not amphoteric. Polyacrylamide is cited as an example for the amphoteric colloids. As can be expected, its pAg/pH dependence of affecting silver halide growth rates resembles exactly the behaviour of native gelatin (Fig. 8).

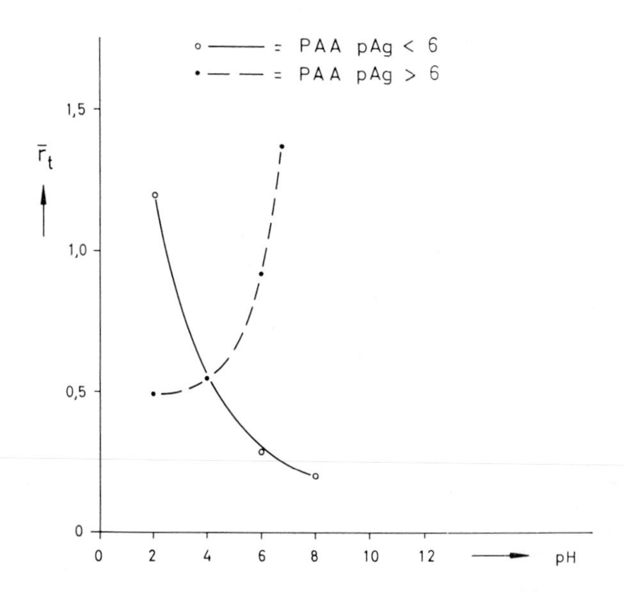

Fig. 8. Same as Fig. 3, but with polyacrylamide.

In the case of polyvinylpyrrolidone, which is not amphoteric, no pH dependence of crystal growth can be observed, except for very low pH values, which may be due to secondary effects (Fig. 9).

It should be mentioned, that these results are somehow related to earlier investigations by Günther and Moisar[7] who observed that the adsorption of a cationic dye at silver bromide crystals increased with increasing pAg, while the adsorption of an anionic dye decreased, with increasing pAg.

So far the complete gelatin molecule has been considered. The question is, are there any peculiar groups within the gelatin molecule which preferentially influence crystal growth. Hydrolytic degradation of the gelatin does not cause any marked effect upon the kinetics of crystal growth (Fig. 10).

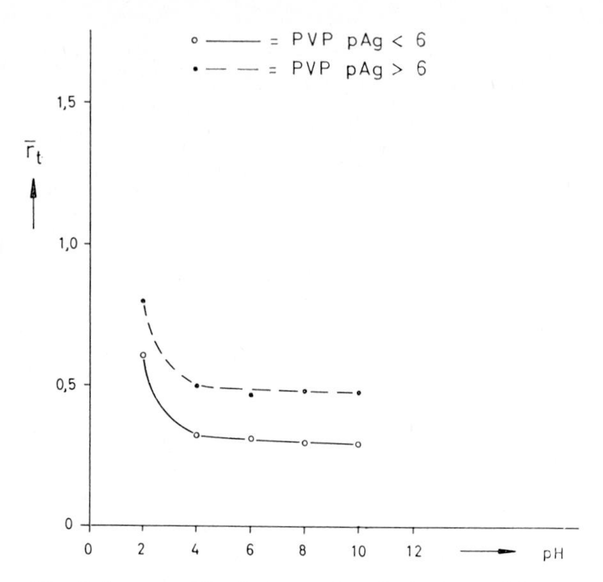

Fig. 9. Same as Fig. 3, but with polyvinylpyrrolidone.

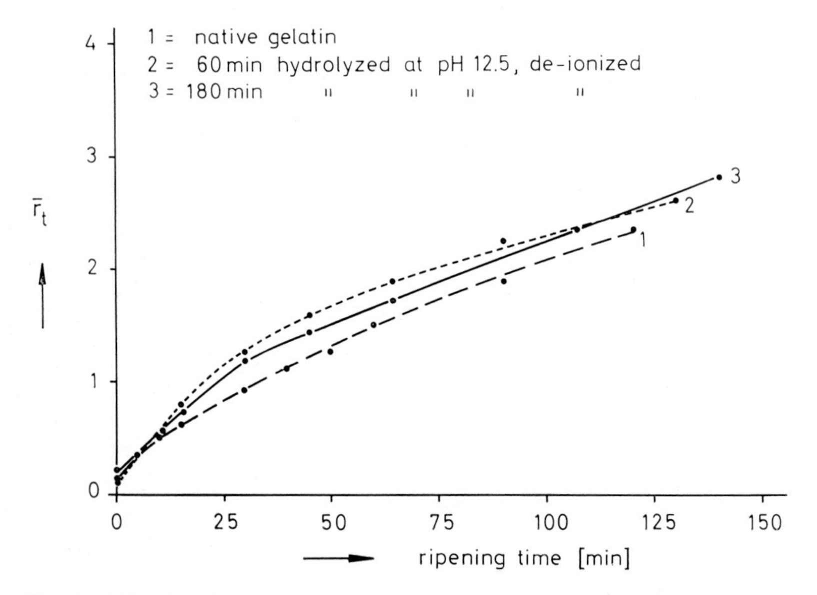

Fig. 10. Kinetics of AgBr crystal growth in the presence of hydrolysed gelatin.

Even single amino acids used instead of gelatin do not considerably change the rate of crystal growth, with two exceptions, arginine and histidine. These two amino acids increase the rate of crystal growth (Fig. 11).

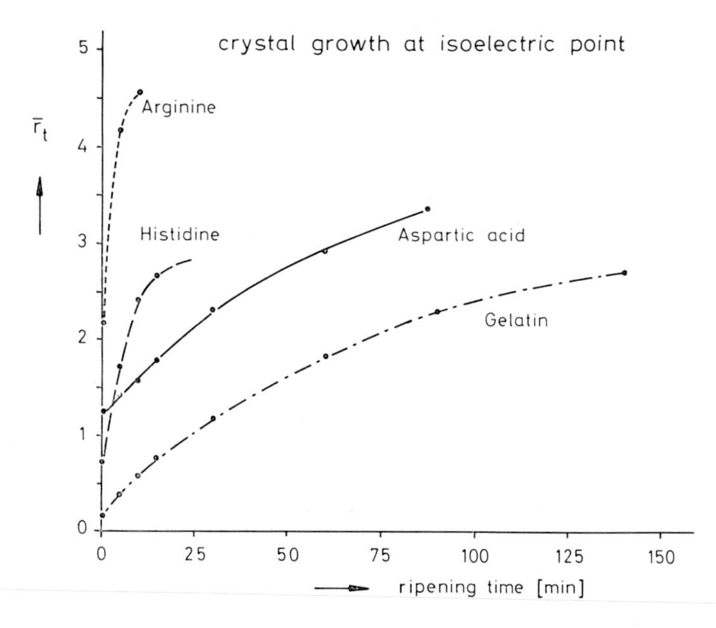

Fig. 11. Kinetics of AgBr crystal growth with different protective colloids. The curve marked "aspartic acid" coincides roughly with growth curves in the presence of other amino acids except arginine and histidine.

This effect is attributed to their ability to form silver complexes and thus to increase the silver halide solubility, which, as has been shown in Fig. 1, must lead to accelerated growth.

CONCLUSION

To summarize the results: the action of pure gelatin as a supporting colloid seems to be due to unspecific adsorption by relatively weak non-polar forces, probably between the numerous carbon amide groups and the silver halide. These adsorption forces are superimposed by electrostatic effects which depend on the pH dependent charge of the gelatin molecule and the pAg dependent charge of the silver halide. A slight specific action may be exerted by the arginine and histidine groups which form silver complexes.

All other acceleration or retardation effects observed with gelatines are not due to intrinsic properties of the gelatin but are caused by impurities, such as sulphite, thiosulphate (as accelerators) or nucleic acids (as retarders).

References

(1) Klein, E. and Moisar, E., *Ber. Bunsenges. Phys. Chem.*, **67,** 349 (1963).
(2) Smoluchowski, M. v., *Zt. Phys. Chem.*, **92,** 129 (1917).
(3) Wagner, C., *Zt. Elektrochem., Ber. Bunsenges. Phys. Chem.*, **65,** 581 (1961).
(4) U.S. Pat. 2.614.931.
(5) French Pat. 994.300.
(6) Bello, J., *Acta Biochim. Biophys.*, **20,** 426 (1956).
(7) Günther, E. and Moisar, E., *J. Photogr. Sci.*, **13,** 280 (1965).

A Technique for Studying the Growth of Silver Halide Crystals. The Effect of Gelatin

J. D. LEWIS and A. M. KRAGH

Research Laboratories, Ilford Limited, Ilford, Essex

ABSTRACT. Single layers of silver bromide crystals about 0·1 μ in diameter attached to microscopic slides were prepared by evaporating silver under vacuum onto the slide and converting this to silver bromide in bromine vapour. The slides were then placed in a gently flowing solution consisting either of 0·1 M ammonium bromide or alternatively, of 0·1 M ammonium bromide and 1% gelatin. The solutions were kept slightly supersaturated with respect to silver bromide by cooling them before they passed over the samples. Under these conditions some of the crystals grew to a diameter of a few microns while remaining attached to the glass slide. Thin tabular crystals were obtained. Gelatin slowed down the growth rate and, under the conditions used, led to the formation of crystals of more regular shape.

INTRODUCTION

When silver halide is precipitated during the preparation of photographic emulsions potassium or ammonium nitrate is formed at a concentration which, in the absence of gelatin, would induce coalescence of the crystals. Gelatin prevents this coalescence while permitting growth of the crystals. Other water-soluble polymers that adsorb to silver halide may prevent coalescence equally well, but many of them interfere too greatly with crystal growth.(1)

The first requirement for a study of the effect of gelatin on crystal growth is that the conditions must not lead to coalescence of crystals in a control sample containing no gelatin. Romer and Sidorowicz(2) achieved this using sols, i.e. very small silver halide crystals produced from dilute solutions. They investigated the effect over a wide range of concentration of ammonia and bromide ion and showed that, although gelatin produced only a small effect under conditions where the solubility of silver halide was high, it greatly reduced the ripening rate under conditions where the solubility of the silver halide was low. The effect was dependent on micro-constituents in the gelatin.

For the limited investigation described here, we have devised a technique for avoiding coalescence by keeping the crystals attached to a rigid support. The technique, which is time-consuming, has proved to be rather inflexible though it could be applied to a wider range of growth conditions. It may also be useful in the study of photographic development.

EXPERIMENTAL

The seed crystals

Pure silver wire was evaporated from a molybdenum boat, under a vacuum of 5×10^{-7} torr, onto a microscope coverglass to give a silver layer about 4 mm thick. The cover-glass was then placed in a dish containing bromine vapour for half an hour at room temperature. This converted the silver to a transparent silver bromide layer. When the cover-glass was placed in a moist atmosphere the transparent layer suddenly became opalescent due to the formation of micro-crystals 0·03–0·1 μ in diameter. The crystals were all separate and not randomly clumped (Fig. 3). This conversion technique for the production of pure silver bromide, was based on the method of Billett and Ottewill[3] for producing thick layers of close-packed crystals of silver iodide.

Growth of the crystals

A diagram of the all-glass apparatus is shown in Fig. 1. Two containers A and B are joined by two horizontal tubes C and D, C being vertically above D. Ammonium bromide solution was saturated with silver bromide at an elevated temperature and added to B. A small quantity of silver bromide powder was also added to B. A glass paddle E, in an opening in the upper surface of tube C, produced a slow flow of liquid from B to A in the upper tube C and in the reverse direction in the lower tube D. Container B was stirred slowly with a separate stirrer to ensure a uniform temperature in the vessel. Container A was jacketed with water thermostated to 49°C, and container B was jacketed with water at 72°C. The measured temperatures of the liquids inside containers A and B, after a steady state had been attained, were respectively 52·6°C and 64·4°C. The ammonium bromide solution in container A was thus supersaturated with silver bromide.

Several microscope cover glasses, G, with seed crystals on their surfaces, were then placed on a low platform in container A and the lid replaced on the container. Samples were removed at intervals and after washing were replicated for electron-micrography.

Gelatin was added to the ammonium bromide solution in container A for some of the experiments. A Rousselot limed ossein gelatin of low restrainer content was used.

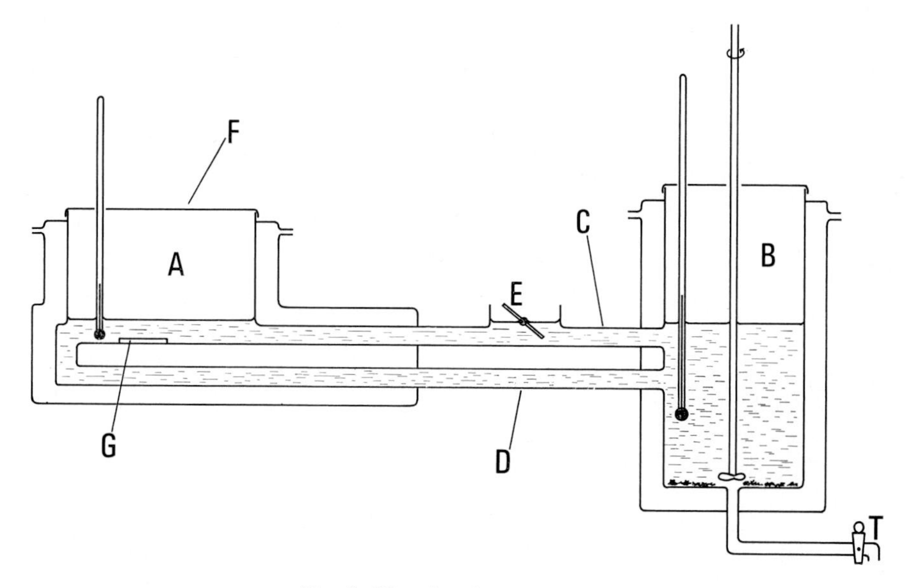

Fig. 1. The ripening apparatus.

Comments on method

Satisfactory growth was obtained only under conditions where the solubility of the silver bromide was fairly low, probably because of the difficulty of preserving a uniform supersaturation. However, very low solubilities made the growth rate inconveniently slow. Supersaturation could not be increased significantly because renucleation occurred on the surface of the glass vessel. More elaborate methods of temperature control would be required to extend the range of the method; a slight temperature increase in A will cause all the crystals to disappear. The most satisfactory concentration of ammonium bromide for ripening in the particular apparatus used was in the range 0·5–1·0 M.

RESULTS

Electronmicrographs of samples taken at different time intervals during growth in 1·0 M ammonium bromide are shown in Fig. 2. The experiments for the two series were identical except for the presence of

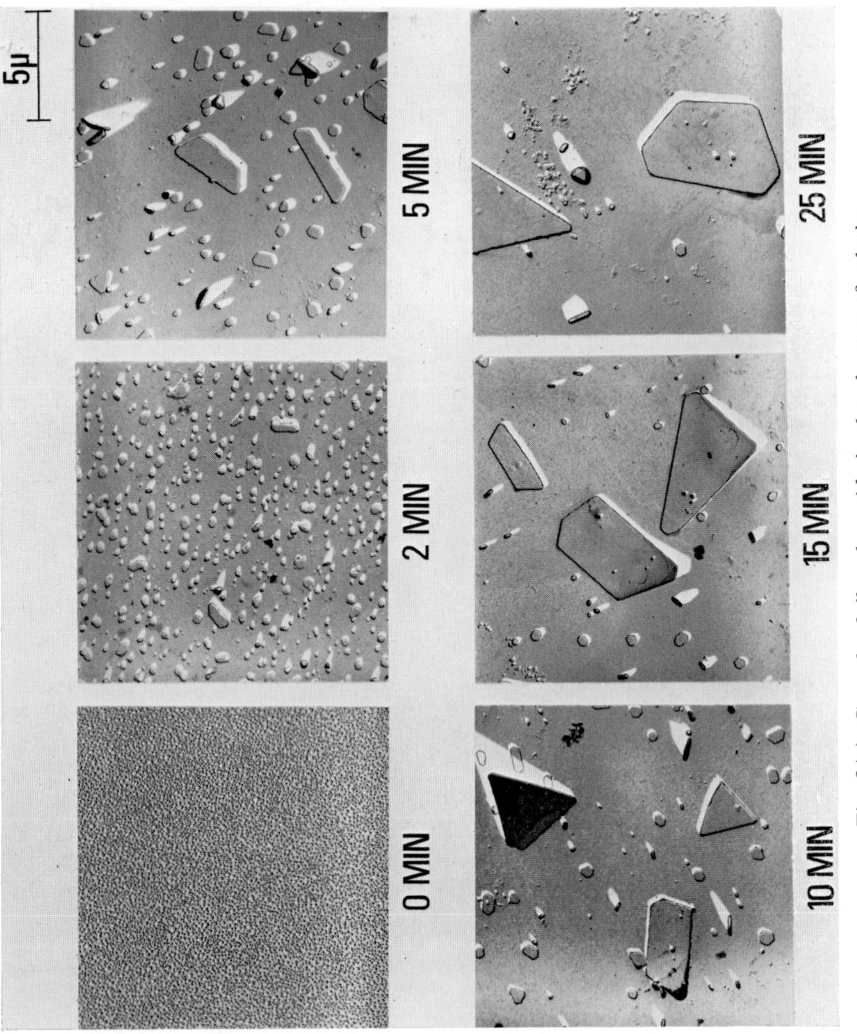

Fig. 2(a). Growth of silver bromide in the absence of gelatin.

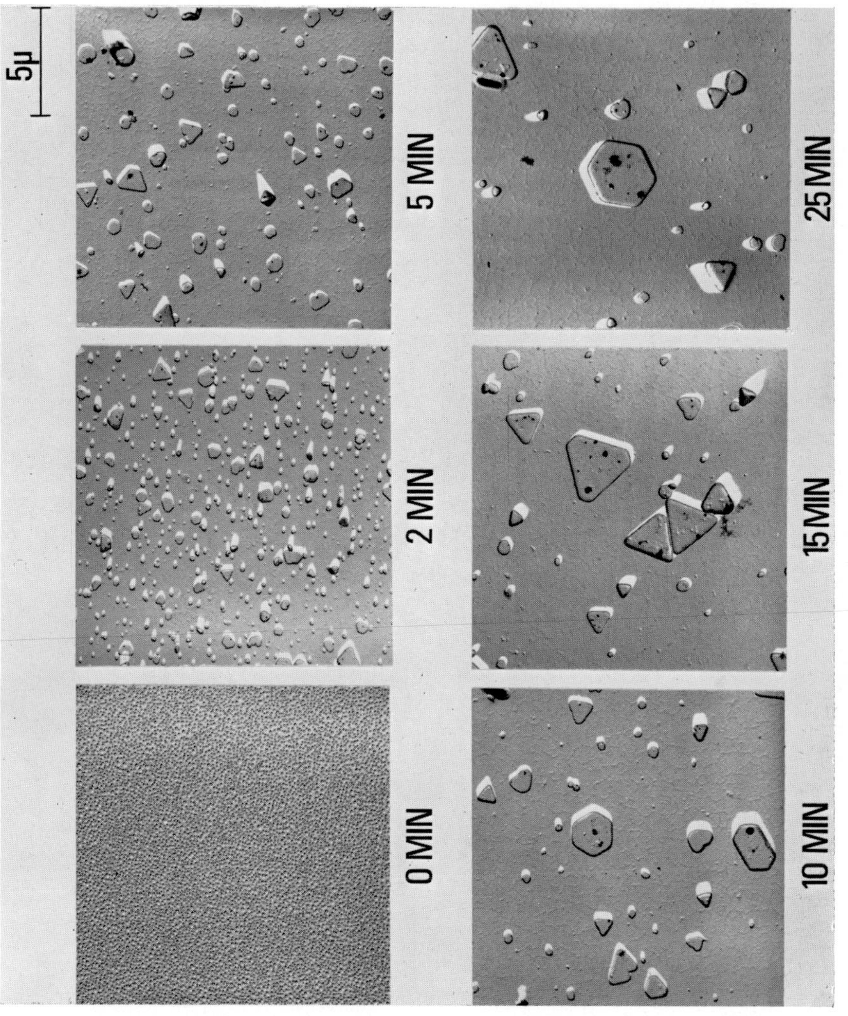

Fig. 2(b). Growth of silver bromide in the presence of 1% gelatin solution.

1% gelatin during growth. Fig. 3 is an enlargement of the sample at zero time, i.e. the seed crystals.

Thin tabular crystals were obtained both with and without gelatin but in the absence of gelatin the crystals were larger, thinner and less regular in shape.

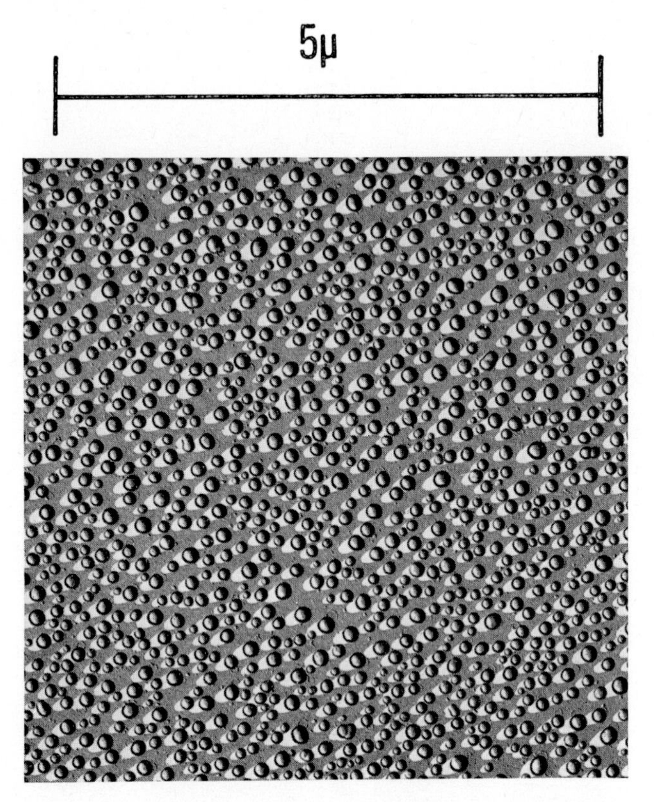

Fig. 3. The seed crystals.

DISCUSSION

It is now recognized that most of the crystals obtained after growth in the presence of excess bromide ions are tabular crystals containing more than one parallel twin plane. Apparently twinning was not significantly influenced by the presence of gelatin, although gelatin slowed the growth rate by a factor of two or three times.

The crystals shown in Fig. 2, which are presumably twinned, are mostly triangular rather than hexagonal and, particularly in the absence of gelatin, tend to be truncated at one corner. The cause of this latter effect is not clear; various changes in the flow and stirring failed to affect the formation of truncated crystals.

The unclumped distribution of crystals on the initial plate is noteworthy.

References

(1) Evva, F., *X. Wiss. Photogr.*, **52,** 1, 64, 136, 237 (1957).
(2) Romer, W. and Sidorowicz, A., *J. Photogr. Sci.*, **15,** 115 (1967).
(3) Billett, D. F. and Ottewill, R. H., *Wetting*, SCI Monographs No. 25, p. 253 (1967).

Physical Ripening of Photographic Emulsions with Hardened Gelatin

A. KATSEV, M. PANCHEVA and N. PANGELOVA
Cinema and Radio Research Institute, Sofia, Bulgaria

ABSTRACT. The paper presents information about the conditions in which the hardeners formaldehyde and chromic acetate can affect the kinetics of the physical ripening of "neutral" and ammoniacal silver bromide emulsions obtained at various excesses of potassium bromide. When a gelatin is partially hardened, there is no effect on the physical ripening of fine-grained emulsions. The crystal growth is restrained as a consequence of the hardening only when the emulsion grains are larger. In this case it is assumed that on the grain surface are formed thicker or more compact adsorption layers of gelatin, which reduce the rate of the diffusion processes and, hence, the rate of crystal growth. Chromic acetate exerts very strong restraining action on ammoniacal emulsions. This effect is explained not by the hardening of gelatin, but by the formation of chromic ammonia complex ions, which block the active centres of crystal growth on grain surface.

INTRODUCTION

Tsariov and co-workers[1] have established that at partial hardening of a gelatin, its compatibility with polyvinyl alcohol is improved. According to the same authors the hardening of gelatin does not exert considerable effect on the process of physical ripening of photographic emulsions. This has been confirmed in our preliminary investigations on the physical ripening of fine-grain emulsions, but in other cases we have observed considerable restraining of the ripening. In this connection we have made it our aim in this paper to find out the conditions in which the hardeners can affect the kinetics of the physical ripening of silver bromide gelatin photographic emulsions. For the explanation of the mechanism of the physical ripening, the probable causes of this effect are undoubtedly of great interest.

EXPERIMENTAL

Ammoniacal emulsions

We have used the following solutions for obtaining ammonical emulsions:

Solution A at 45°C

Potassium bromide	6·55 g
Gelatin	4·0 g
Water up to	80·0 ml

Solution B at 35°C

Silver nitrate	8·50 g
Ammonia/25%/until obtaining clear solution about	8·5 ml
Water up to	50·0 ml

Solution B is poured into solution A for 5 s. The emulsion is ripening at 45°C.

The ripening is carried out at pH = 10·9 and excess of soluble bromide 0·039 mole/l or 1·17 mole/l.

Non-ammoniacal emulsions

The same solutions, but without ammonia, have been used for obtaining "neutral" emulsions. The temperature of solution A is then 70°C and of solution B 50°C. The ripening of the emulsion is at 70°C and pH = 5·8. Here, too, the ripening runs at low or high excess of soluble bromide (0·039 or 1·17 mole/l respectively). At the same temperature and 1·17 mole/l soluble bromide, we have obtained emulsions at pH = 10·9, by preliminary addition of NaOH in solution A.

In all cases the ripening has run at 3% concentration of an "inert" gelatin, Rousselot No. 16080.

Determination of average grain mass

At certain intervals of time 10 ml specimens are taken from the emulsions and are mixed with 10% gelatin solution, which for ammonical emulsions is acidified with acetic acid in order to neutralize the ammonia and to stop the ripening immediately. These specimens, after suitable dilution with 1% gelatin solution, are coated on glass plates. Five photomicrographs are made by optical microscope on every plate. After counting the grains on the photomicrographs and taking into consideration the corresponding dilution and mass of the silver bromide per unit of volume, the average mass ($\bar{m}$) of the emulsion grains is determined. We call "curves of ripening" the graphically represented dependences between $\bar{m}$ and the time of ripening.

Hardeners

We have used formaldehyde (0·0154 mole/l) and chromic acetate (0·0021 mole/l) as hardeners. They are added 1 min prior to the precipitation in the solution A. We have used also preliminary hardened gelatin. After adding chromic acetate to the gelatin solution, it sets and is then washed and dried. We call this gelatin "Cr—gelatin".

Microanalytical determination

The quantity of gelatin adsorbed per cm^2 AgBr surface has been determined on emulsions obtained with and without formaldehyde. The determination has been carried out according to the micro method of Kjeldahl after isolating the solid phase by centrifuging according to the experiments of Sheppard Lambert and Keenan.[2]

RESULTS AND DISCUSSION

Fig. 1 shows curves of ripening of neutral emulsions. When the excess of potassium bromide is small, the ripening is strongly restrained and the chromic acetate or formaldehyde have no effect (curve 2). When the ripening runs at large excess of KBr (1·17 mole/l), the chromic acetate considerably restrains the ripening, if it is added prior to the emulsification (curve 3). When gelatin, previously treated with chromic acetate, i.e. Cr-gelatin is used, the restraining of the ripening is weaker (curve 4). The formaldehyde even exerts a slight acceleration of the ripening. The same curve of ripening is obtained also at four times higher concentrations of hardener (curve 5).

The restraining action of chromic acetate could be due to the adsorption of Cr^{+++} on the emulsion grains, but there is also restraint in the ripening, as we have seen, when a gelatin is used in which Cr^{+++} is involved in the cross-linking reaction. We admit that the restraint in the ripening is due, first of all, to the hardening of gelatin. It is evident that the effect of the hardening on the ripening is stronger when the emulsion grains are larger.

At pH = 5·8 the formaldehyde hardens comparatively weakly, but it blocks nevertheless a part of amino-groups with which the gelatin molecules are adsorbed on the surface of the silver bromide microcrystals. From this point of view one can explain the weak accelerating action of the formaldehyde on the physical ripening.

Fig. 2 shows curves of ripening of ammoniacal emulsions obtained at a small excess of potassium bromide. It is seen that in presence of chromic acetate the emulsion does not ripen (curve 2). When the emulsions ripen with Cr-gelatin the ripening is restrained to a considerably

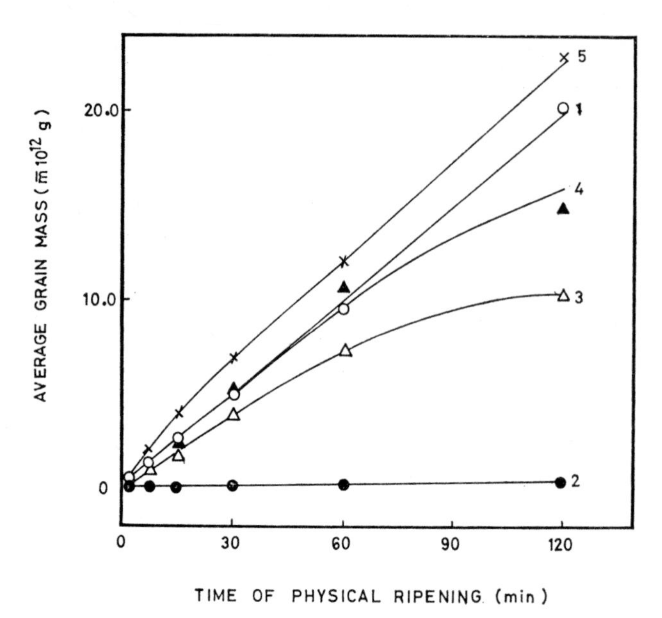

Fig. 1. Effect of hardeners on the physical ripening of "neutral" emulsions (pH = 5, 8, temperature 70°C) at different excess of KBr.

1—Control (C_{KBr} = 1·17 mole/l).
2—Control and with hardeners (C_{KBr} = 0·039 mole/l).
3—With chromic acetate (C_{KBr} = 1·17 mole/l).
4—"Cr-gelatin" is used (C_{KBr} = 1·17 mole/l).
5—With formaldehyde (C_{KBr} = 1·17 mole/l).

weaker extent (curve 3). Contrary to the neutral emulsions, the formaldehyde restrains the ripening of ammoniacal emulsions (curve 4). Restraining of ripening is observed also when formaldehyde is added in the 30th minute of the ripening, but the effect is weaker (curve 5). As a rule, the relative restraining of ripening is more clearly expressed during a longer time of ripening i.e., at larger average masses of emulsion grains. Under "relative restraint", we understand the relation $\bar{m}_1/\bar{m}_2$ where $\bar{m}_1$ is the average mass obtained in absence of hardener and $\bar{m}_2$ is the average mass obtained in the presence of hardener at a determined time of ripening.

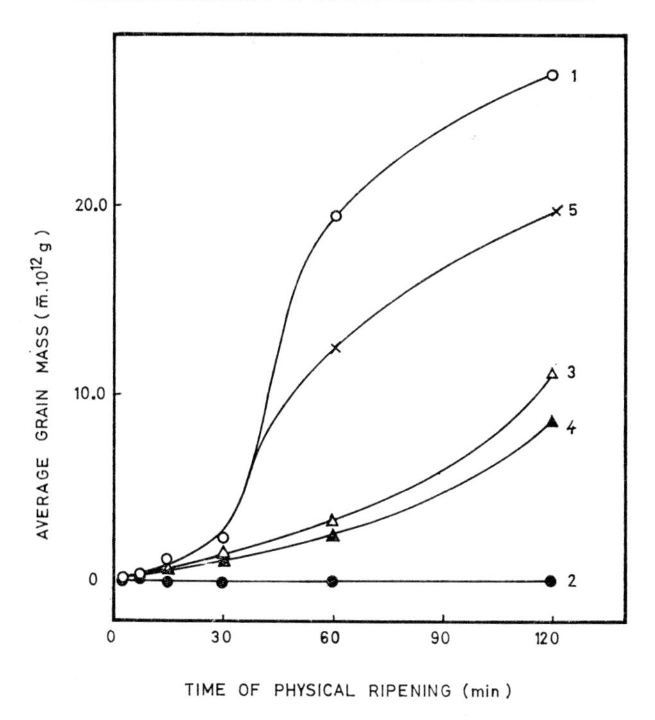

Fig. 2. Effect of hardeners on the physical ripening of ammoniacal emulsions (pH = 10·9; temperature 45°C) at small excess of KBr (C_{KBr} = 0·039 mole/l).

1—Control.
2—With chromic acetate.
3—"Cr-gelatin" is used.
4—With formaldehyde added 1 min prior to precipitation.
5—With formaldehyde added at 30th minute of ripening.

Similar effects of the hardeners are obtained also when ammoniacal emulsions are ripening at large excess of potassium bromide (Fig. 3). The relative restraint of ripening is, however, considerably weaker in comparison with the previous case.

It is known that the chromium salts do not harden at high pH. In such a case, the strong restraining action of the chromic acetate can not be explained by the hardening of the gelatin. This may be possible when a preliminary hardened gelatin, for instance "Cr-gelatin," is used, but then the effect is, as we have seen, much weaker. In such a case, it is quite possible that the restraint in ripening is due to adsorption of $Cr(OH)_3$ or to chromic ammonia complex ions. The first supposition can be tested when the ripening is run at pH = 10·9 in NaOH medium.

Fig. 4 shows that the restraint of the ripening which can be due to adsorption of $Cr(OH)_3$ is comparatively weak (curve 2) and the use of "Cr-gelatin" even leads to an acceleration of ripening (curve 3). In the last case, there seems to be a blocking of carboxyl groups with which the gelatin molecules can be adsorbed in alkali medium.

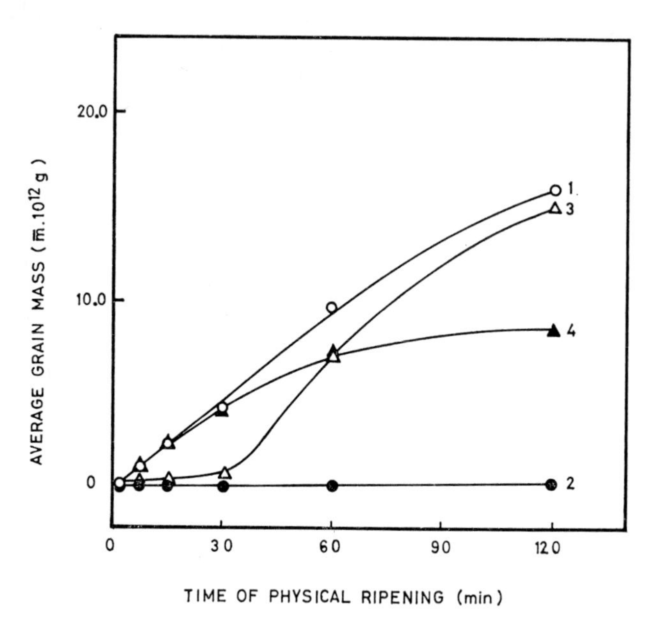

Fig. 3. Effect of hardeners on the physical ripening of ammoniacal emulsions (pH = 10·9; temperature 45°C) at large excess of KBr (C_{KBr} = 1·17 mole/l).

1—Control.
2—With chromic acetate.
3—"Cr-gelatin" is used.
4—With formaldehyde.

On the basis of these experiments we admit that the strong restraining action of Cr^{+++} in ammoniacal emulsions is due to adsorption of chromic ammonia complex ions on the surface of the microcrystals of silver bromide. We do not know the composition of these complex ions, but we suppose they could be of the type of $Cr(NH_3)^{+++}$, where the ammonia may partially be replaced by H_2O or Br^-. The strongly restraining action of the metal ammonia complex ions ($Cd(NH_3)_4^{++}$ $Cu(NH_3)^{++}$ and $Co(NH_3)_6^{+++}$ on the physical ripening of photographic emulsions was established by one of the authors of the present paper.[3][4] Especially strong is the restraining effect caused by

$Co(NH_3)_6^{+++}$: it is supposed[4] that they block the active centres of growth of AgBr microcrystals. Similar explanation may be given also of the effect of the analogical in structure chromic ammonia complex ions.

The restraining action of formaldehyde in ammonia or NaOH medium (Fig. 4—curve 4) could be explained by its reduction properties. Emulsions which are ripening with formaldehyde in alkali medium

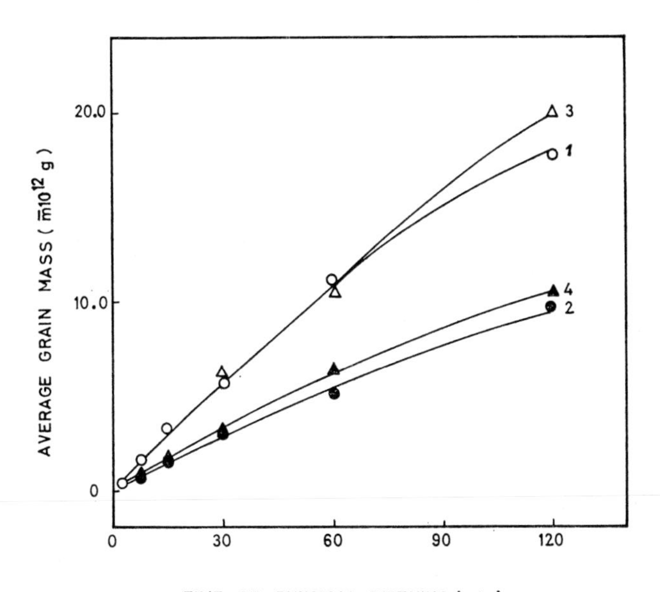

Fig. 4. Effect of hardeners on the physical ripening of emulsions made in NaOH medium (pH = 10·9; temperature 70°C; C_{KBr} = 1·17 mole/l).

1—Control.
2—With chromic acetate.
3—"Cr-gelatin" is used.
4—With formaldehyde.

give a high fog density in the developer. It may be admitted that silver deposit on AgBr microcrystals should restrain their growth. In order to test our supposition we have carried out some experiments with ammoniacal emulsions at small excess of potassium bromide. At first, we have tried the effect of the reducer glucose in concentration 0·0154 mole/l (same as the concentration of the formaldehyde). We have established that the emulsion gives a fog in the developer, but there has been no effect on the ripening. In the second experiment we have shown how the illuminating and obtaining of print-out silver affects the process of ripening. We have established the interesting fact that the physical ripening has been accelerated and that higher values of

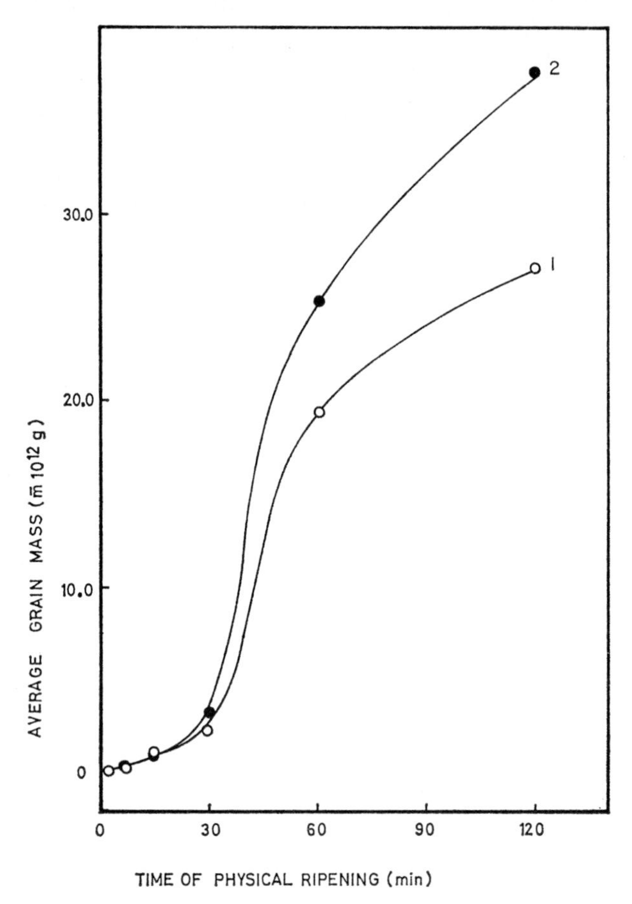

Fig. 5. Effect of illumination on physical ripening of ammoniacal emulsion (pH = 10·9; temperature 45°C; C_{KBr} = 0·039 mole/l).

1—Control.
2—The emulsion is illuminated 6 min after the third minute of ripening.
3—A 75W incandescent lamp is used at 20 cm distance.

the average grain masses have been obtained (Fig. 5). In a third experiment, in an emulsion ripening in the presence of formaldehyde, we have added during the ripening an oxidant (bromine or hydrogenium peroxide). Changes in the control ripening curve have not been observed.

From the last experiments it follows that the main cause which leads to a restraint of the physical ripening by formaldehyde is the hardening of the gelatin. This effect appears stronger when the grains are larger as in the effect of chromic acetate in neutral emulsions.

A probable reason for the restraining action of hardeners in physical ripening is the cross-linking of gelatin, which changes its structural properties and the rate of the diffusion process. In order to explain why the hardener action does not appear in the fine-grain emulsions where there is cross-linking too, but appears only then when the grains reach certain critical sizes, for instance $\bar{m} > 0{\cdot}5 \times 10^{-12}$ g, it could be assumed that on larger grains, after hardening, more compact or thicker adsorption layers of gelatin are formed. This will decrease the rate of the diffusion process, and, hence, the rate of the Ostwald ripening or of the "coalescence".

Under "coalescence" we understand collison of the grains and sticking together, above all, by their protective gelatin layers, subsequent dilution of the smaller grains and deposition of their substance through diffusion on the larger grains. Because of the shorter path of diffusion and the higher concentration gradient, the process of "coalescence" should run with greater rate than the process of Ostwald ripening, where the sticking is excluded.

The microanalytical determination of the amount of adsorbed gelatin of the AgBr surface shows that at hardening by formaldehyde the amount of the adsorbed gelatin increases with about 30%. The determination in both cases has been made at $\bar{m} \approx 4{\cdot}0 \times 10^{-12}$ g. The data shown in Table 1 are in agreement with the above mentioned supposition that hardening creates more compact or thicker adsorption gelatin layers on AgBr surface.

Table 1
Amount of adsorbed gelatin on the emulsion grains in emulsions hardened or not hardened by formaldehyde

Type of emulsion	*mg gelatin adsorbed/cm² AgBr*
not hardened	$0{\cdot}61 \times 10^{-3}$
hardened	$0{\cdot}79 \times 10^{-3}$

The weaker effect of the hardeners as restrainers in emulsions which ripen at a large excess of potassium bromide can be explained to a great extent by the decrease of the degree of hardening caused by the alkali salts. Similar data are known about the hardening of collagen.[(5)]

References

(1) Tsariov, B. A., Ganneman, W. W., Martish, G. G. and Jakowleva, T. P., *Trudy Leningr. Inst. Kinoinzh,* **5,** 159 (1959).
(2) Sheppard, S. E., Lambert, R. H. and Keenan, R. L., *J. Phys. Chem.*, **36,** 174 (1932).
(3) Katsev, A., *III Wiss. und Angew, Photogr. Konferenz*, Budapest, 1961.
(4) Katsev, A., Dr. Thesis, Bulgarian Academy of Science, Institute of Physical Chemistry, Sofia, 1967.
(5) Mikhailow, A. N., *Khimia dubiashchikh veshchestv i protessov dubleniya*, Moskva, 217–218 (1953).

Restrainers in Gelatin

Restraining Properties and Their Determination in Photographic Gelatins

H. AMMANN-BRASS

Laboratory of Photographic Chemistry and Technology, Fribourg (Switzerland)

ABSTRACT. Certain non-collagenous components occurring in photographic gelatins, which slow down or inhibit the physical and chemical ripening processes are designated in the literature as restrainers.

There exists beside the "natural" restrainers other—mostly organic—compounds with similar properties, e.g. anti-foggants and emulsion stabilizers. Such substances are to be considered as "artificial" restrainers. Additions of these to gelatins may control the degree of restraining properties.

Neither the presence, nor the type and the concentration of restrainer components are sufficient criteria for their activity. The reaction conditions in the investigated system are of a particular interest, especially pH.

Evidence by experiment is given, that at constant content of restrainers in gelatin, the degree of restraining is strongly dependent on pH. For instance, Adenine loses its inhibiting properties at pH < 5, but it will react as a powerful restrainer at pH $> 6{\cdot}5$.

The activity of most restrainers increases with pH.

INTRODUCTION

In photographic gelatins usually certain components exist which slow down or inhibit the physical and chemical ripening. These components are designated as "restrainers".

Steigmann[1] first pointed to this important group of active substances. He devised a simple method of evaluating restraining properties by turbidity measurements.[2] Steigmann's original test was modified in my laboratory and its scope was extended.[3]

It may be stated that up to now all methods using the turbidity test for characterizing photographic gelatins are based on the precipitation and physical ripening of silver halide suspensions in presence of the test gelatin. This conventional type of turbidity test has a serious inconvenience, because the ripening characteristics of silver halide suspensions depend on the type and concentration of the gelatin present during precipitation. To prevent the influence of the test gelatin during the precipitation stage, our laboratory has proposed a modified turbidity test,[4],[5] in which precipitation and ripening stages are clearly separated. Starting always under the same working conditions for precipitation (by using an inert-type standard gelatin at one concentration only), the ripening properties of the test gelatin are well determined, if the latter is added at varied concentrations to the silver halide suspension 30 s later.

The limit of detection for sulphur sensitizers and restrainers is improved by increasing the gelatin: silver halide ratio in the suspension.

The selected standard inert gelatin for precipitation has to be practically free of sensitizers (e.g. thiosulphate) and restrainers (e.g. nucleic acids).

Nature of restrainers

Our knowledge regarding the chemical nature of restrainers is still incomplete. The existence of nucleic acids and/or their degradation products in photographic gelatins is generally accepted.[6],[7] However, there are many experimental facts indicating that other restrainers than nucleic acids must still be present.[8] Although until now, we failed to identify such inhibiting components in gelatins by chemical means, we nevertheless succeeded in detecting their influence on physical ripening with some of the modified turbidity tests.[9]

Nucleic acids represent a class of natural restrainers in gelatins. In contrast to these, we have to consider antifoggants and emulsion stabilizers as artificial restrainers. If these synthetic products are added to gelatins, they likewise have pronounced inhibiting effects on the physical ripening. Thus they may be used to adjust the degree of restraining properties.

Dependence of the restraining properties on working conditions

It can be shown experimentally that the restrainer activity depends to a large extent on the chemical constitution of the restrainer, on its concentration and on the silver ion, and the hydrogen ion concentration (pAg, pH) in solution. For this reason the characterization of gelatins with respect to their behaviour in the photographic emulsion is very complex.

It is, therefore, advisable to characterize individual restrainers experimentally in establishing the dependence of their restrainer activity:

1. on the restrainer content;
2. on pH.

Dependence of the restrainer properties on the molecular weight of nucleic acids

Several authors have already stated, that the restrainer activity of nucleic acids is not only a function of their concentration (weight per volume) and of pH, but also of their molecular weight.[10] This fact is not to be forgotten. We do not intend, however, to comment further on this topic.

The aim of the present paper is to deal with the characterization of eight ossein gelatin samples,[11] offered by the manufacturers to participants of the IAG, and to reveal the action of so-called "natural restrainers" (as DNA, RNA, adenine, guanine) added to an inert gelatin depending on the restrainer type and concentration, and on pH.[12]

EXPERIMENTAL

The modified turbidity test as described in detail by the author[5] has proved to be a very sensitive means to demonstrate the restrainer activity in photographic gelatins.

Characterization of various types of gelatins

To characterize various types of gelatins, eight suspensions of silver chloride are prepared, starting under strictly the same conditions with the precipitation at low concentration (1%) of an inert gelatin. After 30 s the resulting silver halide solutions are added consecutively to eight solutions of the test gelatin at various concentrations (0·5–10%) and physical ripening is achieved during 32 min at constant temperature (77°C).

Characterization of the restrainer activity

To characterize the activity of a restrainer (e.g. deoxyribonucleic acid (DNA), ribonucleic acid (RNA), adenine, guanine) at constant gelatin concentration depending on the restrainer content and/or the pH, the physical ripening of eight AgCl suspensions is carried out again with one concentration of gelatin only (7·3%). For this a well defined inert gelatin is used, with various additions of the same restrainer at constant pH or a constant addition of one restrainer but at various pH. The Rousselot ossein inert-type gelatin 16.448 conforms to the prescribed requirements.

Preparation of AgCl suspensions

The formulas serving as the basis for the outlined experiments are as follows:

Precipitation (first to fourth experimental series)

I.	Water	
	Inert-type standard gelatin	0·2 g
	$NaCl/CdCl_2$ (0·707 N)	1·3 ml
	Total volume I	17·3 ml
II.	$AgNO_3$ (0·100 N)	2·7 ml
	Total volume II	2·7 ml
	Total volume of AgCl suspension	20·0 ml

Physical ripening

30 s after precipitation the above volume of 20 ml of AgCl suspension is added to:

First experimental series

III.	Water	
	Test gelatin (IAG sample)	0·75–15 g
	$NaCl/CdCl_2$ (0·707 N)	6·25 ml
	pH for physical ripening adjusted to	6·5 ± 0·2
	Total volume III	130 ml

Second experimental series

III.	Water	
	Test gelatin (IAG sample)	11 g
	$NaCl/CdCl_2$ (0·707 N)	6·25 ml
	pH for physical ripening adjusted to	3–9
	Total volume III	130 ml

Third experimental series

III. Water	
Inert-type standard gelatin (with mentioned restrainer additions)	11 g
$NaCl/CdCl_2$ (0·707 N)	6·25 ml
pH for physical ripening adjusted to	6·5 ± 0·2
Total volume III	130 ml

Fourth experimental series

III. Water	
Inert-type standard gelatin (with mentioned restrainer additions)	11 g
$NaCl/CdCl_2$ (0·707 N)	6·25 ml
pH for physical ripening adjusted to	3–9
Total volume III	130 ml

The final volume of the AgCl suspension is constant (150 ml). Precipitation and physical ripening are performed at 77°C. Samples of 20 ml suspension are removed at 1, 2, 4, 8, 16 and 32 min during ripening. They are diluted with 60 ml water. Acidulation is necessary if the pH value of the sample is above 6·5. Turbidity measurements are carried out in the conventional manner.

RESULTS

Dependence of physical ripening at constant pH on the concentration of the test gelatin

It is commonly accepted that bone gelatins are relatively little restrained.[13] Therefore the characterization of such gelatins with the conventional turbidity test (e.g. method A = standard test[5]) is less suitable. To improve the differentiation, we examined the eight limed type ossein gelatins of IAG with the modified turbidity test (method F) as described above.[14]

The resulting diagrams show considerable differences in the restrainer action (Fig. 1). Rousselot 16.448 is extremely little restrained. Leiner 1701 is much more restrained. It is to be stressed, however, that both types are usually claimed to be little restrained. It depends therefore on the sensitivity of the testing method, whether a clear differentiation of two rather similar gelatins is practicable or not. As in method F the

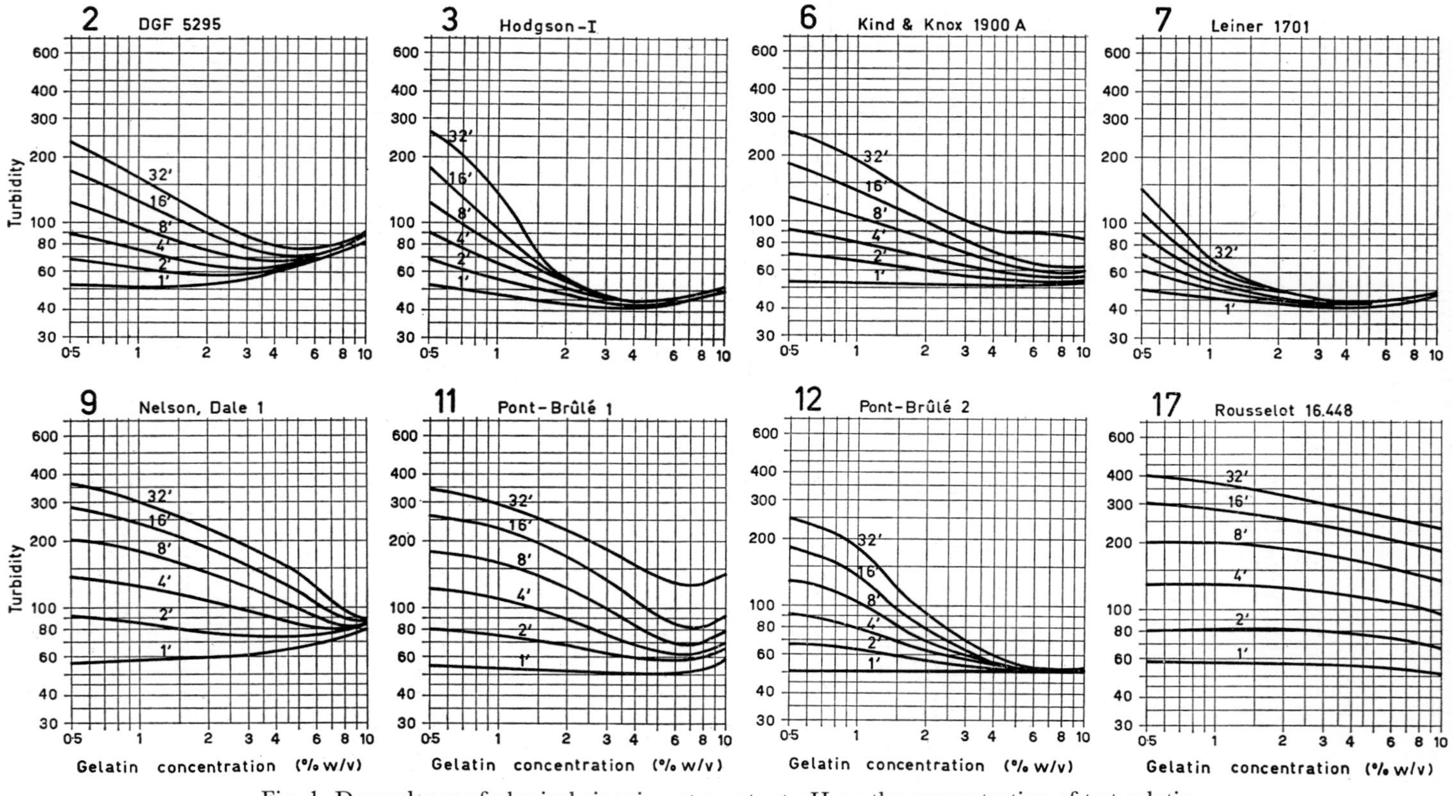

Fig. 1. Dependence of physical ripening at constant pH on the concentration of test gelatin

Precipitation with gelatin Rousselot 14.671: concentration constant 1%
Ripening with test gelatin: concentration varied 0·5–10%; pH constant 6·5 ± 0·2

test gelatin is only present during physical ripening, the respective diagrams characterize specifically the ripening behaviour of examined samples.

All test gelatins were adjusted to pH 6·5 ± 0·2 by addition of adequate volumes of NaOH or HNO_3.[15]

Dependence of physical ripening on pH for various test gelatins

The results presented (Fig. 2) concern the same limed ossein gelatins as above. The diagrams show that the physical ripening with Rousselot 16.448 depends much less on pH than the other samples do. However, Hodgson I and Leiner 1701 are clearly the most restrained of the examined bone gelatins. Physical ripening is completely inhibited with both samples in the pH range from pH 4–7. While ripening with Hodgson I is insignificant from pH 7–9, it becomes again very marked with Leiner 1701 in the same pH range. Pont-Brûlé 1 and Kind & Knox 1900A show a distinct restrainer activity. It is however, much less than that of DGF 5295 and of Pont-Brûlé 2.

In Figs. 1 and 2 the restrainer activity of IAG bone gelatins is conclusively demonstrated. In order to obtain valuable informations on the type of natural restrainers which may be present in these gelatins, the performance of two further experimental series was required.

Dependence of physical ripening at constant pH on restrainer additions

The extremely little restrained IAG gelatin Rousselot 16.448 (a substitute for Rousselot 14.671) was selected as a ripening gelatin. The gelatin was used at a concentration of 7·3% exclusively, but with various additions of restrainer.

The experiments were performed with deoxyribonucleic acid (DNA), ribonucleic acid (RNA), adenine and guanine respectively. The pH of the silver chloride suspensions during ripening was kept constant (pH 6·5 ± 0·2).

The diagrams in Fig. 3 illustrate the variations of restrainer activities with increasing restrainer concentrations. While DNA and RNA already show a characteristic restrainer effect with less than 5 ppm added, adenine requires at least 15 ppm and guanine about 50 ppm for initiation of an inhibiting effect. The turbidity diagrams characterize the specific activity of the four restrainers concerned. In comparing the results, a clear difference between DNA or RNA on the one hand and adenine or guanine on the other hand may be observed.

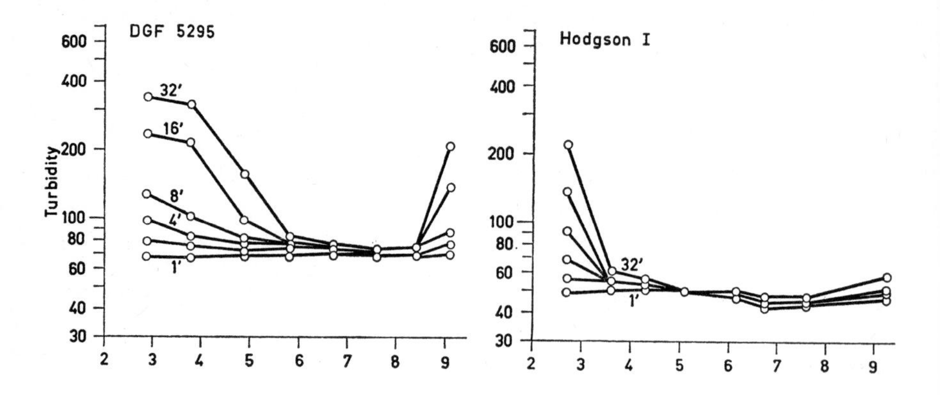
DGF 5295
Turbidity
600
400
200
100
80
60
40
30
32'
16'
8'
4'
1'
2
3
4
5
6
7
8
9
Hodgson I
32'
1'

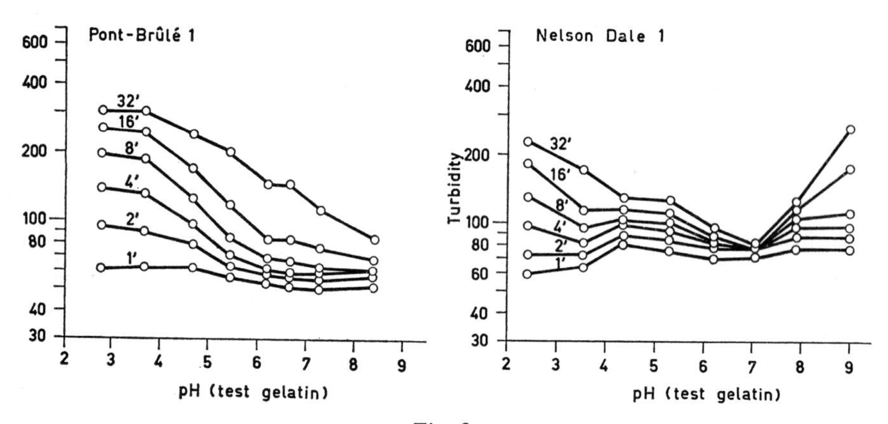
Pont-Brûlé 1
32'
16'
8'
4'
2'
1'
pH (test gelatin)
Nelson Dale 1
Turbidity
32'
16'
8'
4'
2'
1'
pH (test gelatin)

Fig. 2.

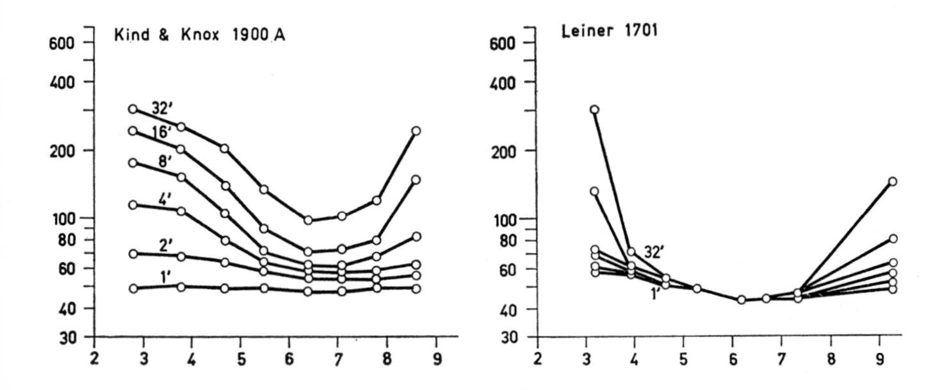

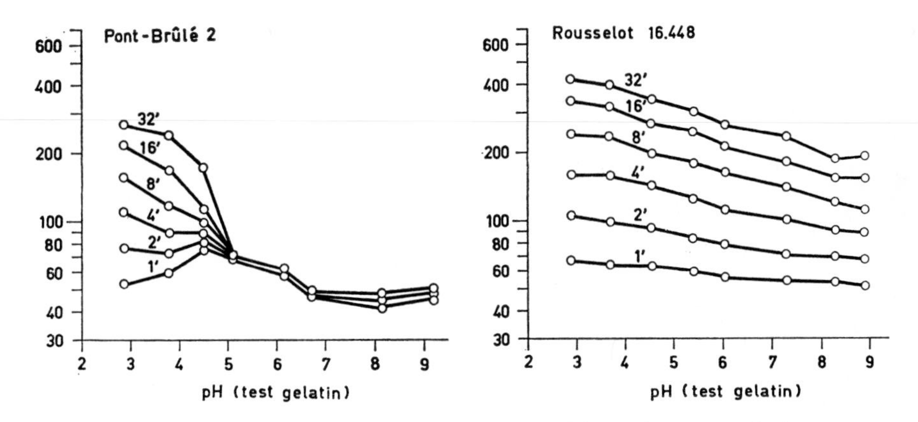

Fig. 2. Dependence of physical ripening on pH for various test gelatins

Precipitation	with gelatin Rousselot 16.448	
	concentration constant	1%
Ripening	with test gelatin	
	concentration constant	7·3%
	pH varied	3–9

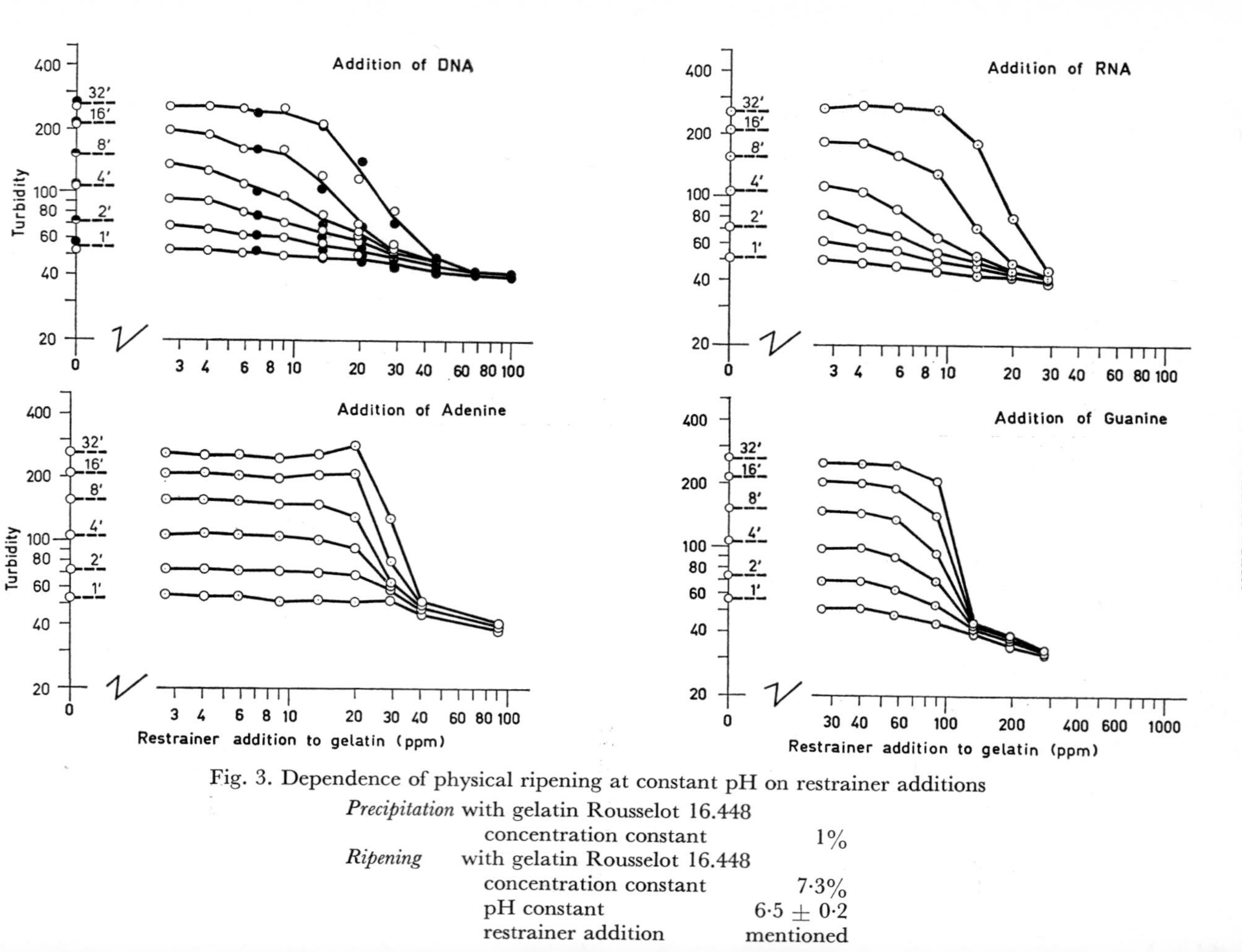

Fig. 3. Dependence of physical ripening at constant pH on restrainer additions

Precipitation	with gelatin Rousselot 16.448	
	concentration constant	1%
Ripening	with gelatin Rousselot 16.448	
	concentration constant	7·3%
	pH constant	6·5 ± 0·2
	restrainer addition	mentioned

Dependence of physical ripening on pH for various restrainer additions

The restrainer action of DNA, RNA, adenine and guanine respectively have been investigated. The variation in concentration within 0 and 80 ppm is performed by addition of adequate volumes of the restrainer dissolved in suitable solvents. The pH is adjusted by addition of HNO_3 respectively NaOH to the ripening gelatin.

The very interesting results are characterized by the diagrams in Fig. 4. With increasing additions of DNA two minima of turbidity (=maxima of restrainer activity) are observed: the first at a pH between 4·5 and 6·5, the second at a pH of more than 8–8·5.

The corresponding test with the inert gelatin Rousselot 16.448 (without any restrainer addition) can be seen in Fig. 2 (=reference diagram).

Addition of RNA shows only one marked minimum of turbidity at a pH between 4·5 and 6·5. Comparing the curves of RNA with DNA characteristic differences appear markedly with additions of 10–40 ppm and with a pH of more than 7·5. While the restrainer activity is very marked for DNA, it is much less evident for RNA.

Adenine and guanine behave quite differently from DNA and RNA. With increasing additions the inhibiting effect shifts from higher to lower pH values. Up to 80 ppm of adenine practically no restrainer effect is observed in the pH range below 5. With more than 40 ppm, adenine inhibits completely the physical ripening at a pH above 6·5. The action of guanine is similar in character to that of adenine but gradually less intense.

CONCLUSIONS

The results presented in Figs. 1–4 demonstrate clearly the efficiency of the modified turbidity test. In using method F the limit of detection[16] for thiosulphate and for deoxyribonucleic acid (low molecular DNA) is 1 ppm $Na_2S_2O_3$ (=0·2 ppm active sulphur) or 5–10 ppm DNA.

Low molecular DNA is a more efficient restrainer than high molecular DNA.[10]

We found under corresponding working conditions that DNA at a low concentration restrains the physical ripening of silver halide suspensions more than adenine. However, at a high concentration adenine may be a more efficient restrainer than DNA.

Moreover, we found that the dependence of the restrainer activity on pH is not the same for various types of restrainers.

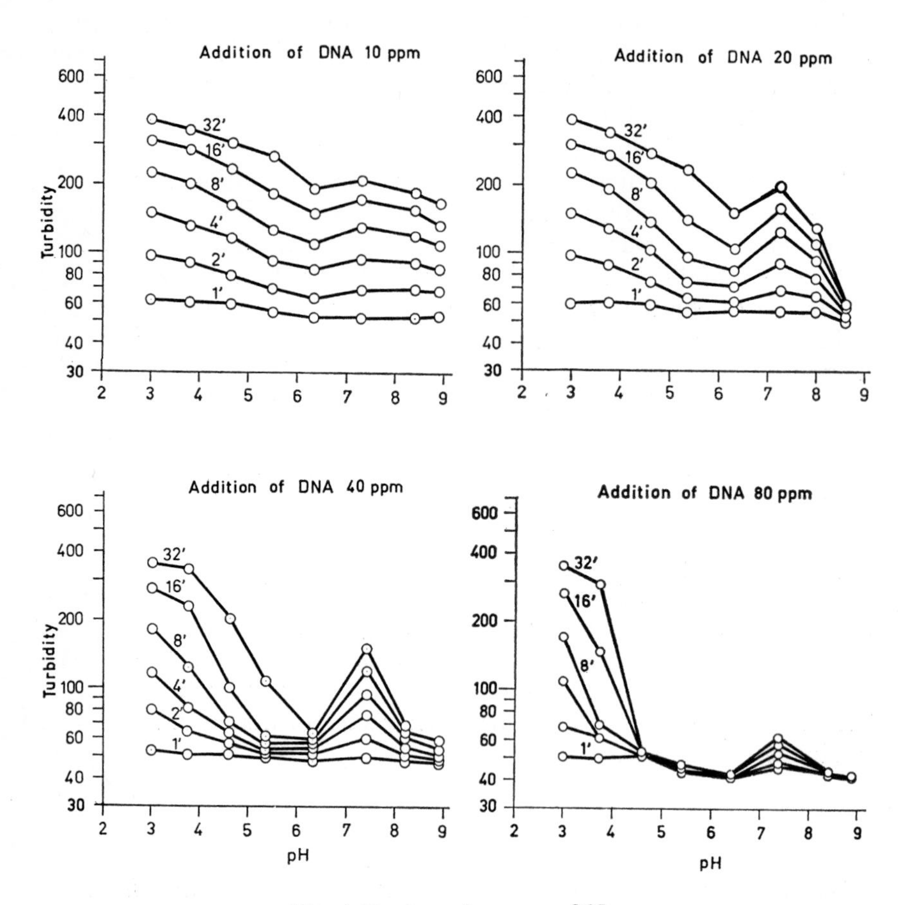

Fig. 4. For legend see page 265.

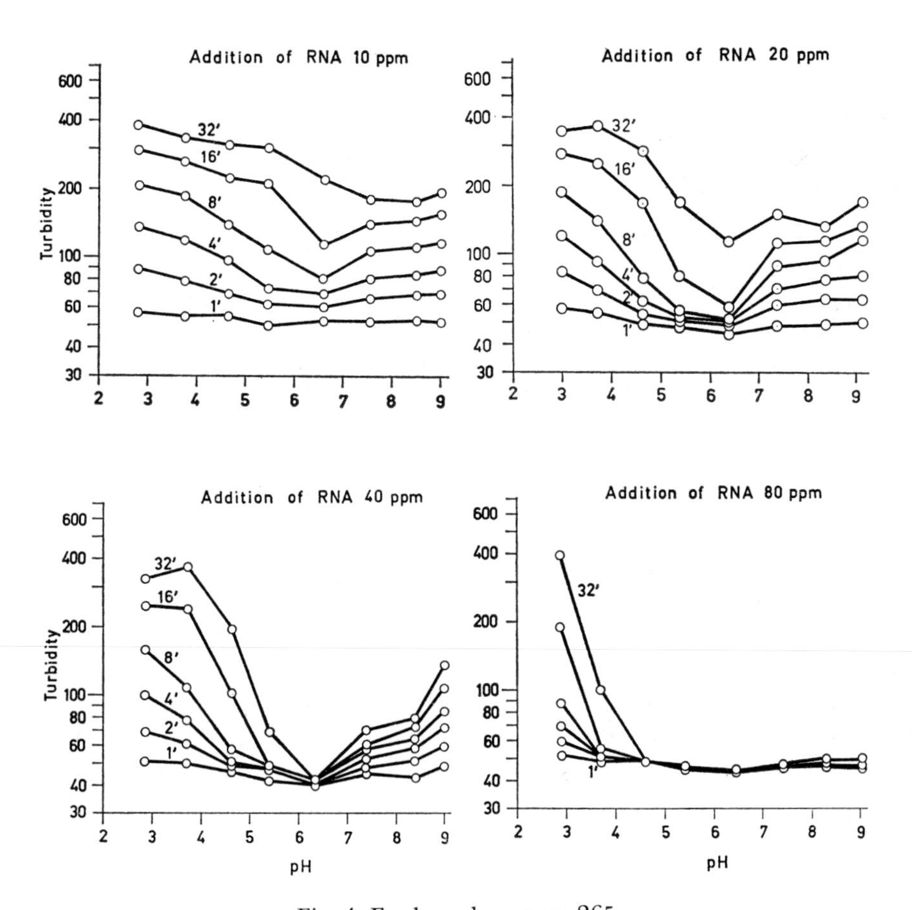

Fig. 4. For legend see page 265.

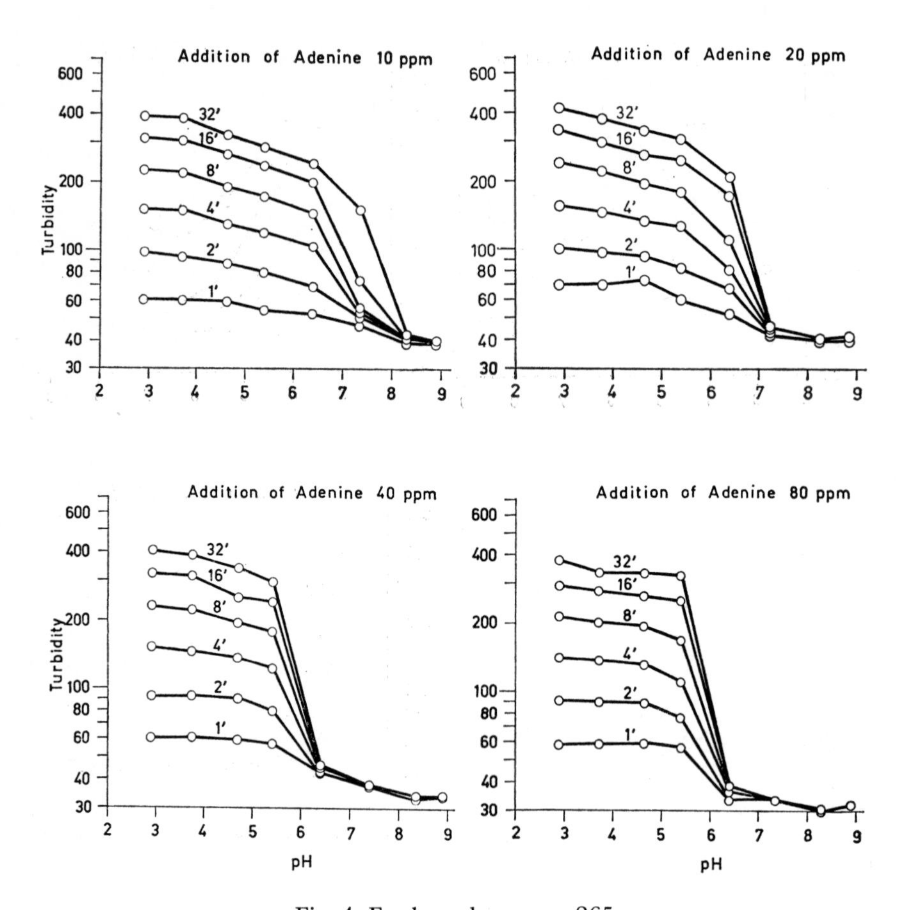

Fig. 4. For legend see page 265.

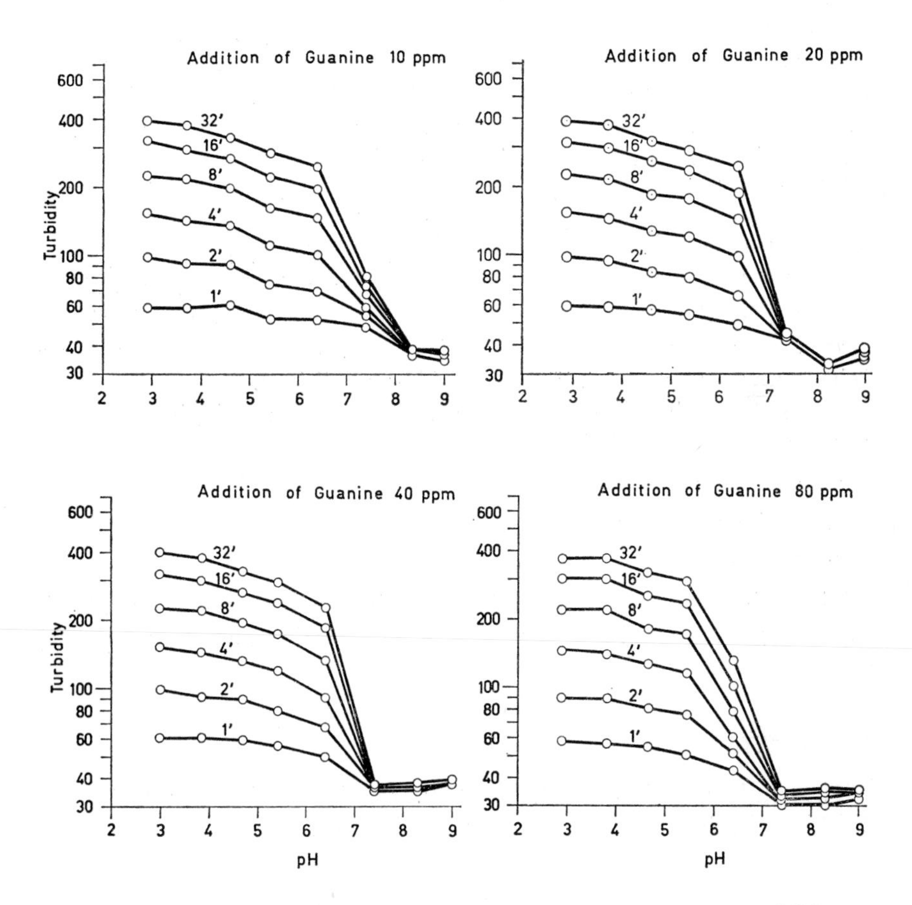

Fig. 4. Dependence of physical ripening on pH for various restrainer additions

Precipitation	with gelatin Rousselot 16.448	
	concentration constant	1%
Ripening	with gelatin Rousselot 16.448	
	concentration constant	7·3%
	pH varied	3–9
	restrainer addition	mentioned

We have to distinguish strictly between the free adenine base and the chemically bound adenine in the nucleic acid molecule. Nucleic acid contains about 10% of its weight of chemically bound adenine[17] and approximately the same proportion of bound guanine.

Our experiments show clearly that the restrainer activity of 100 ppm of DNA does not at all correspond to that of 10 ppm free adenine base at constant pH. Furthermore, the restrainer activity of free and bound adenine show a completely different pH dependence.

The results of the outlined experiments lead to a new criterion[18] for completely inert gelatins. According to the latest conception, such gelatins have to be free of sensitizers and restrainers. The IAG gelatin Rousselot 16.448 is an excellent example for such a type. It is characterized by the exceptionally small dependence of its ripening properties on gelatin concentration and on pH. Therefore, inert gelatins behave unrestrained under most working conditions.

On the other hand, gelatins with a low, medium or high content of restrainer depend in their restraining properties on

1. the restrainer type,
2. on the restrainer concentration, and
3. on pH.

Thus, the same gelatin sample can behave more or less restrained according to type and concentration of the restrainer, and to the pH of the system concerned.[19]

ACKNOWLEDGEMENT

The author wishes to thank Mrs. O. Marbacher for technical assistance in the experimental part of this work.

References

(1) Steigmann, A., *Kolloid. Z.*, **43,** 400 (1927).
(2) Steigmann, A., *Sci. Ind. Photogr.*, [2], **6,** 1 (1935).
(3) Ammann-Brass, H., *Kolloid. Z.*, **110,** 115 (1948). *Sci Ind. Photogr.*, [2], **19,** 406 (1948).
(4) Ammann-Brass, H., *The Photographic Image* (Symposium, Tokyo 1967), p. 15–16 (ed. S. Kikuchi). Focal Press, London (1970).
(5) Ammann-Brass, H., *Photogr. Korresp.*, **106,** 10–32 (1970).
(6) Beersmans, J., *Photographic Science* (Symposium, Zurich 1961), p. 134 (ed. W. F. Berg). Focal Press, London (1963).
(7) Russell, G., *Chemical Analysis in Photography*, p. 77. Focal Press, London (1965).
(8) Möller, G., "Contribution to IAG, in *Restrainer in Photographic Gelatins* (IAG Reports 1965–1969). Ed. H. Ammann-Brass, Fribourg (1971).

(9) Ammann-Brass, H., see Reference 5, p. 29.
(10) Steigmann, A., *Sci. Ind. Photogr.*, [2], **35,** 155 (1964).
(11) Ammann-Brass, H., see Reference 5, p. 11.
(12) Reindorp, J. H., "Contribution to IAG", in *Restrainer in Photographic Gelatins* (IAG Reports 1965–1969). See Reference 8.
(13) Russell, G., *J. Photogr. Sci.*, **15,** 236 (1967).
(14) Ammann-Brass, H., see Reference 5, p. 12, 14, 23.
(15) Ammann-Brass, H., see Reference 5, p. 31.
(16) Ammann-Brass, H., see Reference 5, p. 29.
(17) Janus, J. W. and Nellist, D. R., *J. Photogr. Sci.*, **15,** 147 (1967).
(18) Kelly, W. D., Krummenerl, T., Steigmann, A., Beersmans, J., Tschibissow, K. W., Hautot, A. and Ammann-Brass, H., Discussion in *Scientific Photography* (Symposium, Liège 1959), p. 320–323. Pergamon Press, London (1962).
(19) Ammann-Brass, H., in *Photographic Science* (Symposium, Paris 1965), p. 269. Focal Press, London (1967).

Determination of the Physical Ripening Restraining Properties of Gelatins and Artificial Restrainers

Y. OHYAMA

Mitsubishi Paper Mills Ltd., Photo and Repro Division, Kaiden Nagaoka-machi, Otokuni-gun Kyoto-fu, Japan

ABSTRACT. Restraining properties of some of photographic gelatin and artificial restrainers were examined by turbidity measurement of AgCl (13·3 meq) suspension in 0·1% polyacrylamide solution with various added amounts of a test sample. The report consists of three parts: (1) Restraining behaviours thus examined with some typical samples of photographic gelatin were compared with their accelerating behaviours examined with a similar turbidity test of AgCl suspension in polyvinylalcohol (1%) with added gelatin, which has been formerly proposed by the author. (2) Restraining behaviours of artificial restrainers such as 2-mercapto-benzimidazole, benzotriazole and adenine beside polyvinylalcohol and the effect of pH upon them were examined and accurate data obtained. (3) Using sixteen samples of IAG gelatin, correlations between degrees of restraining (Ha and Hb) based on different criteria in the present method and correlations between the present method and other methods hitherto used were discussed in view of the gelatin/silver ratio, and it was concluded that the simplest way in estimating the practical physical restraining power of photographic gelatin as a grain growth regulator is reduced to the measurement of turbidity of the emulsion in the proposed method at 1% gelatin concentration (=4·4 g gelatin/g $AgNO_3$).

INTRODUCTION

The turbidity test of Ammann-Brass[1] is well known and its usefulness for estimating ripening characteristics of photographic gelatin has been fully recognized in recent years. It seems, however, that this method is not suitable for the determination of restraining behaviours of artificial restrainers, particularly the effect of pH upon them, because of the interference with the behaviour of gelatin used for the experiment as a protective colloid.

A similar turbidity test[2] by the author which uses polyvinyl alcohol (1%) as a major protective colloid, is very useful to detect the existence and to estimate the amount of the accelerating activity for physical ripening (grain growth) in gelatin; it cannot, however, be used to determine the restraining activity of gelatin, in spite of the fact that the turbidity of the emulsion decreases again at higher gelatin concentration, because the phenomenon seems due to the fact that at higher concentration gelatin loses its inherent activity as an accelerator for grain growth and there appears again the extraordinary powerful restraining property of polyvinylalcohol itself alone or in cooperation with that of added gelatin.

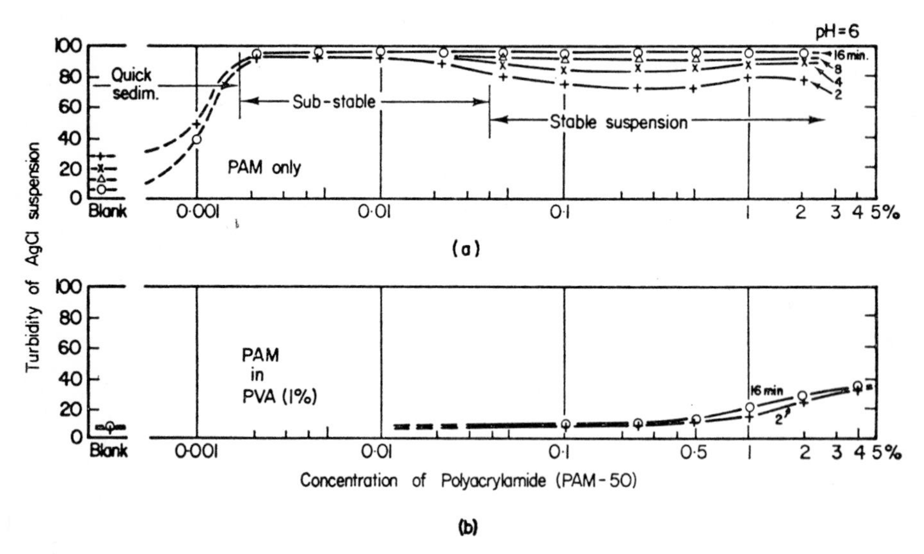

Fig. 1

In the present method, polyvinylalcohol (1%) is replaced by polyacrylamide (0·1–0·5%), and the restraining property of gelatin or of other substances for physical ripening can be determined almost free from their accelerating property, because polyacrylamide seems to be completely inert and to have no restraining property; it sustains the grain growth of silver chloride suspension quite well and the grain growth is stable in the broad range of its concentration (0·04–2%) as shown in Fig. 1(a). It also has no accelerating activity under 0·5% as shown in Fig. 1(b), and in the author's assumption the accelerating property of gelatin is only detectable at rather lower concentration in the presence of suitable restrainers in the emulsion, and is not detectable in the environment where the grains grow freely as in polyacrylamide. On the other hand the restraining property of gelatin can only be detected at a rather higher concentration (usually over 0·3%).

Hitherto the determination of the restraining property of an artificial restrainer at various pH of the emulsion has been hampered by the interference with the restraining property of gelatin, which in spite of its inertness, is used as a protective colloid in the experiment. In the present method however, the restraining property of an artificial restrainer can be determined independently at any pH, because in this method a completely inert medium, as polyacrylamide, is used in lieu of inert gelatin which has inherently some restraining property at a certain pH range.

EXPERIMENTAL

Procedure

To 32 ml of an aqueous solution of gelatin or other substance at various concentrations (10 ml of water in this solution may be replaced by alcohol when necessary for sparingly soluble substances), 10 ml of 0·6% solution of polyacrylamide,* 10 ml of an acetate buffer solution for controlling the pH of the suspension and 4 ml of 0·6 M sodium chloride solution are added. The mixture is heated to 70°C, and under agitation 4 ml of 0·2 M silver nitrate solution (70°C) is added in about 15 s.

2 ml portions of this suspension of silver chloride are drawn off at 2, 4, 8 and 16 min after the addition of silver ions. A portion is diluted with 20 ml of cold water and the turbidity is measured in a glass cuvette (1 cm thick). The turbidity measurement adopted in this experiment is similar to the method of Ammann-Brass[1] and the turbidity is expressed in a linear scale from 0–100.

Acetate buffer solutions† used for the experiment (10 ml for 60 ml of the suspension) are all equivalent to 0·6 M acetic acid and made up by mixing a variable amount of 0·6 M sodium acetate and 0·6 M acetic acid solution in cases of pH between 3 and 8, and at lower or higher pH (2 and 10), the addition of a small portion of sulphuric acid or sodium carbonate solution is sufficient. Buffering action of these solutions, however, is not sufficient at a higher concentration of gelatin and sometimes

* "Polyacrylamide (PAM-50)" manufactured by American Cyanamid Co. was used through the experiments.

† Phosphate or borate buffer is not suitable for the purpose, because either of them interfere with silver ion.

it was necessary to adjust the final pH of the gelatin solution, before addition of silver solution, with a smallest portion of suphuric acid or sodium carbonate solution.

Materials tested

Part 1: Photographic gelatins of five different types

Designation of samples and types are as follows:

Nippi IN-1	Inertized ossein
Nitta bone	Ordinary limed ossein
Atlantic 24488	Very active
Atlantic 27186	Medium restrained
Union 11193	Highly restrained

Part 2: Artificial restrainers

2-Mercapto-benzimidazole, benzotriazole and adenine are tested together with polyvinylalcohol.

Part 3: Eight pairs of IAG photographic gelatin

They are supplied by eight different makers in Europe for "Internationale Arbeitgemeinschaft zum Stadium der Hemmkörper in Photogelatinen" (IAG) under the chairmanship of Prof. H. Ammann-Brass since 1964. Each pair consists of gelatins differing in restraining property. Numbers and designations of samples are shown in Table 3.

Presentation of restraining behaviours and degrees of restraining

The turbidity of silver chloride suspensions, prepared according to the above mentioned procedure, is measured for ripening times of 2, 4, 8 and 16 min, and the values are plotted against the logarithm of the concentration of the gelatin or the restrainer added. Characteristic curves thus prepared are shown in Figs. 2, 4, 6 and 7.

Restraining behaviours of a gelatin or a restrainer are best shown in the form of characteristic curves but degrees of restraining in various gelatins or restrainers can be more conveniently compared and numerically determined from two types of criteria, i.e.

(a) Intensity: the turbidity decrease of the suspension at adequate concentration of addition.

(b) Sensitivity: the minimum concentration (or addition) which causes a certain adquate decrease of turbidity.

The degree of restraining (*Ha*) in criterion (a) is expressed simply by substracting the measured turbidity (T at 16 min ripening) from 100 and in the case of gelatin one of the four levels of concentration (i.e. 1, 2, 4 and 8%) may be chosen for the purposes and designated as for example, $Ha(1\%) = 100 - T(1\%)$ etc. In the case of artificial restrainers, usually 0·001% ($\fallingdotseq$0·1 mmole), 0·002% or 0·004% may be preferred.

As the degree of restraining in criterion (b), *Hb* values are derived from the reciprocal of concentration (*Ch*) at a chosen level of turbidity ($T = 90$ or 80) and calculated from the equation $Hb = 0{\cdot}1/Ch$. Lower turbidity (as for instance, $T = 50$) can be used in some cases, but in the case of gelatin of lower restraining property (e.g. ossein gelatin) turbidity of the suspension at 16 min ripening usually does not decrease under 70.

RESULTS AND DISCUSSION

Part 1: photographic gelatin samples of five different types

Restraining behaviours of these gelatin samples are shown as characteristic curves in Fig. 2. Curves are shown in the order of increasing restraining (from top to bottom) and degrees of restraining (*Ha* and *Hb*) measured on the curves are tabulated in Table 1. In the

Table 1

Restraining and accelerating behaviours of various types of gelatin

Samples of gelatin	*Restraining behaviours**							*Accelerating behaviours†*				
	Ha (= 100 − T) 16 *min ripening* C =			Hb (= 0·1/*Ch*)				A (= 0·1/*Ca*) T = 20		Hp (= 100 − T) 16 *min ripening* C =		
				T = 90		T = 80						
	1%	2%	4%	*C*%	Hb	*C*%	Hb	*C*%	A	1%	2%	4%
Nippi IN-1	10	34	38	1·03	9·7	1·35	7·4	0·038	2·7	58	43	15
Nitta bone	32	35	34	0·53	18·9	0·70	14·3	0·0076	13·2	9	26	52
Atlantic 24 488	28	49	58	0·50	20·0	0·78	12·8	0·0012	98·0	16	67	63
Atlantic 27 186	34	60	70	0·37	27·0	0·60	16·7	0·0045	22·2	17	13	51
Union 11 193	54	70	87	0·115	87·0	0·225	44·5	0·017	5·9	60	66	89

* Fig. 2.
† Fig. 3.

table, accelerating activity, A, of these gelatins for physical ripening and degrees of pseudo-restraining, *Hp*, are also tabulated, both of which are determined from the similar characteristic curves of accelerating behaviours of these gelatin samples, obtained by the author's method,[2] which has been published in his paper, but is briefly described below for convenience.

To 160 ml of water, 50 ml of 6% polyvinylalcohol and 20 ml of 0·6 M sodium chloride solution are added. The mixture is heated to 70°C and 20 ml of 0·2 M silver nitrate solution, at a temperature of 70°C, is added

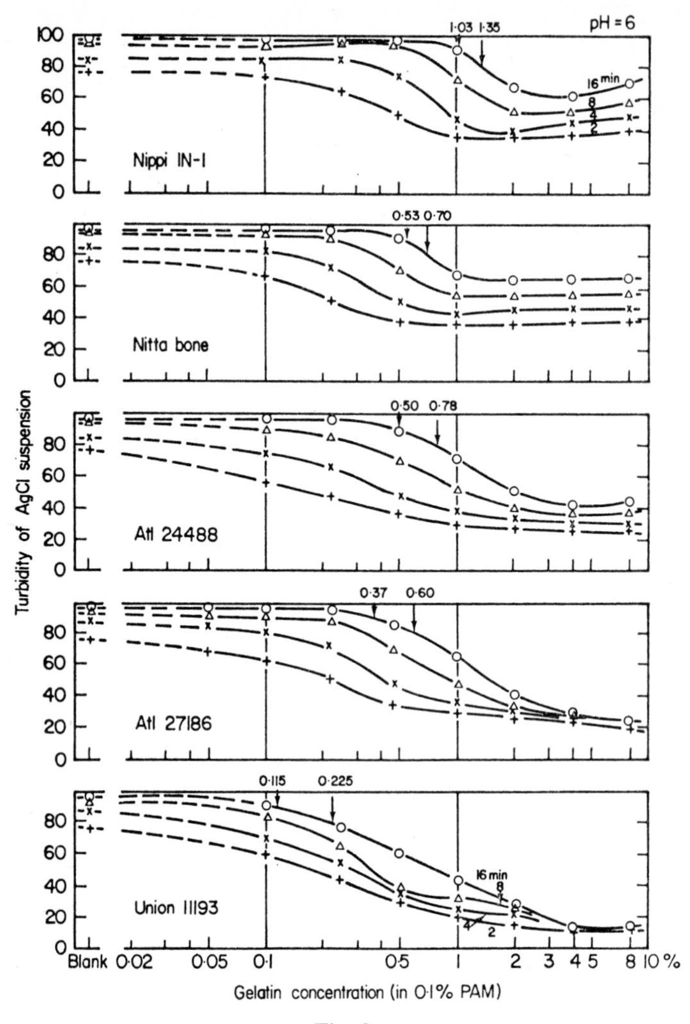

Fig. 2

in about 30 s. Four portions, 50 ml each, are drawn off from this neutral emulsion (pH = 6) of 250 ml. A variable, but known, amount of gelatin is dissolved (or swelled) with 10 ml of water and added to each of the four drawn off portions. After the addition of the gelatin, four portions of 2 ml are drawn off from each of the final emulsions at

2, 4, 8 and 16 min intervals. The four portions are then diluted with 20 ml of cold water and the turbidity is measured and characteristic curves are drawn by plotting the turbidity against the logarithm of concentration of added gelatin.

Acceleration characteristic curves thus obtained* are shown in Fig. 3. From the minimum concentration (*Ca*) to attain a certain increase of turbidity (ΔT) or to reach a definite level of turbidity (e.g. $T = 20$, and $\Delta T = 20 -$ initial T_0) of the emulsion (at 16 min ripening), degree of acceleration (*A*) can be determined as the reciprocal of the concentration, i.e. $A = 0{\cdot}1/Ca$.

At higher concentration (far right) on Fig. 3, curves usually tend to go downward or grain growth of the emulsion retards, as if the restraining property of gelatin reveals itself here. This apparent restraining, however, cannot be connected directly to the real restraining property of gelatin itself and should be called "pseudo-restraining", because there is always acting an extraordinary powerful restraining of polyvinylalcohol (1%) which is far more powerful than the restraining tendency of gelatin itself. The phenomenon seems to show that gelatin is losing its inherent accelerating property for grain growth of silver halide, which is only detectable at lower concentration and in the presence of suitable restrainers, and there appears again an extraordinary powerful restraining action of polyvinylalcohol intact or in cooperation with rather weaker restraining property of gelatin. It is also evident that degrees of this "pseudo"-restraining ($Hp = 100 - T$) measured at various gelatin concentration (1, 2 or 4%, *Hp* values are also tabulated in Table 1) do not correlate with degrees of restraining (*Ha* or *Hb*) measured by the present method.

Part 2: restraining behaviours of some artificial restrainers and the effect of pH

Behaviours of artificial restrainers, such as 2-mercapto-benzimidazole and benzotriazole at pH 6 are shown, together with that of polyvinylalcohol, in Fig. 4 ((c), (b) and (a) respectively). The former two restrainers show high restraining tendency at about $0{\cdot}0003 \sim 0{\cdot}002\%$ ($\fallingdotseq 0{\cdot}03 \sim 0{\cdot}2$ mM) and at higher concentration above $0{\cdot}002\%$ rapid grain growth again occurs and flocculation of coarse grains often results. The fact is due to the dual character of these compounds, which act as a restrainer for physical ripening at lower concentration and act as an accelerator at higher concentration and this dual character is often

* Experimental work described here was performed by T. Iwasaki in 1957.

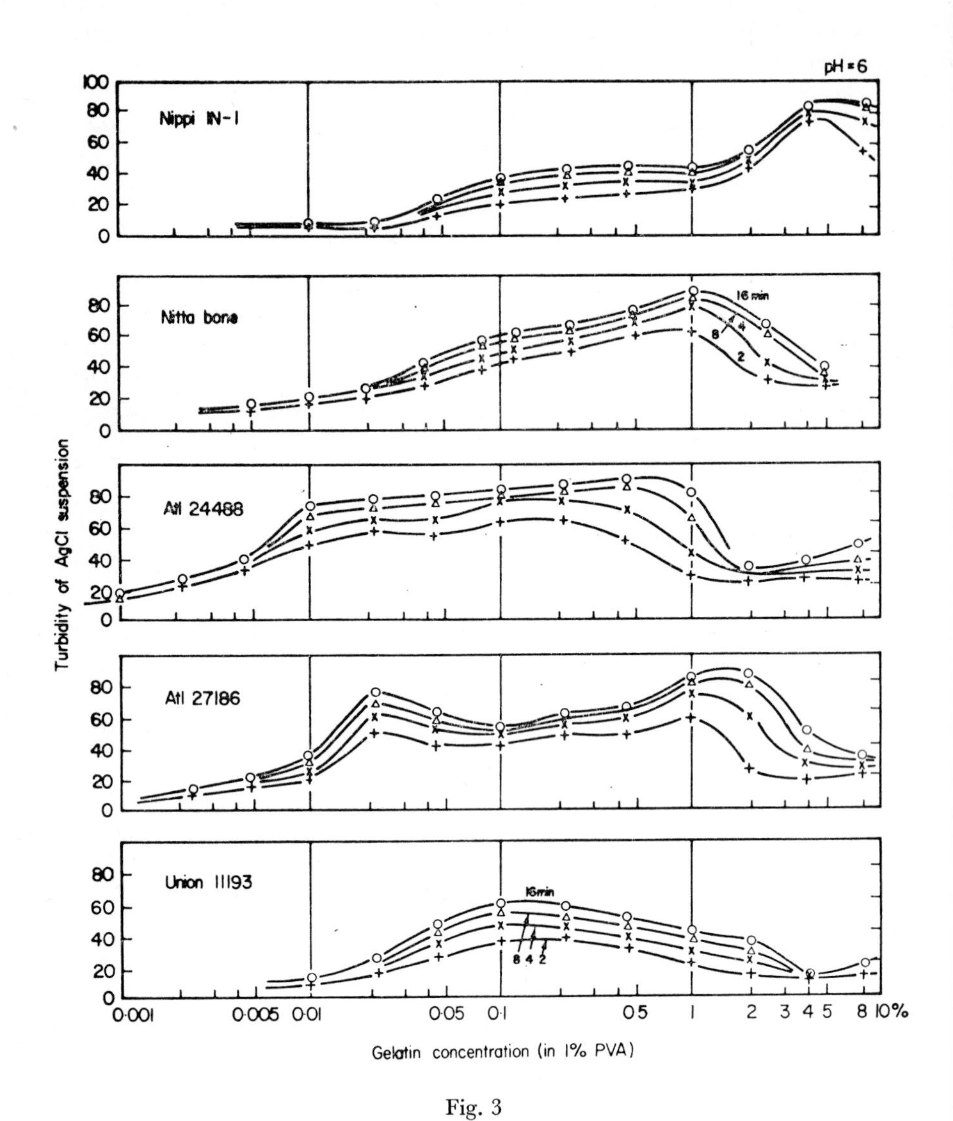
pH = 6
Nippi IN-1
Nitta bone
16 min
8
4
2
Atl 24488
Atl 27186
Union 11193
16min
8 4 2
Turbidity of AgCl suspension
0
20
40
60
80
100
0·001
0·005
0·01
0·05
0·1
0·5
1
2
3
4
5
8
10%
Gelatin concentration (in 1% PVA)

Fig. 3

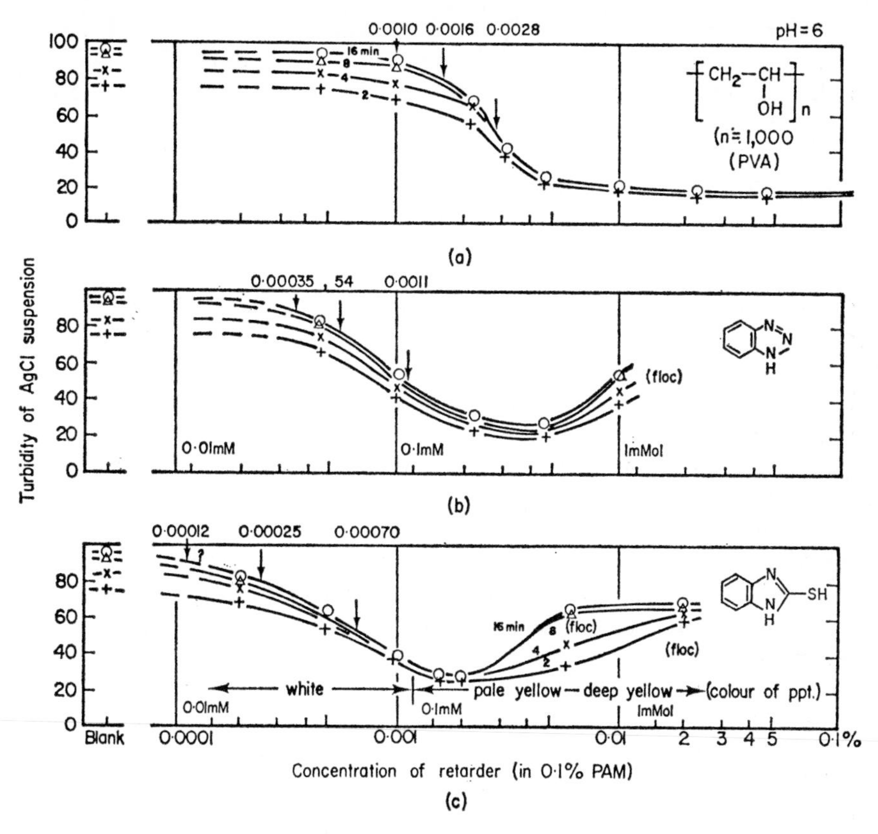

Fig. 4

observed in some of mercapto compounds or thiones, e.g. 2-mercapto benzothiazole, N-methyl-benzothiazoline-2-thione, N-methyl-quinoline-2-thione and N,N-dimethyl-benzimdazoline-2-thione, as already previously reported.[3] With some mercapto compounds, at their acceleration range of addition, precipitated grains change colour from pure white, through pale yellow to final deep yellow, with increasing concentration of the compounds in the emulsion as shown, for example in Fig. 4(c).

Polyvinylalcohol also acts as powerful restrainer at the concentration of about 0·002 ~ 0·005%, probably due to its extraordinary high adsorptive tendency onto the surface of silver halide and it inhibits almost completely the grain growth of AgCl suspension at the concentration over 0·005% (Fig. 4(a)).

Degrees of restraining calculated according to two sorts (a and b) of the criterion (see Presentation of restraining behaviours and degree of restraining), namely *Ha* values at 0·001, 0·002 and 0·004% additions and *Hb* values at $T = 90$, 80 and 50 are tabulated in Table 2. *Hb* values

Table 2

Degrees of restraining (Ha and Hb) of some artificial restrainers at pH 6

Artificial restrainers tested	Ha (= 100 − *T*) 16 *min ripening* $C =$			Hb (= 0·1/*Ch*, *at* 16 *min ripening*) $T = 90$		$T = 80$		$T = 50$	
	0·001%	0·002%	0·004%	*Ch*%	Hb	*Ch*%	Hb	*Ch*%	Hb
Polyvinylalcohol	10	27	70	0·001 00	10 000	0·001 60	6300	0·0028	3600
Benzotriazole	46	67	73	0·000 35	28 600	0·000 54	18 500	0·0011	9100
2-Mercapto-benzimidazole	60	72	(50)	0·000 12	85 000	0·000 25	40 000	0·0007	14 300

are usually extraordinary larger compared with that of gelatin, but it is reasonable because an ordinary gelatin contains only very small amount (few milligrammes per gramme of gelatin) of the compounds analogous to adenine or related active compounds.

It is well known fact that the restraining activities of these artificial restrainers depend not only on concentration, but on pH of the emulsion.[4] The effect of pH on the restraining activity of typical artificial restrainers such as 2-mercapto-benzimidazole, benzotriazole and adenine at adequate level of concentration is shown in Fig. 5. They show their restraining properties at their optimum pH ranges of $3 \sim 6$, $6 \sim 9$ and $6 \sim 10$ respectively, at almost same level of addition (0·001% ≒ 0·1 mmole).*

These results are in good accordance with the results of an earlier turbidity test with benzimidazole and 2-mercapto-benzimidazole by E. J. Birr,[4] who used gelatin as a protective colloid. However, the delicate difference as shown in Fig. 5 between benzotriazole and adenine could only be detected with the present method, because polyacrylamide is the best possible protective colloid which has no restraining at any pH as shown in the figure and even inert gelatin has some restraining and accelerating properties at some pH range, and the effect of pH on the restraining or accelerating activity of various gelatins has never been thoroughly investigated even with the intensive study of J. H. Reindorp.[5]

Part 3: restraining behaviours of IAG gelatin samples†

In Figs. 6 and 7 the restraining behaviours of IAG gelatin samples are shown. Curves of ossein gelatin (Fig. 6) are similar to each other and

* Which corresponds to about 10 mMole/Mole AgCl (=0·133 mMole/13·3 mMole $AgNO_3$).

† Experimental work described here was performed by H. Sumitani.

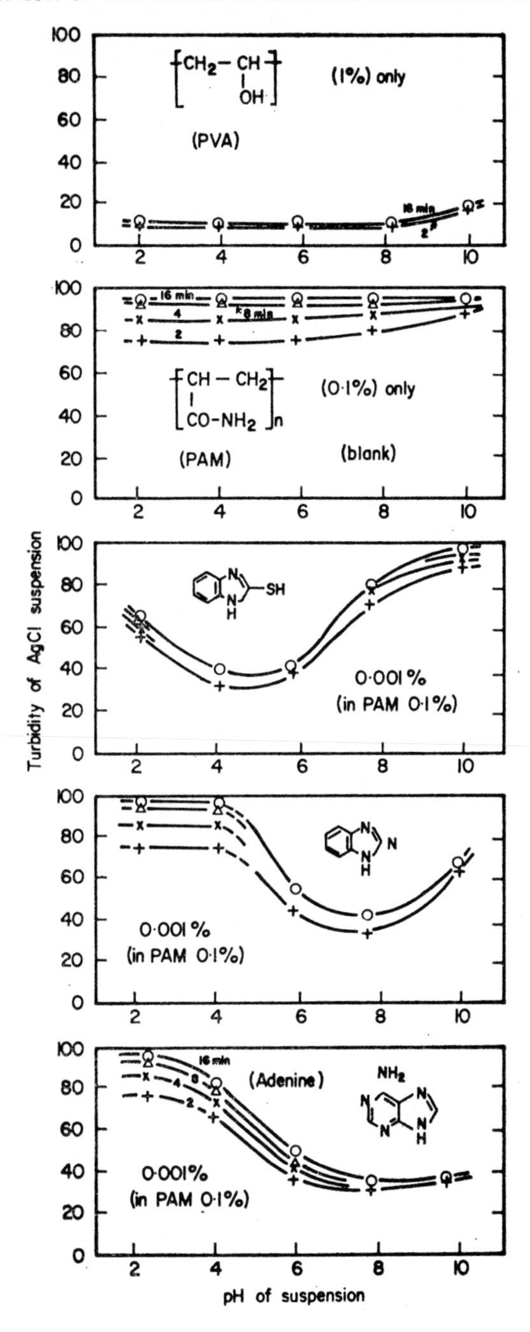
(1%) only
(PVA)
16 min
2
(0·1%) only
(PAM)
(blank)
16 min
8 min
4
2
0·001 %
(in PAM 0·1%)
SH
N
0·001 %
(in PAM 0·1%)
(Adenine)
NH_2
0·001%
(in PAM 0·1%)
Turbidity of AgCl suspension
pH of suspension

Fig. 5

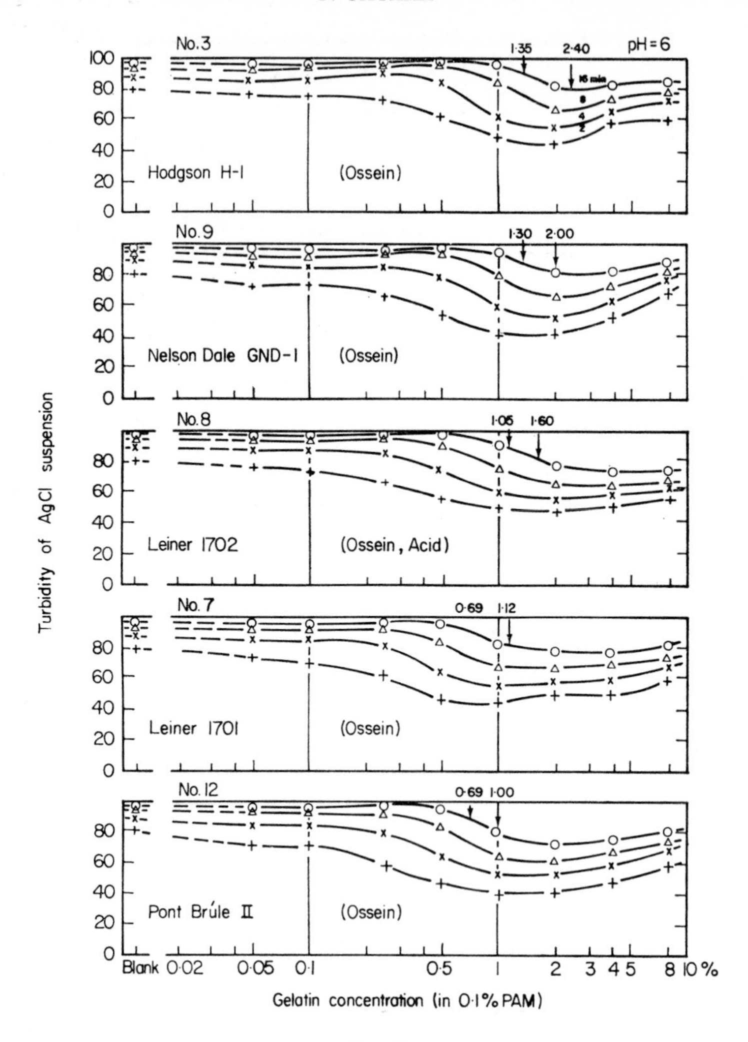

Fig. 6

differ with those of hide gelatin (Fig. 7). Restraining behaviours of ossein gelatin are generally moderate and turbidity (T) at 16 min ripening usually over 70 and does not decrease with the increase of gelatin concentration above 2% and sometimes minimum point is seen on the curve between 1 $\sim$ 2%, namely turbidity of the emulsion is apt to increase at higher concentration in ossein gelatin.

Of course, restraining does not depend really on the concentration of gelatin, but depends on the gelatin/silver ratio in the emulsion. The

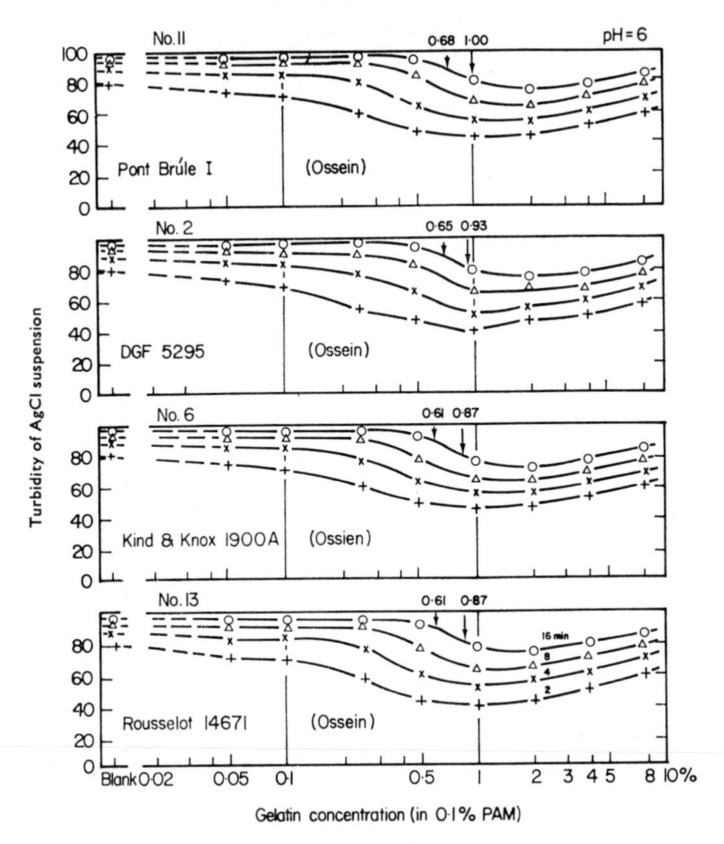

Fig. 6. (*continued*)

fact will be discussed later and in this case 1% of gelatin concentration is equivalent to 4·4 g gelatin/g $AgNO_3$ (=10 g gelatin/13·3 mmole AgCl).

Characteristic curves of hide gelatins are also similar to each other as shown in Fig. 7, with the exception of acid pigskin gelatin (above top, No. 5, K & K 2006) which is almost identical with that of a highly restrained ossein gelatin, and the turbidity of the emulsion tends to decrease with increasing gelatin concentration, in this case from 70 ~ 30 at 2% to 40 ~ 15 at 8%. Therefore, it seems reasonable to state that hide gelatin is generally superior to ossein gelatin in restraining at higher concentration.

The degrees of restraining (*Ha* and *Hb* values) determined on these curves are tabulated on Table 3 together with values of restraining factors of "Nelson Dale" test[5] which was performed by A. M. Kragh[6]

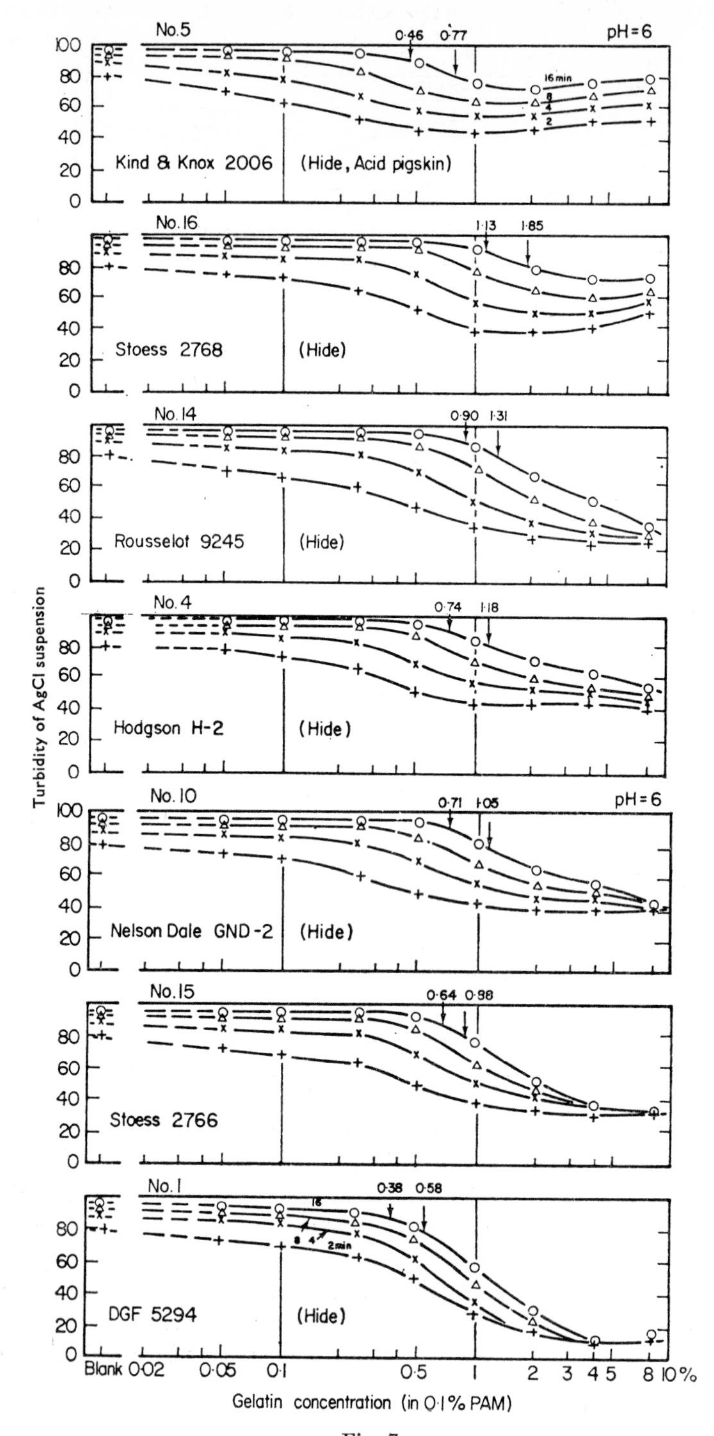

No.5
0·46
0·77
pH=6
16 min
8
4
2
Kind & Knox 2006
(Hide, Acid pigskin)
No.16
1·13
1·85
Stoess 2768
(Hide)
No.14
0·90
1·31
Rousselot 9245
(Hide)
No.4
0·74
1·18
Hodgson H-2
(Hide)
No.10
0·71
1·05
pH=6
Nelson Dale GND-2
(Hide)
No.15
0·64
0·88
Stoess 2766
No.1
0·38
0·58
16
8
4
2min
DGF 5294
(Hide)
Turbidity of AgCl suspension
Blank 0·02 0·05 0·1 0·5 1 2 3 4 5 8 10%
Gelatin concentration (in 0·1% PAM)

Fig. 7

Table 3

Degrees of restraining (Ha and Hb) of 16 gelatin samples from 1 AG

Gelatin samples	Ha (= 100 − *T*) 16 *min ripening* *C* = 1%	2%	4%	8%	Hb (= 0·1/*Ch*) *at* 16 *min R*, *T* = 90, *C*%	Hb	*T* = 80, *C*%	Hb	*Raw Material*	*Nelson* Dale Test*	*Physik.† Hemm. (Ammann)*	Ha (8%) −Ha (1%) +10
1. DGF 5294	41	68	88	87	0·38	26·3	0·58	17·2	Hide	0·03	13·4	56
2. DGF 5295	22	25	23	15	0·65	15·4	0·93	10·8	Ossein	0·33	1·03	3
3. Hodgson-1	4	19	17	15	1·35	7·4	2·40	4·2	Ossein	0·49	2·22	21
4. Hodgson-2	16	31	36	45	0·74	13·5	1·18	8·5	Hide	0·12	3·74	39
5. K & K 2006	25	28	23	22	0·47	21·8	0·77	13·0	Acid Hide	0·07	1·20	7
6. K & K 1900A	24	29	22	16	0·61	16·4	0·87	11·5	Ossein	0·36	1·81	2
7. Leiner 1701	19	23	25	20	0·69	14·5	1·12	8·9	Ossein	0·32	2·61	11
8. Leiner 1702	9	23	27	26	1·05	9·5	1·60	6·3	Acid Os.	0·21	1·26	27
9. Nelson D-1	5	20	18	11	1·30	7·7	2·00	5·0	Ossein	0·59	1·07	16
10. Nelson D-2	18	36	44	56	0·71	14·1	1·05	9·5	Hide	0·12	3·73	48
11. Pont Brúle-I	20	26	21	15	0·68	14·7	1·00	10·0	Ossein	0·49	0·93	5
12. Pont Brúle-II	20	27	23	15	0·69	14·5	1·00	10·0	Ossein	0·35	1·49	5
13. Rouss 14 671	23	26	20	14	0·61	16·4	0·87	11·5	Ossein	0·50	0·98	1
14. Rouss 9245	12	32	46	63	0·90	11·1	1·31	7·6	Hide	0·04	3·17	51
15. Stoess 2766	24	48	63	67	0·64	16·6	0·88	11·4	Hide	0·04	11·3	53
16. Stoess 2768	8	22	28	27	1·13	8·9	1·85	5·4	Hide	0·17	2·75	29

* By A. M. Kragh May 1968 (IAG Report).

† H. Ammann-Brass (IAG Report No. 12, Dec. 1965).

of Ilford Ltd. and "Physik. Hemmung" of H. Ammann-Brass.[7] The fact that degrees of restraining of hide gelatin are generally larger than that of ossein gelatin is clearly shown in *Ha* values, particularly at higher gelatin concentration, but the difference between two kinds of gelatin is not so distinct in *Hb* values. Accordingly the correlation between *Ha* and *Hb* values is not good in general, but the correlation

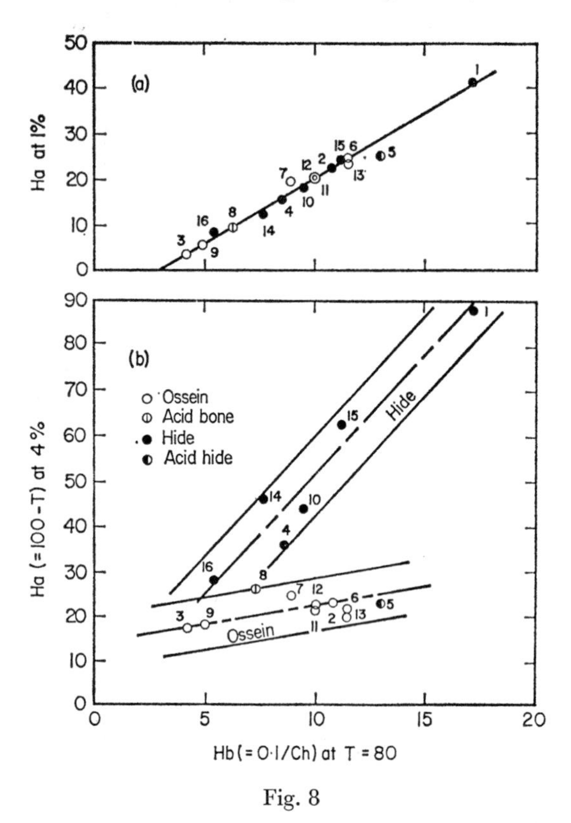

Fig. 8

at lower gelatin concentration is exceptionally good as shown in Fig. 8(a) and because of the fact that *Hb* values of ossein gelatin do not increase with concentration as mentioned before, correlation between *Ha* and *Hb* values generally divides into two groups, one for ossein and the other for hide gelatin at higher concentration, with the exception of acid processed ones as shown in Fig. 8(b). It is also concluded that at lower gelatin concentration or the gelatin/silver ratio which is the usual practice in emulsion making, there is no distinction in restraining activity between hide and ossein gelatins.

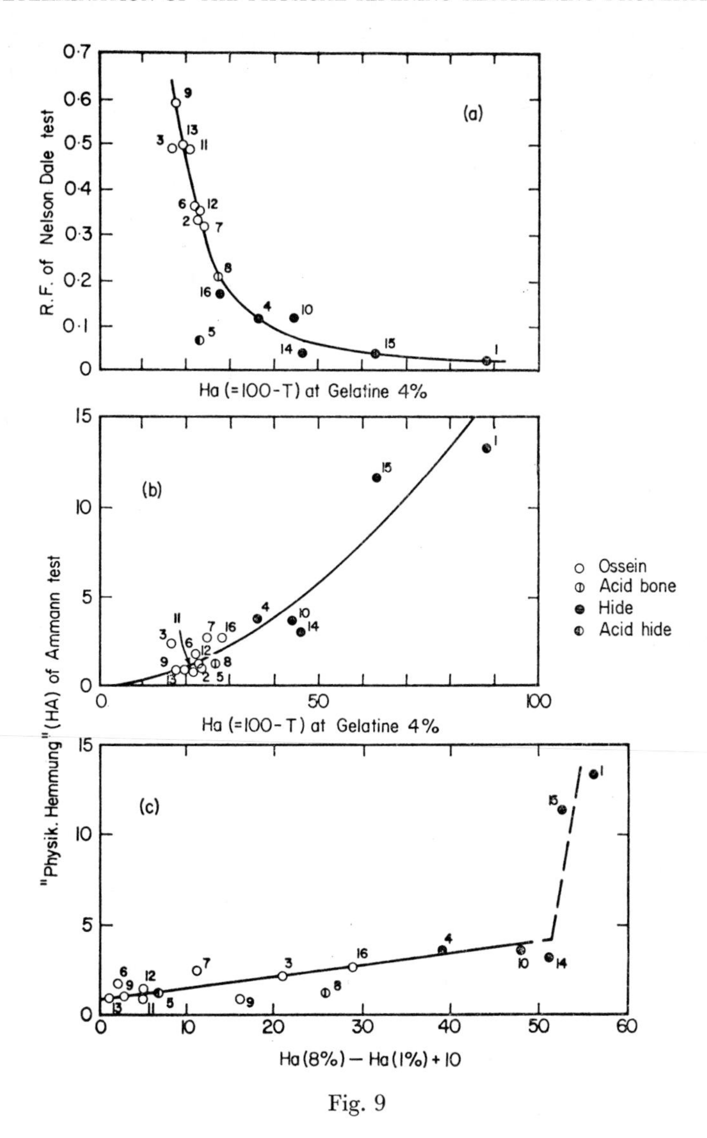

Fig. 9

The correlations between data by the present method and other methods hitherto designed and used were found usually better at higher gelatin concentration or the gelatin/silver ratio, where usually the powerful restraining property of hide gelatin reveals itself. *Ha* values at 4% gelatin concentration correlate quite well with the results of "Nelson Dale" test conducted by A. M. Kragh[6] with the only exception of acid pigskin gelatin (No. 5, K & K 2006) as shown in Fig. 9(a), and the correlation between "Physik. Hemmung" (HA) values of Ammann-Brass method[7] and the present method is expected at $Ha_{(4\%)}$ or $Ha_{(8\%)}$, because in Ammann-Brass method HA value is defined as follows:

$$\mathrm{HA} = 10 - \log \{\mathrm{T}(1{\cdot}0\%)/\mathrm{T}(7{\cdot}3\%)\}$$

and the turbidities of emulsions by the Ammann-Brass method at 1% gelatin concentration are almost nearly constant ($250 \sim 400$, $\log T = 2{\cdot}5 \pm 0{\cdot}1$) in various gelatins except for highly restrained gelatin. Therefore the above equation can be simplified as follows:

$$\mathrm{HA} \fallingdotseq \mathrm{K} + \log \mathrm{T}(7{\cdot}3\%)$$

and the linear scale of T values in the present method is almost proportional to the logarithm of T values in the Ammann-Brass method, hence:

$$\mathrm{HA} \fallingdotseq \mathrm{K} + \log \mathrm{T}(7{\cdot}3\%) \propto \mathrm{K}' + \mathrm{Ha}_{(8\%)}$$

where K and K' are constants.

However, the correlation of HA to $Ha_{(8\%)}$ is not better than that to $Ha_{(4\%)}$ and naturally the correlation of HA to $\{Ha_{(8\%)} - Ha_{(1\%)}\}$ is quite good except for highly restrained gelatin as shown in Figs. 9(b) and 9(c).

Effect of gelatin/silver ratio and the practical physical restraining power of gelatin

As the range of gelatin concentration in the original "Nelson Dale" test lies in $0{\cdot}2 \sim 4\%$ (logarithmic scale) and in the revised method by A. M. Kragh it lies in $0{\cdot}2 \sim 2\%$ (arithmetic scale), the effective mean concentration in both methods lies in around 1%, but the emulsion contains only 1·0 mmoles of silver chloride (equivalent to 170 mg $AgNO_3$/l), therefore the gelatin/silver ratio has an extraordinary high value of 59·0 g gelatin/g $AgNO_3$. Whereas in our present method even at 4% gelatin concentration, the ratio has a rational value of about 17·6 g gelatin/g $AgNO_3$, and in the Ammann-Brass method,[7] where the silver content of emulsion is 13·3 mmoles, 7·3% of gelatin concentration corresponds to the gelatin/silver ratio of almost 32·2 g gelatin/g $AgNO_3$. These values of the gelatin/silver ratio, however, are only usual for "Stop" gelatin which inhibits the grain growth of silver halide at the final stage of emulsion making and is not practical for the grain growth regulation during usual emulsion making, where the ratio is recognized to be in the range of $1 \sim 10$ g gelatin/g $AgNO_3$, which corresponds to gelatin concentration of about $0{\cdot}2 \sim 2{\cdot}3\%$ in the present method ($\fallingdotseq 2{\cdot}26 \sim 22{\cdot}6$ g G/13·3 mmoles AgCl).

Therefore the estimation of restraining power of gelatin at the practical emulsion making as grain growth regulator is best based on *Hb* values of the present method, because the corresponding gelatin concentration (*Ch*) lies just in this region ($0{\cdot}2 \sim 2\%$). But the determination of *Hb* value of the gelatin is rather tedious, as it necessitates at least three times, sometimes four or five times determinations of turbidity at different levels of gelatin concentration. However, as was demonstrated above, *Ha* values at 1% gelatin concentration correlate quite well to *Hb* values in various gelatin samples (Fig. 8(a)), the simplest and easiest way in the estimation of the practical restraining power of photographic gelatins as grain growth regulator is, therefore, reduced to the measurement of turbidity of the emulsion in the present method at 1% gelatin concentration (one point only) and the method is supplemented by the determination of *Ha* values at 4% of gelatin concentration, which corresponds to the estimation of restraining power as "Stop" gelatin.

In the practical restraining power thus estimated at the lower gelatin/silver ratio or gelatin concentration (1% in the present method), there is no large difference between hide and ossein gelatin as shown in Fig. 8(a) and generally hide gelatin is always superior for "Stop" gelatin as shown in Fig. 9(a).

Determination of practical physical restraining power of photographic gelatin

On the basis of the fact described in the preceding section, determination of physical restraining power of photographic gelatin can be simplified as follows:

To 32 ml of deionized water, 10 ml of 6% aqueous solution of a sample of gelatin (100 ml is made up from 6 g of gelatin and sufficient water), 10 ml of 0·6% aqueous solution of polyacrylamide and 4 ml of 0·6 M sodium chloride solution are added. The mixture is heated at 70°C and under agitation 4 ml of 0·2 M silver nitrate solution (70°C) is added in about 15 s. After 16 min ripening 2 ml of the suspension is drawn out and diluted with 20 ml of cold water and the turbidity (T, $0 \sim 100$) of the suspension is measured, then the value of $100 - T$ ($=Ha_{(1\%)}$) is used for the expression of power of physical restraining.

As a supplementary test, a modified method which use 2 ml of deionized water and 40 ml of 6% gelatin solution, instead of 32 ml of water and 10 ml of 6% gelatin solution in the above mentioned procedure, may be selected for the determination of the stopping power of gelatin to inhibit physical ripening.

ACKNOWLEDGEMENT

The author is indebted to Prof. H. Ammann-Brass and colleagues of the IAG organization, and the makers of photographic gelatin, foreign and domestic, for furnishing valuable gelatin samples and the many helpful contributions from IAG. Thanks are also due to Mr. T. Iwasaki and Mr. H. Sumitani for carrying out parts of the experimental work. He also wishes to thank the Director of Mitsubishi Paper Mills Limited for permission to publish this work.

References

(1) Ammann-Brass, H., *Koll. Z.*, **110,** 105, 161 (1948).
(2) Ohyama, Y., *Science and Application of Photography*, published by Royal Photographic Society, London (1955), p. 37.
(3) Ohyama, Y. and Futaki, K., *Photogr. Sci. Eng.*, **2,** 128 (1958).
(4) Birr, E. J., *Z. Wiss. Photogr.*, **48,** 103 (1953).
(5) Reindorp, J. H., IAG Report No. 13 (Dec. 1965), "Some Factors which Influence the Interpretation of Silver Chloride Ripening Test".
(6) Kragh, A. M., IAG Report No. 14 (Dec. 1965), and IAG Report May 1968.
(7) Ammann-Brass, H., IAG Report No. 12 (Nov. 1965).

Increase of the Density of the Silver Image during Storage after Processing

S. COUPRIÉ, A. DE CUGNAC-PAILLIOTET and J. POURADIER

Centre de Recherches Kodak-Pathé, 30, rue des Vignerons 94-Vincennes

ABSTRACT. When kept at low humidity, the density of the processed image increases slightly during storage. This increase is roughly proportional to the initial density and, among other factors, depends on the nature of the film.

INTRODUCTION

It has long been realized that the density of processed films varies during drying and this effect was attributed to two opposing causes:[1],[2]

a mechanical orientation of the grains;
a compression and a collapse of the grains.

The stresses exerted by gelatin remain in the dry coat,[3] and during a study on the keeping of processed films, we were surprised to observe that under some conditions of storage the image density increased slowly.

EXPERIMENTAL

For obvious reasons, it was desirable to make measurements on emulsions of very different grain sizes. The two emulsions examined in detail in this work are:

a coarse grain emulsion: No screen X-ray film Kodirex;
a fine grain emulsion: Eastman Positive Code 5303

but experiments made on other commercial and experimental emulsions gave similar results.

After exposure to light and development in D19b (Kodirex) and KRX(5303), the films were fixed, washed and dried in open air.

Each film being cut into two portions, the two samples were kept under control at constant humidity and temperature, one at 25°C and RH $\leq 8\%$ in a dessicator with Silicagel, and the other at 30°C and RH $= 50\%$ in an air conditioned cabinet.

The densities were measured regularly and the changes were followed until equilibrium was reached. These measurements show that the behaviour depends on the photosensitive layer and on the storage conditions.

RESULTS

The density of samples kept in dry atmosphere (RH $< 8\%$) increased for about 3 days and levelled afterwards (solid line of Fig. 1). The increase is a function of the initial density and is roughly proportional

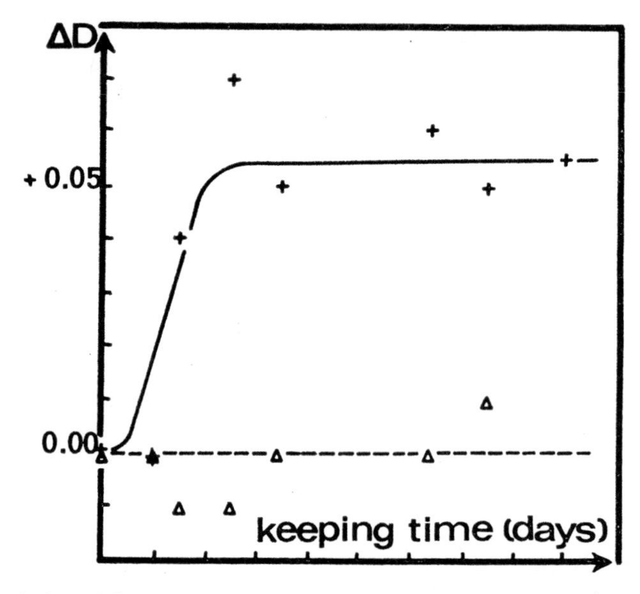

Fig. 1. Variation of density during storage of processed Kodirex films. ——— ≤8% RH at 25°C; ---- 50% RH at 30°C. Initial density 1·80.

to this parameter (solid line of Fig. 2). It is more accentuated with Kodirex films than with Eastman Positive 5303 (solid and dotted lines of Fig. 2).

The change of density is irreversible (or very slowly reversible) and after a few days storage in moist atmosphere the film does not recover its initial density.

The behaviour of samples kept at higher humidities is quite different and for these conditions we never succeeded in detecting any significant change of density during storage. The difference of behaviour at low and high humidities is rather unexpected but may be connected with the greater stresses exerted by the layer at low relative humidities. The density increase might conceivably be caused by several mechanisms:

(a) Stored at low humidity, gelatin loses about 10% of water and the thickness of the image layer decreases proportionately. So, the silver grains are closer in the dry film than in samples stored at higher humidity and the close packing of the grains increases the diffuse density.

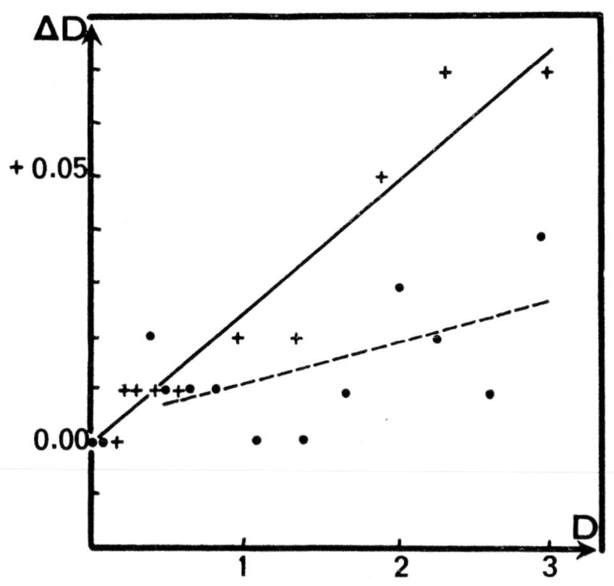

Fig. 2. Influence of the initial density on the variation of density during 10 day storage, RH ≤8% at 25°C of ——— Kodirex and - - - - Eastman Positive 5303 films.

(b) Contraction of the gelatin during dehydration increases probably the stresses exerted on developed silver. This effect is perhaps purely mechanical, but it may also be enhanced by the adsorption of gelatin on the silver grains.[4] Because of their loose filamentary structure, silver grains are deformed by dry gelatin when the stresses are sufficient to overcome their rigidity, and their projective areas are modified.

References

(1) Pinoir, R., *Sci. Ind. Photogr.*, (2), **14,** 241–252 (1943).
(2) Blake, R. K. and Meerkamper, B., *J. Photogr. Sci.*, **9,** 14–25 (1961).
(3) de Cugnac, A. and Pouradier, J., "Photographic Science", Paris Symposium (1965). J. Pouradier, Editor, the Focal Press, pp. 519–521.
(4) Wood, H. W., *J. Photogr. Sci.*, **9,** 84–92 (1961).

On the pH Dependence of the Emulsion Turbidity Test of Photographic Gelatins

H. IRIE and T. ISHIDA
Chiba University, Japan

ABSTRACT. Photographic gelatins are more characteristically classified on the basis of their pH dependence of the emulsion turbidity test. Restraining gelatins are discriminated in three types that are highly restraining, (i) over wide pH range of 4 to 10; (ii) in the pH range 3 to 5; and (iii) only at narrow pH range near 10. Some of these differences may be ascribed to the thiosulphate-nucleic acid balance in gelatin; effects of these additives will be reported and discussed.

EXPERIMENT

1. Test emulsion

A.	NaCl solution (35 g l^{-1})	10 ml
	Gelatin gel (16·6% wt./vol.)	30 g
	Distilled water	(25–x) ml
	Alkali or acid solution*	x ml
B.	$AgNO_3$ solution (17 g l^{-1})	20 ml

Precipitation: B is poured into A in about 25 s. Both solutions are kept at 70°C before precipitation.

The ripening condition of the emulsion: 70°C for 20 min shaking the sample flask every 3 min.

Turbidity test emulsion dilution: 11 times v/v with distilled water.

The turbidity test results are shown in Figs. 1–8 in terms of the physical retardance.

2. The turbidity of the test emulsion is replaced by the transmittance in the experiment, since the restraining power of gelatin is expressed as the "physical retardance", which is in turn expressed as one tenth of the relative transmittance value, rounded off at one digit above the decimal in accordance with the test standard of photographic gelatin in Japan.

* Any one of the following solutions is used to adjust the emulsion pH: 0·2 N NaOH, 2·0 N NaOH, 1 N HNO_3.

The transmittance of the diluted emulsion in a 10 mm width curvette is measured by a photocell at a distance of 20 cm with reference to 100% value at zero distance. The incident light is specular and passes through a Toshiba V-Y1 glass filter (yellow) in front of the curvette.

Sixteen sorts of IAG gelatins were tested over pH range 1–10.

These gelatins can be arranged in four groups by their characteristic pH dependence of physical retardance.

Group 1. Most highly restraining over wide pH range 4 to 10. DGF 5294 and Stoess 2766 in Fig. 1.

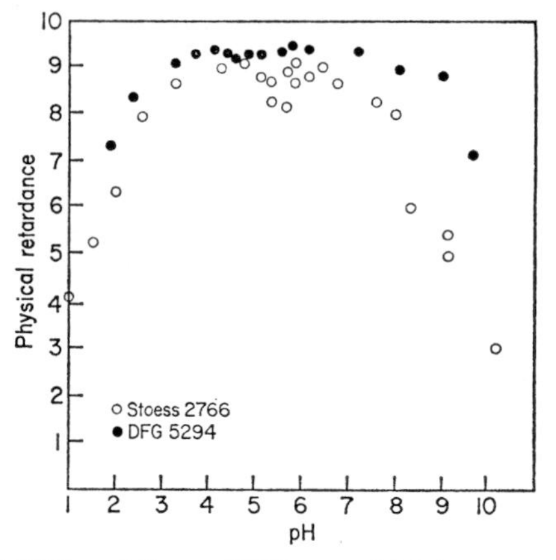

Fig. 1. Gelatins DGF 5294 and Stoess 2766, most highly restraining over a wide pH range.

Group 2. Highlyrestraininginrathernarrow pHrange. Rousselot 9245, Stoess 2768, Hodgson 2 and GND 2 in Fig. 2.

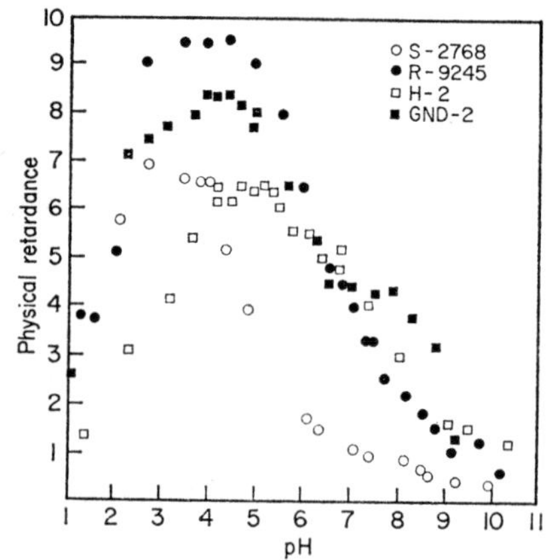

Fig. 2. Gelatins Rousselot 9245, Stoess 2768, Hodgson 2 and GND 2, highly restraining in a rather narrow pH range.

Group 3. Highly restraining only in a very narrow pH range near pH 10. Kind and Knox 2006 in Fig. 3(a).

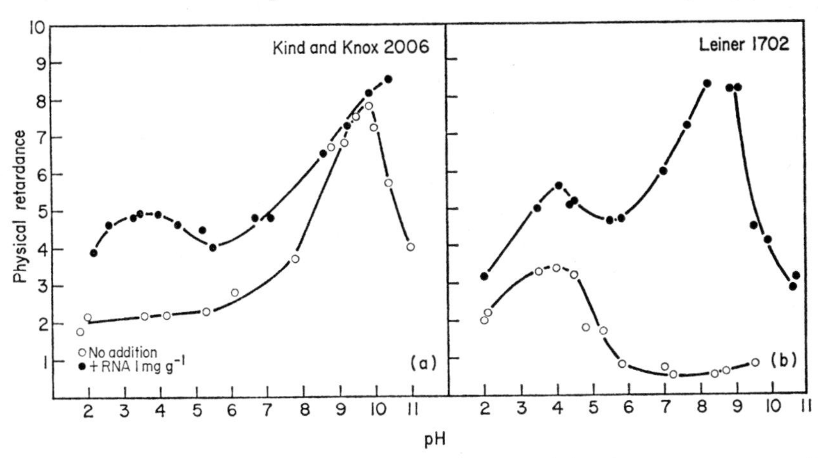

Fig. 3(a). Gelatin Kind and Knox 2006, highly restraining in a very narrow pH range, near pH 10. (b) Gelatin Leiner 1702; low restraining.

Group 4. General low restraining gelatins. Leiner 1702 in Fig. 3(b). GND 1, PB 1, PB 2, Rousselot 14671 and DGF 5295 in Fig. 4. Leiner 1701, Kind and Knox 1900A and Hodgson 1 in Fig. 5.

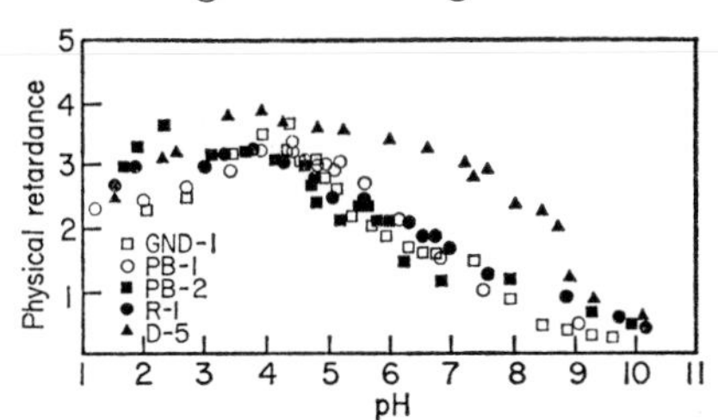

Fig. 4. Gelatins GND 1, PB 1, PB 2, Rousselot 14671 and DGF 5295, low restraining.

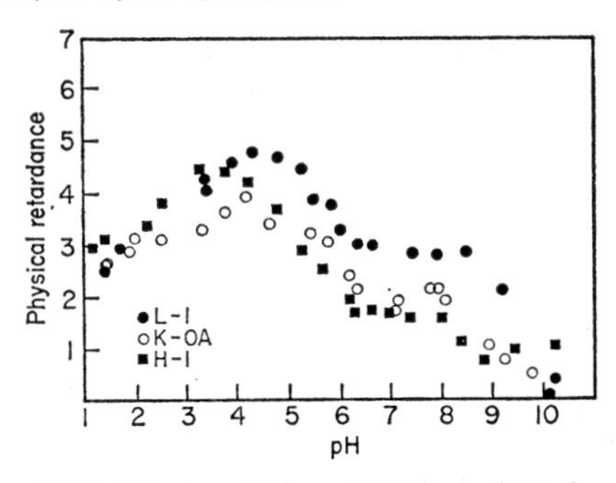

Fig. 5. Gelatins Leiner 1701, Kind and Knox 1900A and Hodgson 1, low restraining.

The first two types of gelatins, both highly restraining groups, may be able to stimulate their turbidity behaviour in the emulsion ripening by adding RNA and thiosulphate to low restraining gelatins.

RNA addition to a low restraining gelatin makes it more highly restraining mainly in the alkali region in contrast with thiosulphate which depresses it in the same region and raises it in the acid region. (Figs. 6 and 7). A balanced addition of an RNA and thiosulphate

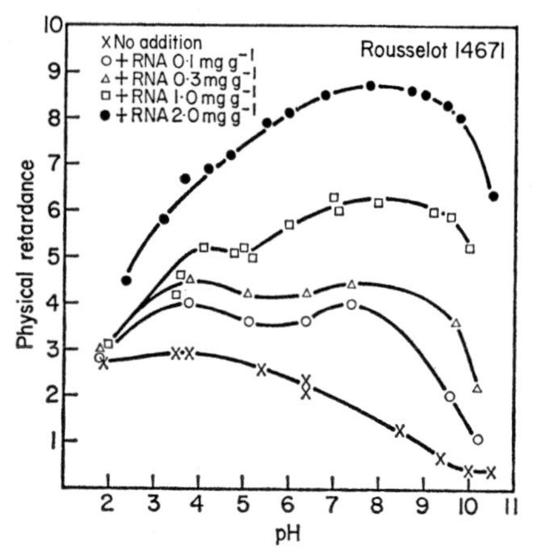

Fig. 6. RNA addition to a low restraining gelatin, DGF 5294.

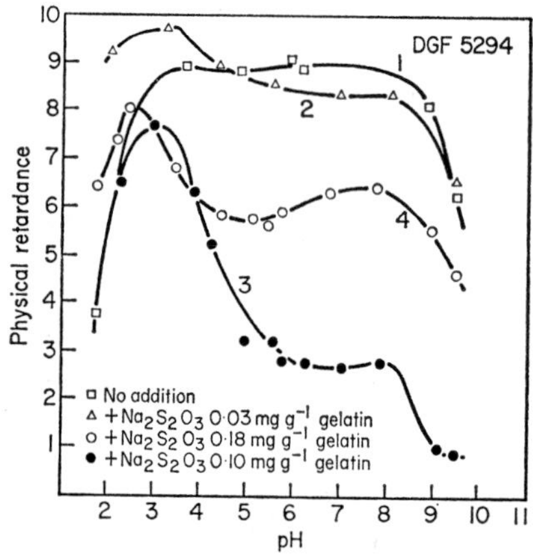

Fig. 7. Thiosulphate addition to a low restraining gelatin, Rousselot 14671.

combination makes a low restraining gelatin, type 1, that is highly restraining over a wide pH region (Fig. 8, curve 3). Over weighted addition of thiosulphate against RNA to a type 1 highly restraining gelatin makes it a type 2 gelatin, depressing physical retardance in the alkali region (Fig. 7, curves 3 and 4). Type 3 gelatin cannot be made with a limed inert gelatin adding RNA, but is simulated with an acid process Leiner 1702 gelatin by adding RNA (Fig. 3(b)).

The above observations are consistent with the analytical data of other authors.[(1),(2),(3),(4)] In Table 1, analytical data of labile sulphur,

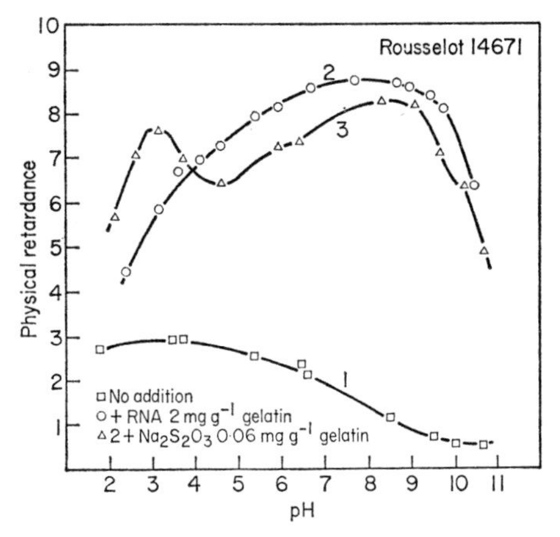

Fig. 8. Balanced addition of an RNA and thiosulphate combination to gelatin, Rousselot 14671.

adenine and guanine are listed. Stoess 2766 and DGF 5294 contain an exceptionally high quantity of adenine and guanine in comparison with the other gelatins and their labile sulphur content is also quite high; in the case of GND 1 and 2, Rousselot 9245 and Hodgson 2 there is a high level of labile sulphur as compared to the adenine and guanine content. Thus it appears that the reduction effect of physical retardance in the alkali region might have become predominant.

Table 1

Analytical data of DNA, adenine, thiosulphate and labile sulphur in IAG gelatins by other authors

Gelatin	*DNA* (*Nawn and Steigmann*[1])	*Adenine* (*Janus and Nellist*[2])	$Na_2S_2O_3$ (*Janus and Nellist*[3])	*Labile sulphur* (*Awa*[4])
	μg g^{-1} *gelatin*		mg g^{-1} *gelatin*	
Stoess 2766	1·980	310	0·022	0·025
DGF 5294	1·410	245	0·028	0·044
Rousselot 9245	0·735	92	0·047	0·074
GND 2	0·610	60	0·019	0·024
Stoess 2768	0·315	27	0·021	0·026
Hodgson 2	0·550	25	0·020	0·015
Pont Brûlé 1	0·005	3	0	0·017
Pont Brûlé 2	0·005	6	0	0·015
Leiner 1701	0·030	5	0	0·011
Hodgson 1	0·005	5	0	0·014
DGF 5295	0·005	2	0	0·014
K & K 1900A	0·005	1	0	0·023
GND 1	0·025	0·5	0	0·013
Rousselot 14671	0	1	0	0·011
K & K 2006	0	25	0	0·024
Leiner 1702	0	6	0	0·011

Abbreviations used in the figures

D–4	DGF 5294	L–1	Leiner PL/EX/1701
D–5	DGF 5295	L–2	Leiner PL/EX/1702
G–1	GND 1	P–1	Pont Brûlé 1
G–2	GND 2	P–2	Pont Brûlé 2
H–1	Hodgson 1	R–1	Rousselot 14671
H–2	Hodgson 2	R–5	Rousselot 9245
K–OA	Kind & Knox 1900A	S–6	Stoess 2766
K–6	Kind & Knox 2006	S–8	Stoess 2768

References

(1) Nawn, G. E. and Steigmann, A. E., IAG Report.
(2) Janus, J. W. and Nellist, D. R., *J. Photogr. Sci.*, **15,** 147 (1967).
(3) Janus, J. W. and Nellist, D. R., *J. Photogr. Sci.*, **15,** 274 (1967).
(4) Awa, T., IAG Report.

Surface Phenomena

The Influence of the Protective Colloid on the Course of Surface Reactions at Silver Bromide Crystal Faces

E. KLEIN, E. MOISAR and E. ROCHE

Agfa-Gevaert AG, Leverkusen, Germany

ABSTRACT. Spectrophotometric investigations of the rate of Ag_2S formation during thiosulphate digestion on mono-disperse AgBr emulsions accompanied by an evaluation of the photographic properties reveal that foreign additives as well as intrinsic properties of the protective colloid markedly influence the course of surface reactions. The results are discussed under the general viewpoint of homogeneous crystal growth according to the classic theories of Stanski and Kaischew.

INTRODUCTION

Numerous publications have described the use of synthetic polymers as supporting agents for silver halide emulsions. From these publications it can be roughly deduced that no particular photographic property of synthetic polymers justifies at the present time the substitution of gelatin by such compounds. The majority of emulsions prepared with synthetic binding agents lead generally to photographic speeds inferior to those of gelatin emulsions.

The photographic speed of any silver halide emulsion is, as we know, a rather complex property which depends on the mean grain dimensions of the silver halide crystals as well as on the chemical composition of the grain surface and particularly on the presence of so-called sensitivity specks. These are formed at the grain surface by decomposition, e.g. of sulphur compounds during chemical ripening.

If the use of a certain synthetic polymer leads to an emulsion which is, say, less sensitive than a gelatin emulsion prepared and treated under similar conditions, the question may arise whether this fact is due to a restrained grain growth in the presence of the synthetic polymer, or to an insufficient formation of sensitivity specks, or both.

Investigations have been performed with the aim of studying the behaviour of a few typical polymers in photographic emulsions, and some preliminary results are reported here, which show that both silver halide crystal growth as well as the course of chemical ripening is strongly influenced by the respective polymers. The results are discussed in terms of the classical theories of crystal growth as developed by Volmer, Kaischew, Stranski *et al.*[(1)–(4)]

CRYSTAL GROWTH

The influence of the supporting colloid on the crystal growth was investigated by turbidimetric measurements of the mean particle size. Silver nitrate and potassium bromide solutions were mixed in the presence of a supporting colloid such as gelatin, polyvinylpyrrolidone

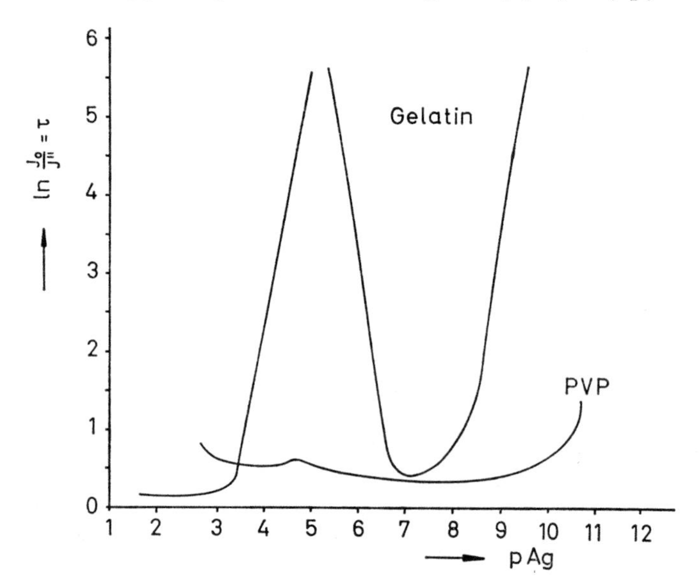

Fig. 1. Turbidity (which is proportional to the mean particle size) of AgBr dispersions versus pAg for gelatin and PVP.

(PVP) or polyvinylalcohol (PVA). By adding various amounts of excess silver nitrate or KBr solutions a wide region of pAg values has been covered. A typical curve obtained in the presence of gelatin is shown in Fig. 1.

The ordinate values represent the rate of crystal growth while the pAg values are shown in the abscissa. One observes a rapid crystal growth at extremely high pAg values and also a very pronounced maximum of the growth rate in the vicinity of the equivalence point. Such curves have been discussed in detail in the other paper presented by us.[5] If gelatin is substituted by PVP the rate of crystal growth strongly decreases as can be seen from the curve marked PVP. The same is true if we use PVA as supporting colloid.

As we know, the mean particle size of the silver halide crystal is a result of a recrystallization process, the rate of which is given by the Wagner equations for diffusion controlled process by

$$r_{t,D} = \text{const. } [\sigma D c_{\infty} t]^{\frac{1}{3}} \tag{1}$$

and for reaction-rate controlled process by

$$r_{t,K} = \text{const. } [\sigma K c_{\infty} t]^{\frac{1}{2}} \tag{2}$$

when r_t is the mean particle size after the recrystallization time t, σ the surface energy, D the diffusion coefficient, and c_{∞} the solubility of AgBr.[6]

Neither the solubility nor the diffusion coefficient of AgBr are much influenced by the various polymers. The drastic decrease of the rate of crystal growth in the presence of PVP and PVA must, therefore be, due to a decrease of σ, the surface energy, or of K, the reaction rate constant. Both are attributed to a strong adsorption of the synthetic polymers to the AgBr surface which inhibits crystal growth. The strong adsorption of PVP at AgBr surfaces can also be deduced from other experiments, e.g. as with pAg controlled double-jet precipitations.

Contrary to the experiments mentioned above, practically no random recrystallization occurs during double-jet precipitations; in the initial stage of precipitation a certain number N of AgBr crystal nuclei is formed which remains nearly constant during the subsequent stages of precipitation. If such double-jet precipitations are carried out either in the presence of gelatin or in presence of PVP, the resulting crystals in the latter case are much smaller, or their number is much greater, as in the presence of gelatin as shown in Fig. 2.

The total amount of AgBr precipitated is of course the same in both runs. This means that more, and consequently smaller, AgBr nuclei are formed in the presence of PVP as compared to gelatin. Nucleation requires a certain amount of nucleation energy which, according to classical theories, is given by

$$A_k = \frac{4}{3} \pi r^2 \sigma \tag{3}$$

If σ is lowered due to strong adsorption this results in a decrease of nucleation energy A_k and consequently in an increase of the rate of nucleation

$$\frac{dN}{dt} = \text{const. exp}\left[-\frac{A_k}{RT}\right] \tag{4}$$

Thus the formation of nuclei is facilitated by adsorption.

A closer observation of the electron micrograph reveals a small, but nevertheless interesting difference in the AgBr crystal shapes. In presence of gelatin, pure cubes with exclusively (100) faces are formed.

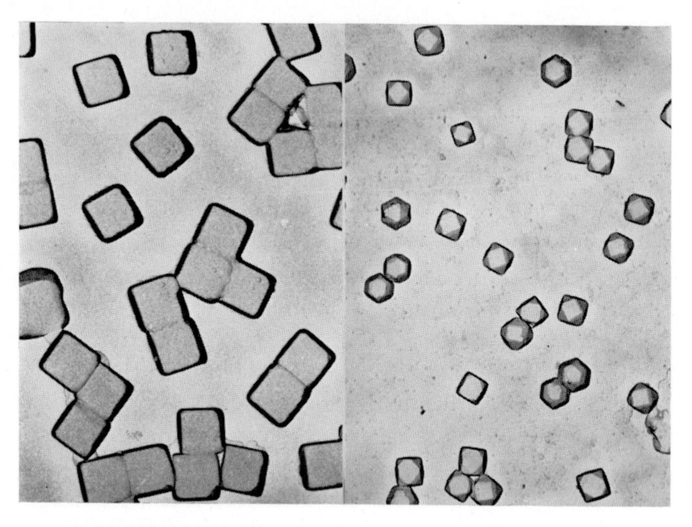

Fig. 2. Electron micrographs of AgBr crystals (carbon replica) obtained by double-jet precipitation, at pAg ~8 with gelatin (*left*) or PVP (*right*) as supporting colloid.

When PVP is used one observes in addition the formation of a certain amount of (111) faces. According to the rule of Gibbs–Curie–Wulff the faces with the smallest surface energy appear as crystal planes. Consequently one must assume that PVP is more strongly adsorbed to (111) faces than to (100) faces.

INFLUENCE OF POLYMERS ON CHEMICAL SENSITIZATION

The chemical sensitization with sulphur compounds proceeds according to the scheme[(7)–(9)]

$$2AgBr + S_2O_3^{2-} + H_2O \rightarrow Ag_2S + SO_4^{2-} + 2H^+ + 2Br^- \tag{5}$$

and leads to the formation of Ag_2S at the crystal faces. These Ag_2S

specks, the so-called sensitivity specks, act as electron traps during exposure, and they are the sites where the latent image specks are formed.

In order to investigate the influence of different supporting colloids on the course of the chemical sensitization and to separate clearly this influence from the action of these colloids on crystal growth, a monodisperse AgBr emulsion was used which had been prepared by double-jet precipitation in the presence of only an extremely small amount of

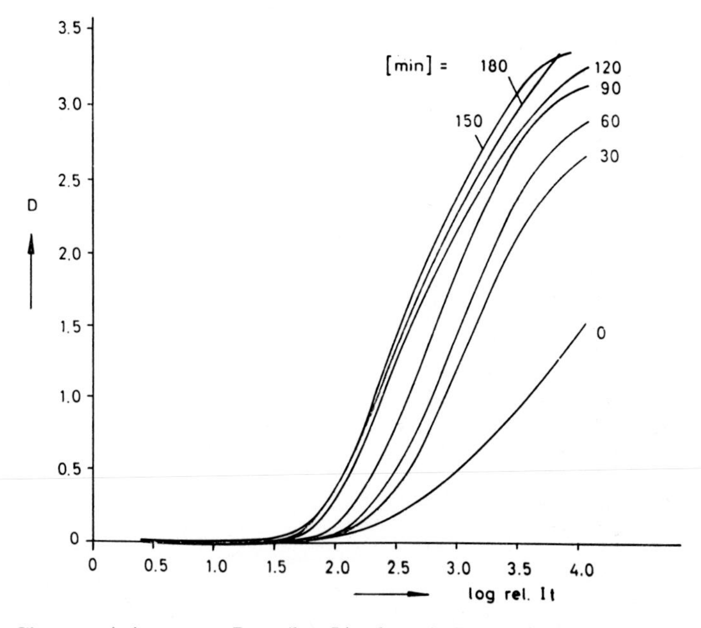

Fig. 3. Characteristic curves D — (log It) of an AgBr emulsion digested with thiosulphate for the periods of time indicated at the curves. The supporting colloid is gelatin.

gelatin. To parts of this starting emulsion relatively large amounts of gelatin, PVP and PVA and small amounts of thiosulphate as sulphur compound were added. During digestion samples were taken in certain intervals which were used for coating on film base.

Upon exposure and development characteristic curves were obtained which are shown in Figs. 3–5 for gelatin, PVA and PVP respectively.

If the emulsion is digested in the presence of gelatin (see Fig. 3), the usual effect of chemical sensitization can be observed, i.e. the speed increases with increasing ripening time and no fog appears.

When PVA instead of gelatin is used as the supporting colloid during ripening, we observe a less pronounced sensitivity increase, but a very strong formation of fog (see Fig. 4).

PVP used as a supporting colloid finally leads to a surprising result: the threshold sensitivity decreases upon ripening as is shown in Fig. 5.

In all three cases equal ripening conditions, such as temperature and the thiosulphate concentration, have been employed. The ripening times, at which digestion has been stopped, are indicated by the curves.

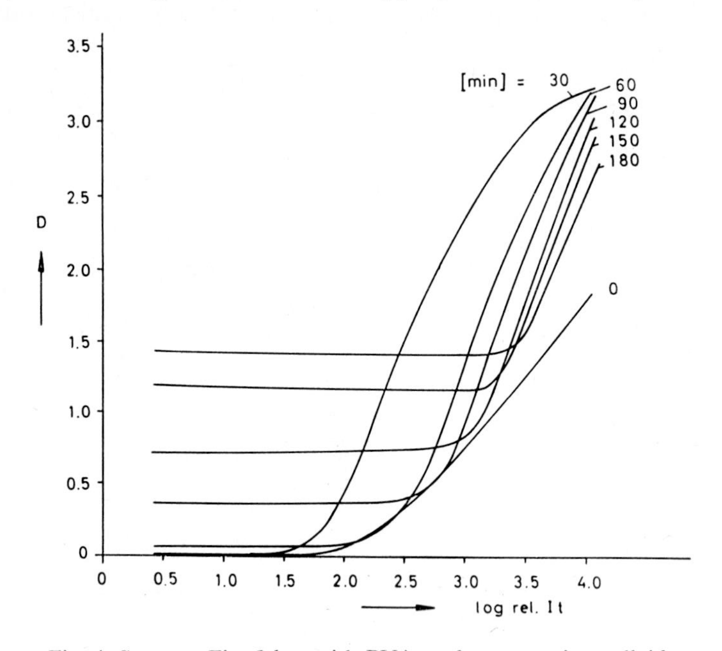

Fig. 4. Same as Fig. 3 but with PVA as the supporting colloid.

When we measure the amount of Ag_2S formed during ripening we obtain the curves shown in Fig. 6, again for the same three supporting colloids.

While Ag_2S formation proceeds relatively slowly in the presence of gelatin, it is much faster in the presence of PVA and finally proceeds very quickly in the presence of PVP. We do not know what causes this different behaviour of the three supporting colloids during chemical ripening. We are however in the position to discuss some of the observed effects on the basis of crystal growth theories. Previous investigations had shown that the growth of Ag_2S upon an AgBr (100) face can be similarly treated as homogenous crystal growth;[10] due to thermal activation/deactivation processes adsorbed silver-thiosulphate

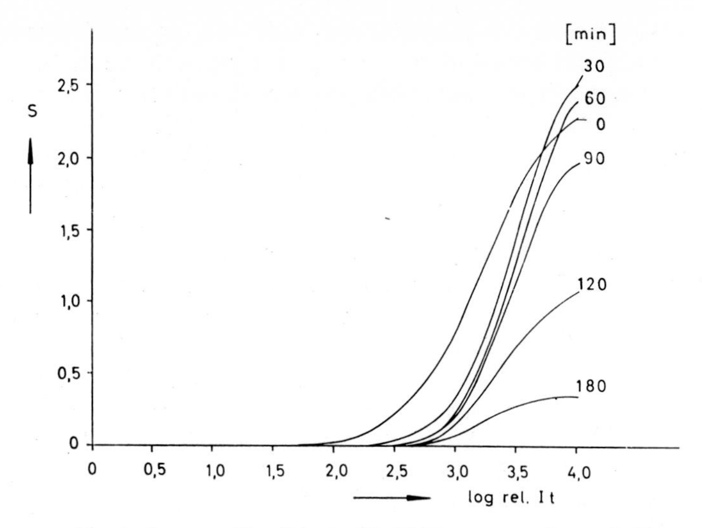

Fig. 5. Same as Fig. 3 but with PVP as supporting colloid.

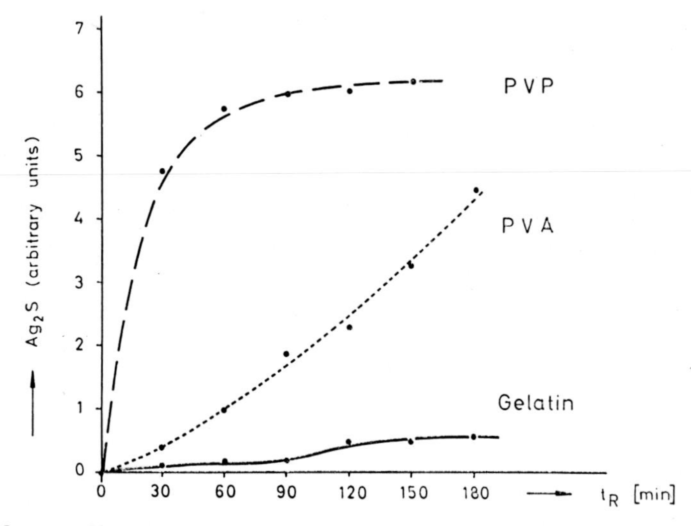

Fig. 6. Formation of Ag_2S versus ripening time of AgBr emulsion upon thiosulphate digestion in the presence of gelatin, PVA and PVP respectively.

complex can disintegrate to a two-dimensional Ag_2S nucleus at the AgBr crystal surface. This process requires a nucleation energy, which in analogy to the above mentioned nucleation energy for a three-dimensional crystal nucleus is given by

$$A_{k(2)} \approx \rho l \tag{6}$$

where ρ is the specific peripheral energy and l the circumference of the Ag_2S nucleus. Once such a nucleus has been formed at the surface of an AgBr microcrystal the decomposition of more thiosulphate is facilitated, and the newly formed Ag_2S deposits at the periphery of the initial Ag_2S nucleus. This autocatalytic mechanism of Ag_2S formation has been proved in previous investigations. We must therefore distinguish between two different steps of Ag_2S formation, namely primary nucleation and subsequent growth at the periphery of the nuclei. When the peripheral energy ρ is lowered by adsorption, the activation energy $A_{k(2)}$ of nucleation is consequently decreased or, in other words, the rate of Ag_2S nucleation is increased. This leads to an increase of the number of Ag_2S specks formed at each microcrystal. When more Ag_2S specks are present they may compete in photoelectron trapping and the practical sensitivity of the AgBr crystal is reduced.[11] This explains the rather unexpected experimental result, that a highly increased rate of Ag_2S formation, as in the case of the PVP-emulsion, leads to a sensitivity decrease rather than to an increase of speed as one may expect. So we must conclude that PVP is very strongly adsorbed at Ag_2S; much more strongly than to AgBr, and likewise more strongly than gelatin to Ag_2S.

PVA, as we have seen, promotes fog formation and, contrary to PVP, no desenstization in the early ripening stages. We are quite sure that an Ag_2S speck which initially is a sensitivity centre becomes a fog centre after it has grown to a certain size. In other words, while small Ag_2S specks merely act as photo electron traps, large Ag_2S specks can accept electrons also from the developer and thus form fog centres. As this is the case when an AgBr emulsion is sulphur digested in presence of PVA, we must conclude that PVA does not facilitate the initial Ag_2S nucleation, but does increase the speed of subsequent growth to large Ag_2S specks.

SUMMARY

The supporting colloids influence both crystal growth and the course of surface reactions, such as chemical sensitization. Both processes have been separately investigated with gelatin, PVA and PVP. Both synthetic polymers restrain crystal growth due to adsorption at AgBr. PVP is apparently also strongly adsorbed to Ag_2S. It therefore facilitates Ag_2S nucleation and leads to highly disperse formation of small Ag_2S specks.

PVA is apparently not adsorbed to Ag_2S. For some reason not yet known it increases the rate of Ag_2S speck growth and thus leads to large Ag_2S specks which very soon grow to fog centres.

The chemical background of the different behaviour of the three protective colloids has still to be investigated in the future.

References

(1) Knacke, O. and Stranski, I. N., *Ergeb. exakte Naturwiss.*, **26,** 383 (1952).
(2) Stranski, I. N., *Z. Phys. Chem.*, **17B,** 127 (1932).
(3) Stranski, I. N. and Kaischew, R., *Phys. Z.*, **36,** 393 (1935).
(4) Volmer, M., *Kinetik der Phasenbildung*. Th. Steinkopf, Dresden (1939).
(5) Klein, E., Moisar, E. and Roche, E., "An Investigation of the Role of the Functional Groups of Gelatin on Silver Halide Crystal Growth (see this volume).
(6) Wagner, C., *Z. Elektrochem., Ber. Bunsenges. Phys. Chem.*, **65,** 581 (1961).
(7) Duranté, M. and Pouradier, J., *Sci. Ind. Photogr.*, **28,** 194 (1957).
(8) Venet, A. M., Chateau, H. and Pouradier, J., *Sci. Ind. Photogr.*, **29,** 219 (1958).
(9) Chateau, H. and Pouradier, J., *Sci. Ind. Photogr.*, **31,** 261 (1960).
(10) Moisar, E., *Ber. Bunsenges. Phys. Chem.*, **72,** 3, 467 (1968).
(11) Klein, E. and Langner, G., *Z. Wiss. Photogr. Photophys. Photochem.*, **55,** 93 (1961).

Effect of Molecular Size on the Photographic Action of Gelatin

Y. TSUBAI and H. IRIE
Chiba University, Japan

ABSTRACT. Characteristics of fractionated photogelatins are tested. It was found that dye adsorption and the clearing time of silver bromide depend upon molecular weight of gelatin.